Shojo Beat

OTOMEN

Story & Art by
Aya Kanno

Volume
NINE

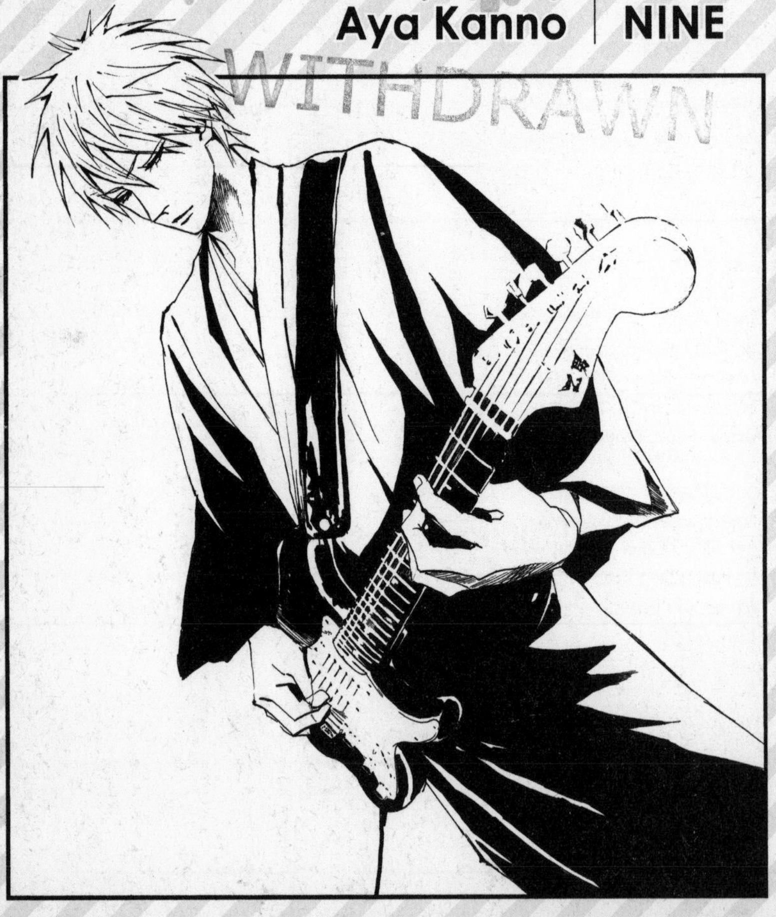

:OTOMEN CHARACTERS & STORY

What is an OTOMEN?

O・to・men *[OH-toe-men]*
1) A young man with girlish interests and thoughts.
2) A young man who has talent for cooking, needlework and general housework.
3) A manly young man with a girlish heart.

Asuka Masamune

The captain of Ginyuri Academy High School's kendo team. He is handsome, studious and (to the casual observer) the perfect high school student. But he is actually an *otomen*, a man with a girlish heart. He loves cute things ♥, and he has a natural talent for cooking, needlework and general housekeeping. He's even a big fan of the shojo manga *Love Chick*.

STORY

Asuka Masamune, the kendo captain, is actually an *otomen* (a girlish guy)— a man who likes cute things, housework and shojo manga. When he was young, his father left home to become a woman. His mother was traumatized, and ever since then, he has kept his girlish interests a secret. However, things change when he meets Juta, a guy who is using Asuka as the basis for the female character in the shojo manga he is writing (←top secret). Asuka also starts having feelings for a tomboy girl who is good at martial arts. Because of this, he's slowly reverting to his true *otomen* self!

Ryo Miyakozuka

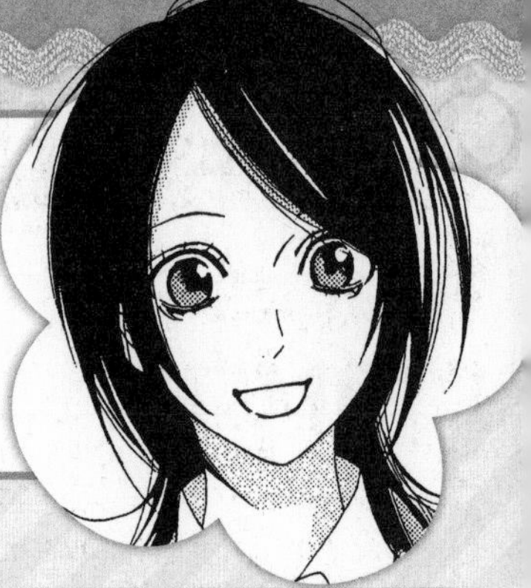

Asuka's classmate for whom he has feelings. She has studied martial arts under her father ever since she was little, and she is very good at it. On the other hand, her housekeeping skills are disastrous. She's a very eccentric beauty.

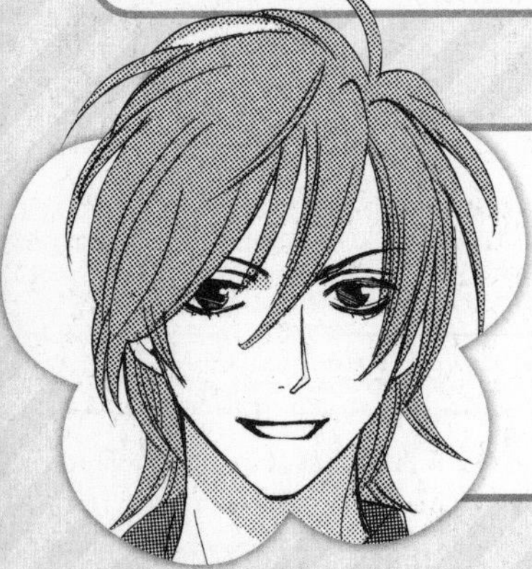

Juta Tachibana

Asuka's classmate. He's flirtatious, but he's actually the popular shojo manga artist Jewel Sachihana. He is using Asuka and Ryo as character concepts in his manga *Love Chick*, which is being published in the shojo magazine *Hana to Mame*. His personal life is a mystery! He has ten younger sisters!!

Yamato Ariake

Underclassman at Asuka's school. He looks like a girl, but he admires manliness and has long, delusional fantasies about being manly…

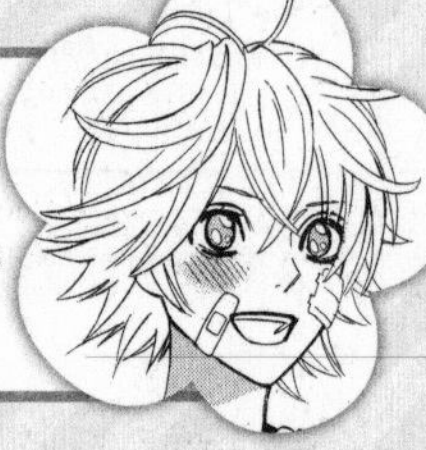

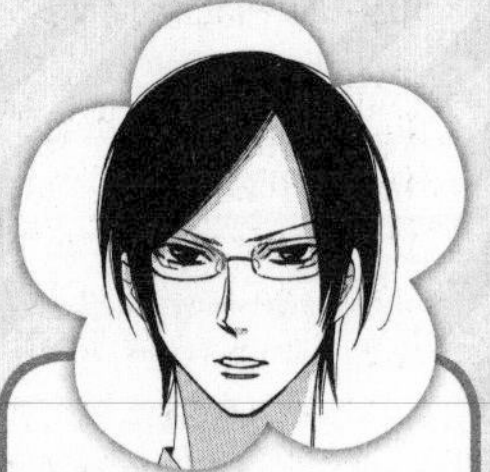

Hajime Tonomine

The captain of Kinbara High School's kendo team, he sees Asuka as his lifelong rival. He is the strong and silent type but is actually an *otomen* who is good with makeup. A *Tsun-sama*.

("Tsun-sama" © Juta Tachibana.)

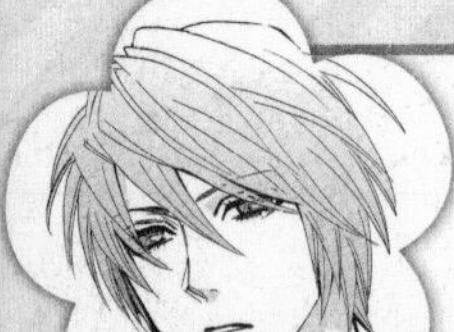

Kitora Kurokawa

Asuka's classmate. He is obsessed with the beauty of flowers. He is an *otomen* who refers to himself as the Flower Evangelist.

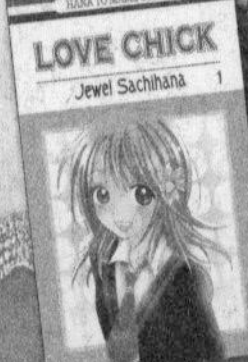
HANA TO MAME COMICS
LOVE CHICK
Jewel Sachihana 1

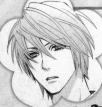

Asuka is also a BIG FAN!

Hana to Mame Comics

LOVE CHICK by Jewel Sachihana

(Now serialized in *Hana to Mame*)

The very popular shojo comic that Juta writes (under the pen name Jewel Sachihana).

OTOMEN

volume 9

CONTENTS

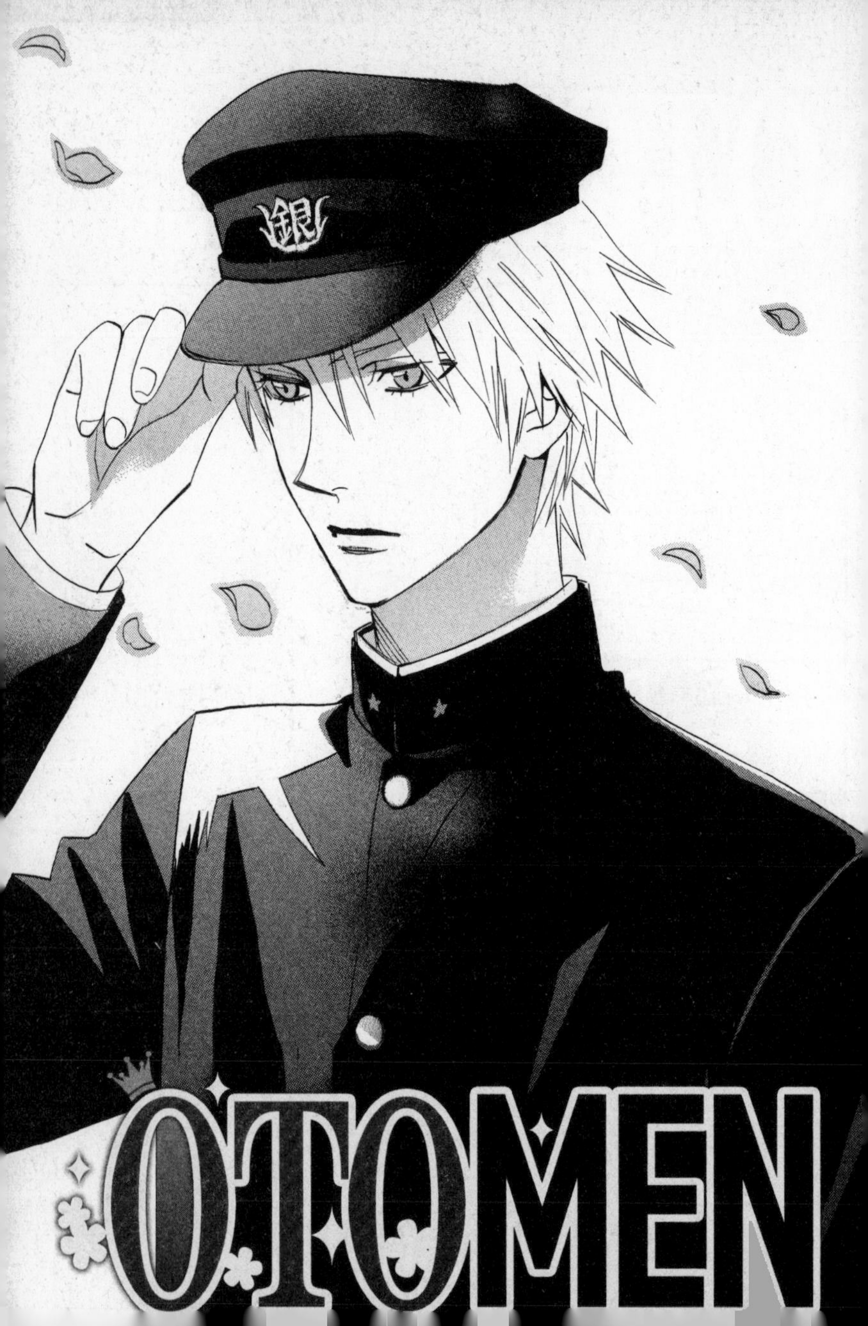
OTOMEN

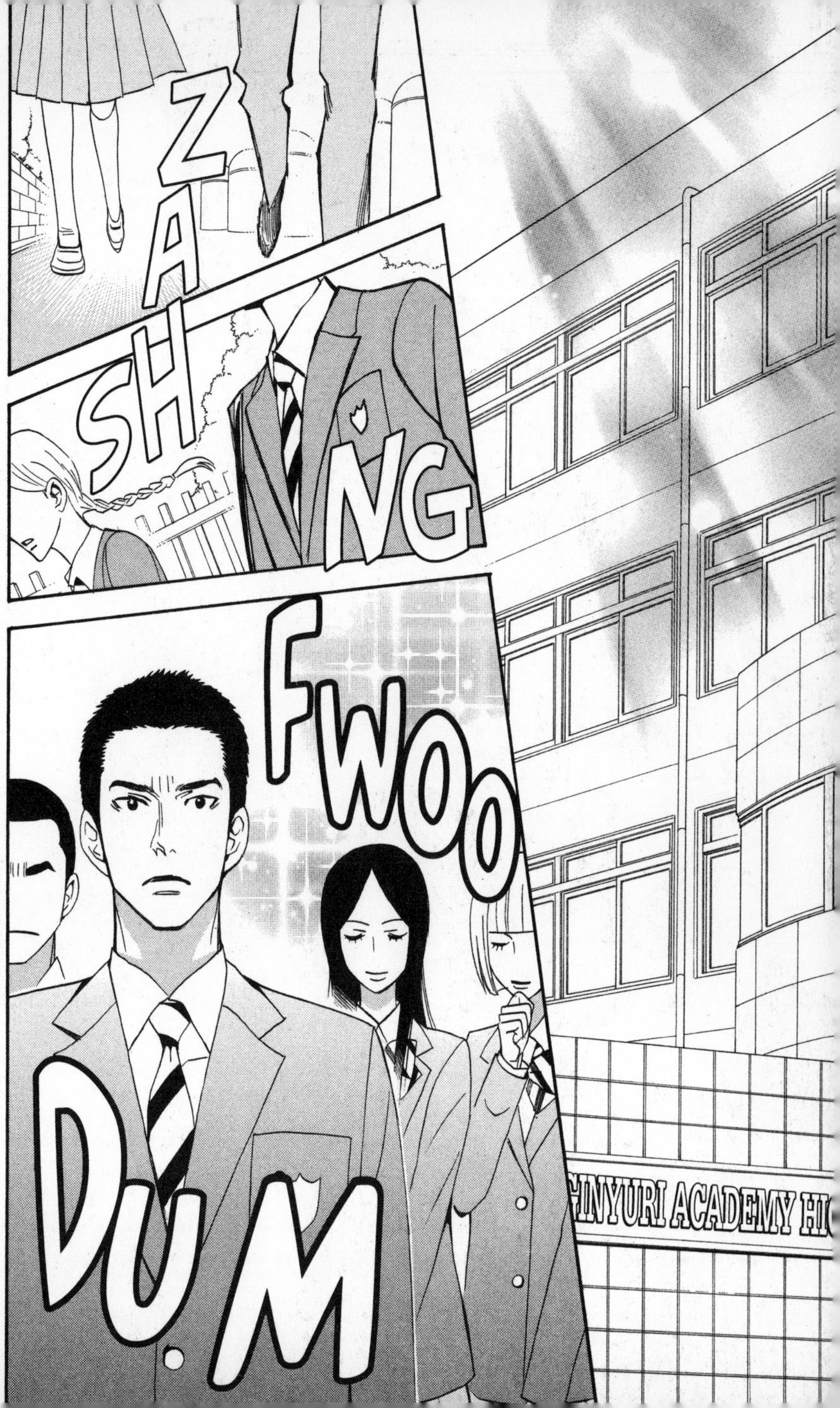
GINYURI ACADEMY HI
ZA
SH
NG
FWOO
DUM

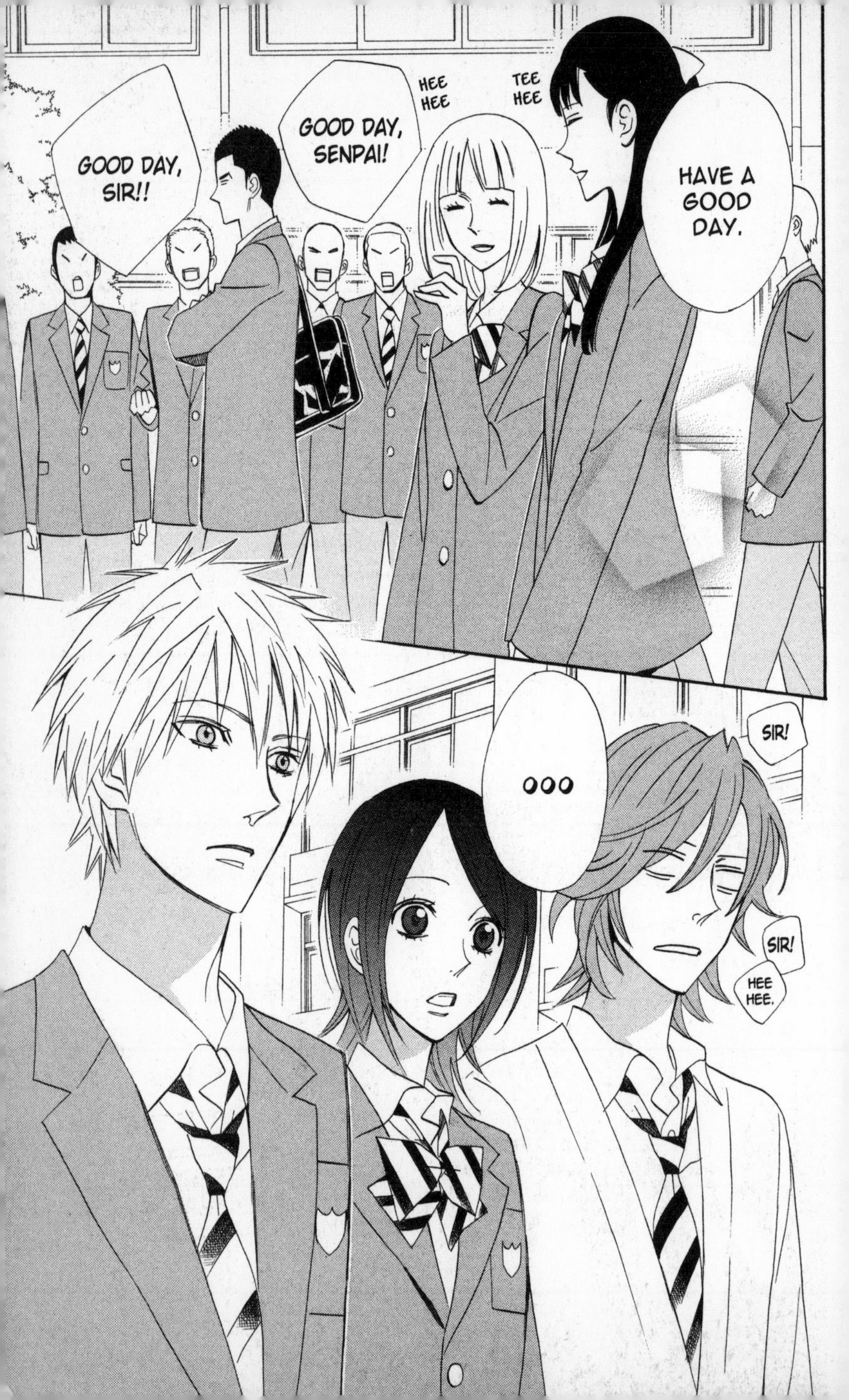

HAVE A GOOD DAY.
TEE HEE
HEE HEE
GOOD DAY, SENPAI!
GOOD DAY, SIR!!
SIR!
...
SIR!
HEE HEE.

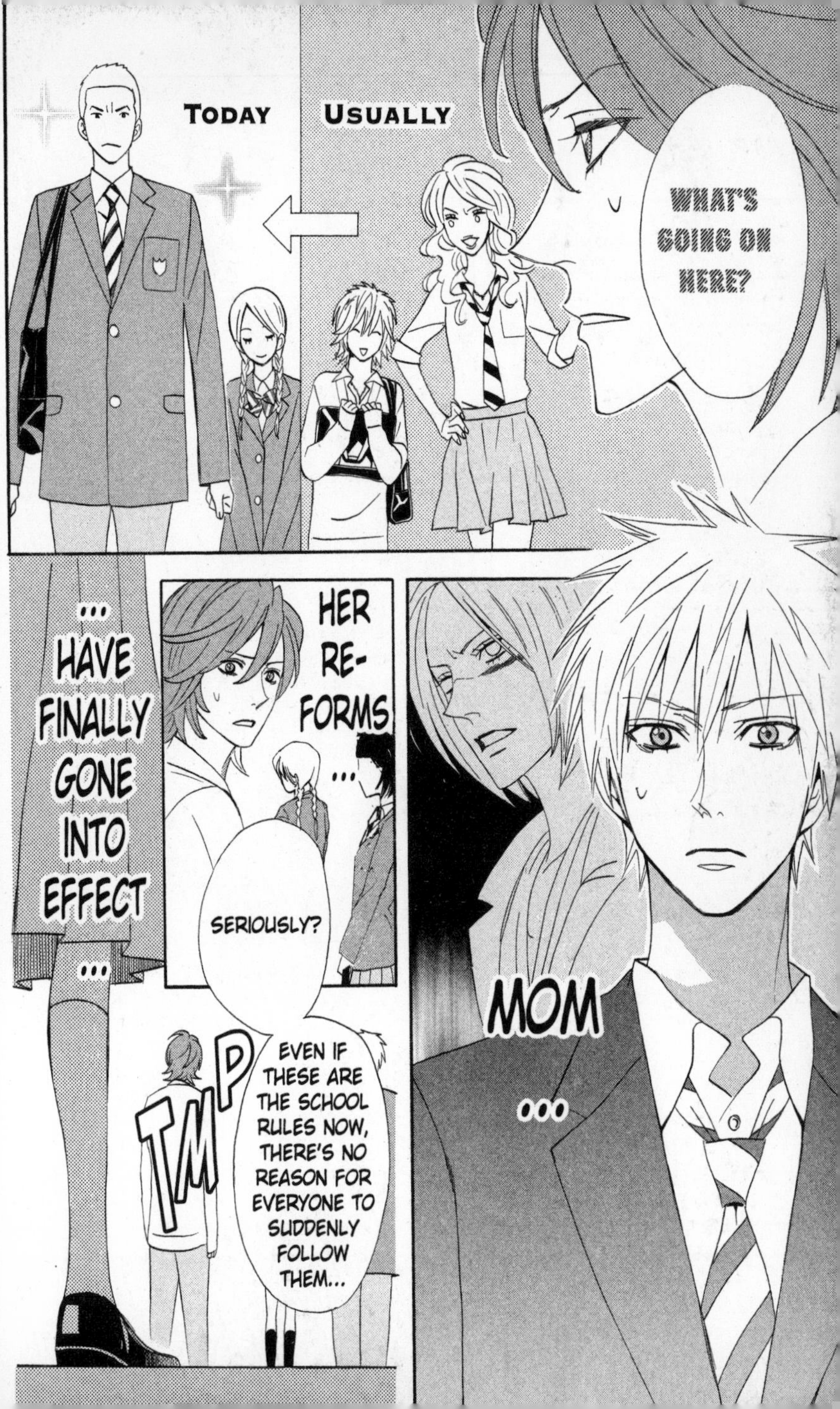

WHAT'S GOING ON HERE?
USUALLY
TODAY
MOM
...
HER RE-FORMS
...
SERIOUSLY?
... HAVE FINALLY GONE INTO EFFECT ...
EVEN IF THESE ARE THE SCHOOL RULES NOW, THERE'S NO REASON FOR EVERYONE TO SUDDENLY FOLLOW THEM...
TMP

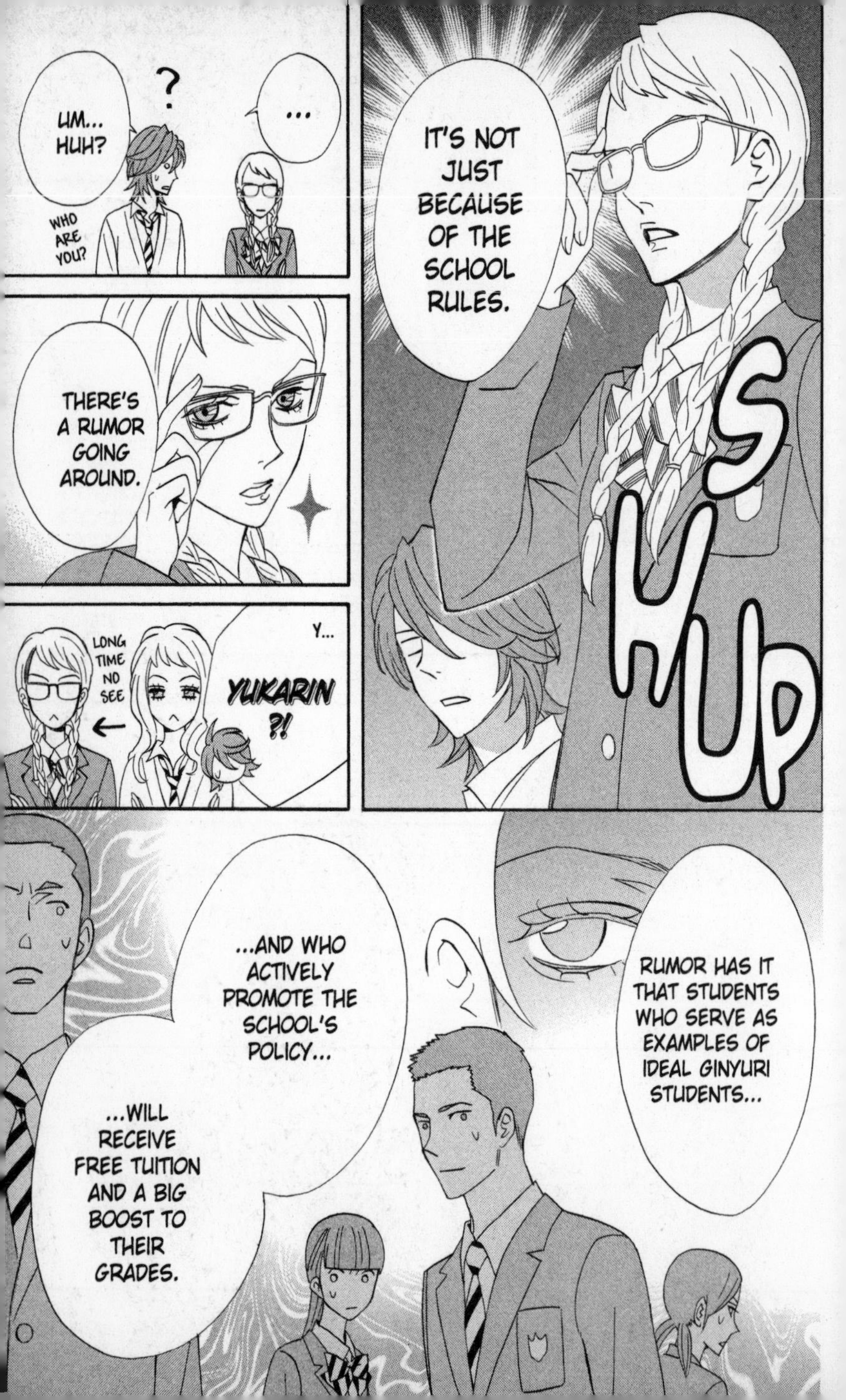

IT'S NOT JUST BECAUSE OF THE SCHOOL RULES.
SHUP
...
?
UM... HUH?
WHO ARE YOU?
THERE'S A RUMOR GOING AROUND.
Y...
YUKARIN ?!
LONG TIME NO SEE
RUMOR HAS IT THAT STUDENTS WHO SERVE AS EXAMPLES OF IDEAL GINYURI STUDENTS...
...AND WHO ACTIVELY PROMOTE THE SCHOOL'S POLICY...
...WILL RECEIVE FREE TUITION AND A BIG BOOST TO THEIR GRADES.

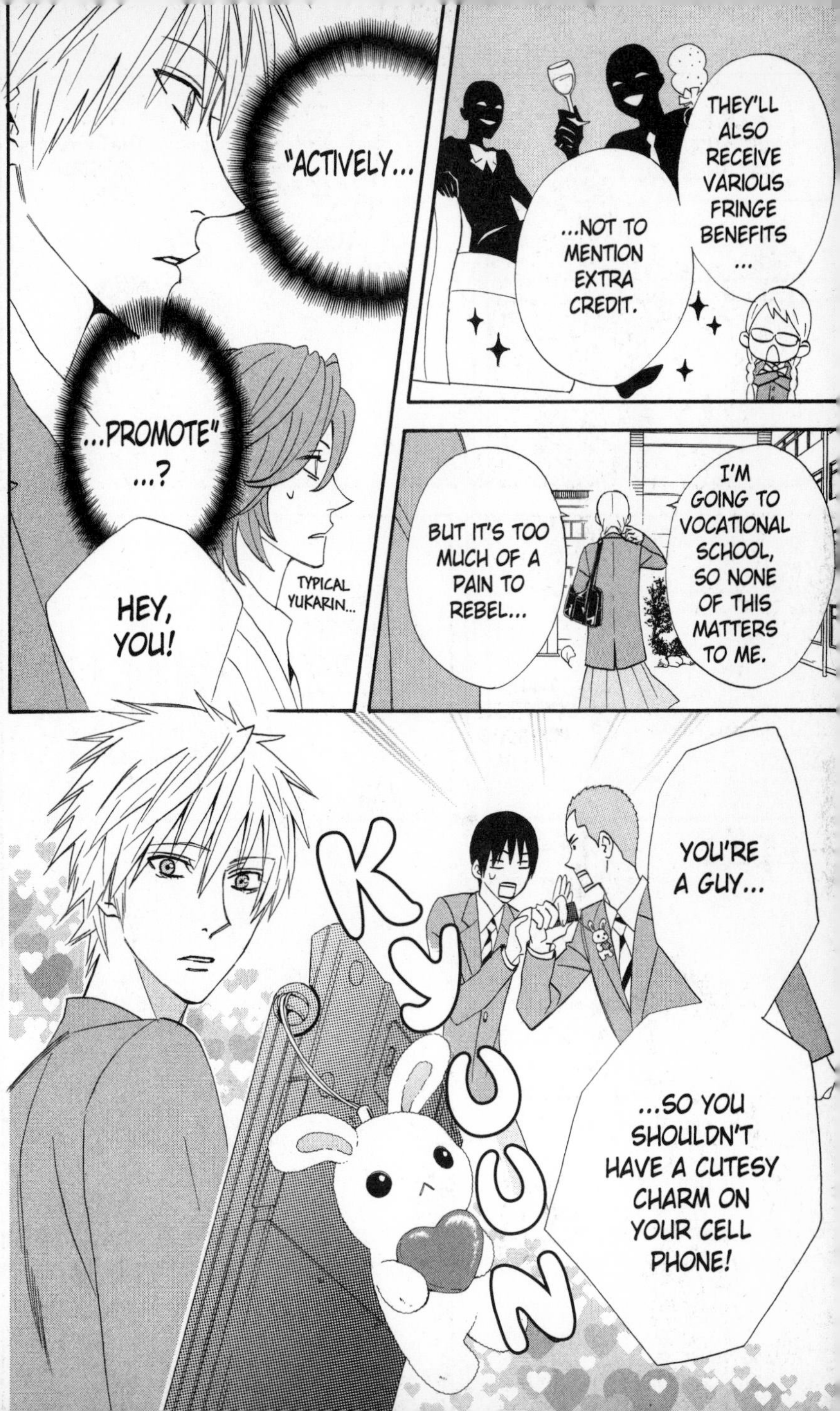
THEY'LL ALSO RECEIVE VARIOUS FRINGE BENEFITS ...
...NOT TO MENTION EXTRA CREDIT.
I'M GOING TO VOCATIONAL SCHOOL, SO NONE OF THIS MATTERS TO ME.
BUT IT'S TOO MUCH OF A PAIN TO REBEL...
"ACTIVELY...
...PROMOTE" ...?
TYPICAL YUKARIN...
HEY, YOU!
YOU'RE A GUY...
...SO YOU SHOULDN'T HAVE A CUTESY CHARM ON YOUR CELL PHONE!
KYUUN

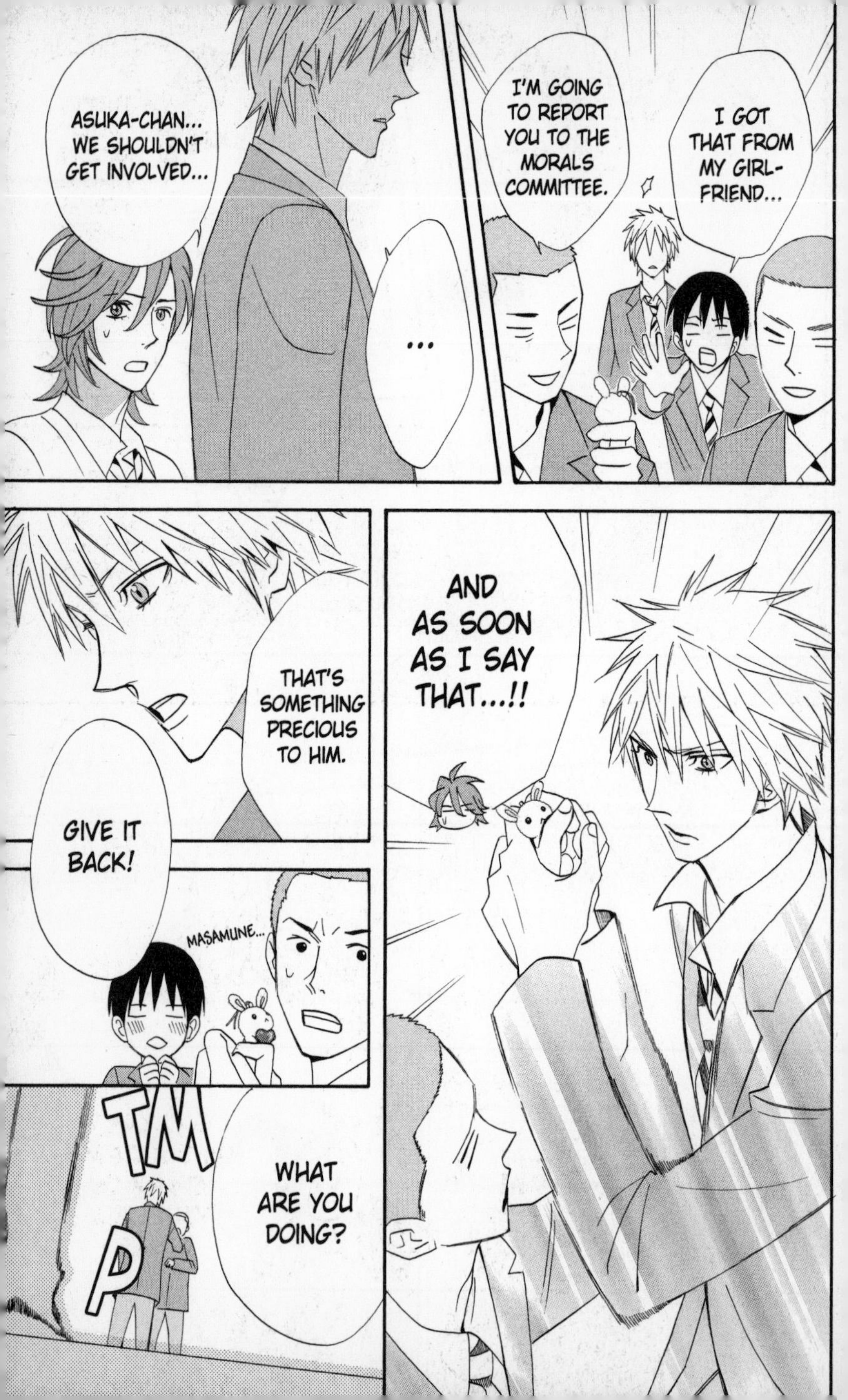
I GOT THAT FROM MY GIRL-FRIEND...
I'M GOING TO REPORT YOU TO THE MORALS COMMITTEE.
ASUKA-CHAN... WE SHOULDN'T GET INVOLVED...
...
AND AS SOON AS I SAY THAT...!!
THAT'S SOMETHING PRECIOUS TO HIM.
GIVE IT BACK!
MASAMUNE...
WHAT ARE YOU DOING?
TMP

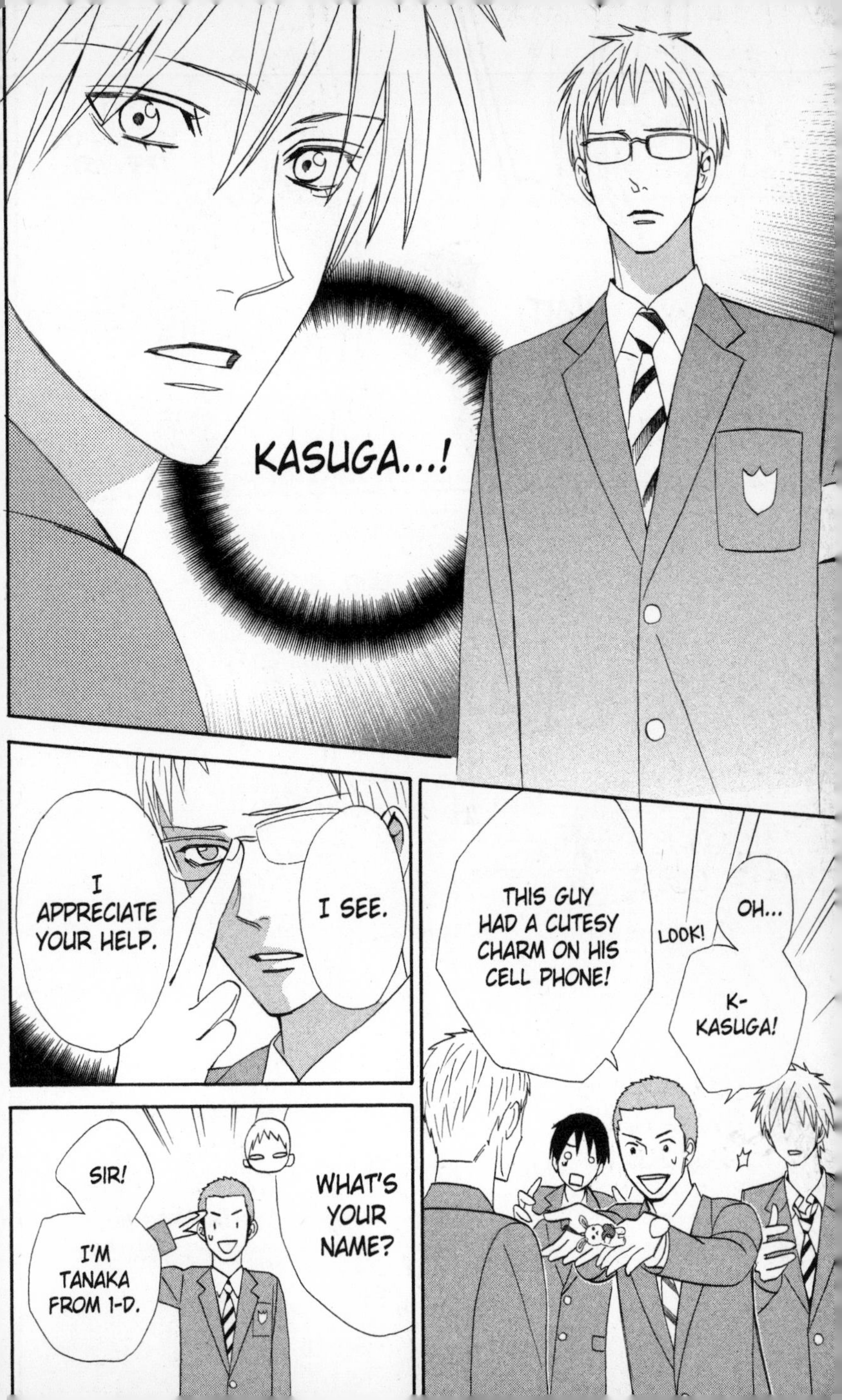
KASUGA...!
OH... K-KASUGA!
LOOK!
THIS GUY HAD A CUTESY CHARM ON HIS CELL PHONE!
I SEE.
I APPRECIATE YOUR HELP.
WHAT'S YOUR NAME?
SIR! I'M TANAKA FROM 1-D.

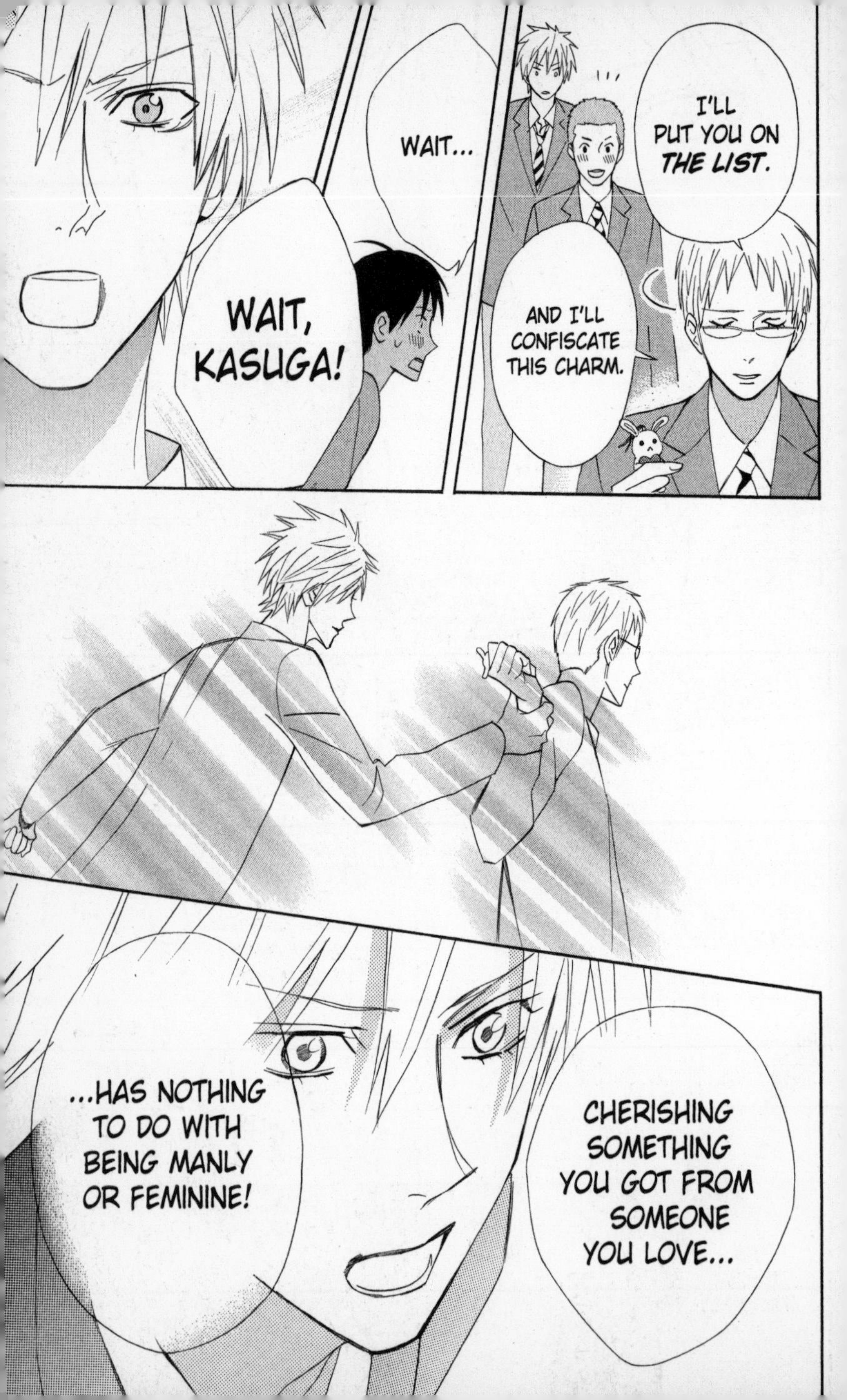
I'LL PUT YOU ON *THE LIST*.
AND I'LL CONFISCATE THIS CHARM.
WAIT...
WAIT, KASUGA!
CHERISHING SOMETHING YOU GOT FROM SOMEONE YOU LOVE...
...HAS NOTHING TO DO WITH BEING MANLY OR FEMININE!

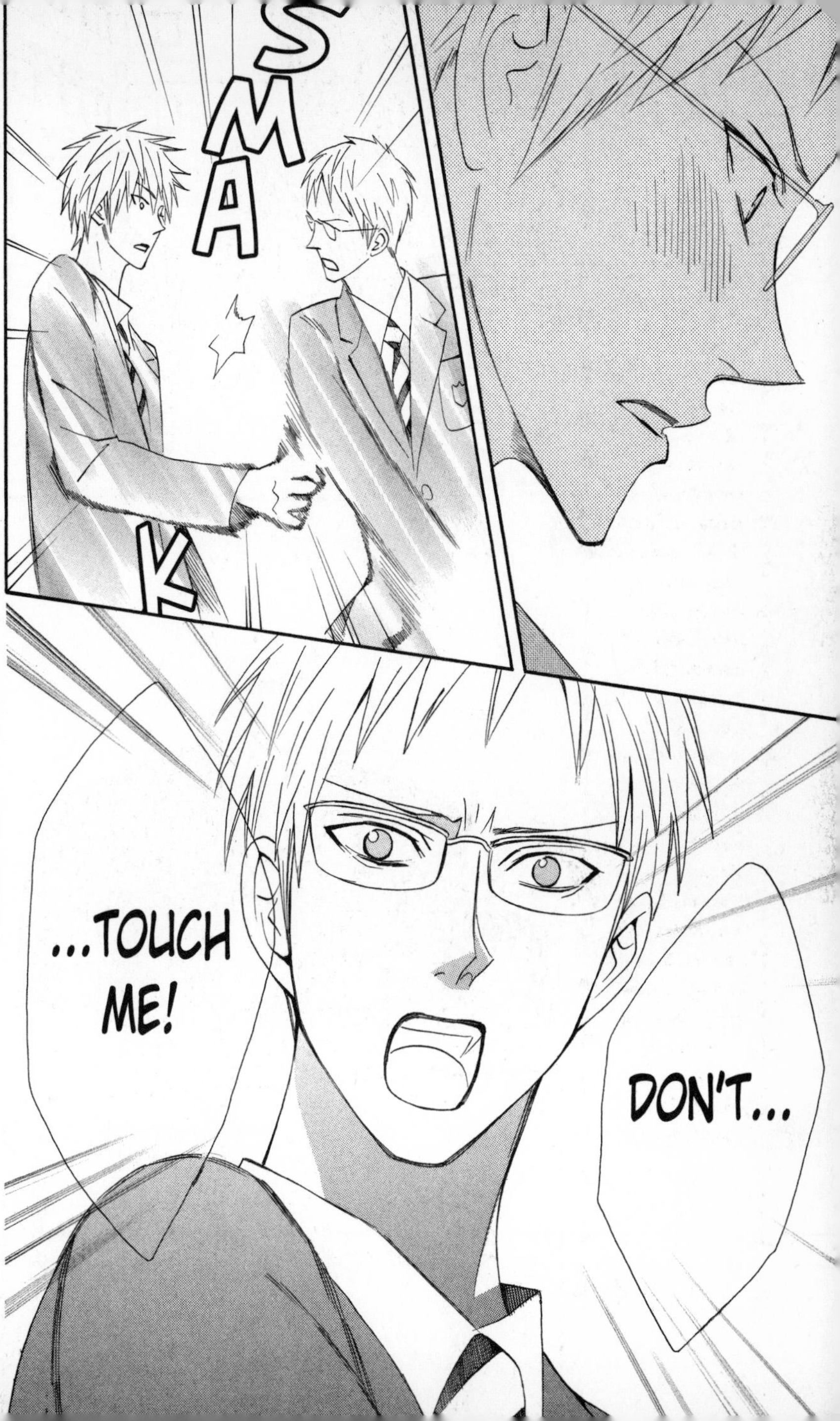
SMACK
DON'T...
...TOUCH ME!

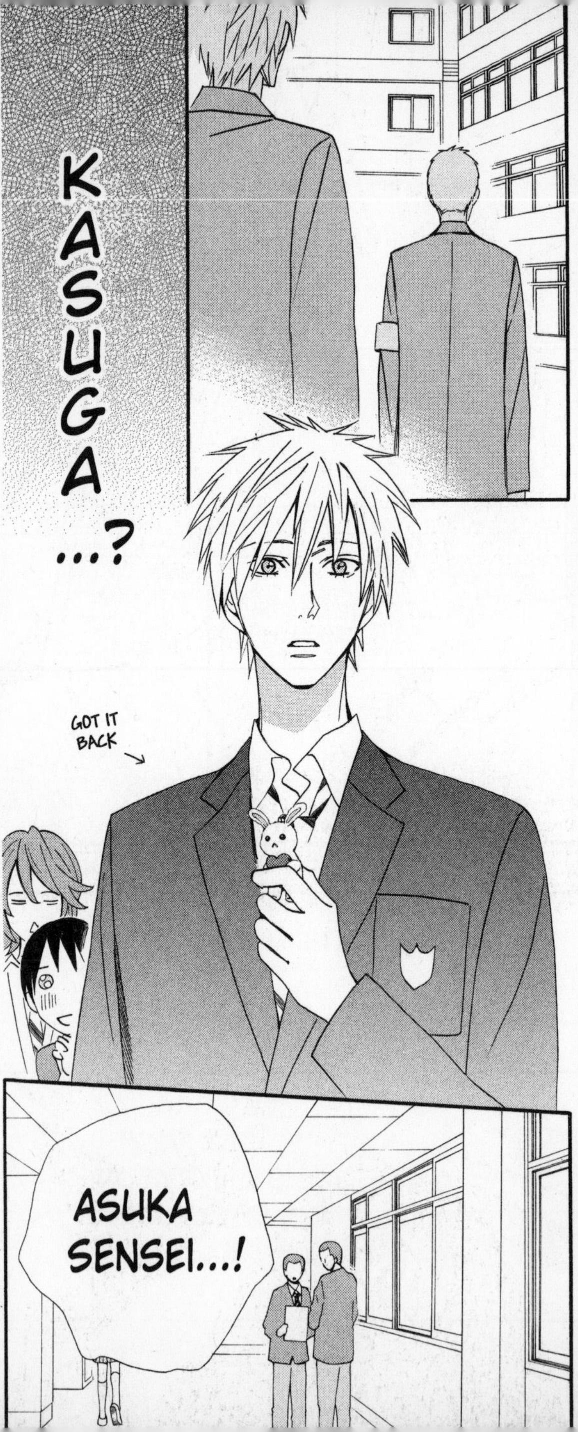
KASUGA...?
GOT IT BACK
ASUKA SENSEI...!

Hi there.
This is volume 9.

A lot of new characters have appeared. All the teachers have strong personalities. They almost overshadow the main characters. Kasuga and Amakashi both wear glasses. Bespectacled characters are becoming more common in *Otomen*, but I don't particularly care much for men with glasses. However, I like men who don't normally wear glasses but actually have bad eyesight and wear them at home. They're the "Actually, I wear glasses" type.

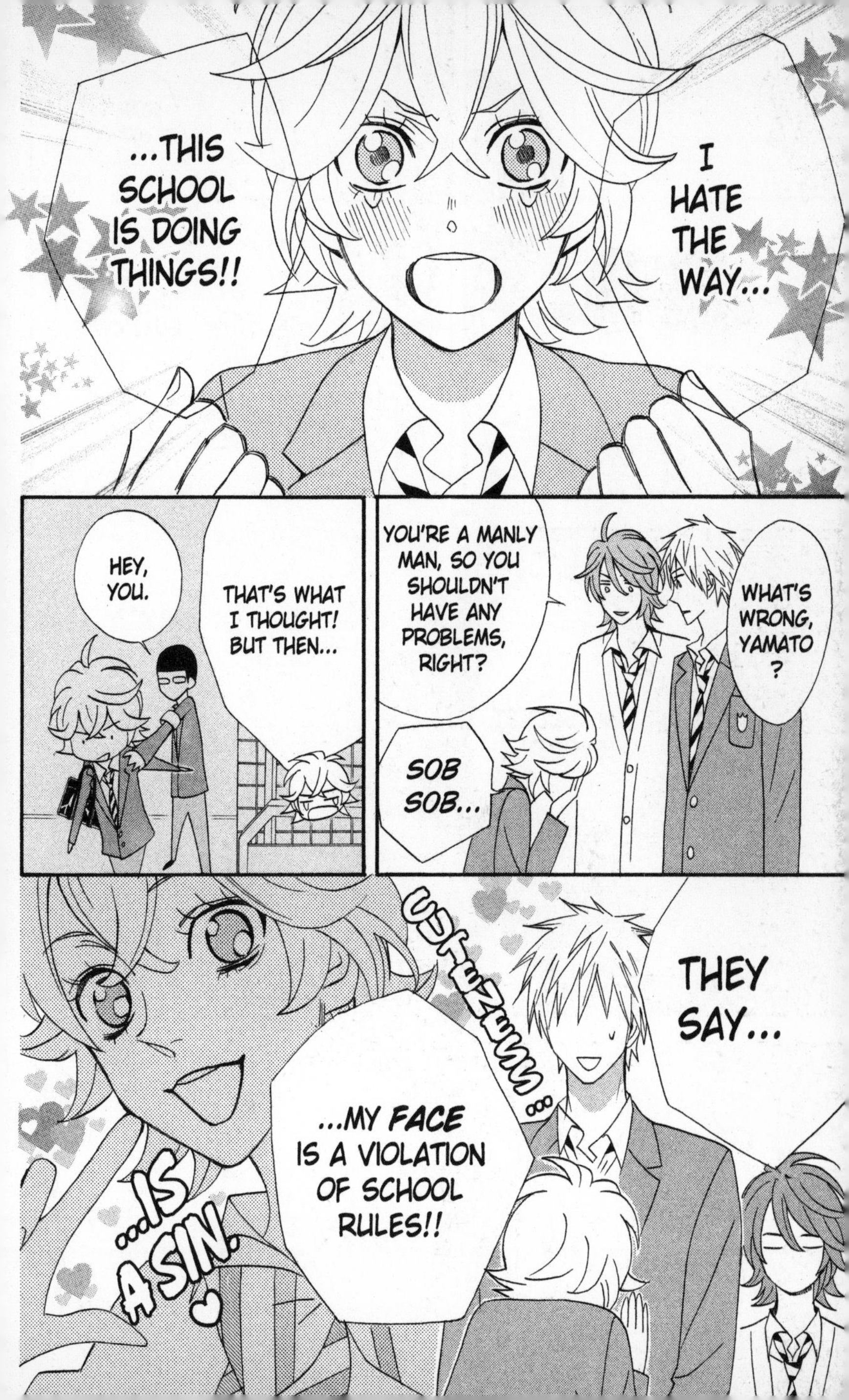
I HATE THE WAY...
...THIS SCHOOL IS DOING THINGS!!
WHAT'S WRONG, YAMATO?
YOU'RE A MANLY MAN, SO YOU SHOULDN'T HAVE ANY PROBLEMS, RIGHT?
SOB SOB...
THAT'S WHAT I THOUGHT! BUT THEN...
HEY, YOU.
THEY SAY...
...MY FACE IS A VIOLATION OF SCHOOL RULES!!
...IS A SIN.

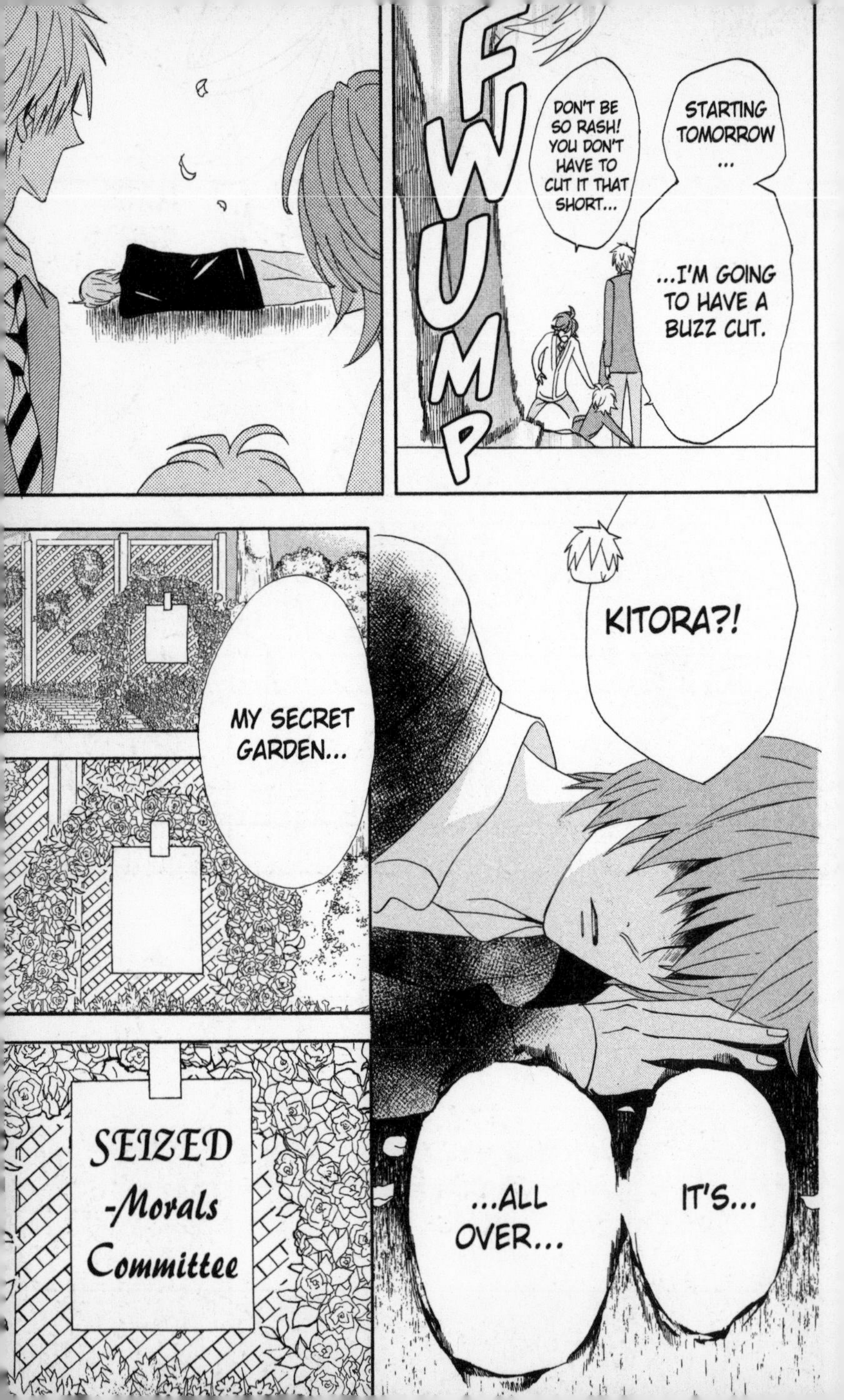
STARTING TOMORROW ...
...I'M GOING TO HAVE A BUZZ CUT.
DON'T BE SO RASH! YOU DON'T HAVE TO CUT IT THAT SHORT...
FWUMP
KITORA?!
IT'S...
...ALL OVER...
MY SECRET GARDEN...
SEIZED
-Morals Committee

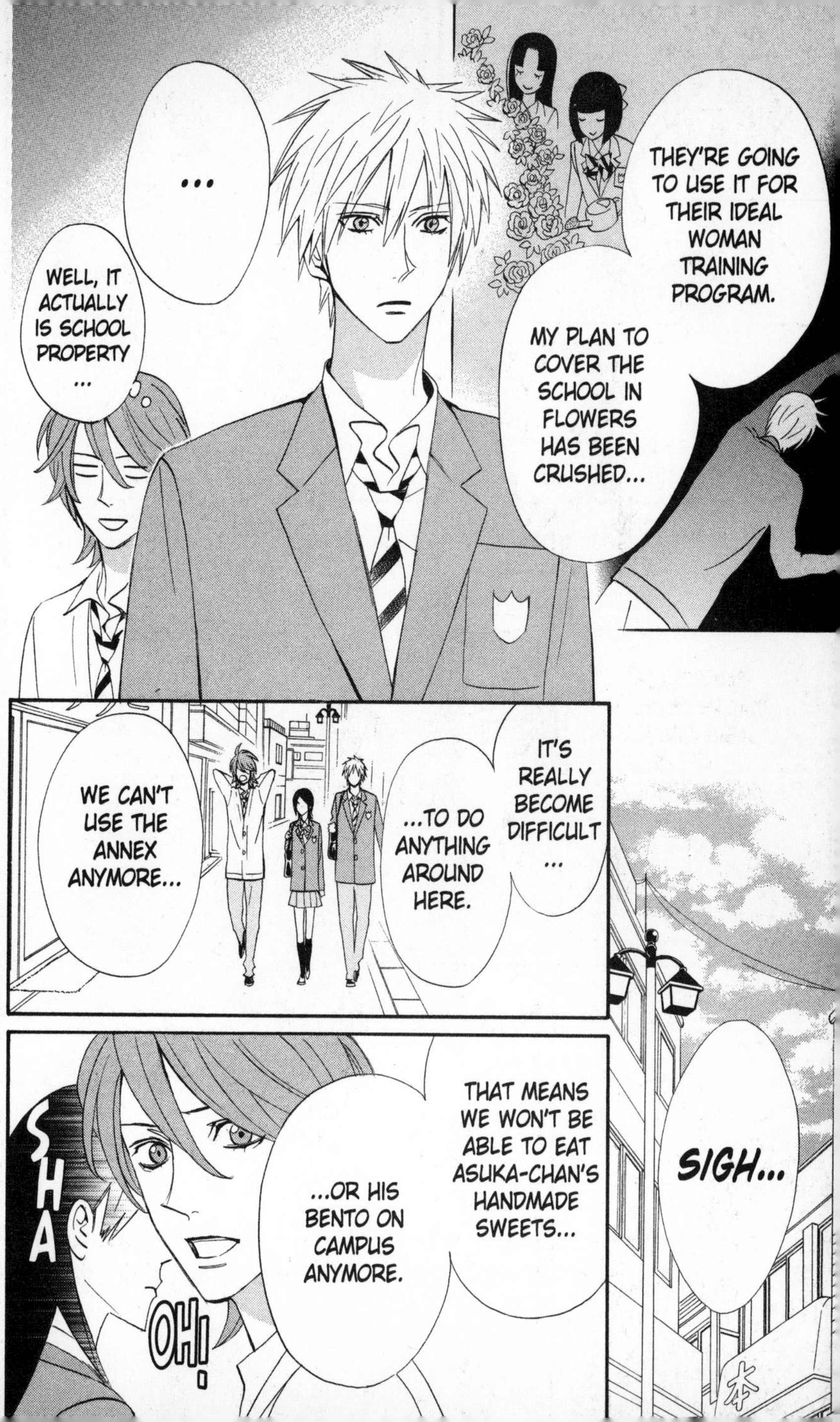
THEY'RE GOING TO USE IT FOR THEIR IDEAL WOMAN TRAINING PROGRAM.
MY PLAN TO COVER THE SCHOOL IN FLOWERS HAS BEEN CRUSHED...
...
WELL, IT ACTUALLY IS SCHOOL PROPERTY...
IT'S REALLY BECOME DIFFICULT...
...TO DO ANYTHING AROUND HERE.
WE CAN'T USE THE ANNEX ANYMORE...
SIGH...
THAT MEANS WE WON'T BE ABLE TO EAT ASUKA-CHAN'S HANDMADE SWEETS...
...OR HIS BENTO ON CAMPUS ANYMORE.
OH!
SHA

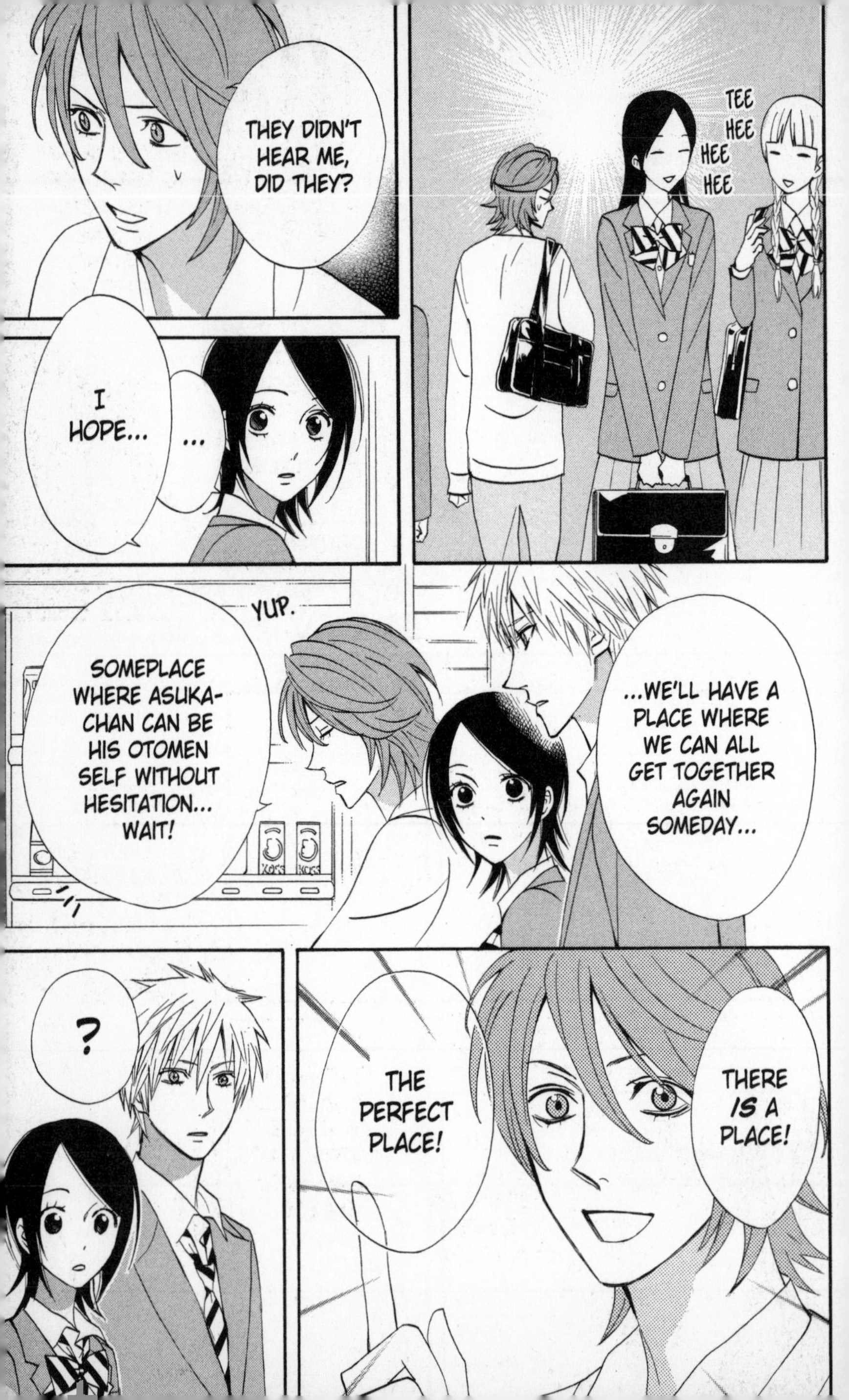
TEE HEE
HEE HEE
THEY DIDN'T HEAR ME, DID THEY?
I HOPE...
...
...WE'LL HAVE A PLACE WHERE WE CAN ALL GET TOGETHER AGAIN SOMEDAY...
YUP.
SOMEPLACE WHERE ASUKA-CHAN CAN BE HIS OTOMEN SELF WITHOUT HESITATION... WAIT!
THERE *IS* A PLACE!
THE PERFECT PLACE!
?

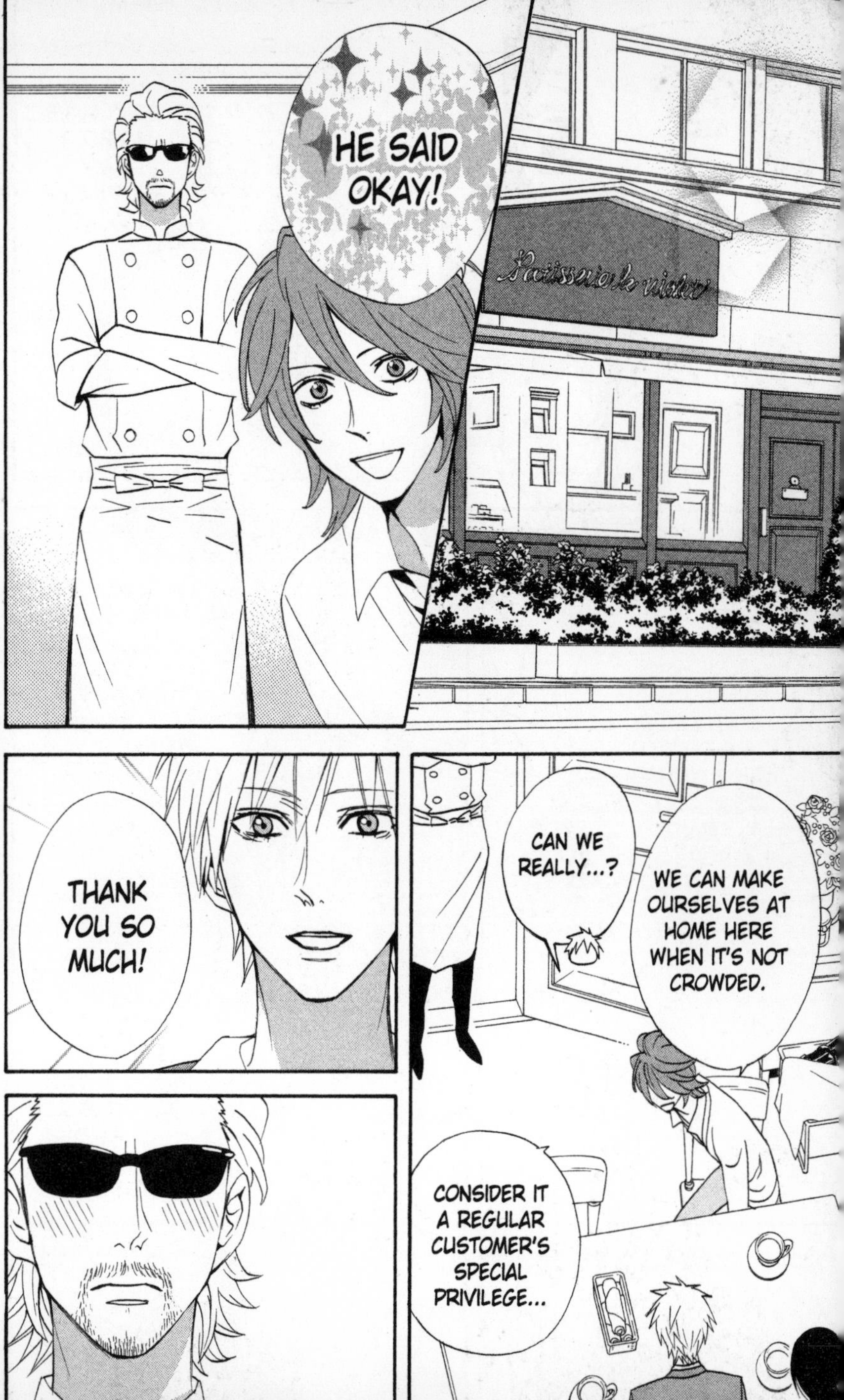
HE SAID OKAY!
WE CAN MAKE OURSELVES AT HOME HERE WHEN IT'S NOT CROWDED.
CAN WE REALLY...?
CONSIDER IT A REGULAR CUSTOMER'S SPECIAL PRIVILEGE...
THANK YOU SO MUCH!

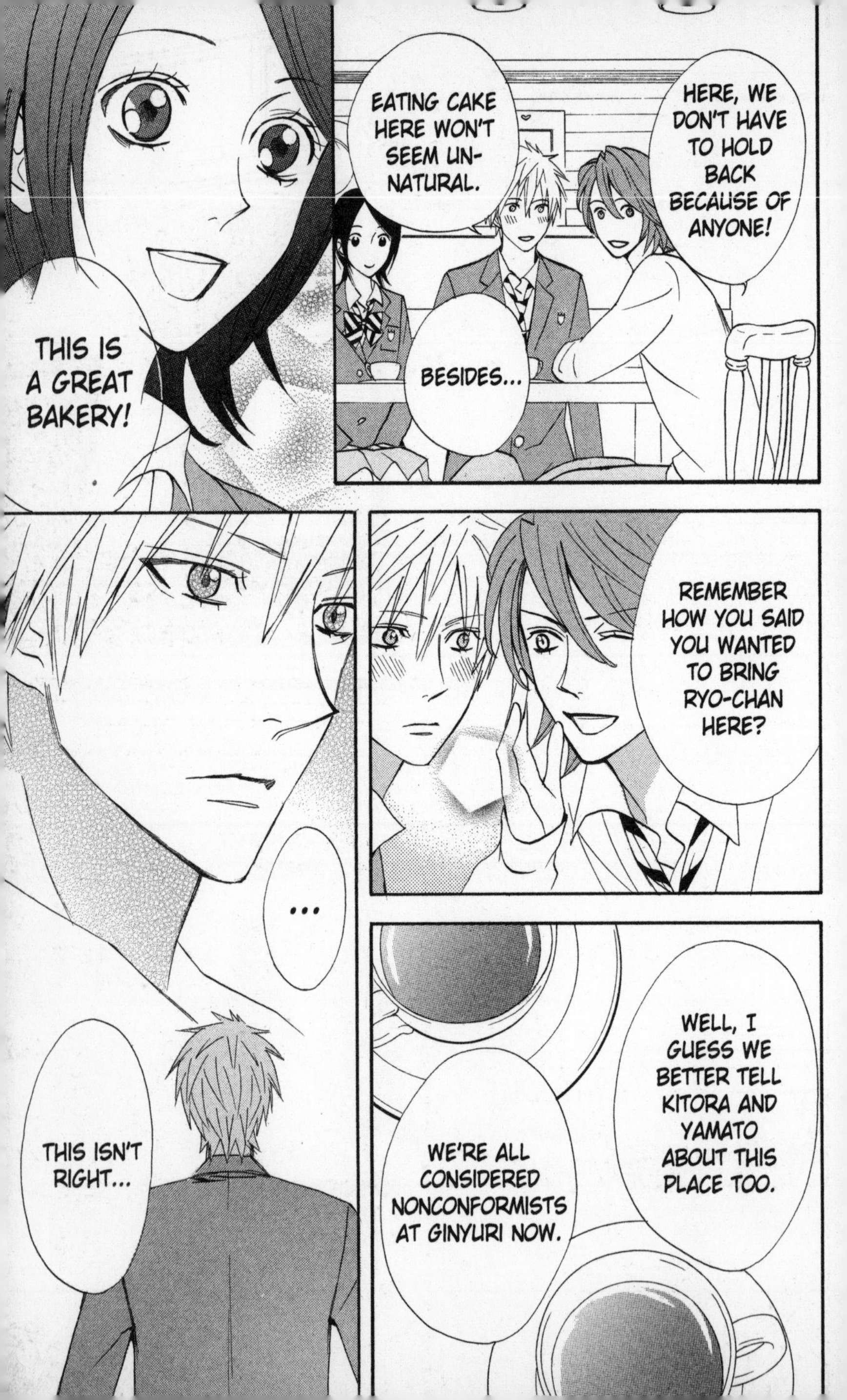
HERE, WE DON'T HAVE TO HOLD BACK BECAUSE OF ANYONE!
EATING CAKE HERE WON'T SEEM UN-NATURAL.
BESIDES...
THIS IS A GREAT BAKERY!
REMEMBER HOW YOU SAID YOU WANTED TO BRING RYO-CHAN HERE?
WELL, I GUESS WE BETTER TELL KITORA AND YAMATO ABOUT THIS PLACE TOO.
WE'RE ALL CONSIDERED NONCONFORMISTS AT GINYURI NOW.
...
THIS ISN'T RIGHT...

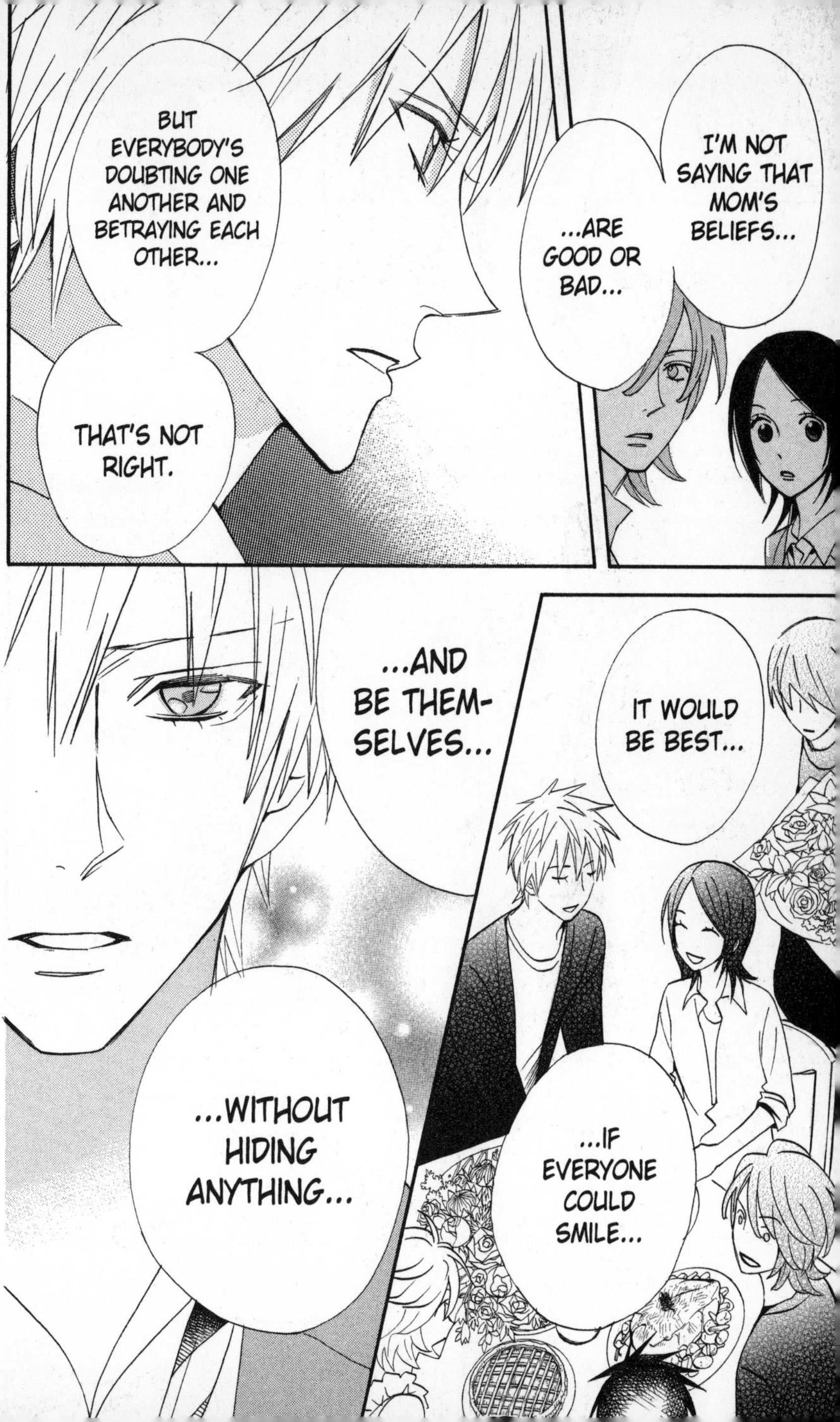
I'M NOT SAYING THAT MOM'S BELIEFS...
...ARE GOOD OR BAD...
BUT EVERYBODY'S DOUBTING ONE ANOTHER AND BETRAYING EACH OTHER...
THAT'S NOT RIGHT.
IT WOULD BE BEST...
...IF EVERYONE COULD SMILE...
...AND BE THEM-SELVES...
...WITHOUT HIDING ANYTHING...

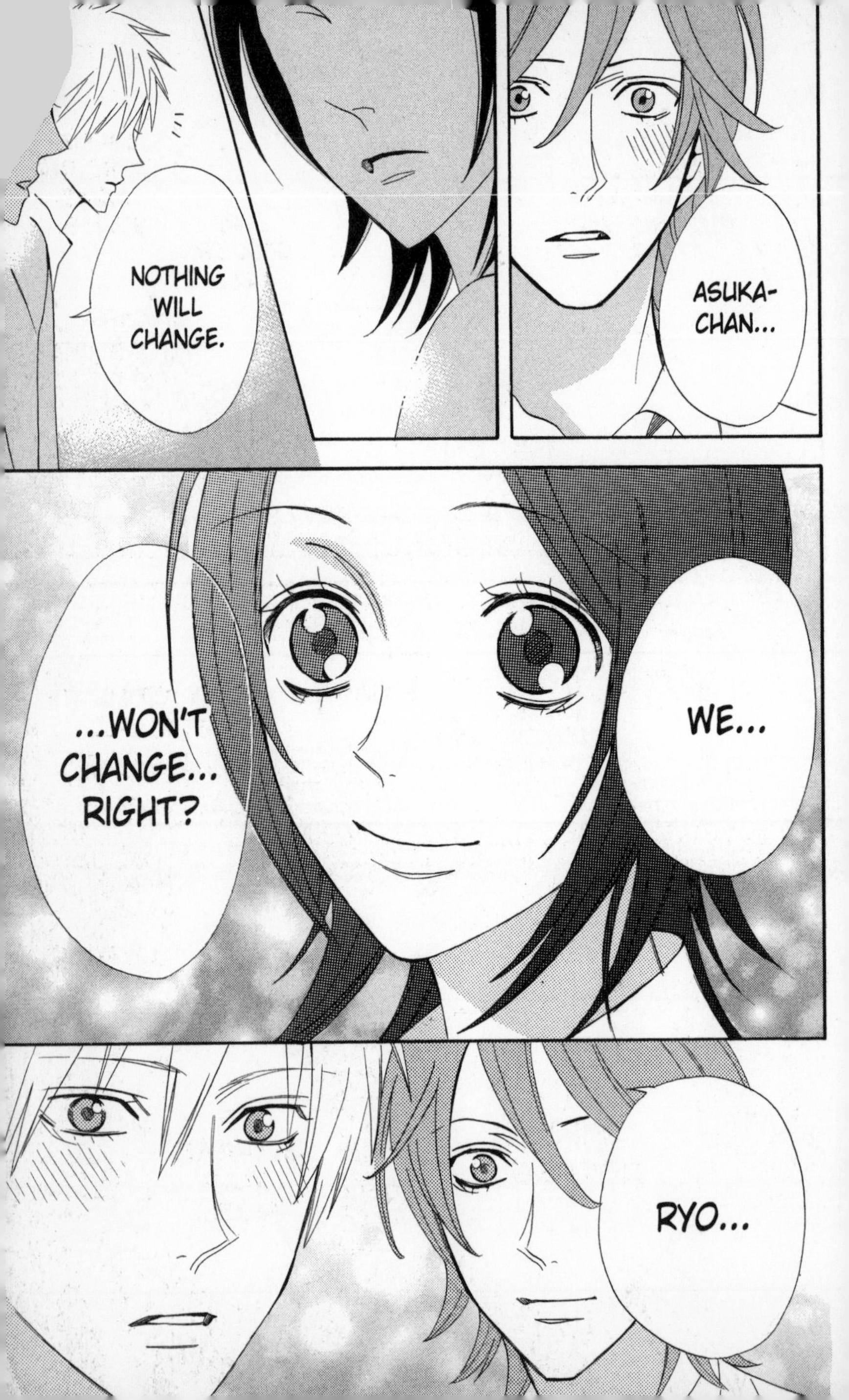
ASUKA-CHAN...
NOTHING WILL CHANGE.
WE...
...WON'T CHANGE... RIGHT?
RYO...

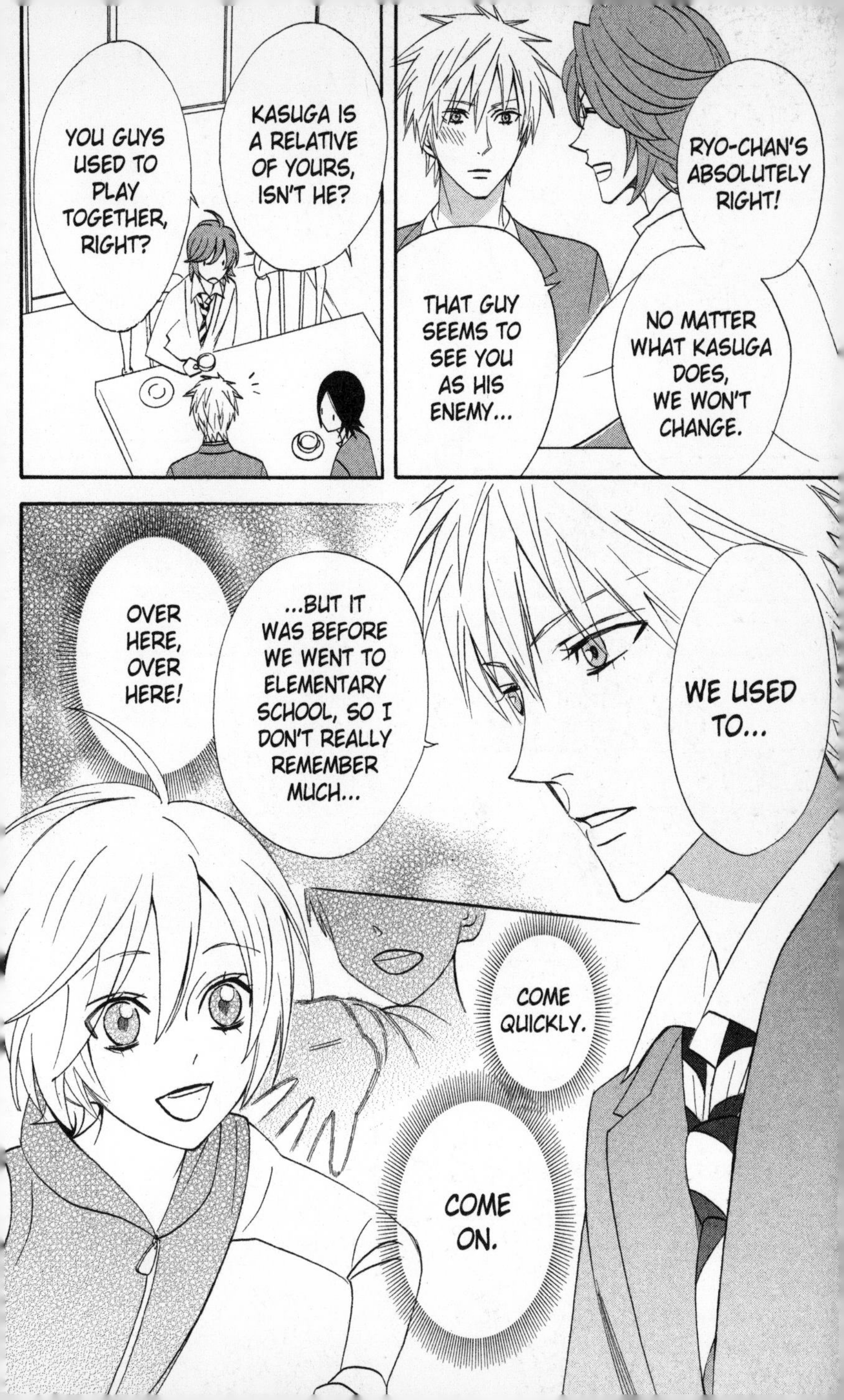
RYO-CHAN'S ABSOLUTELY RIGHT!
NO MATTER WHAT KASUGA DOES, WE WON'T CHANGE.
THAT GUY SEEMS TO SEE YOU AS HIS ENEMY...
KASUGA IS A RELATIVE OF YOURS, ISN'T HE?
YOU GUYS USED TO PLAY TOGETHER, RIGHT?
WE USED TO...
...BUT IT WAS BEFORE WE WENT TO ELEMENTARY SCHOOL, SO I DON'T REALLY REMEMBER MUCH...
OVER HERE, OVER HERE!
COME QUICKLY.
COME ON.

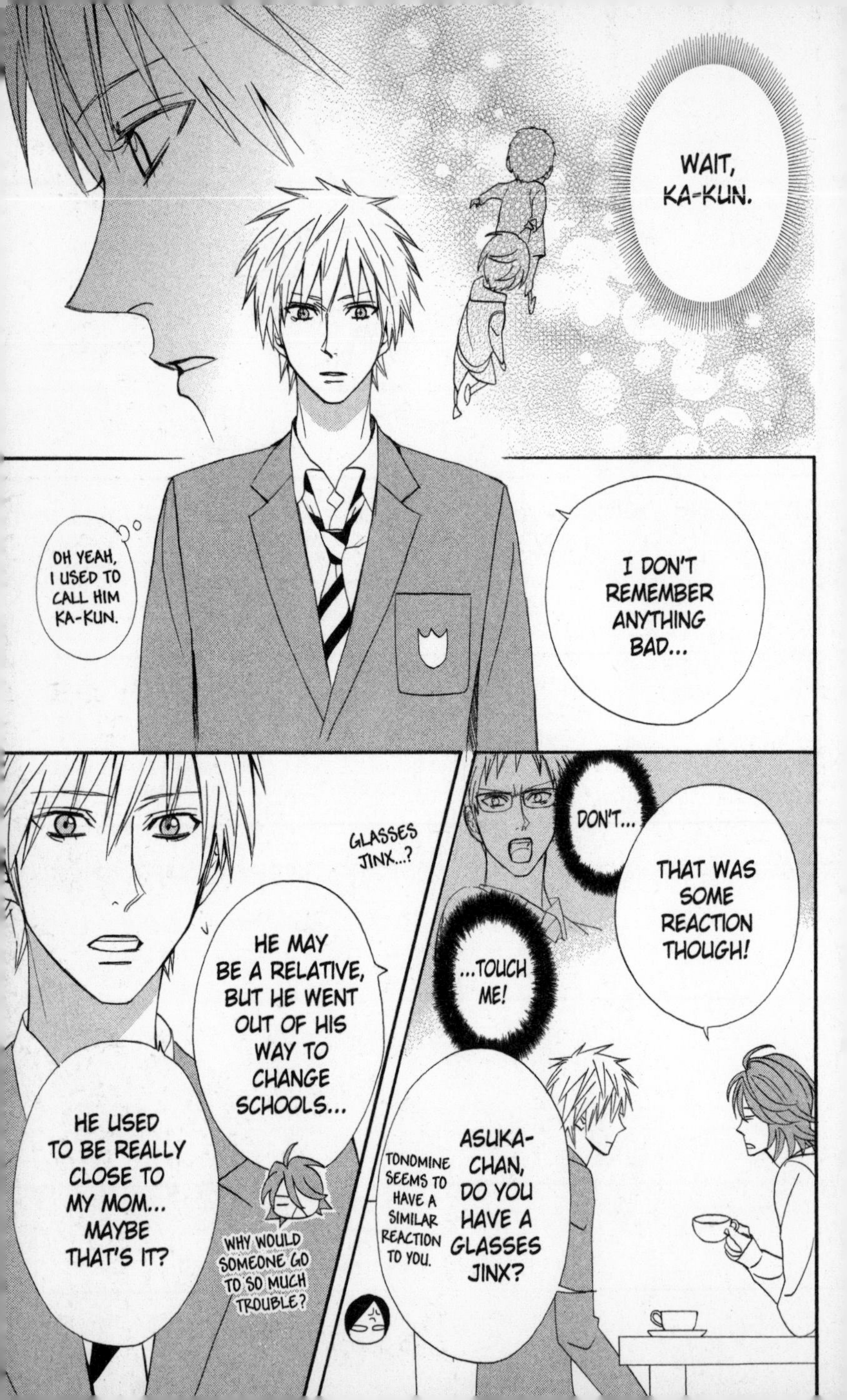
WAIT, KA-KUN.
I DON'T REMEMBER ANYTHING BAD...
OH YEAH, I USED TO CALL HIM KA-KUN.
DON'T...
...TOUCH ME!
THAT WAS SOME REACTION THOUGH!
ASUKA-CHAN, DO YOU HAVE A GLASSES JINX?
TONOMINE SEEMS TO HAVE A SIMILAR REACTION TO YOU.
GLASSES JINX...?
HE MAY BE A RELATIVE, BUT HE WENT OUT OF HIS WAY TO CHANGE SCHOOLS...
HE USED TO BE REALLY CLOSE TO MY MOM... MAYBE THAT'S IT?
WHY WOULD SOMEONE GO TO SO MUCH TROUBLE?

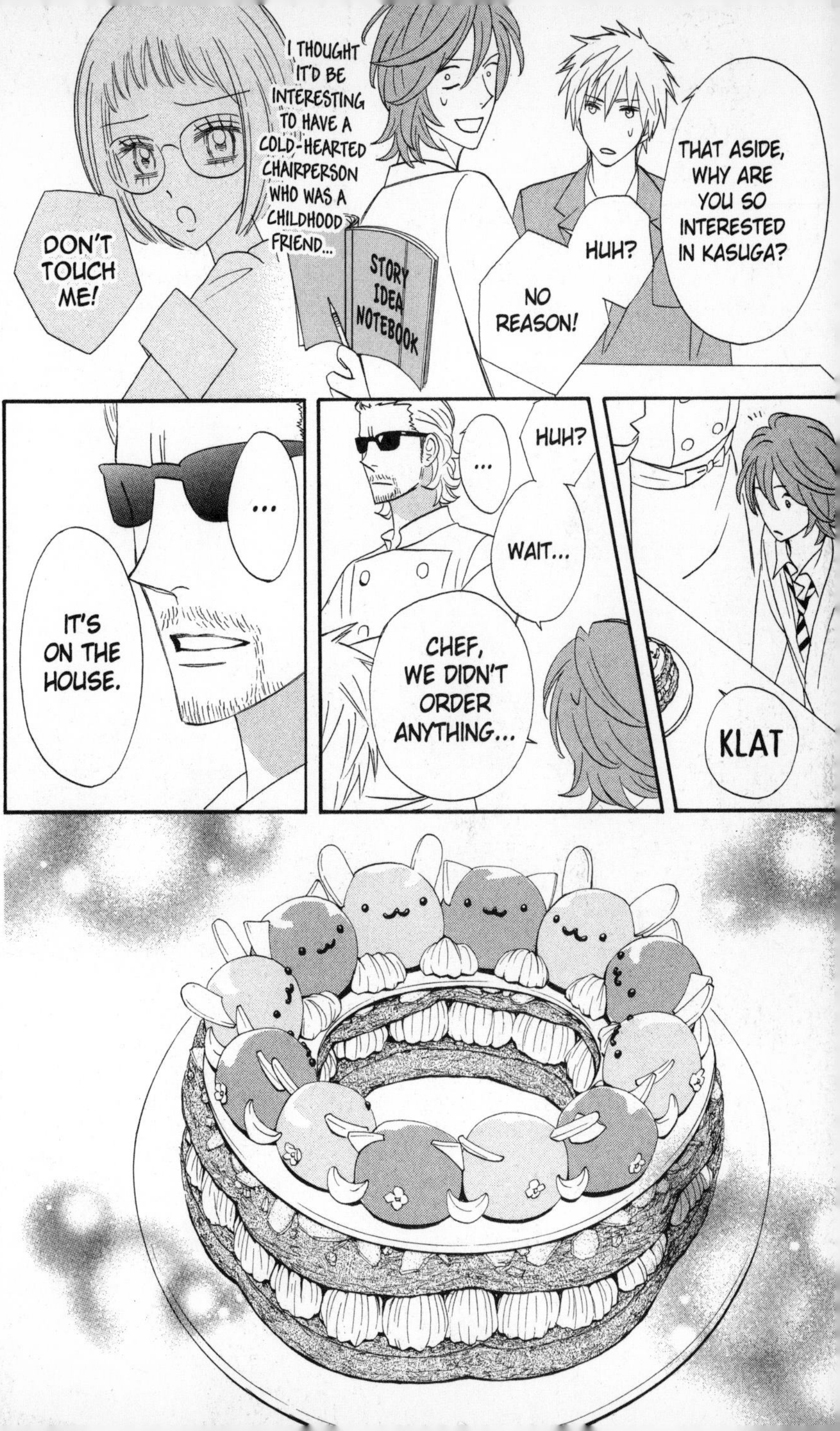
THAT ASIDE, WHY ARE YOU SO INTERESTED IN KASUGA?
HUH?
NO REASON!
I THOUGHT IT'D BE INTERESTING TO HAVE A COLD-HEARTED CHAIRPERSON WHO WAS A CHILDHOOD FRIEND...
STORY IDEA NOTEBOOK
DON'T TOUCH ME!
KLAT
HUH?
...
WAIT...
CHEF, WE DIDN'T ORDER ANYTHING...
...
IT'S ON THE HOUSE.

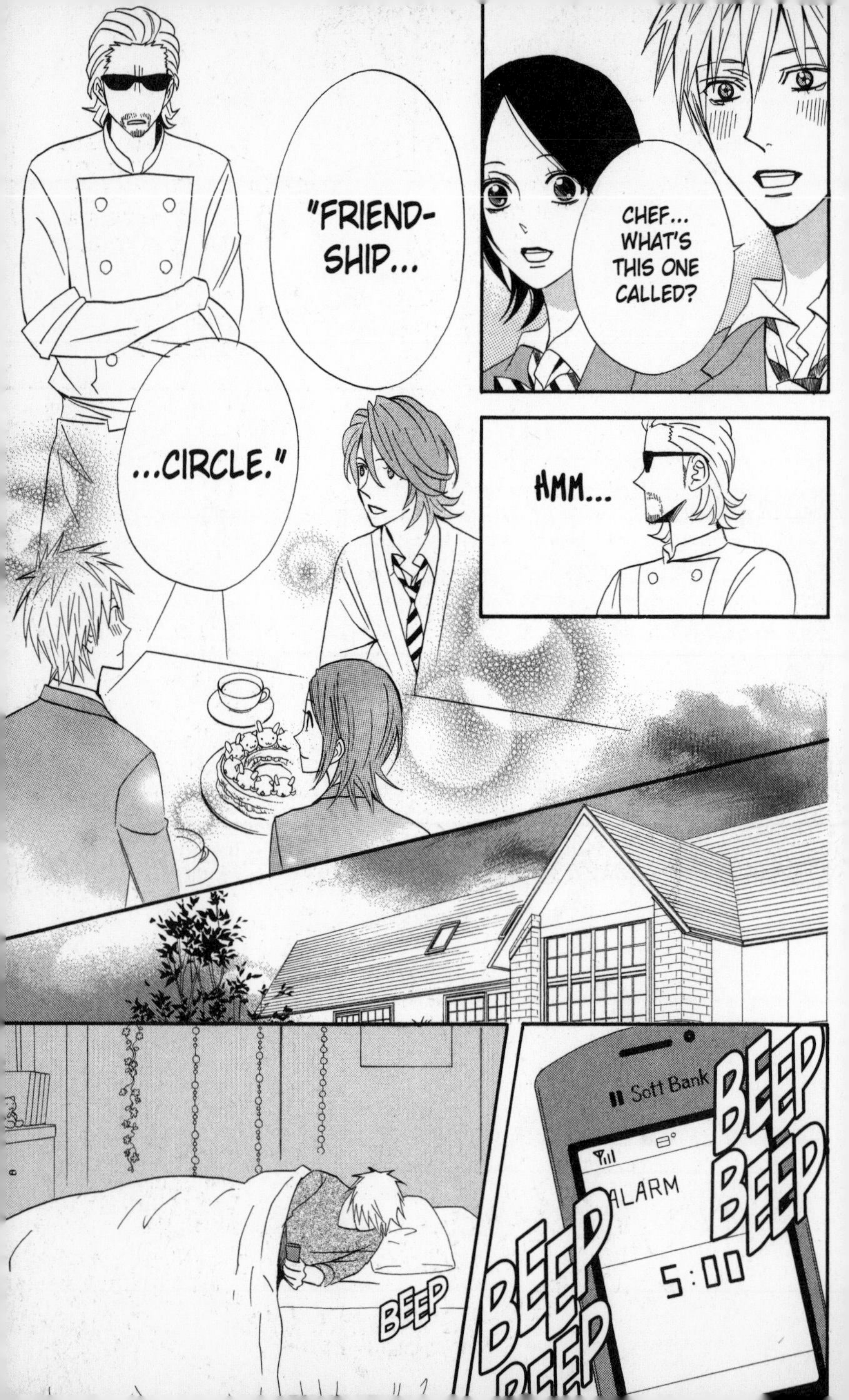
CHEF... WHAT'S THIS ONE CALLED?
HMM...
"FRIEND-SHIP...
...CIRCLE."
Soft Bank
ALARM
5:00
BEEP BEEP
BEEP BEEP
BEEP
BEEP

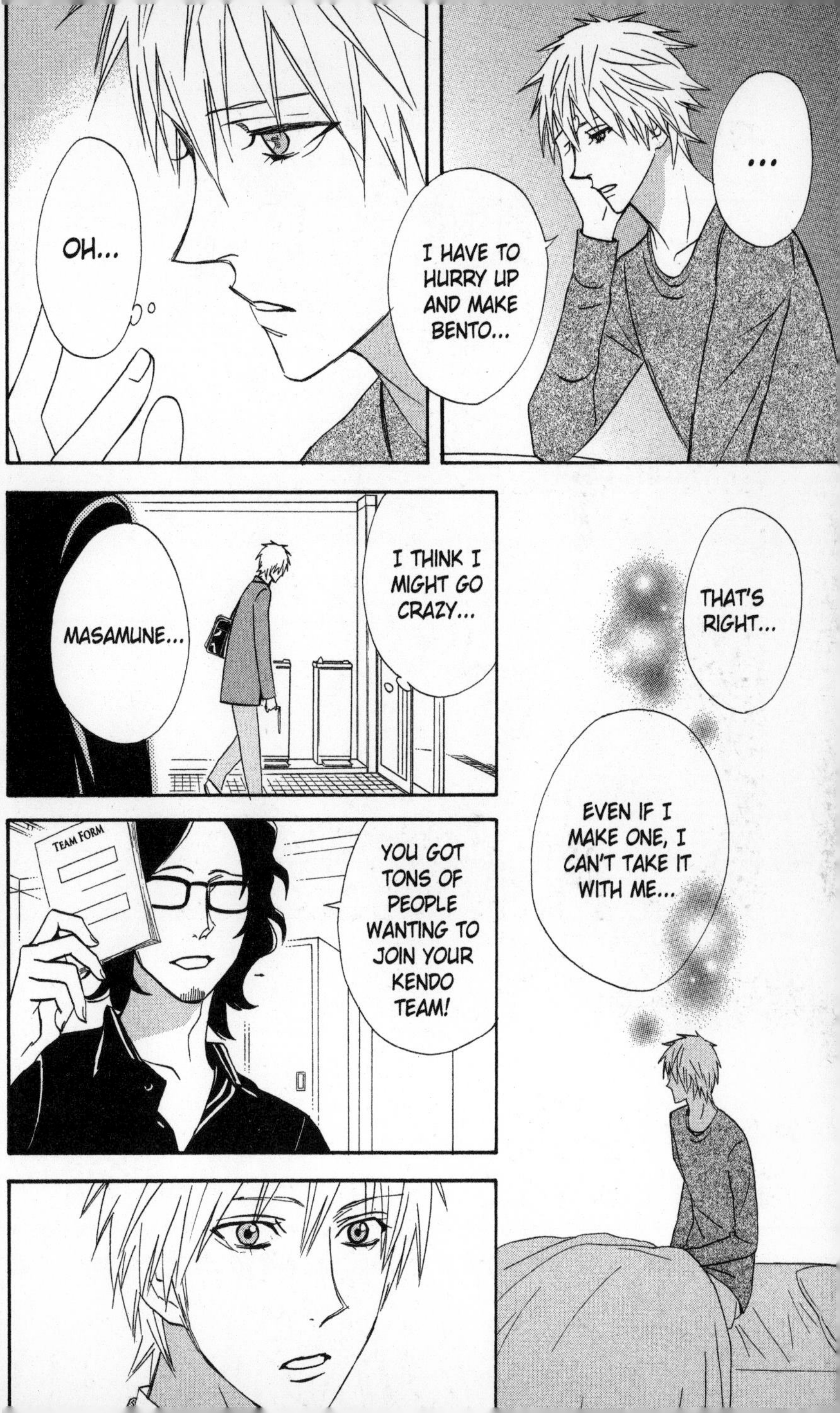
...
I HAVE TO HURRY UP AND MAKE BENTO...
OH...
THAT'S RIGHT...
EVEN IF I MAKE ONE, I CAN'T TAKE IT WITH ME...
I THINK I MIGHT GO CRAZY...
MASAMUNE...
TEAM FORM
YOU GOT TONS OF PEOPLE WANTING TO JOIN YOUR KENDO TEAM!

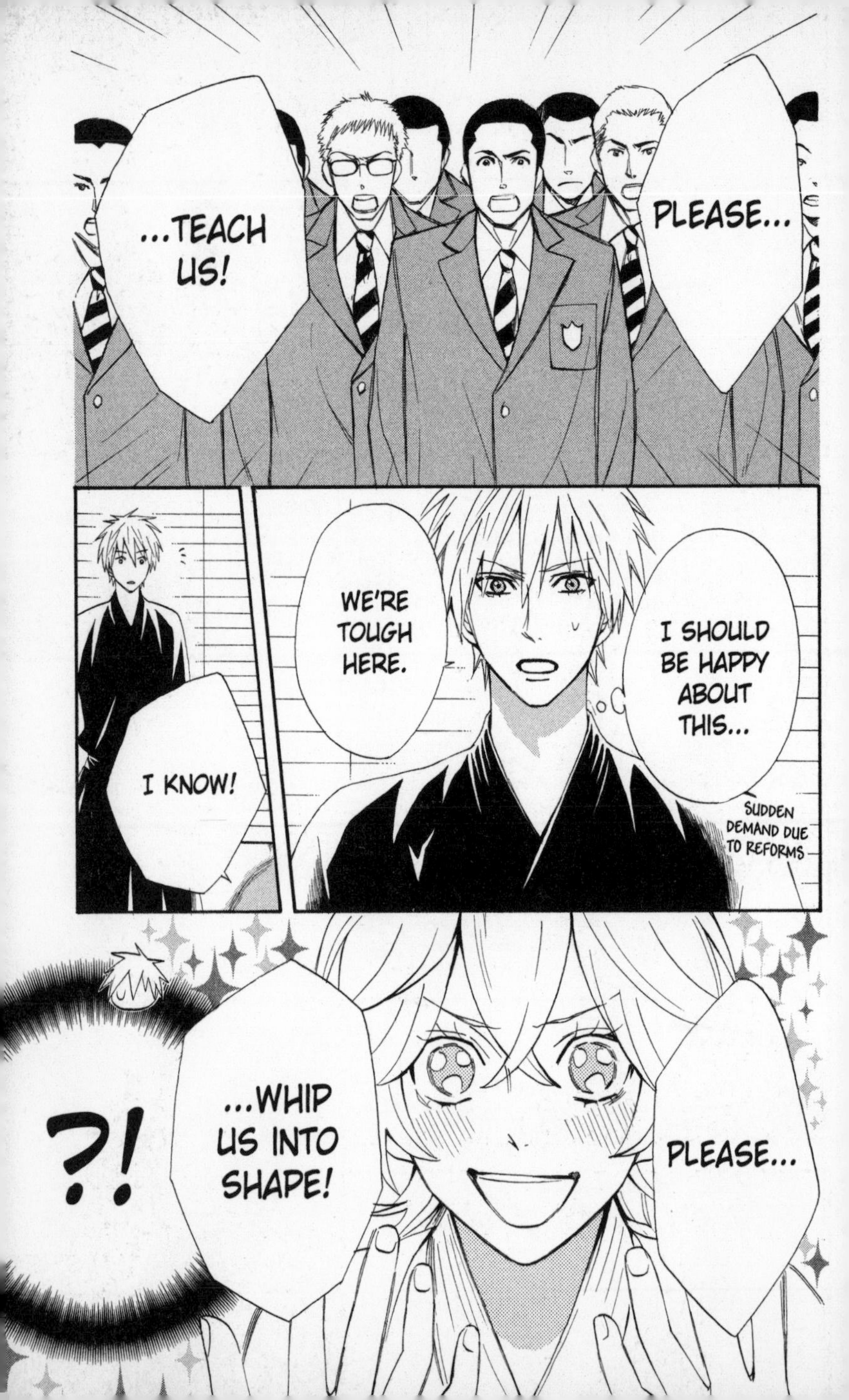
PLEASE...
...TEACH US!
I SHOULD BE HAPPY ABOUT THIS...
WE'RE TOUGH HERE.
SUDDEN DEMAND DUE TO REFORMS
I KNOW!
PLEASE...
...WHIP US INTO SHAPE!
?!

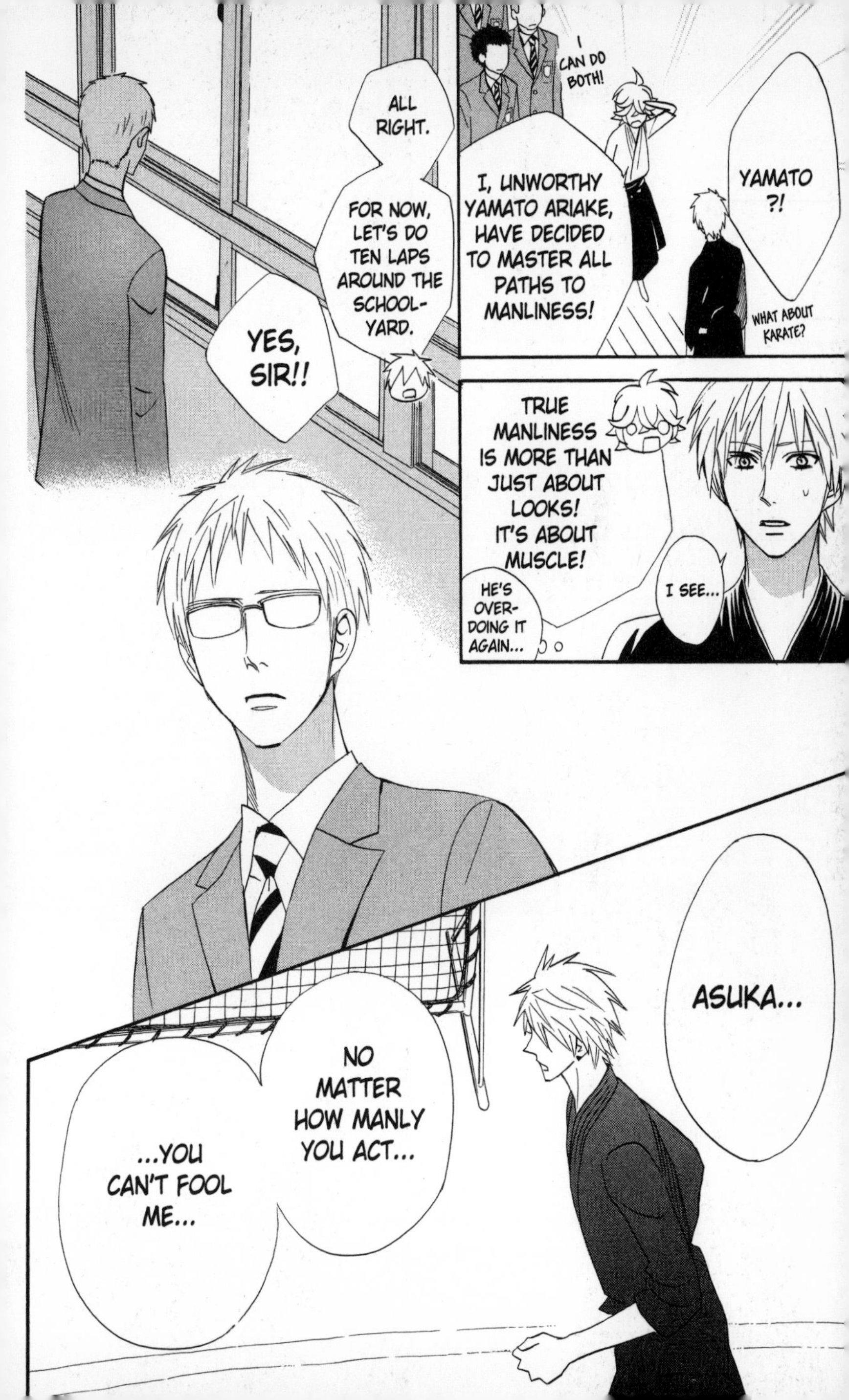
YAMATO ?!
WHAT ABOUT KARATE?
I CAN DO BOTH!
I, UNWORTHY YAMATO ARIAKE, HAVE DECIDED TO MASTER ALL PATHS TO MANLINESS!
TRUE MANLINESS IS MORE THAN JUST ABOUT LOOKS! IT'S ABOUT MUSCLE!
I SEE...
HE'S OVER-DOING IT AGAIN...
ALL RIGHT.
FOR NOW, LET'S DO TEN LAPS AROUND THE SCHOOL-YARD.
YES, SIR!!
ASUKA...
NO MATTER HOW MANLY YOU ACT...
...YOU CAN'T FOOL ME...

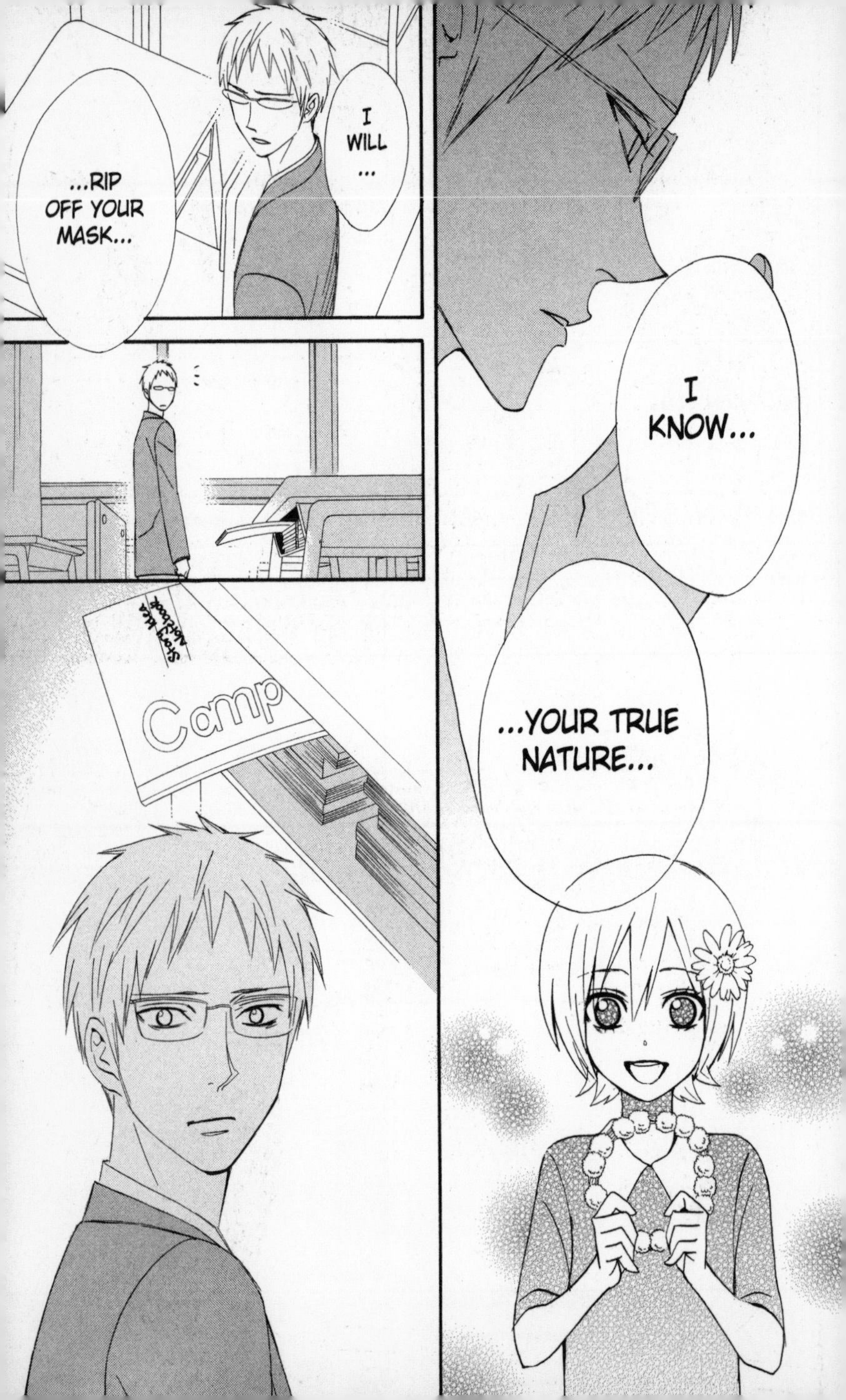
I KNOW...
...YOUR TRUE NATURE...
I WILL...
...RIP OFF YOUR MASK...
Story Idea Notebook
Camp

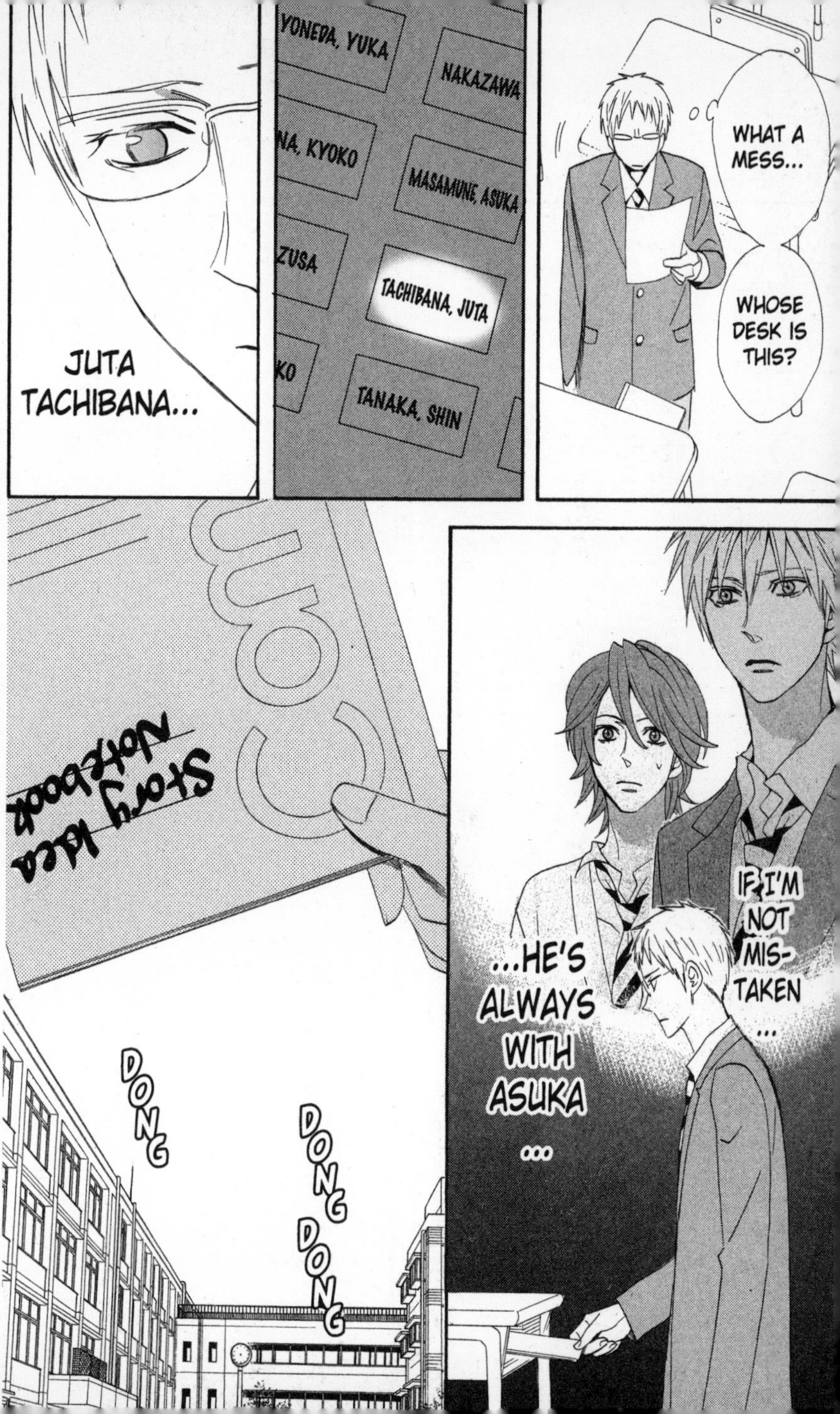
WHAT A MESS...
WHOSE DESK IS THIS?
YONEDA, YUKA
NAKAZAWA
MASAMUNE, ASUKA
TACHIBANA, JUTA
TANAKA, SHIN
JUTA TACHIBANA...
IF I'M NOT MIS-TAKEN...
...HE'S ALWAYS WITH ASUKA...
Story Idea Notebook
DONG
DONG DONG DONG

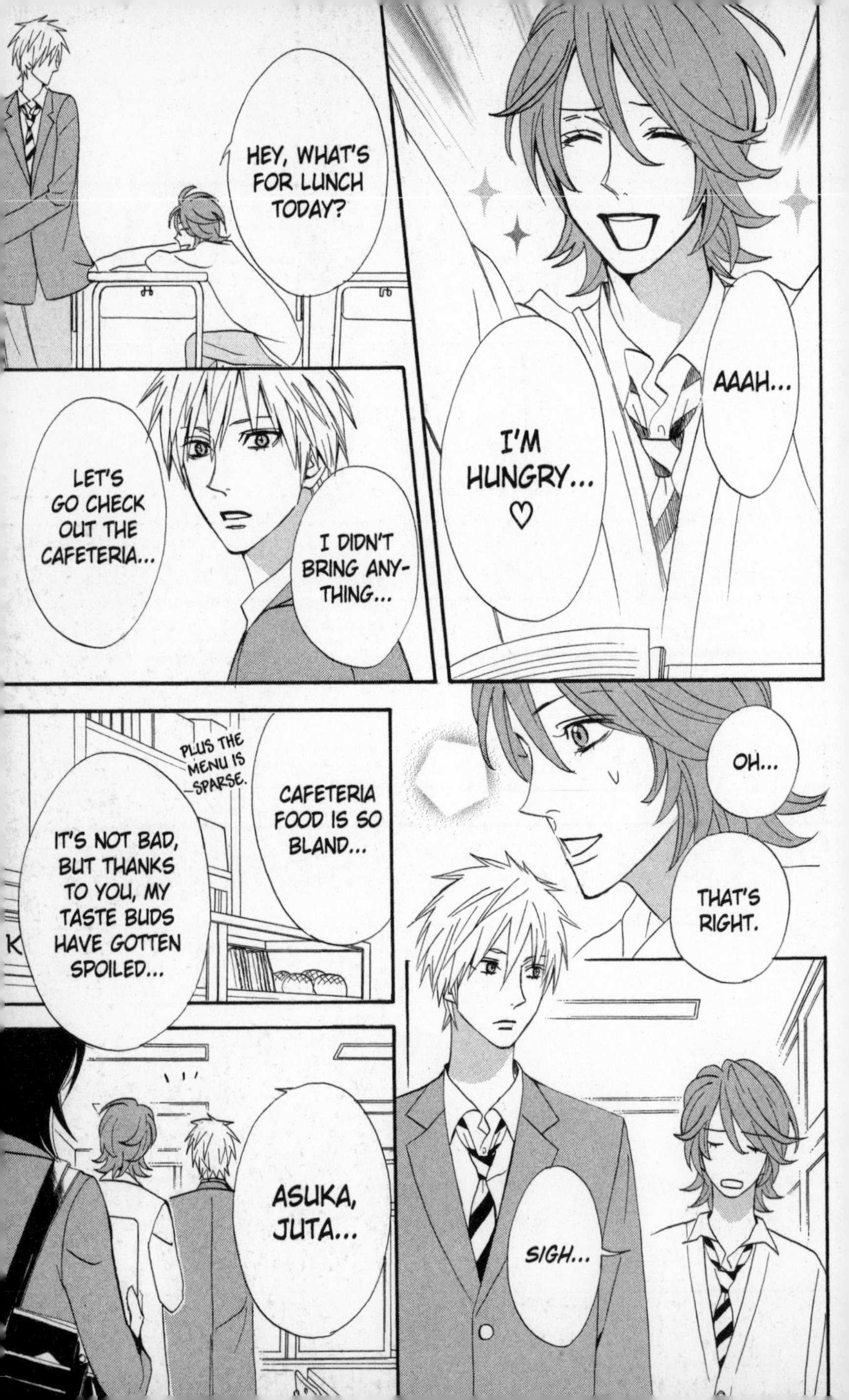
AAAH...
I'M HUNGRY... ♡
HEY, WHAT'S FOR LUNCH TODAY?
I DIDN'T BRING ANY-THING...
LET'S GO CHECK OUT THE CAFETERIA...
OH...
THAT'S RIGHT.
CAFETERIA FOOD IS SO BLAND...
PLUS THE MENU IS SPARSE.
IT'S NOT BAD, BUT THANKS TO YOU, MY TASTE BUDS HAVE GOTTEN SPOILED...
SIGH...
ASUKA, JUTA...

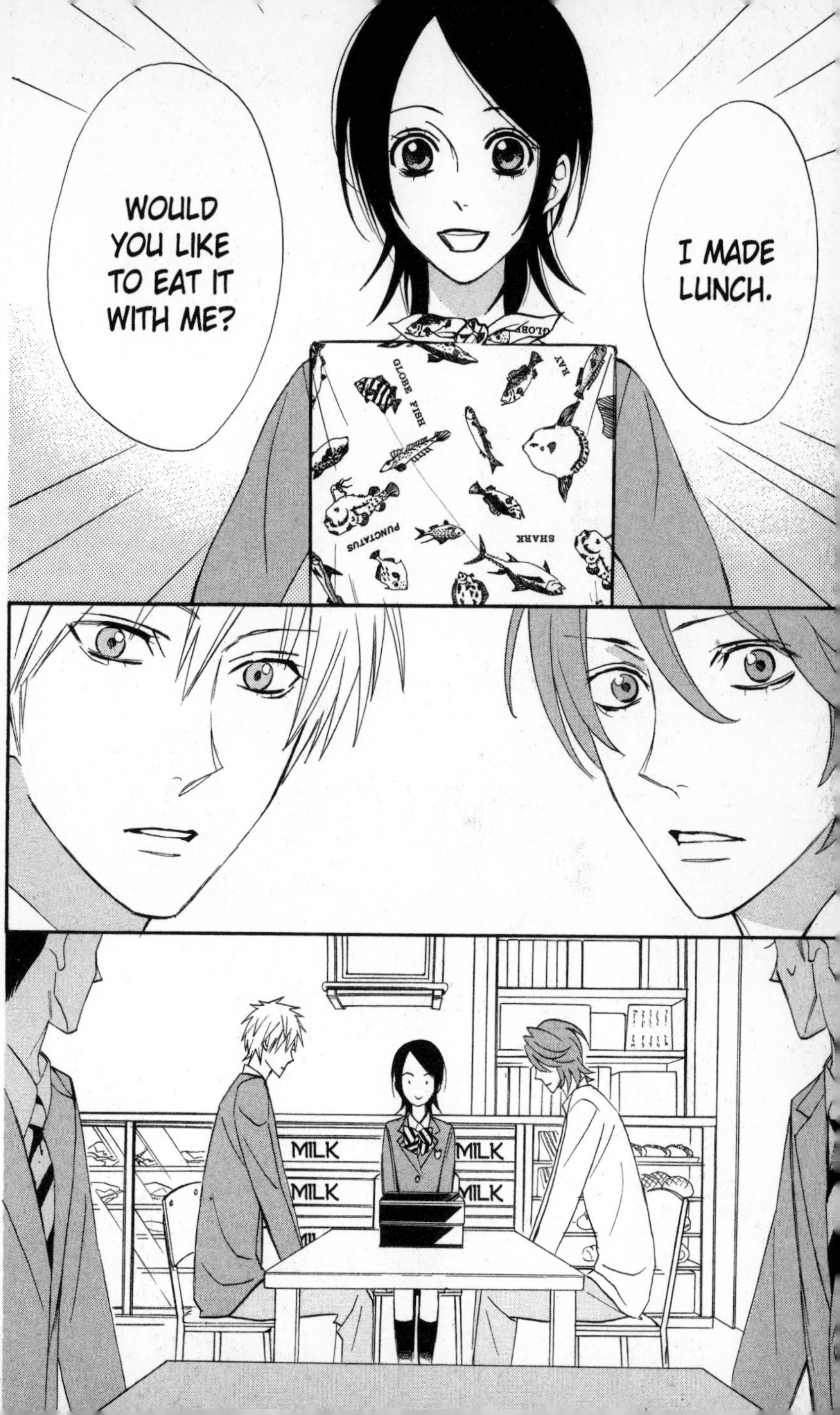
I MADE LUNCH.
WOULD YOU LIKE TO EAT IT WITH ME?
GLOBE FISH
RAY
MILK
MILK
MILK
MILK

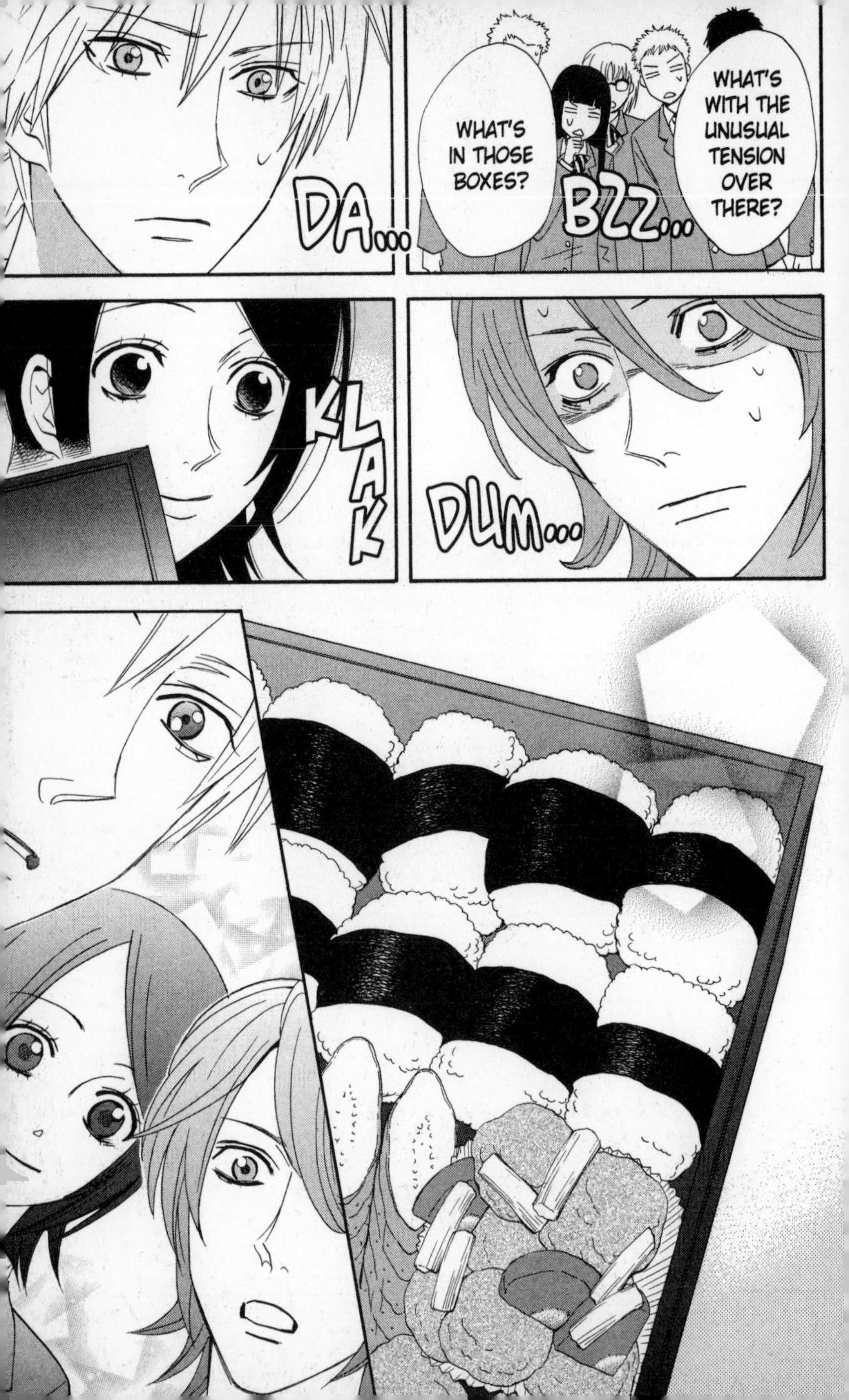

WHAT'S WITH THE UNUSUAL TENSION OVER THERE?
WHAT'S IN THOSE BOXES?
BZZ...
DA...
DUM...
KLAK

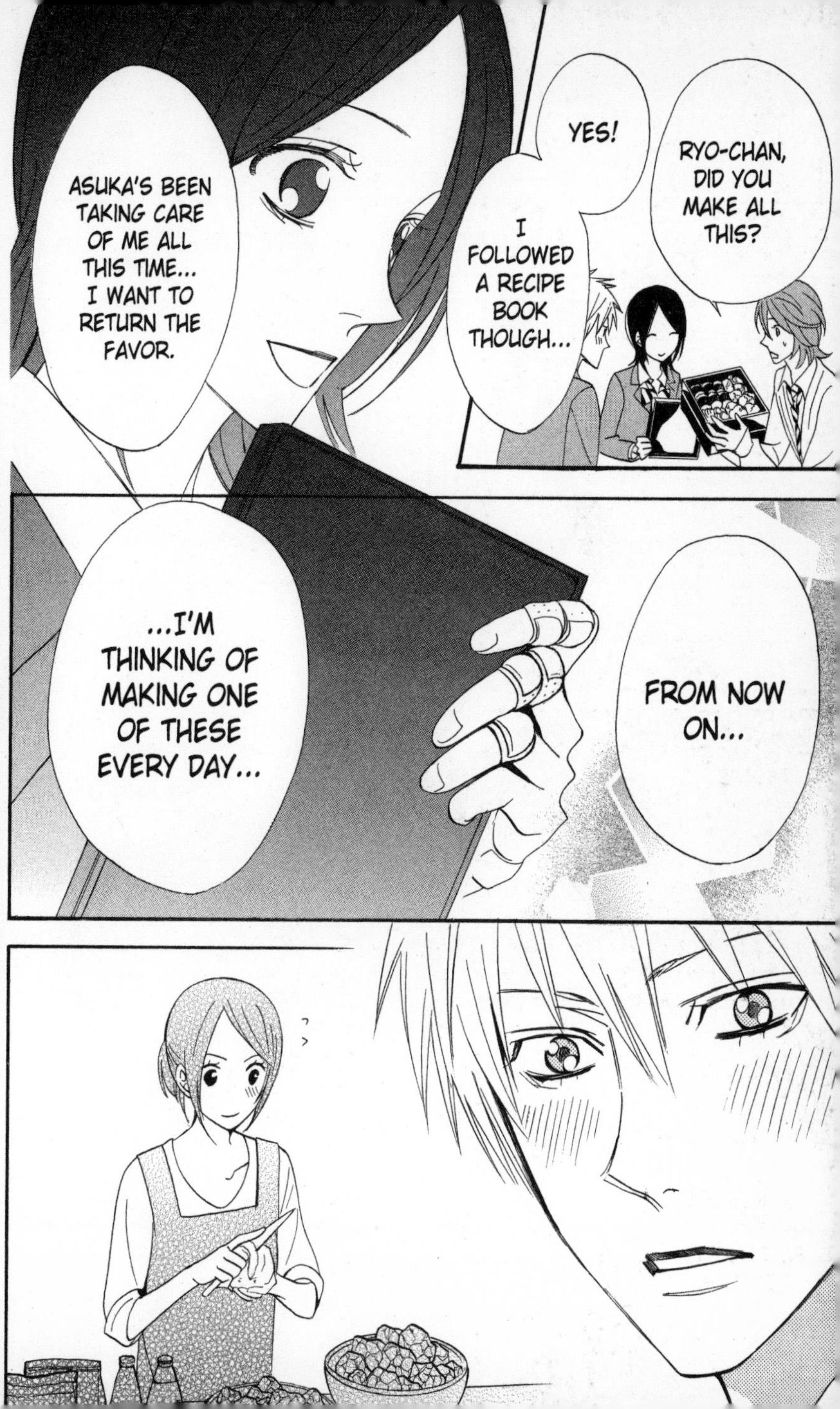
RYO-CHAN, DID YOU MAKE ALL THIS?
YES!
I FOLLOWED A RECIPE BOOK THOUGH...
ASUKA'S BEEN TAKING CARE OF ME ALL THIS TIME... I WANT TO RETURN THE FAVOR.
FROM NOW ON...
...I'M THINKING OF MAKING ONE OF THESE EVERY DAY...

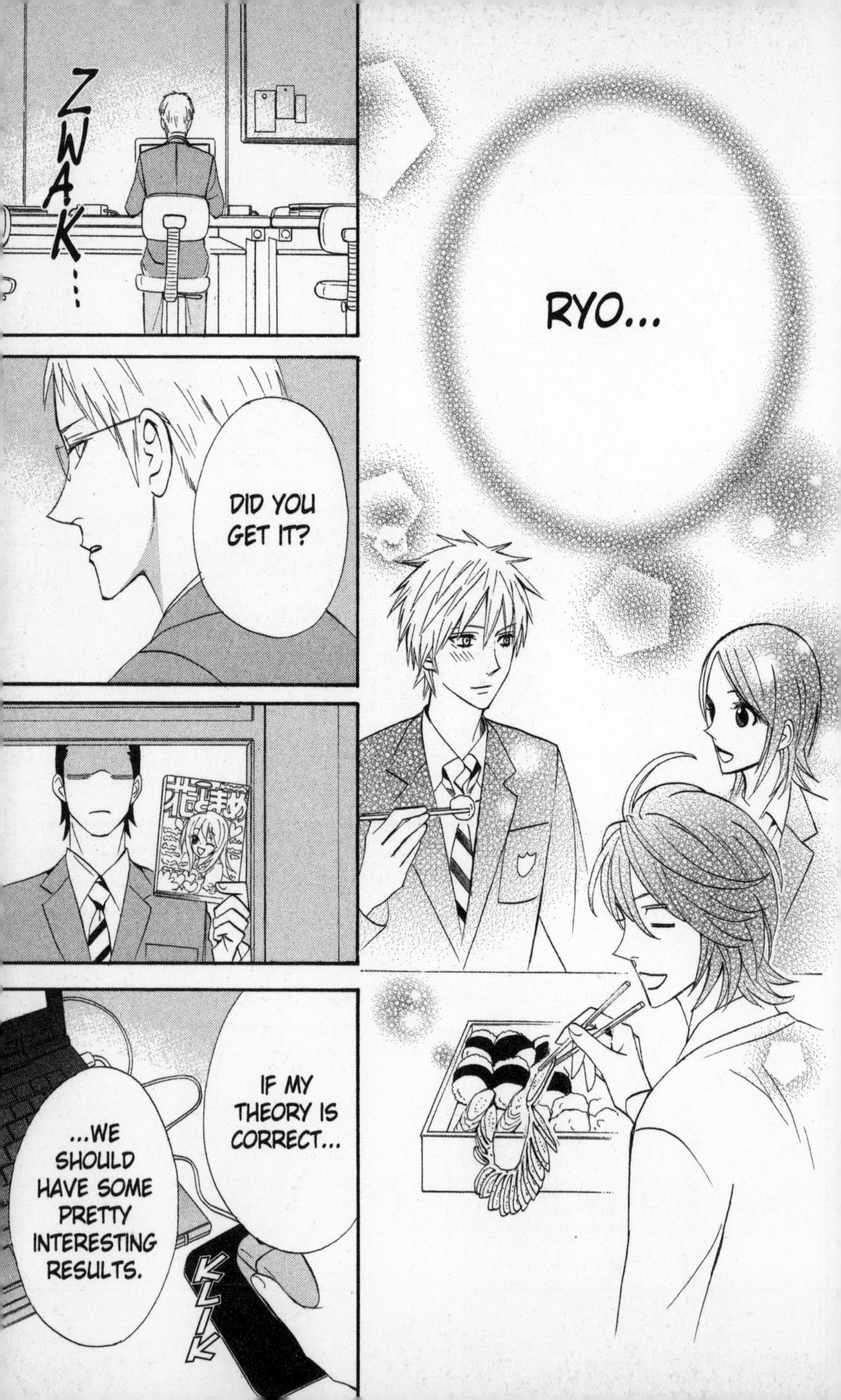
RYO...
ZWAK...
DID YOU GET IT?
IF MY THEORY IS CORRECT...
...WE SHOULD HAVE SOME PRETTY INTERESTING RESULTS.
KLIK

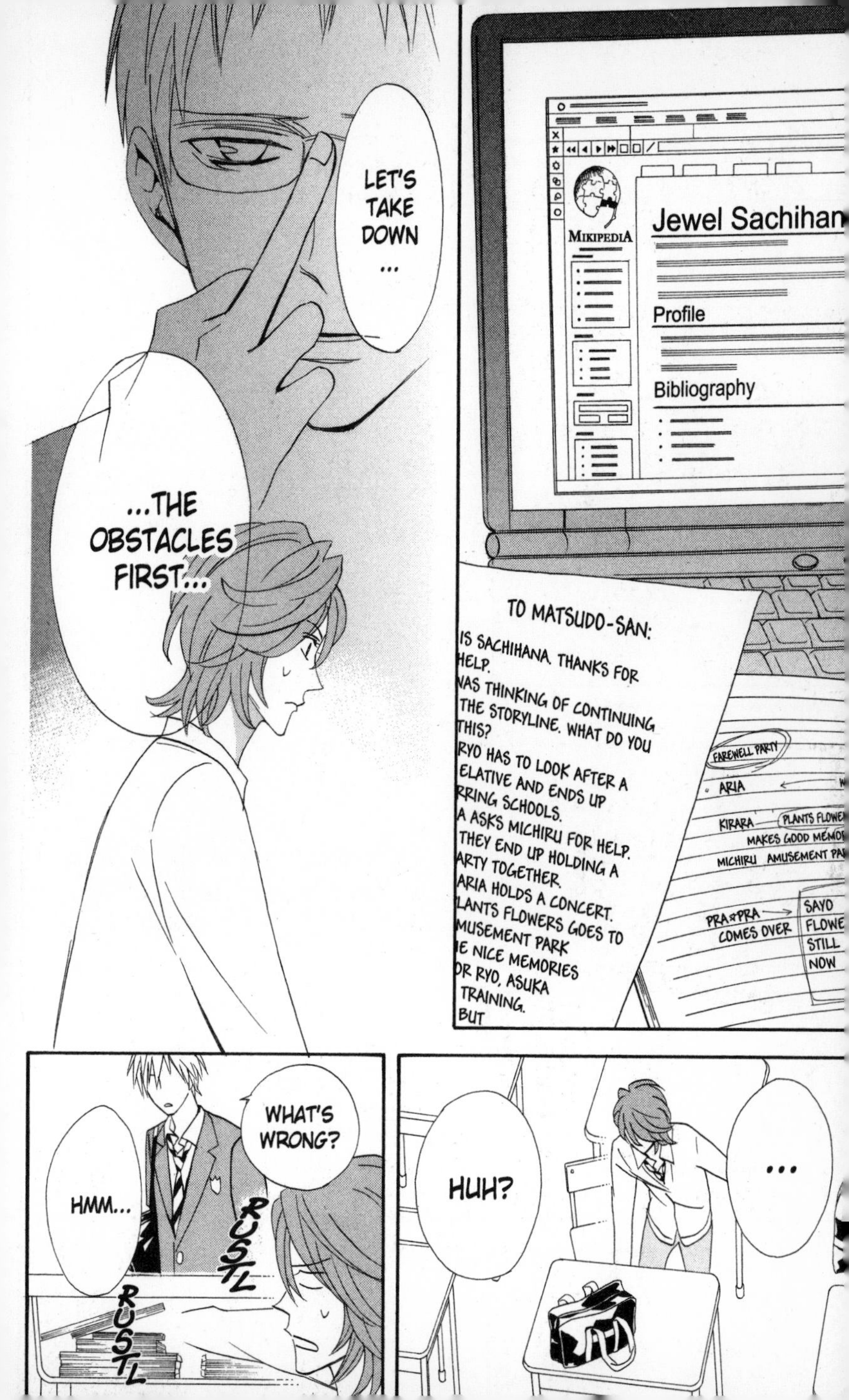
MIKIPEDIA
Jewel Sachihan
Profile
Bibliography
TO MATSUDO-SAN:
IS SACHIHANA. THANKS FOR
HELP.
NAS THINKING OF CONTINUING
THE STORYLINE. WHAT DO YOU
THIS?
RYO HAS TO LOOK AFTER A
ELATIVE AND ENDS UP
RRING SCHOOLS.
A ASKS MICHIRU FOR HELP.
THEY END UP HOLDING A
ARTY TOGETHER.
ARIA HOLDS A CONCERT.
LANTS FLOWERS GOES TO
MUSEMENT PARK
E NICE MEMORIES
R RYO, ASUKA
TRAINING.
BUT
FAREWELL PARTY
ARIA
KIRARA
PLANTS FLOWE
MAKES GOOD MEMO
MICHIRU
AMUSEMENT PA
PRA☆PRA
COMES OVER
SAYO
FLOWE
STILL
NOW
LET'S TAKE DOWN...
...THE OBSTACLES FIRST...
...
HUH?
WHAT'S WRONG?
RUSTL
HMM...
RUSTL

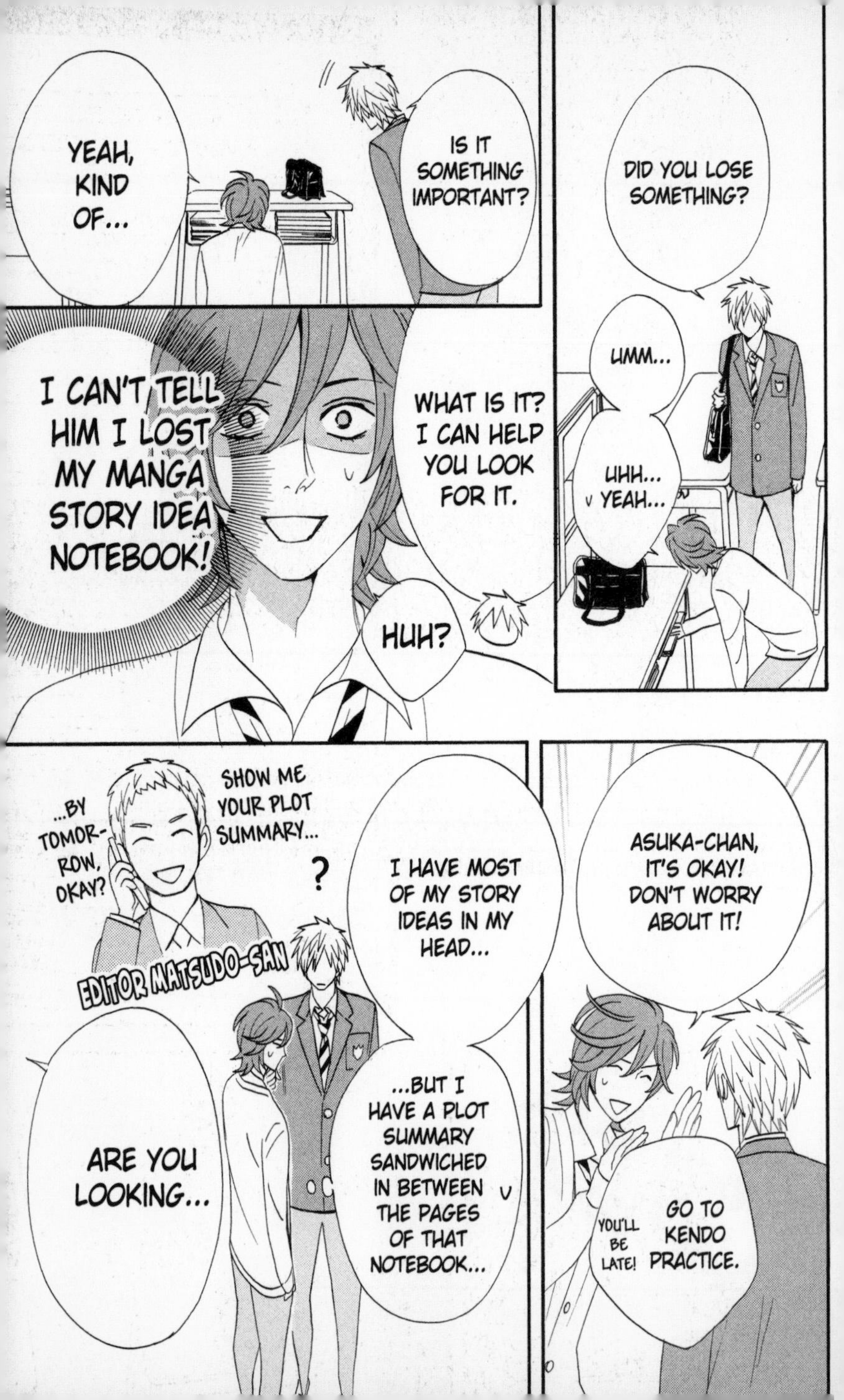
DID YOU LOSE SOMETHING?
UMM...
UHH... YEAH...
IS IT SOMETHING IMPORTANT?
YEAH, KIND OF...
WHAT IS IT? I CAN HELP YOU LOOK FOR IT.
I CAN'T TELL HIM I LOST MY MANGA STORY IDEA NOTEBOOK!
HUH?
ASUKA-CHAN, IT'S OKAY! DON'T WORRY ABOUT IT!
GO TO KENDO PRACTICE.
YOU'LL BE LATE!
I HAVE MOST OF MY STORY IDEAS IN MY HEAD...
SHOW ME YOUR PLOT SUMMARY...
...BY TOMOR-ROW, OKAY?
?
EDITOR MATSUDO-SAN
...BUT I HAVE A PLOT SUMMARY SANDWICHED IN BETWEEN THE PAGES OF THAT NOTEBOOK...
ARE YOU LOOKING...

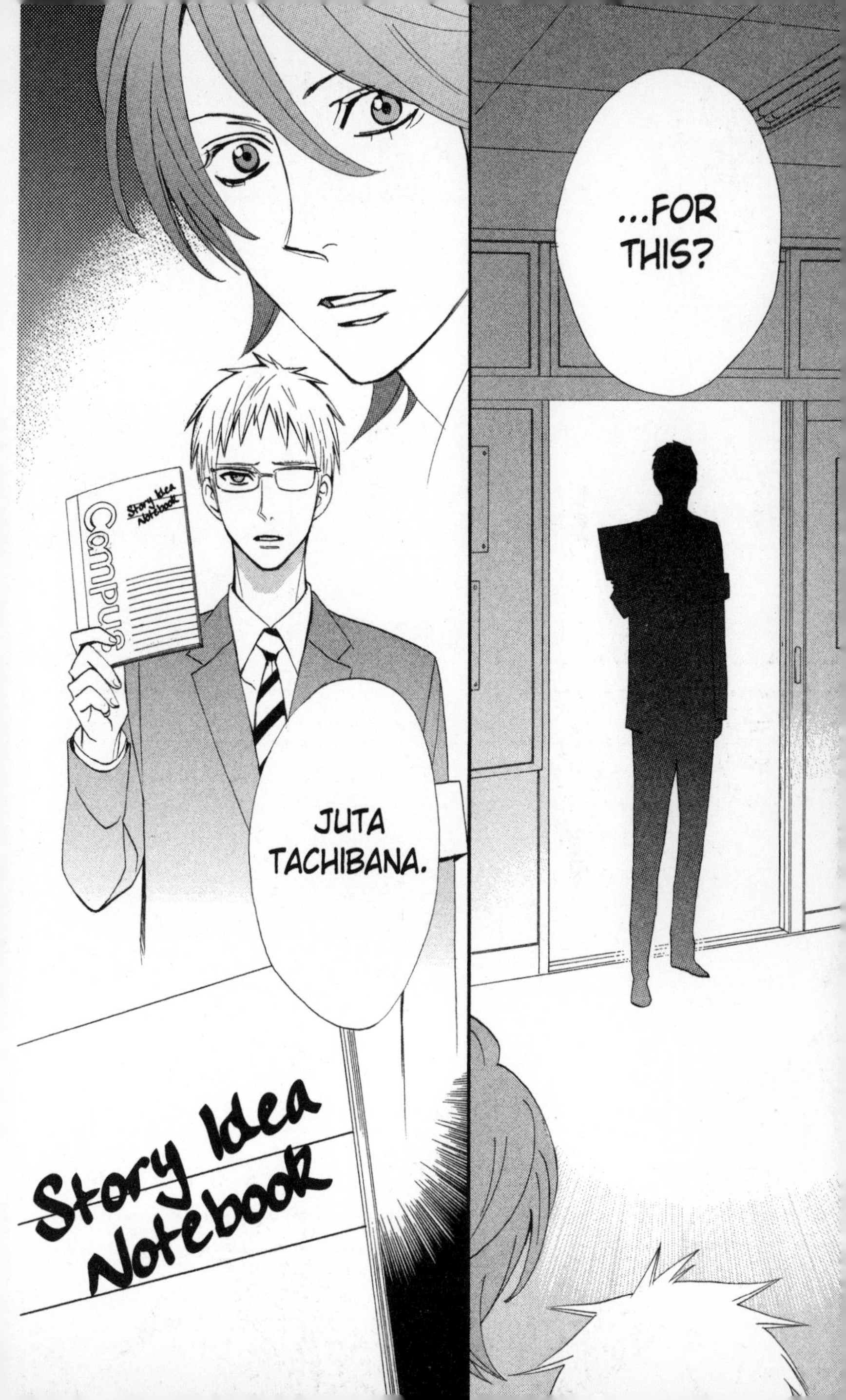
...FOR THIS?
Story Idea Notebook
Campus
JUTA TACHIBANA.
Story Idea Notebook

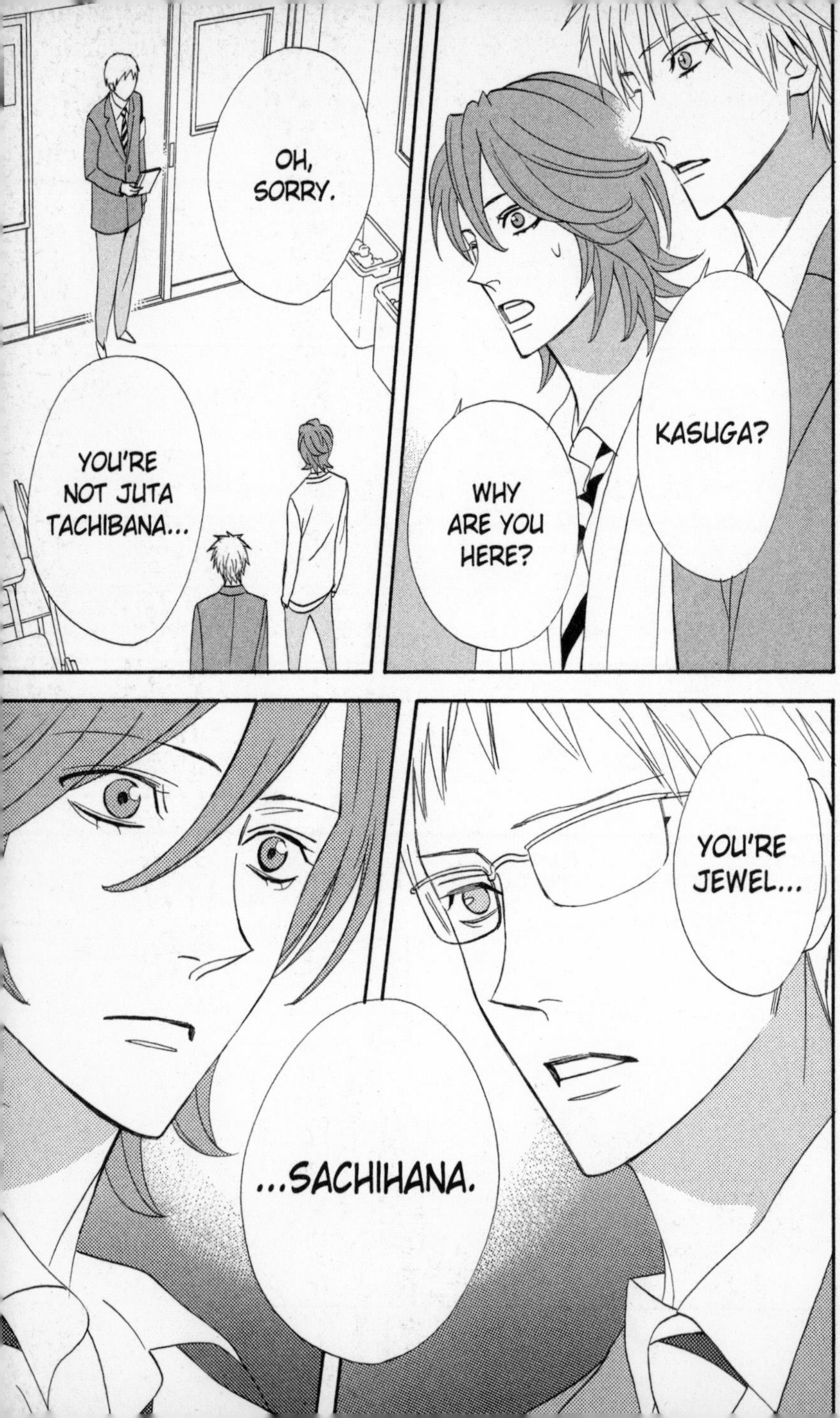
KASUGA?
WHY ARE YOU HERE?
OH, SORRY.
YOU'RE NOT JUTA TACHIBANA...
YOU'RE JEWEL...
...SACHIHANA.

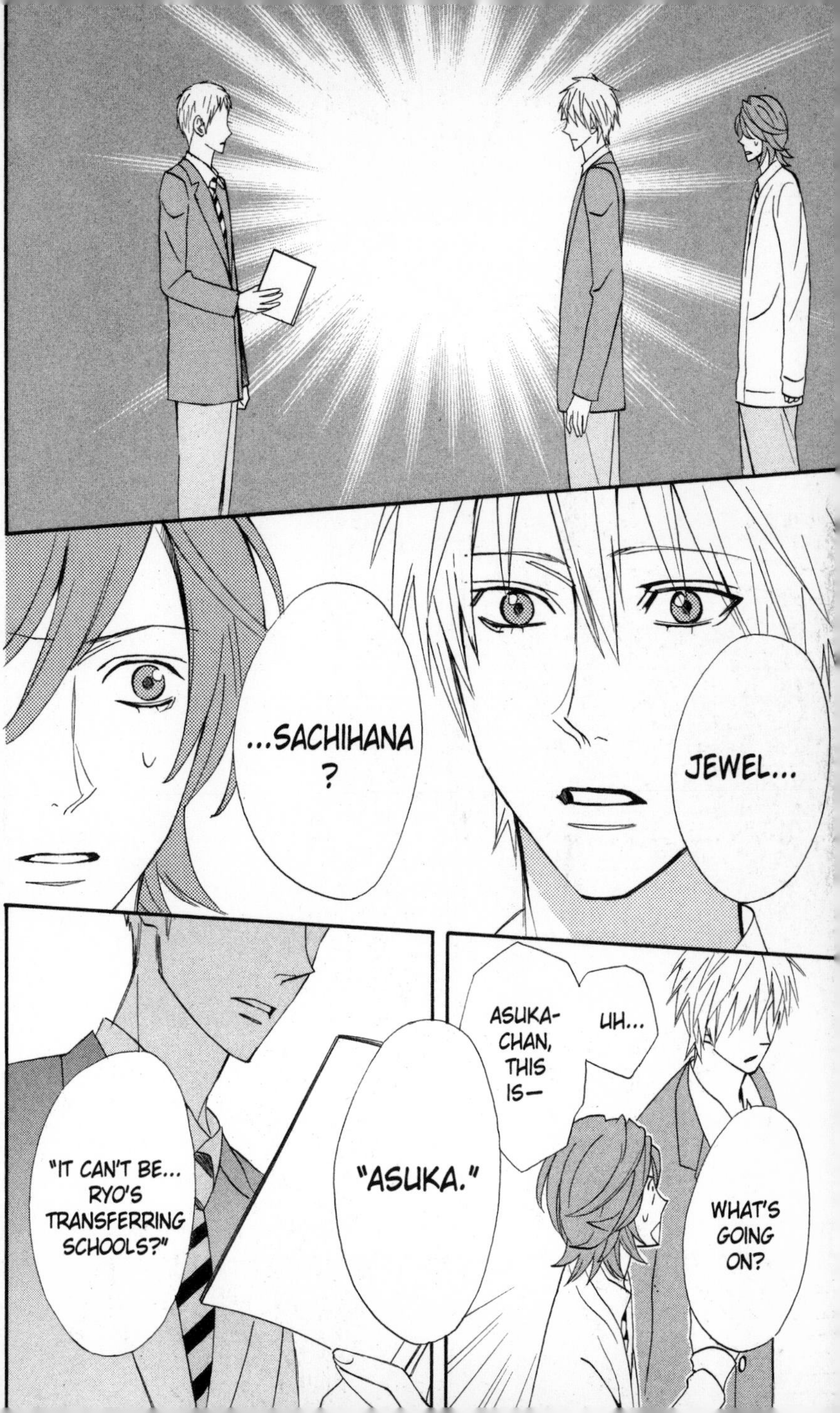
JEWEL...
...SACHIHANA?
UH...
ASUKA-CHAN, THIS IS—
WHAT'S GOING ON?
"ASUKA."
"IT CAN'T BE... RYO'S TRANSFERRING SCHOOLS?"

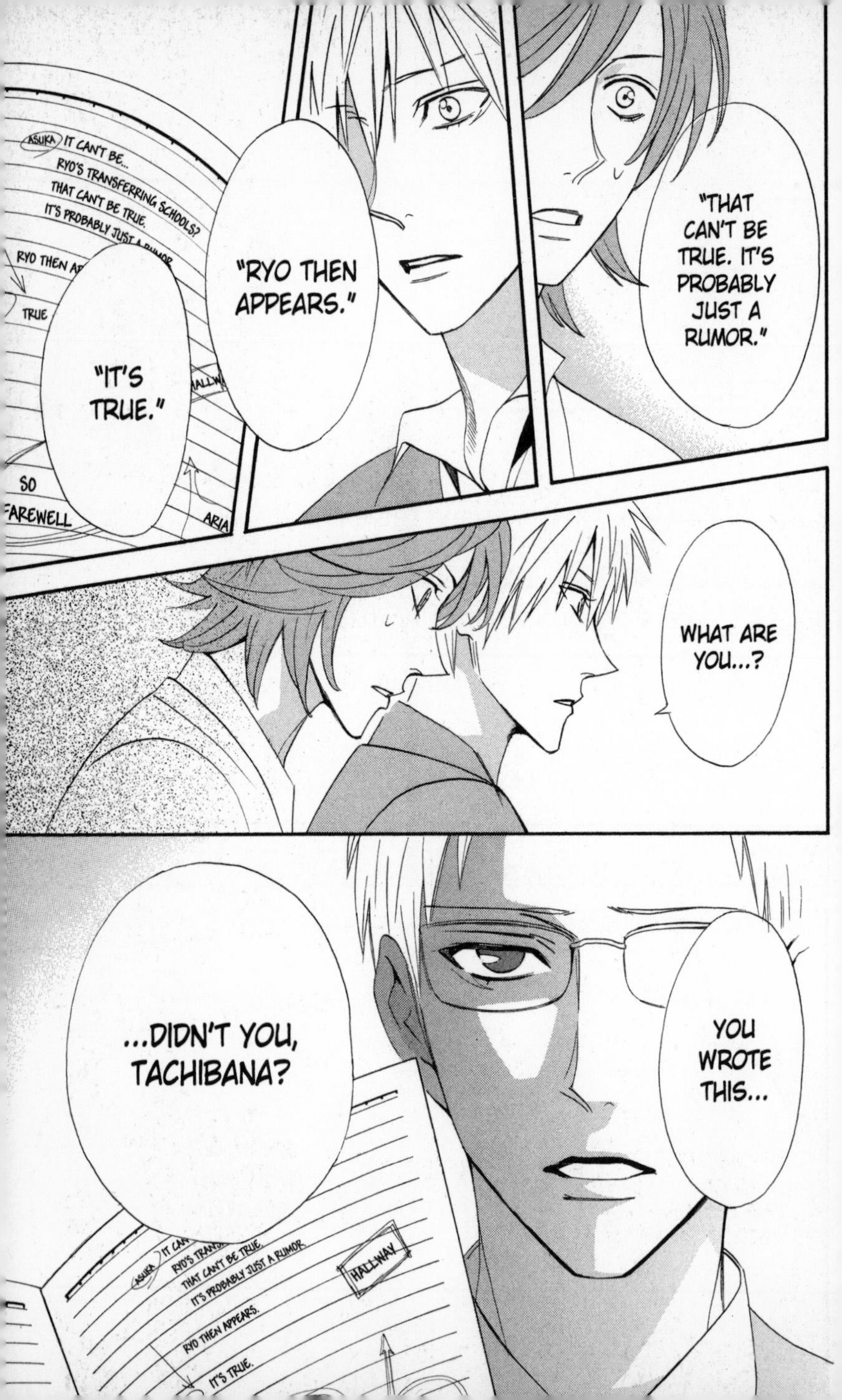
"THAT CAN'T BE TRUE. IT'S PROBABLY JUST A RUMOR."
"RYO THEN APPEARS."
ASUKA IT CAN'T BE..
RYO'S TRANSFERRING SCHOOLS?
THAT CAN'T BE TRUE.
"IT'S TRUE."
SO
FAREWELL
WHAT ARE YOU...?
YOU WROTE THIS...
...DIDN'T YOU, TACHIBANA?
THAT CAN'T BE TRUE.
IT'S PROBABLY JUST A RUMOR.
HALLWAY
RYO THEN APPEARS.
IT'S TRUE.

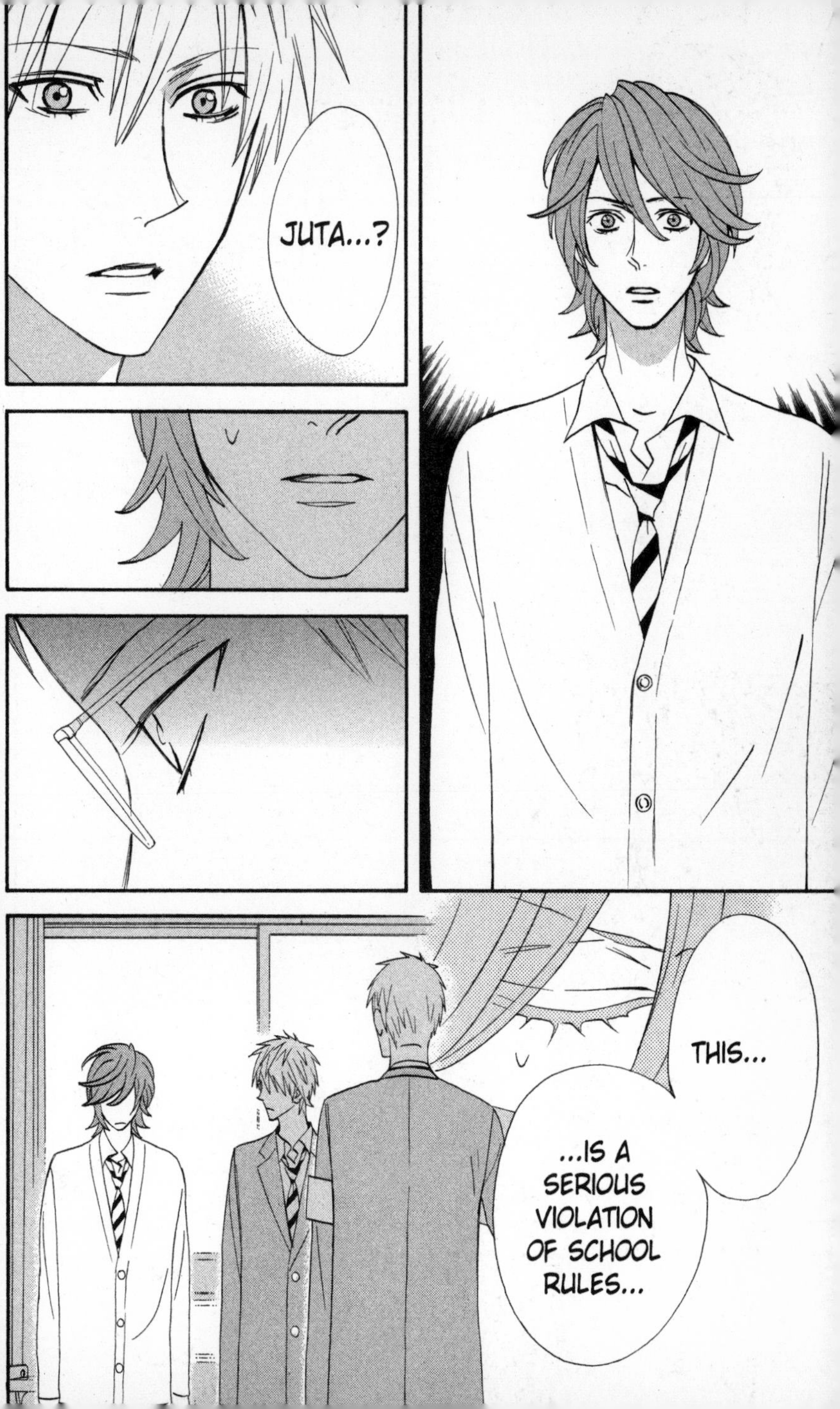
JUTA...?
THIS...
...IS A SERIOUS VIOLATION OF SCHOOL RULES...

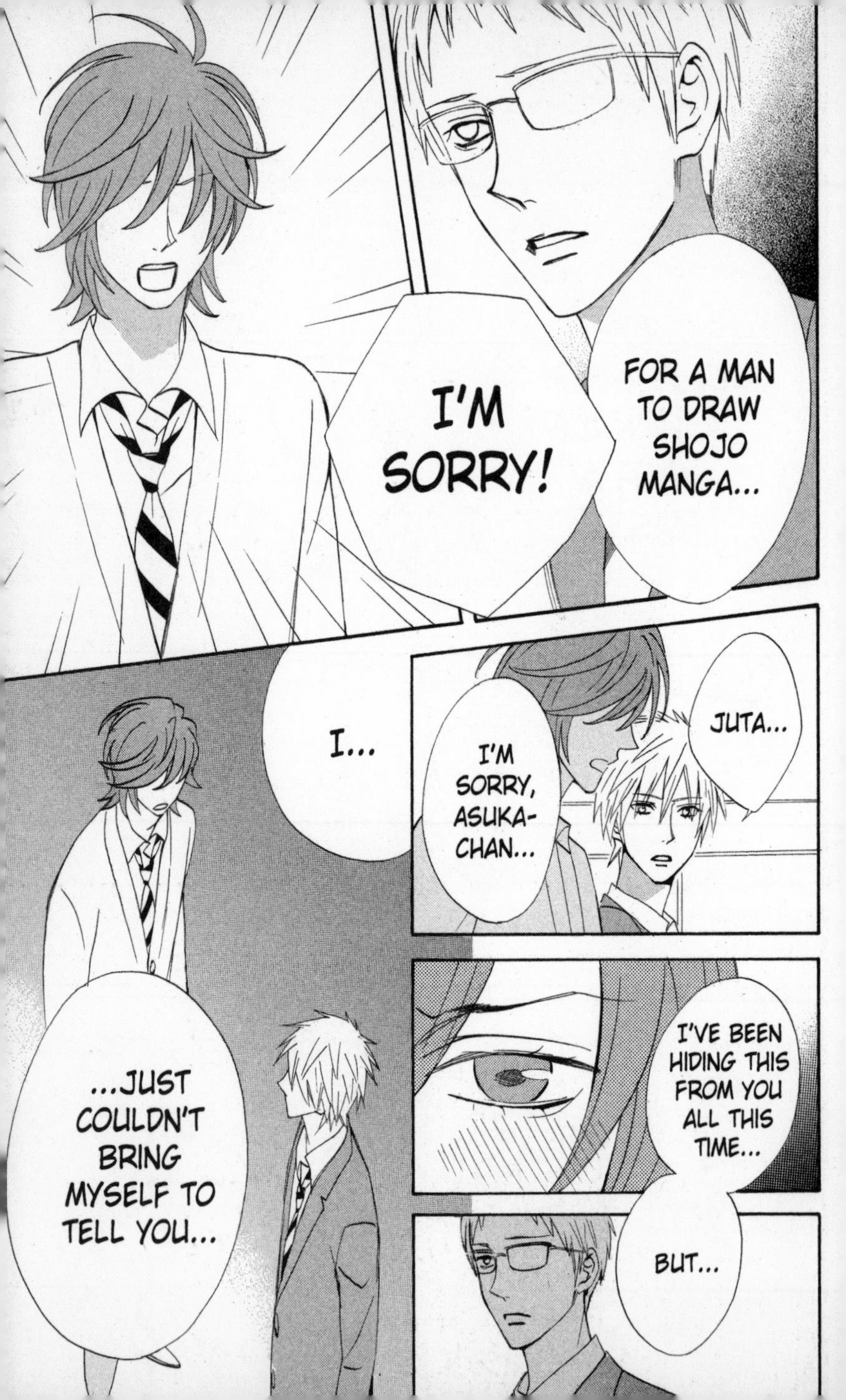
FOR A MAN TO DRAW SHOJO MANGA...
I'M SORRY!
JUTA...
I'M SORRY, ASUKA-CHAN...
I'VE BEEN HIDING THIS FROM YOU ALL THIS TIME...
BUT...
I...
...JUST COULDN'T BRING MYSELF TO TELL YOU...

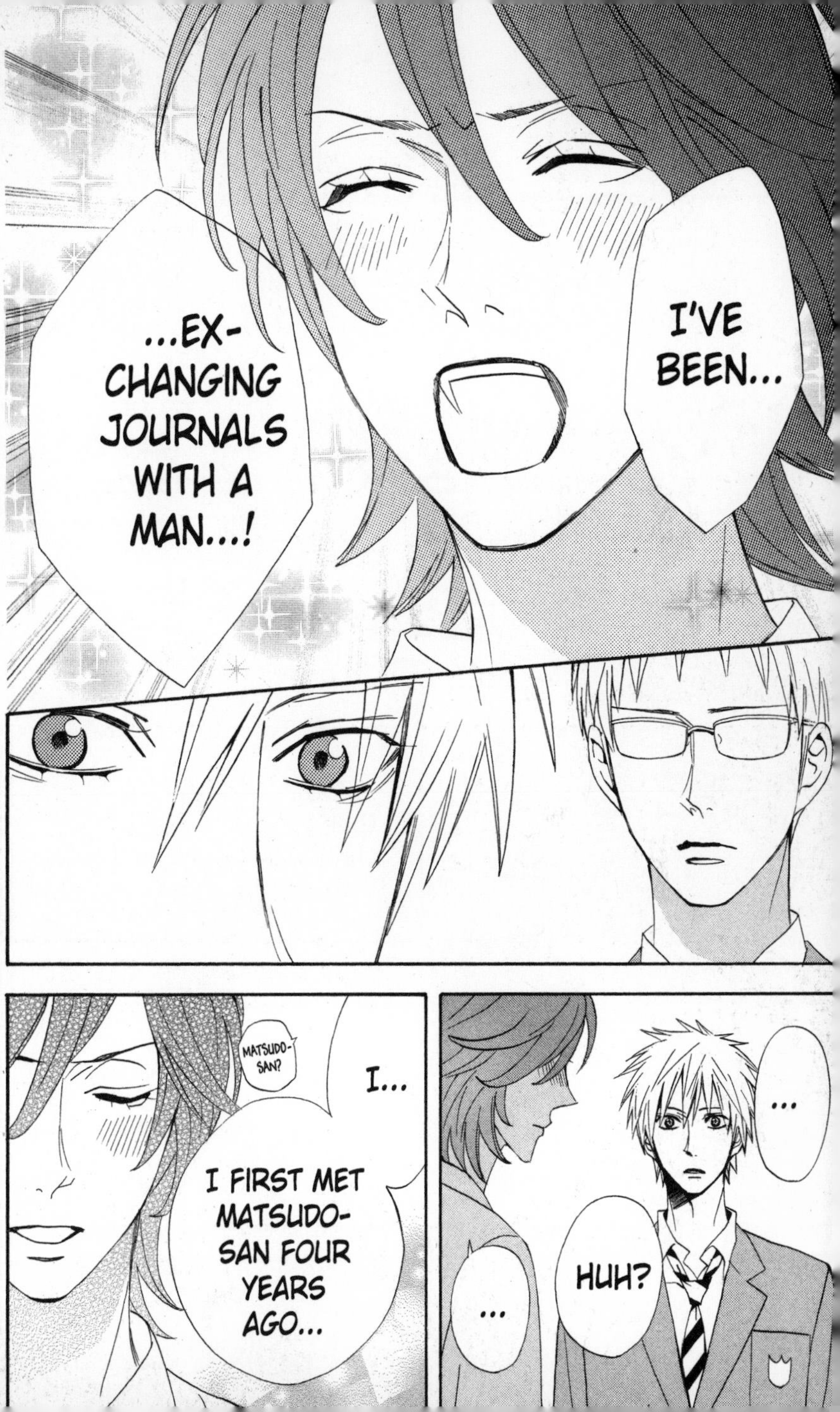
I'VE BEEN...
...EX-CHANGING JOURNALS WITH A MAN...!
...
HUH?
...
I...
MATSUDO-SAN?
I FIRST MET MATSUDO-SAN FOUR YEARS AGO...

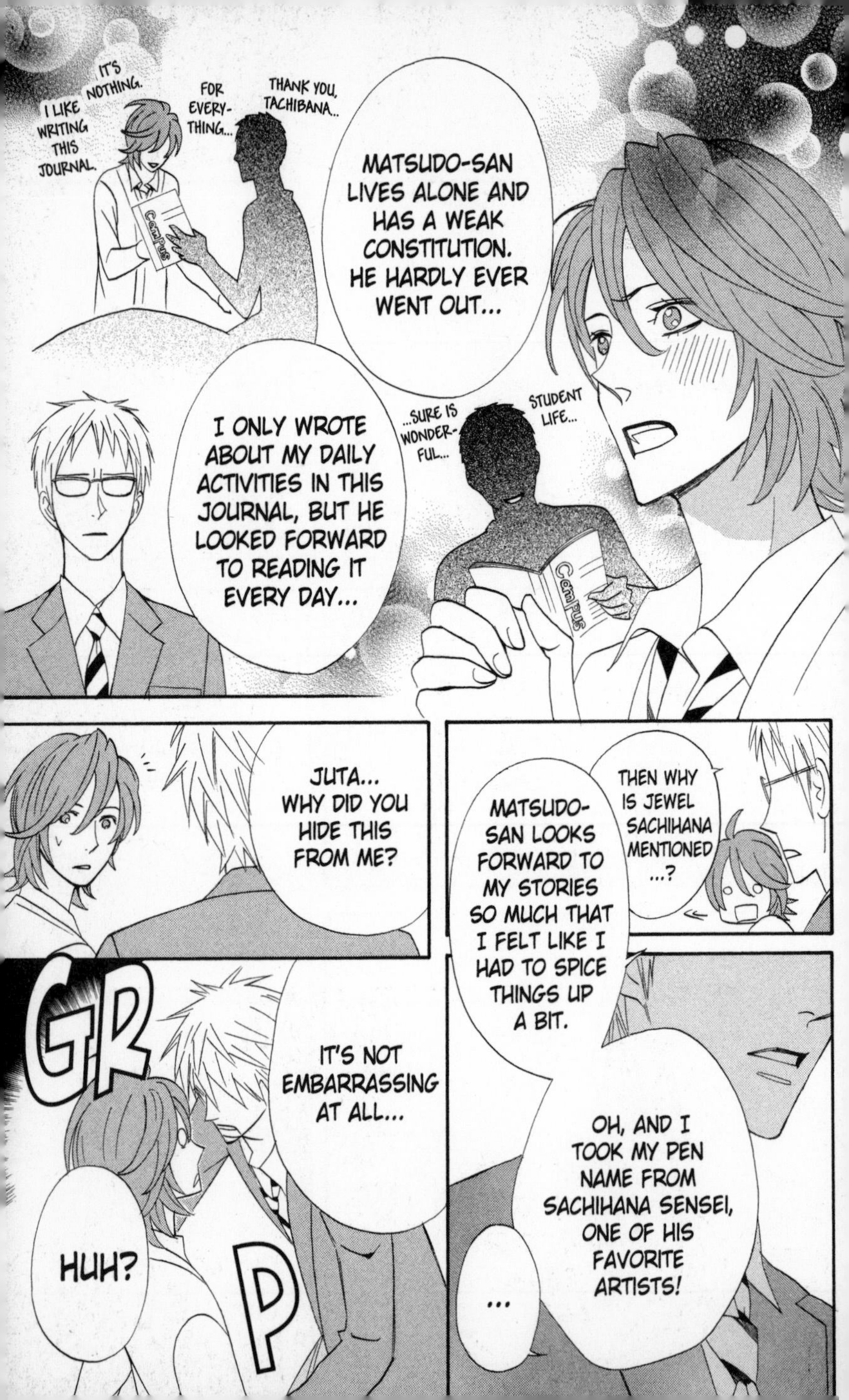
MATSUDO-SAN LIVES ALONE AND HAS A WEAK CONSTITUTION. HE HARDLY EVER WENT OUT...
THANK YOU, TACHIBANA...
FOR EVERY-THING...
IT'S NOTHING.
I LIKE WRITING THIS JOURNAL.
CAMPUS
STUDENT LIFE...
...SURE IS WONDER-FUL...
CAMPUS
I ONLY WROTE ABOUT MY DAILY ACTIVITIES IN THIS JOURNAL, BUT HE LOOKED FORWARD TO READING IT EVERY DAY...
THEN WHY IS JEWEL SACHIHANA MENTIONED ...?
MATSUDO-SAN LOOKS FORWARD TO MY STORIES SO MUCH THAT I FELT LIKE I HAD TO SPICE THINGS UP A BIT.
JUTA... WHY DID YOU HIDE THIS FROM ME?
OH, AND I TOOK MY PEN NAME FROM SACHIHANA SENSEI, ONE OF HIS FAVORITE ARTISTS!
...
IT'S NOT EMBARRASSING AT ALL...
GR
P
HUH?

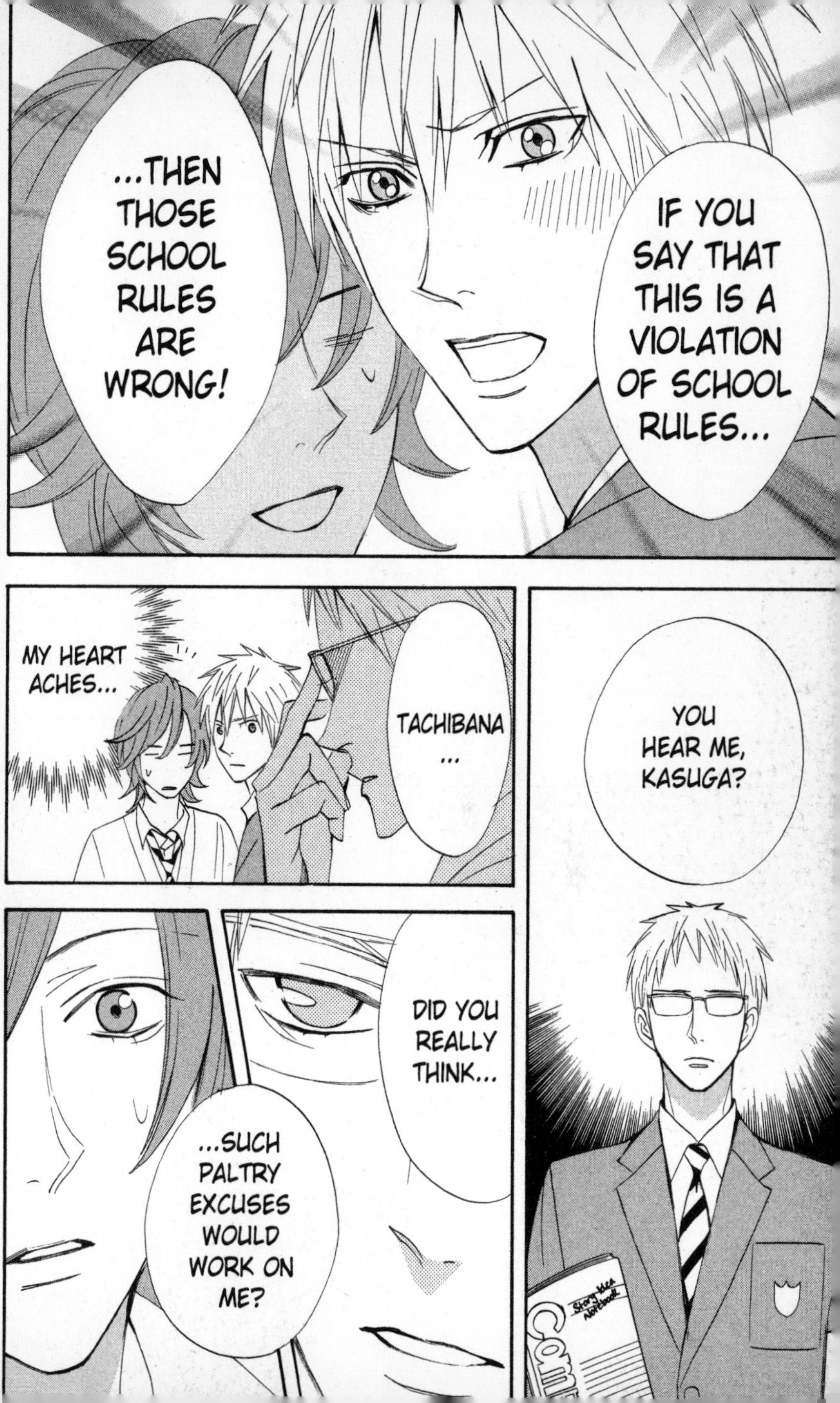
IF YOU SAY THAT THIS IS A VIOLATION OF SCHOOL RULES...
...THEN THOSE SCHOOL RULES ARE WRONG!
YOU HEAR ME, KASUGA?
TACHIBANA...
MY HEART ACHES...
DID YOU REALLY THINK...
...SUCH PALTRY EXCUSES WOULD WORK ON ME?

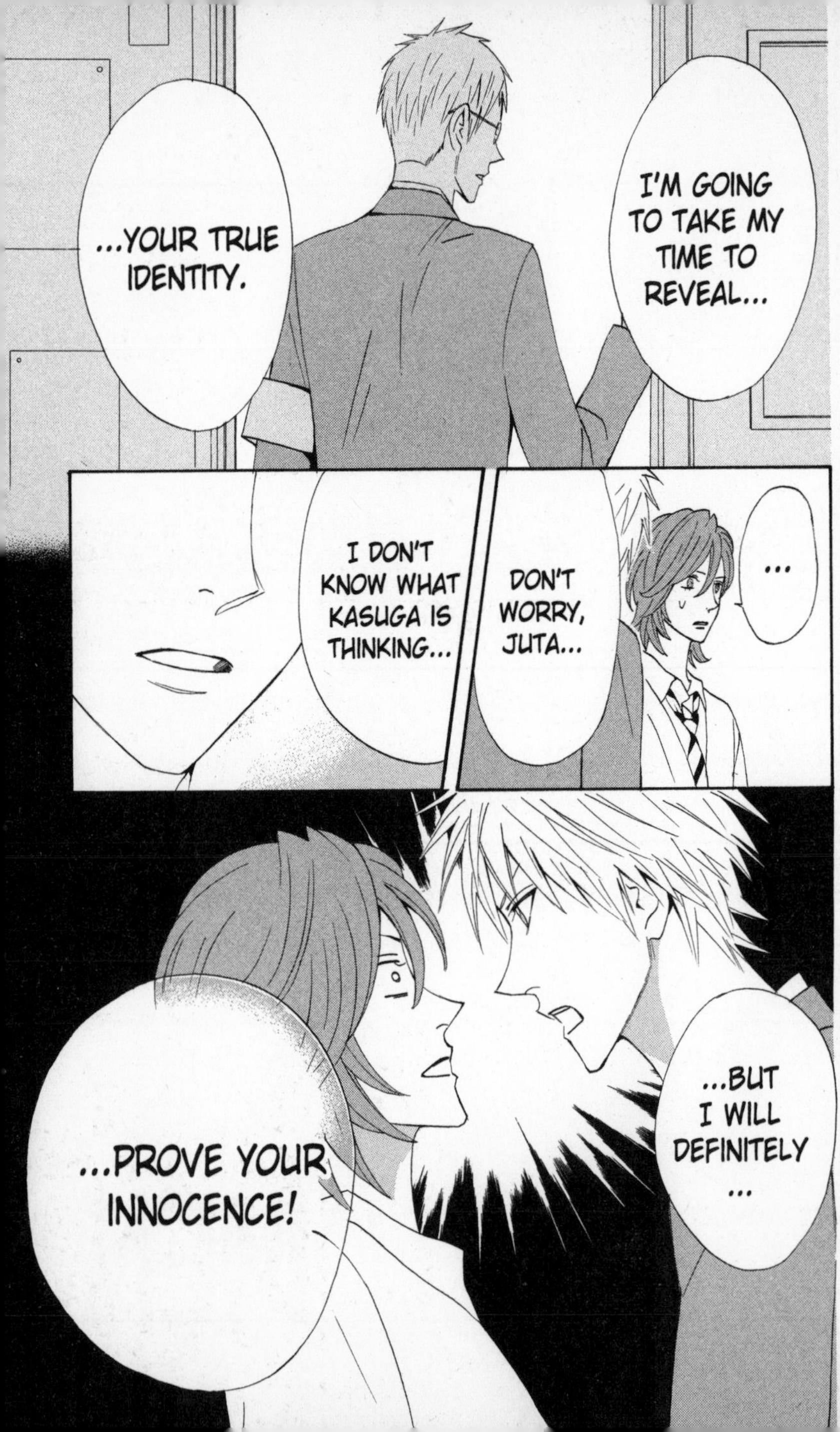
I'M GOING TO TAKE MY TIME TO REVEAL...
...YOUR TRUE IDENTITY.
...
DON'T WORRY, JUTA...
I DON'T KNOW WHAT KASUGA IS THINKING...
...BUT I WILL DEFINITELY ...
...PROVE YOUR INNOCENCE!

OTOMEN

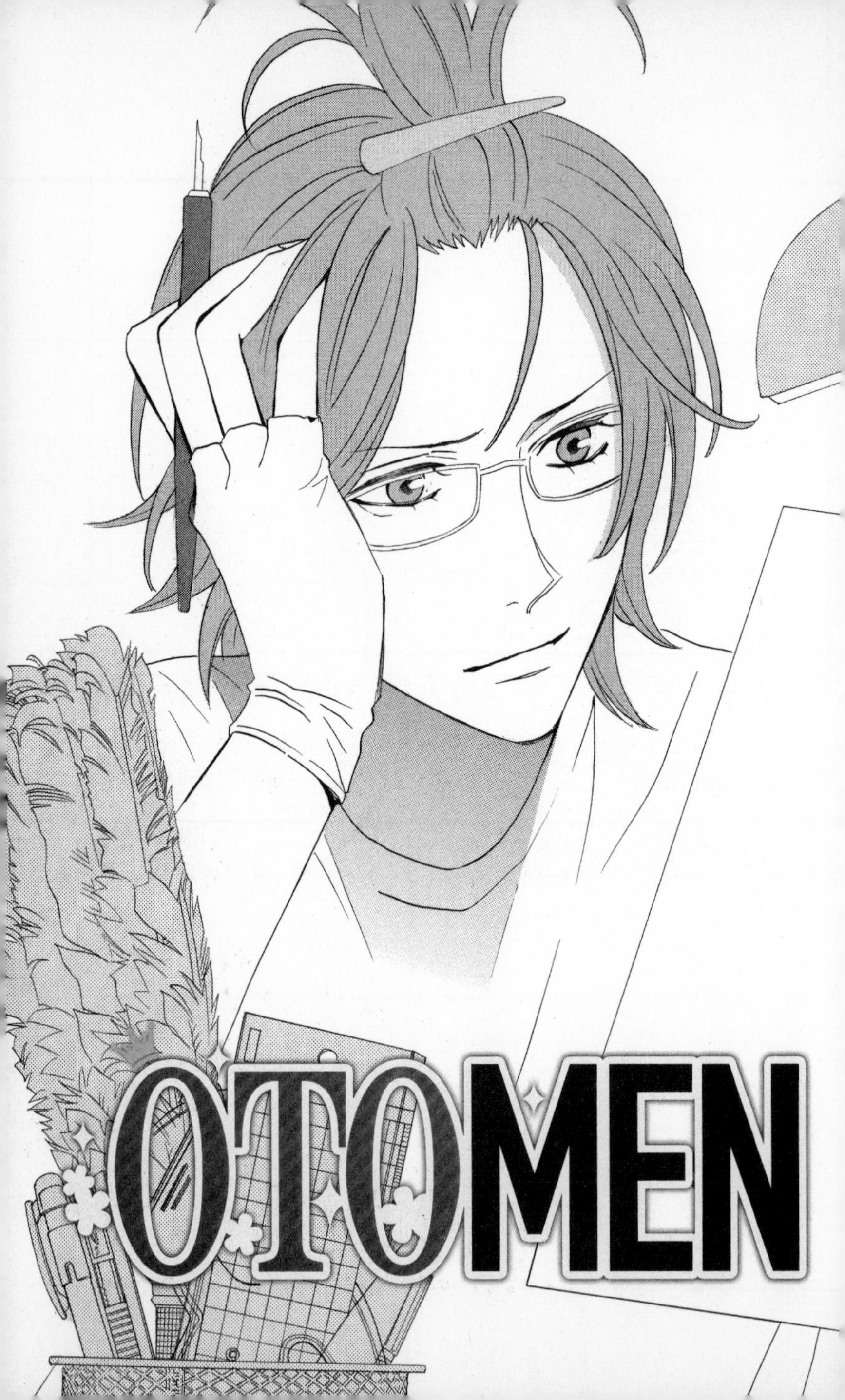
OTOMEN

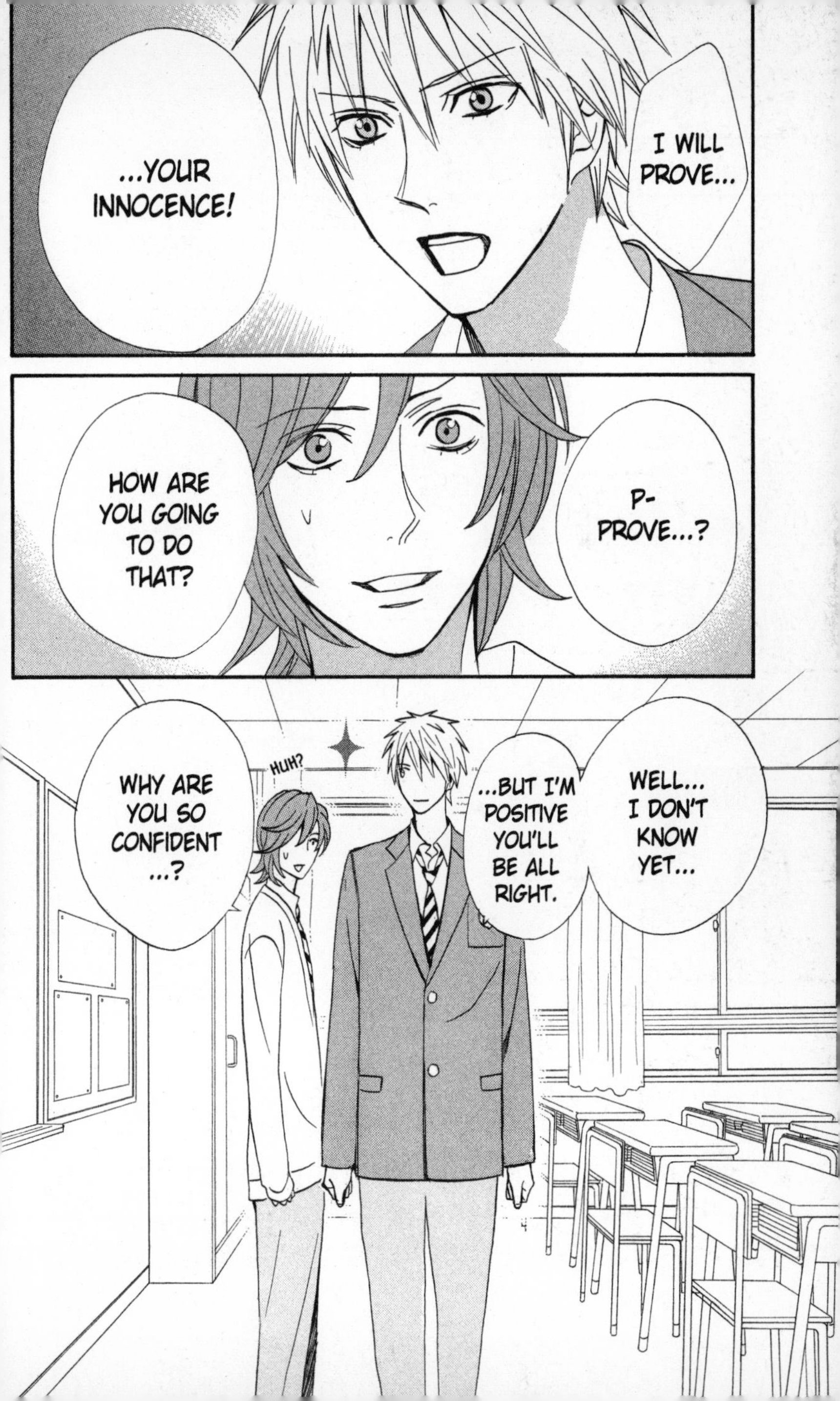
I WILL PROVE...
...YOUR INNOCENCE!
P-PROVE...?
HOW ARE YOU GOING TO DO THAT?
WELL... I DON'T KNOW YET...
...BUT I'M POSITIVE YOU'LL BE ALL RIGHT.
HUH?
WHY ARE YOU SO CONFIDENT ...?

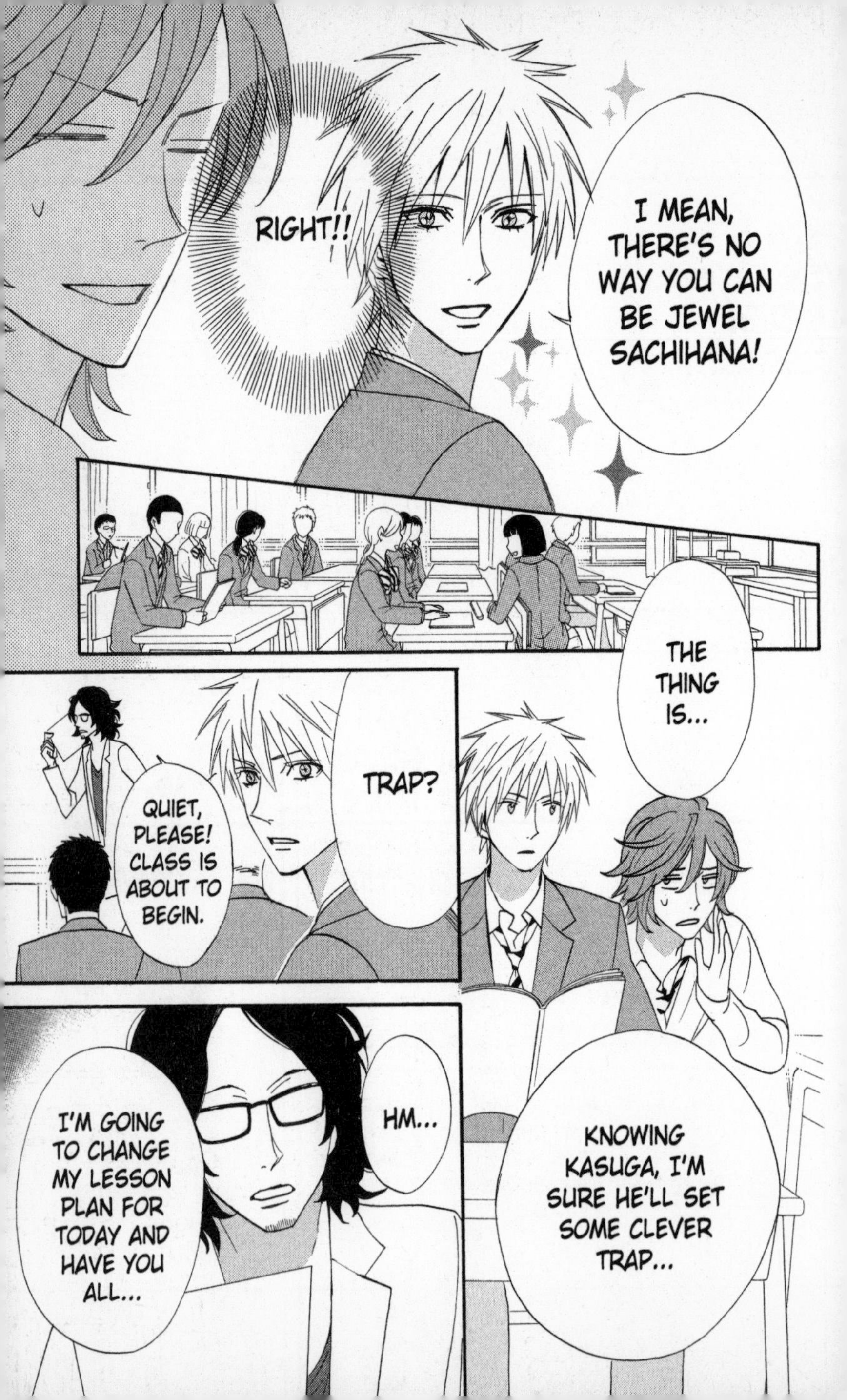
I MEAN, THERE'S NO WAY YOU CAN BE JEWEL SACHIHANA!
RIGHT!!
THE THING IS...
KNOWING KASUGA, I'M SURE HE'LL SET SOME CLEVER TRAP...
TRAP?
QUIET, PLEASE! CLASS IS ABOUT TO BEGIN.
HM...
I'M GOING TO CHANGE MY LESSON PLAN FOR TODAY AND HAVE YOU ALL...

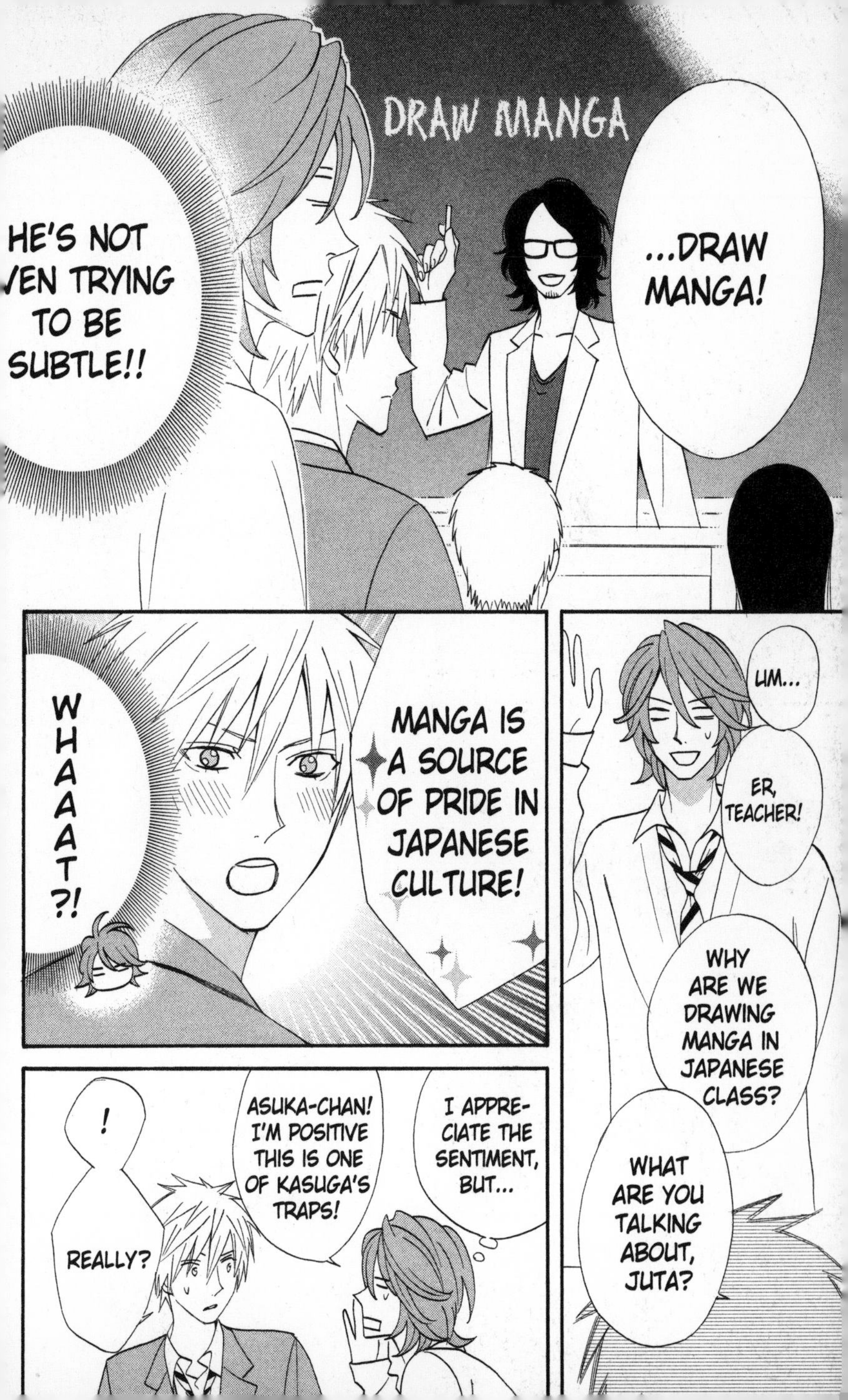

DRAW MANGA
...DRAW MANGA!
HE'S NOT VEN TRYING TO BE SUBTLE!!
UM...
ER, TEACHER!
WHY ARE WE DRAWING MANGA IN JAPANESE CLASS?
WHAT ARE YOU TALKING ABOUT, JUTA?
MANGA IS A SOURCE OF PRIDE IN JAPANESE CULTURE!
WHAAAAT?!
I APPRE-CIATE THE SENTIMENT, BUT...
ASUKA-CHAN! I'M POSITIVE THIS IS ONE OF KASUGA'S TRAPS!
!
REALLY?

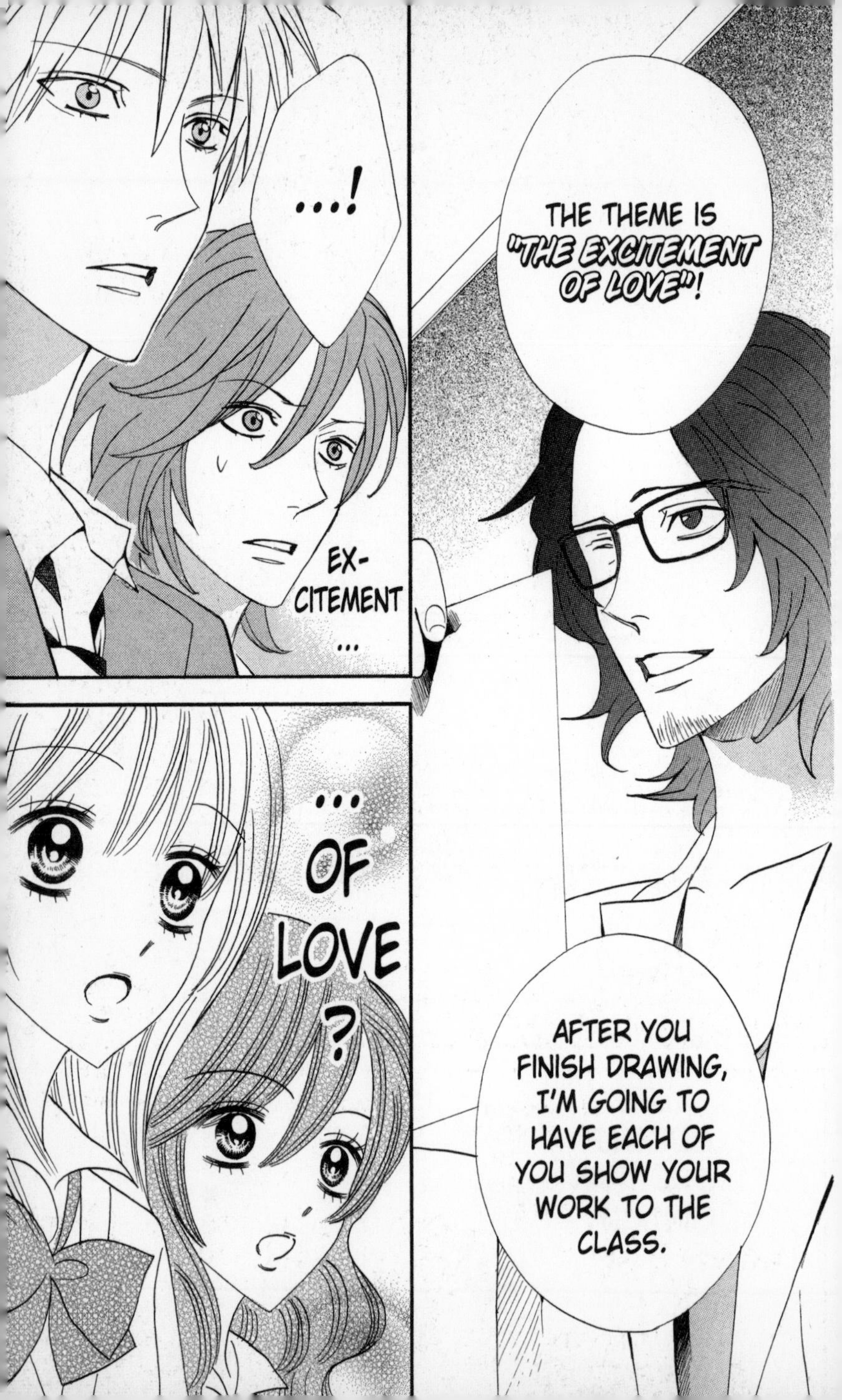
THE THEME IS "THE EXCITEMENT OF LOVE"!
AFTER YOU FINISH DRAWING, I'M GOING TO HAVE EACH OF YOU SHOW YOUR WORK TO THE CLASS.
...!
EX-CITEMENT ...
...OF LOVE?

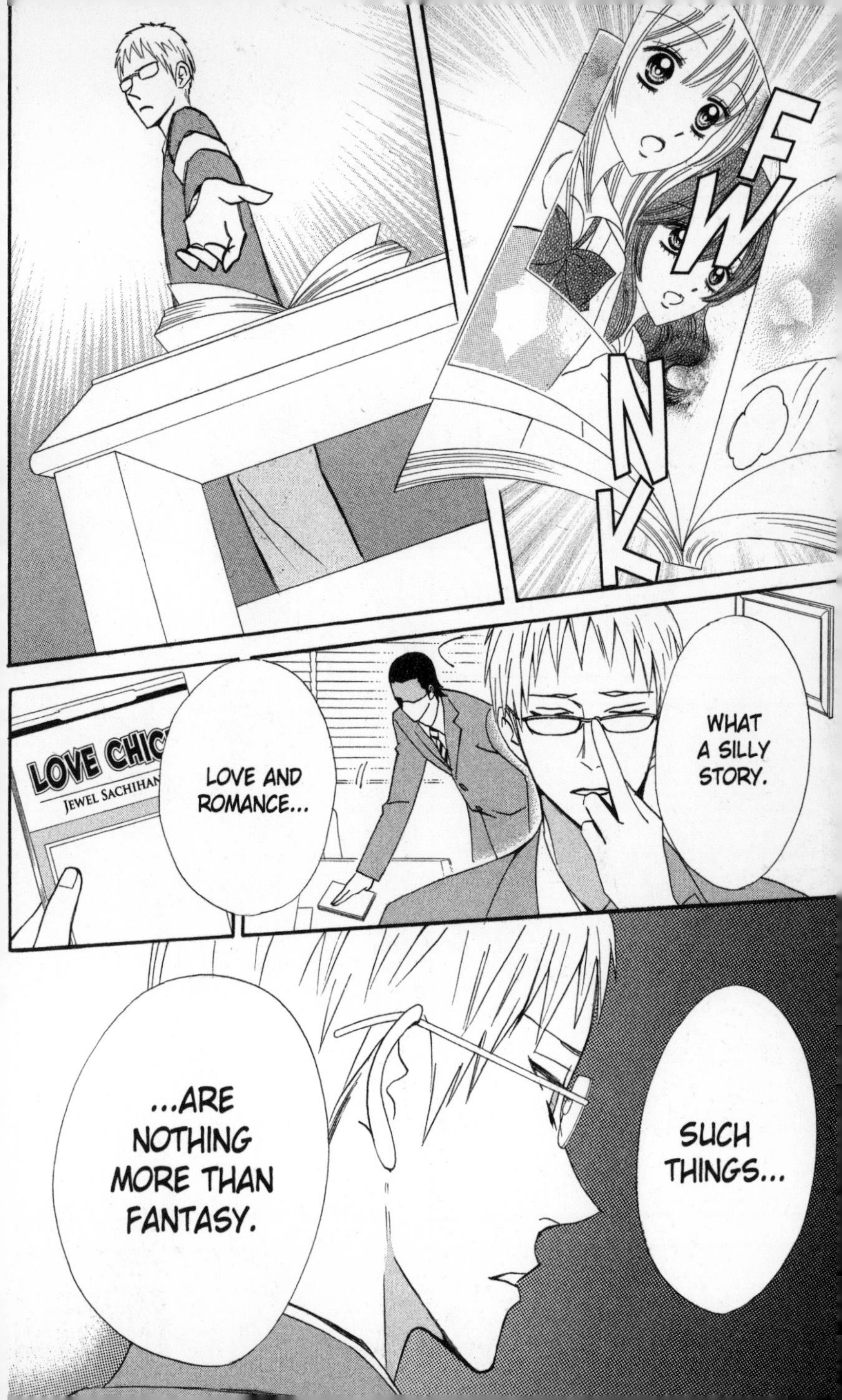
FWNK
WHAT A SILLY STORY.
LOVE AND ROMANCE...
LOVE CHIC
JEWEL SACHIHAN
SUCH THINGS...
...ARE NOTHING MORE THAN FANTASY.

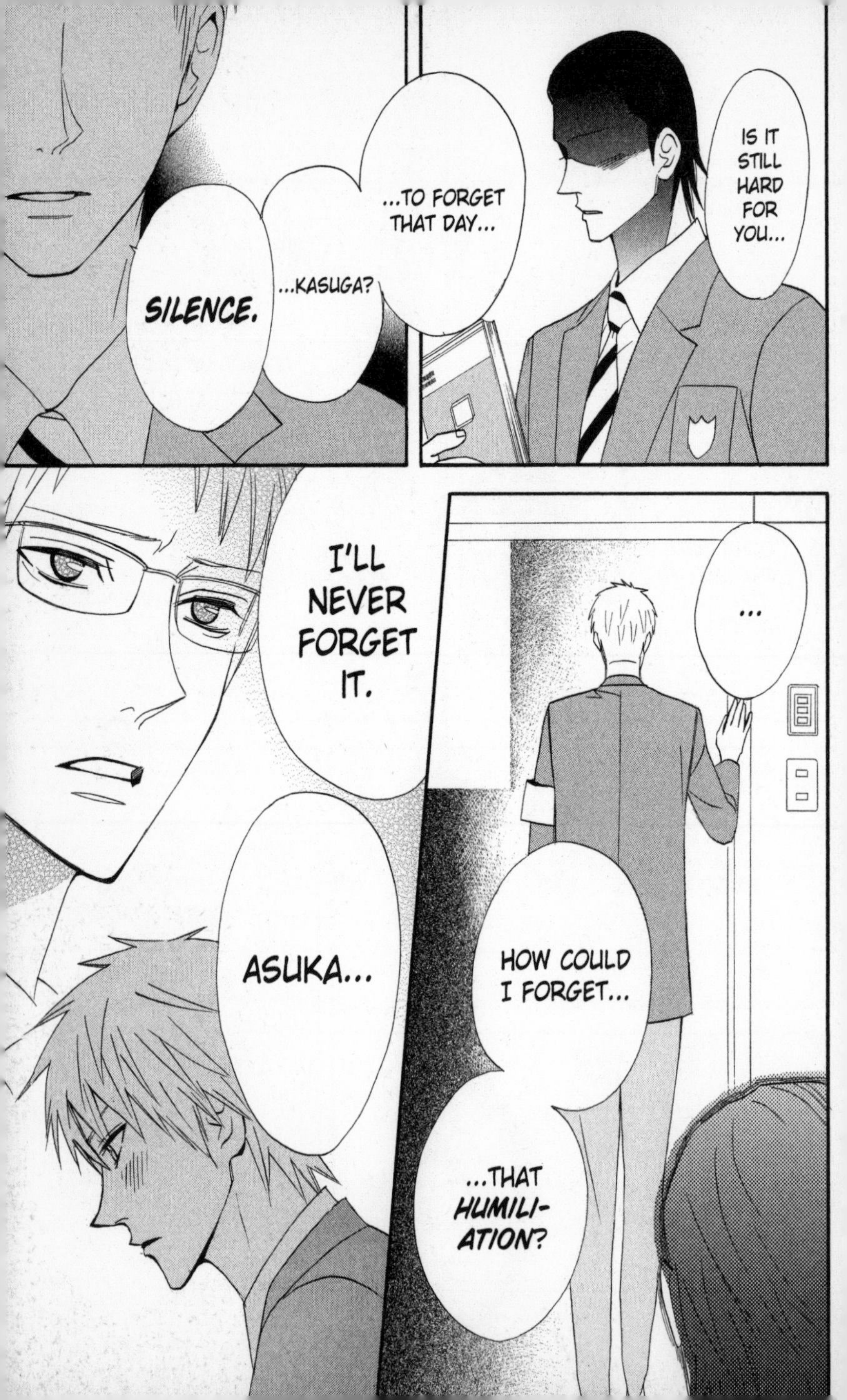
IS IT STILL HARD FOR YOU...
...TO FORGET THAT DAY...
...KASUGA?
SILENCE.
...
HOW COULD I FORGET...
...THAT HUMILIATION?
I'LL NEVER FORGET IT.
ASUKA...

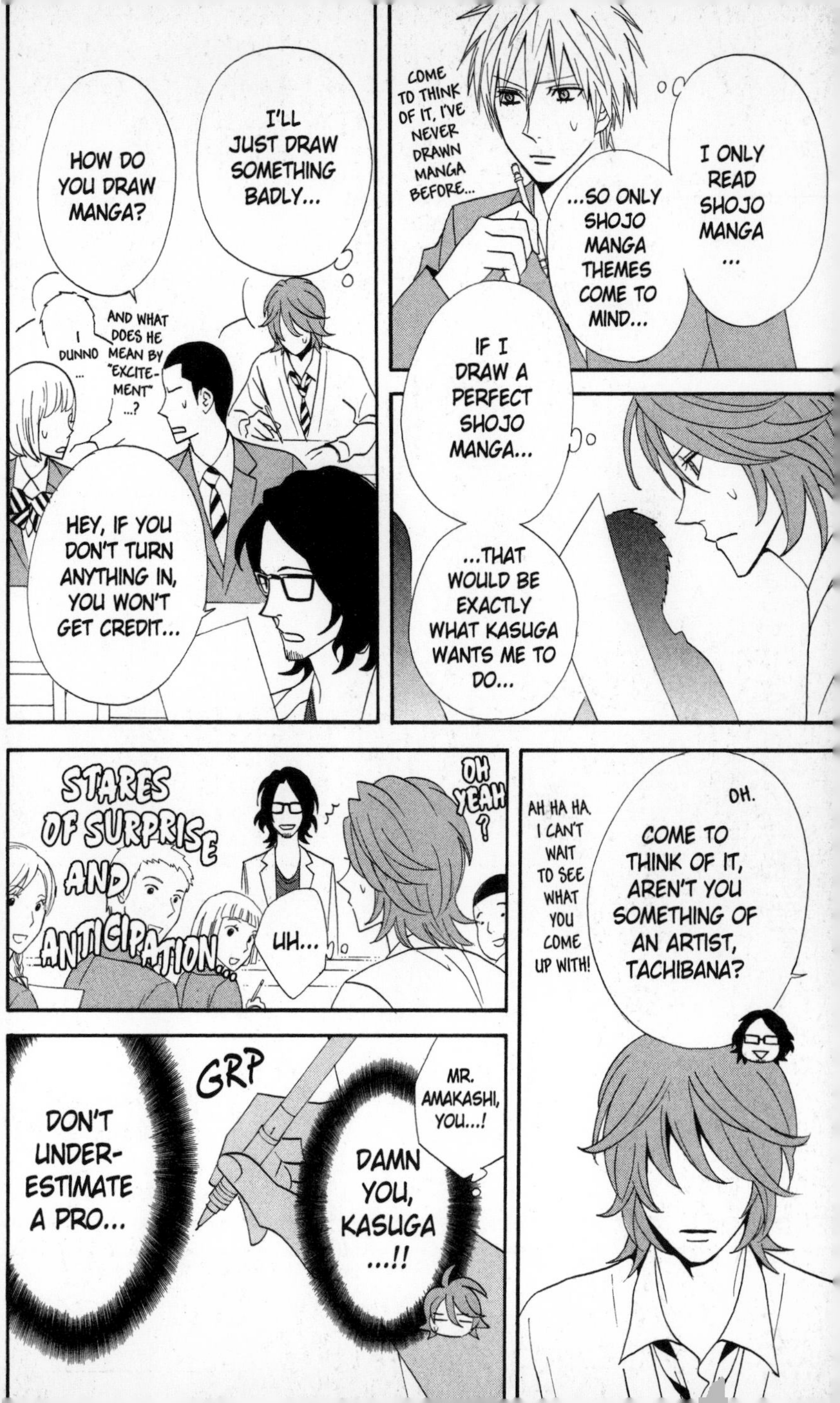
I ONLY READ SHOJO MANGA...
COME TO THINK OF IT, I'VE NEVER DRAWN MANGA BEFORE...
...SO ONLY SHOJO MANGA THEMES COME TO MIND...
IF I DRAW A PERFECT SHOJO MANGA...
...THAT WOULD BE EXACTLY WHAT KASUGA WANTS ME TO DO...
I'LL JUST DRAW SOMETHING BADLY...
HOW DO YOU DRAW MANGA?
AND WHAT DOES HE MEAN BY "EXCITEMENT"...?
I DUNNO...
HEY, IF YOU DON'T TURN ANYTHING IN, YOU WON'T GET CREDIT...
OH.
COME TO THINK OF IT, AREN'T YOU SOMETHING OF AN ARTIST, TACHIBANA?
AH HA HA. I CAN'T WAIT TO SEE WHAT YOU COME UP WITH!
OH YEAH?
UH...
STARES OF SURPRISE AND ANTICIPATION...
MR. AMAKASHI, YOU...!
GRP
DAMN YOU, KASUGA...!!
DON'T UNDER-ESTIMATE A PRO...

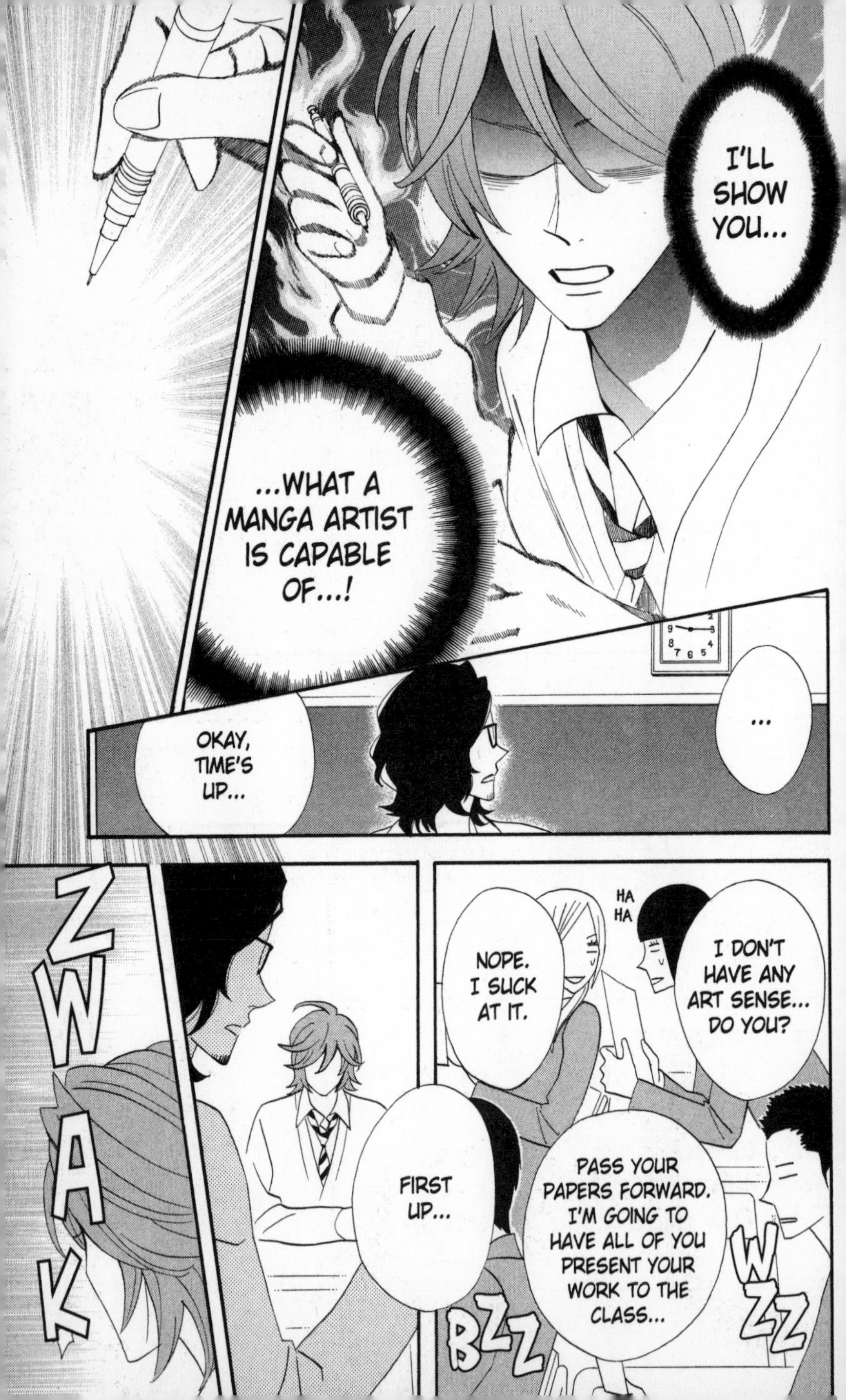
I'LL SHOW YOU...
...WHAT A MANGA ARTIST IS CAPABLE OF...!
...
OKAY, TIME'S UP...
I DON'T HAVE ANY ART SENSE... DO YOU?
HA HA
NOPE. I SUCK AT IT.
PASS YOUR PAPERS FORWARD. I'M GOING TO HAVE ALL OF YOU PRESENT YOUR WORK TO THE CLASS...
WZZ
BZZ
FIRST UP...
ZWAK

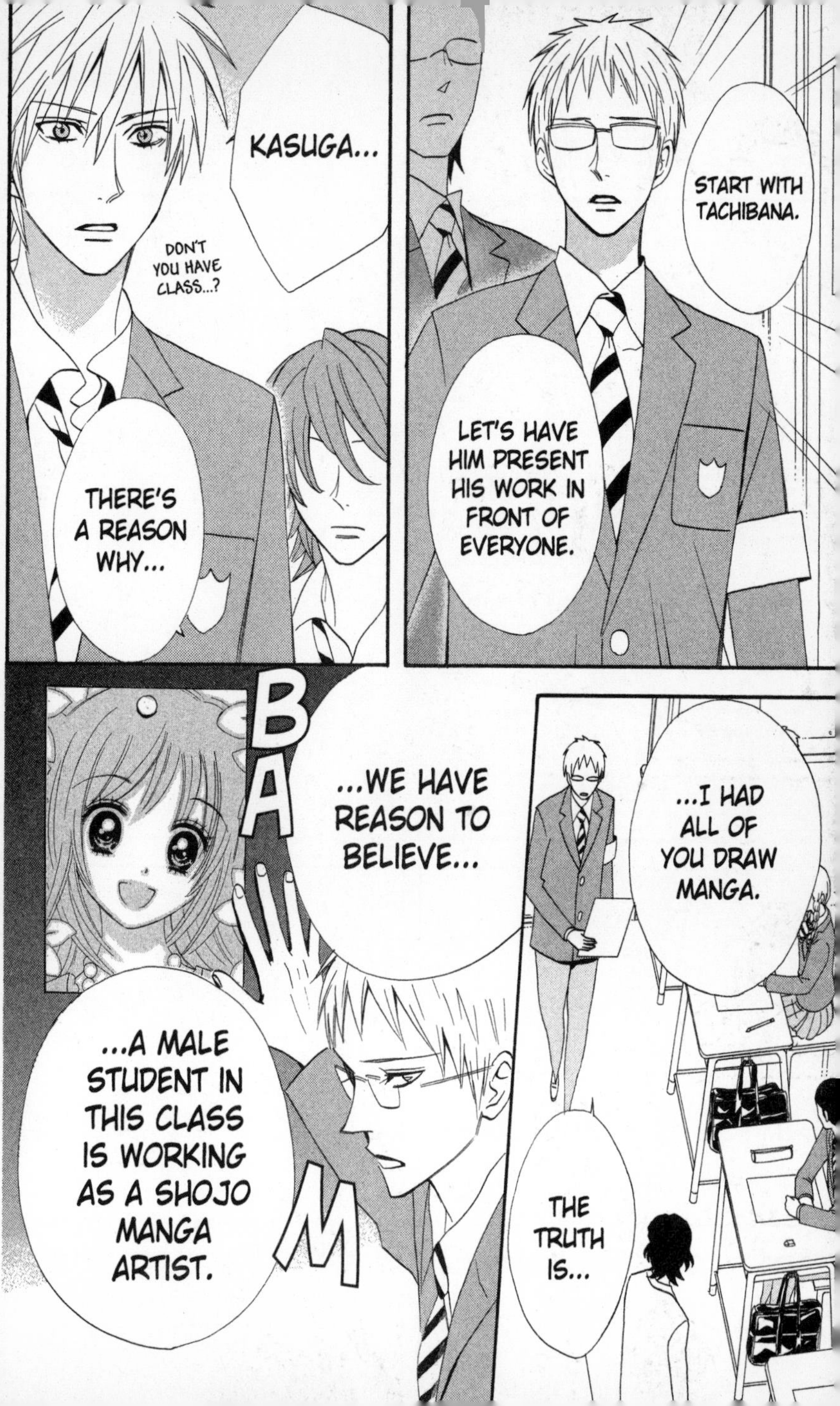
START WITH TACHIBANA.
LET'S HAVE HIM PRESENT HIS WORK IN FRONT OF EVERYONE.
KASUGA...
DON'T YOU HAVE CLASS...?
THERE'S A REASON WHY...
...I HAD ALL OF YOU DRAW MANGA.
THE TRUTH IS...
BAM
...WE HAVE REASON TO BELIEVE...
...A MALE STUDENT IN THIS CLASS IS WORKING AS A SHOJO MANGA ARTIST.

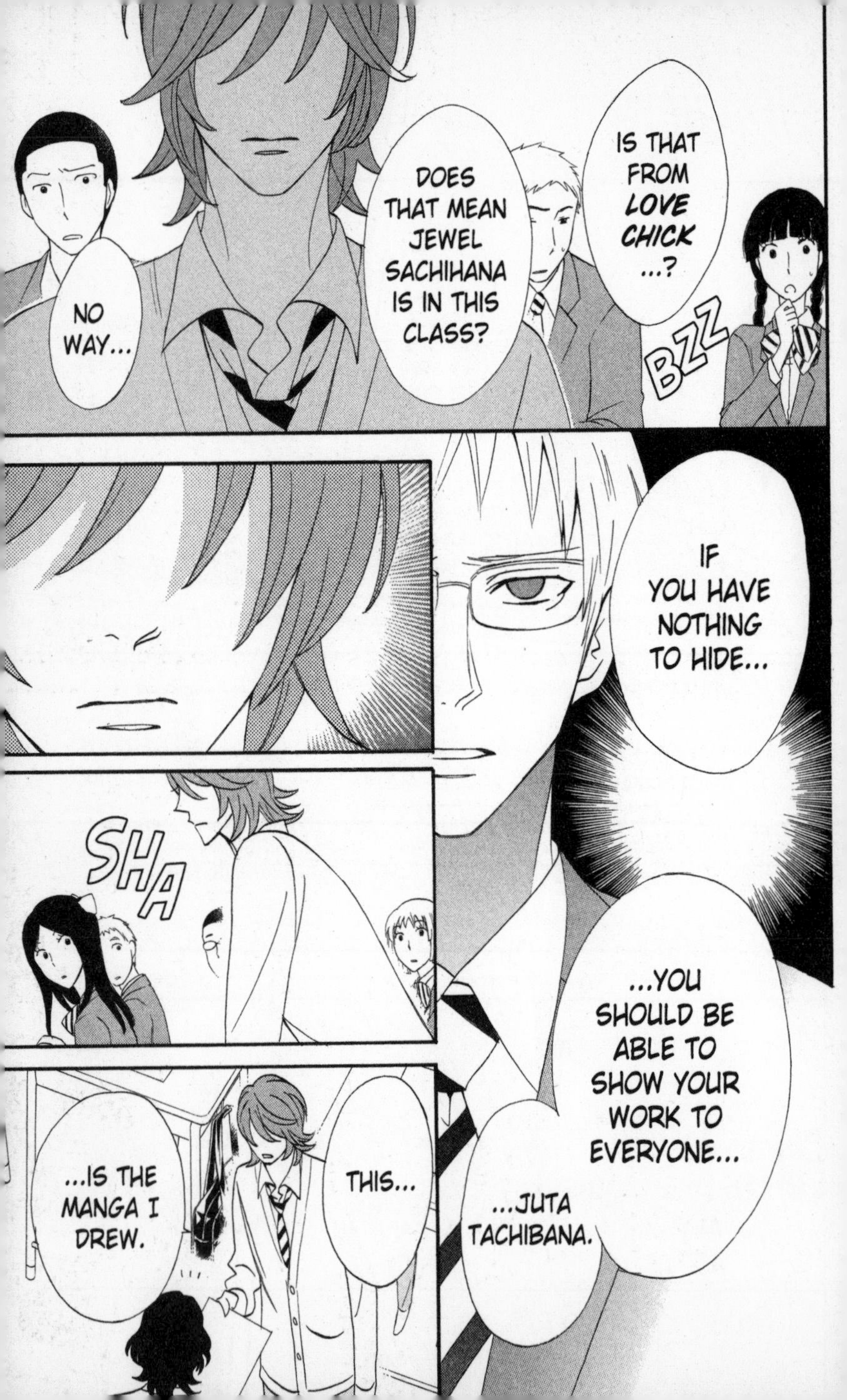
IS THAT FROM *LOVE CHICK* ...?
BZZ
DOES THAT MEAN JEWEL SACHIHANA IS IN THIS CLASS?
NO WAY...
IF YOU HAVE NOTHING TO HIDE...
...YOU SHOULD BE ABLE TO SHOW YOUR WORK TO EVERYONE...
...JUTA TACHIBANA.
SHA
THIS...
...IS THE MANGA I DREW.

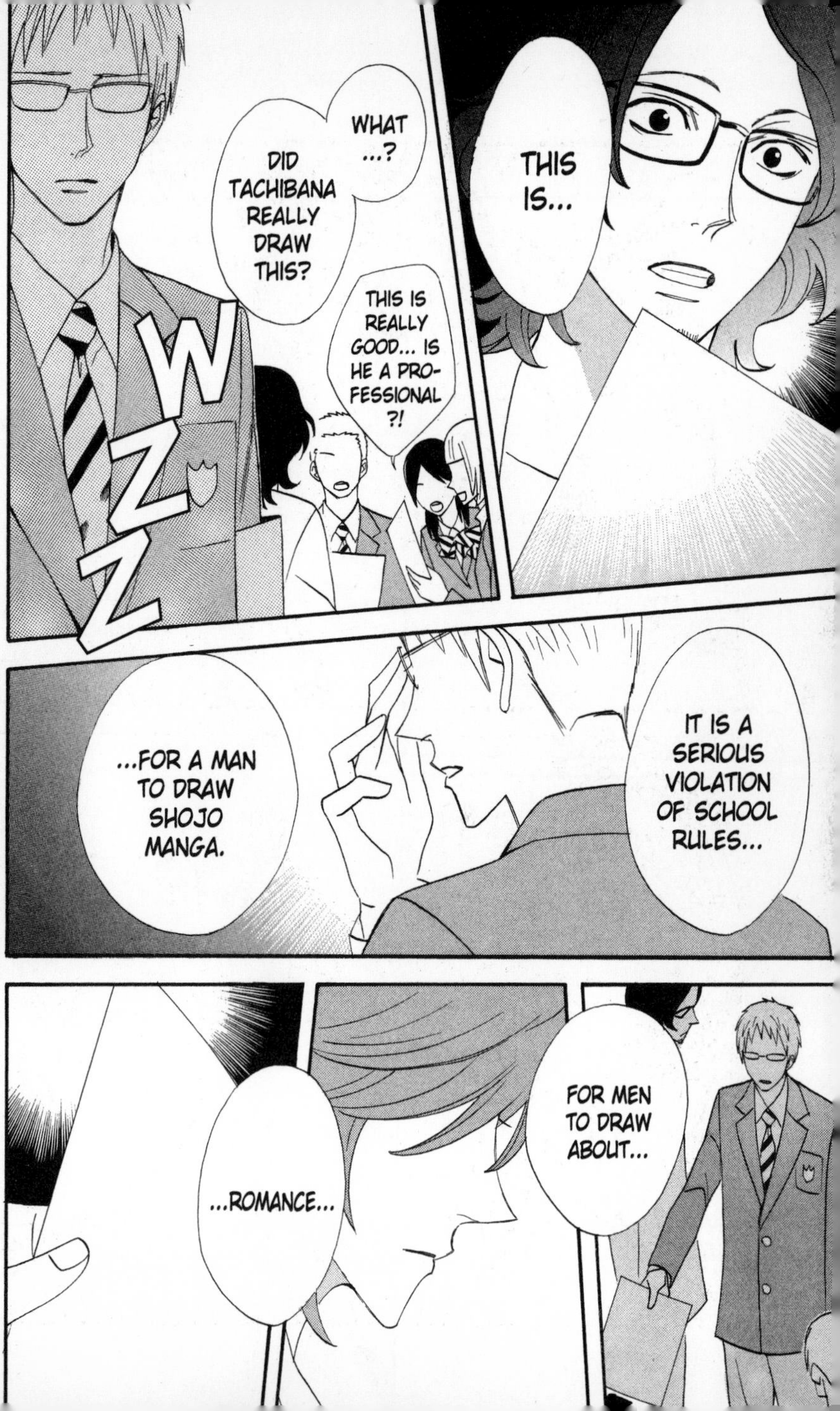
THIS IS...
WHAT ...?
DID TACHIBANA REALLY DRAW THIS?
THIS IS REALLY GOOD... IS HE A PRO-FESSIONAL ?!
WZZ
IT IS A SERIOUS VIOLATION OF SCHOOL RULES...
...FOR A MAN TO DRAW SHOJO MANGA.
FOR MEN TO DRAW ABOUT...
...ROMANCE...

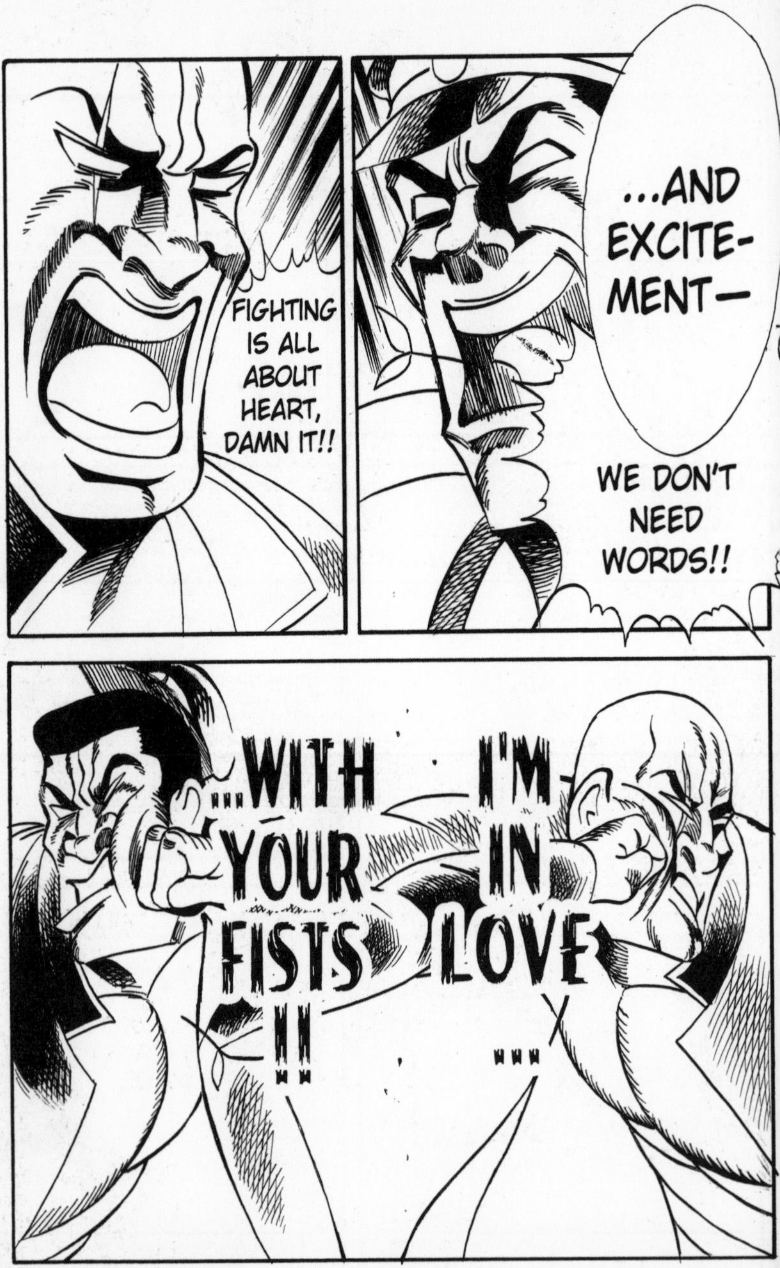
...AND EXCITE-MENT—
WE DON'T NEED WORDS!!
FIGHTING IS ALL ABOUT HEART, DAMN IT!!
I'M IN LOVE...
...WITH YOUR FISTS!!

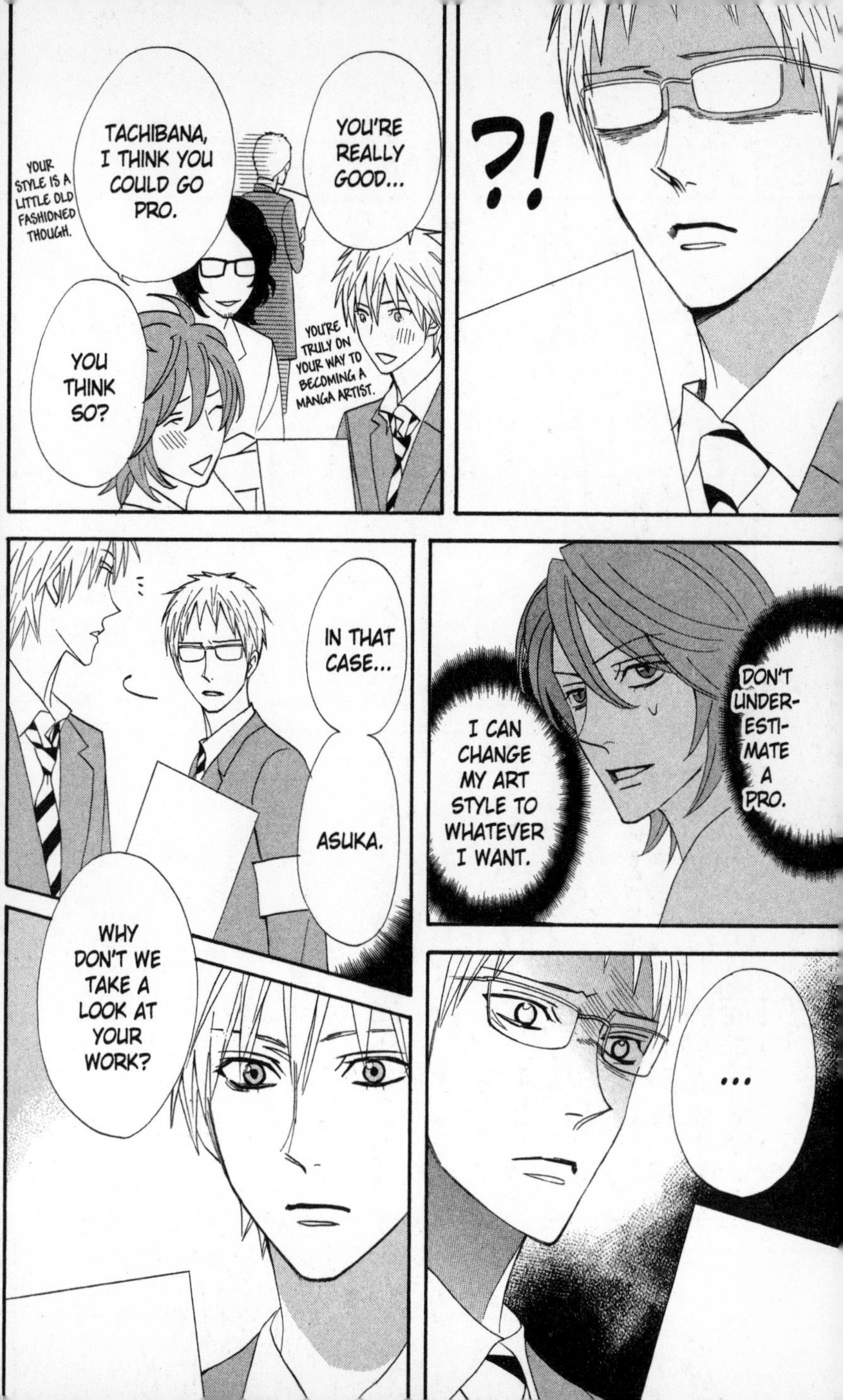
?!
YOU'RE REALLY GOOD...
YOU'RE TRULY ON YOUR WAY TO BECOMING A MANGA ARTIST.
TACHIBANA, I THINK YOU COULD GO PRO.
YOUR STYLE IS A LITTLE OLD FASHIONED THOUGH.
YOU THINK SO?
DON'T UNDER-ESTI-MATE A PRO.
I CAN CHANGE MY ART STYLE TO WHATEVER I WANT.
IN THAT CASE...
ASUKA.
...
WHY DON'T WE TAKE A LOOK AT YOUR WORK?

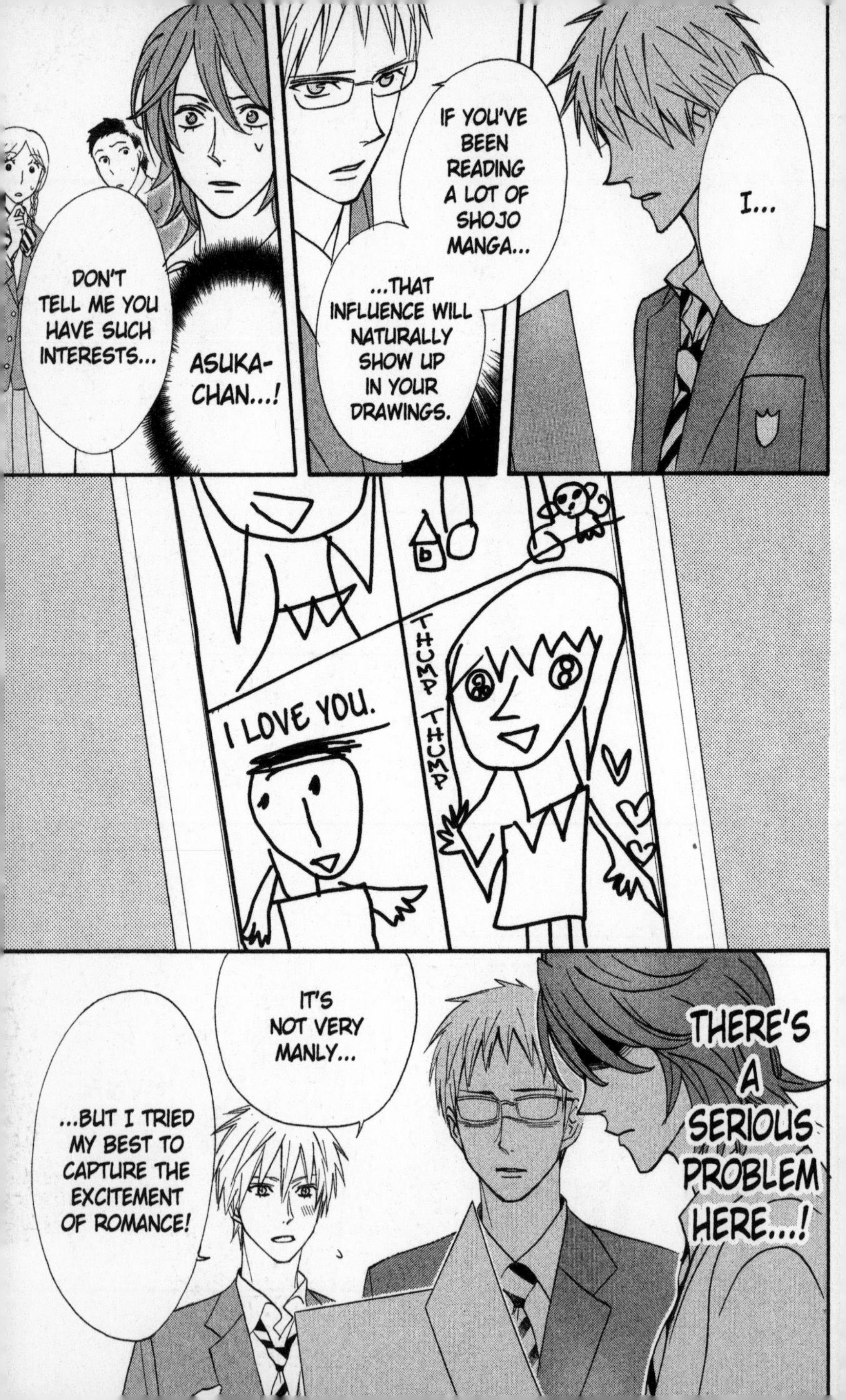
I...
IF YOU'VE BEEN READING A LOT OF SHOJO MANGA...
...THAT INFLUENCE WILL NATURALLY SHOW UP IN YOUR DRAWINGS.
DON'T TELL ME YOU HAVE SUCH INTERESTS...
ASUKA-CHAN...!
THUMP THUMP
I LOVE YOU.
THERE'S A SERIOUS PROBLEM HERE...!
IT'S NOT VERY MANLY...
...BUT I TRIED MY BEST TO CAPTURE THE EXCITEMENT OF ROMANCE!

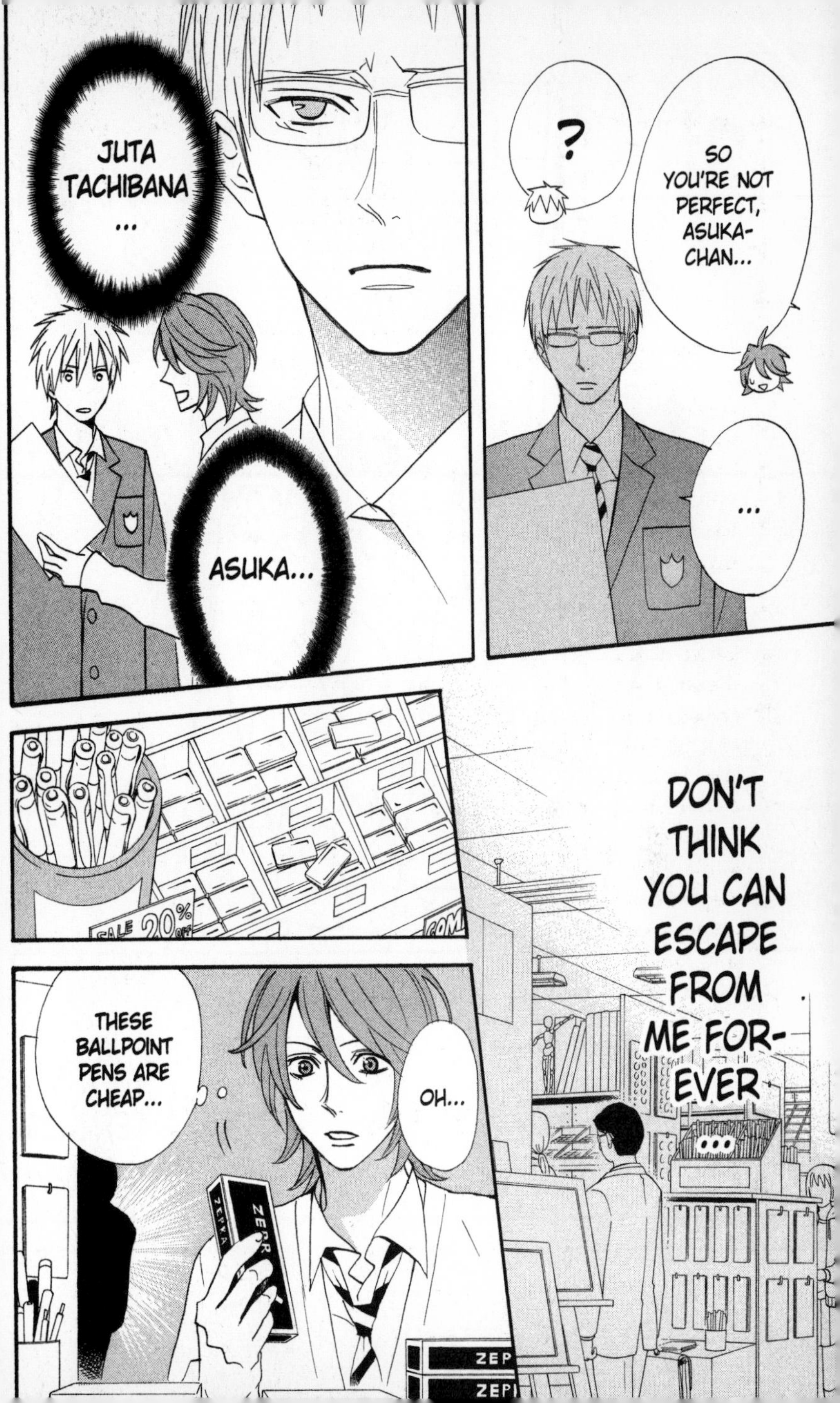
?
SO YOU'RE NOT PERFECT, ASUKA-CHAN...
...
JUTA TACHIBANA ...
ASUKA...
DON'T THINK YOU CAN ESCAPE FROM ME FOR-EVER
...
SALE 20%
THESE BALLPOINT PENS ARE CHEAP...
OH...

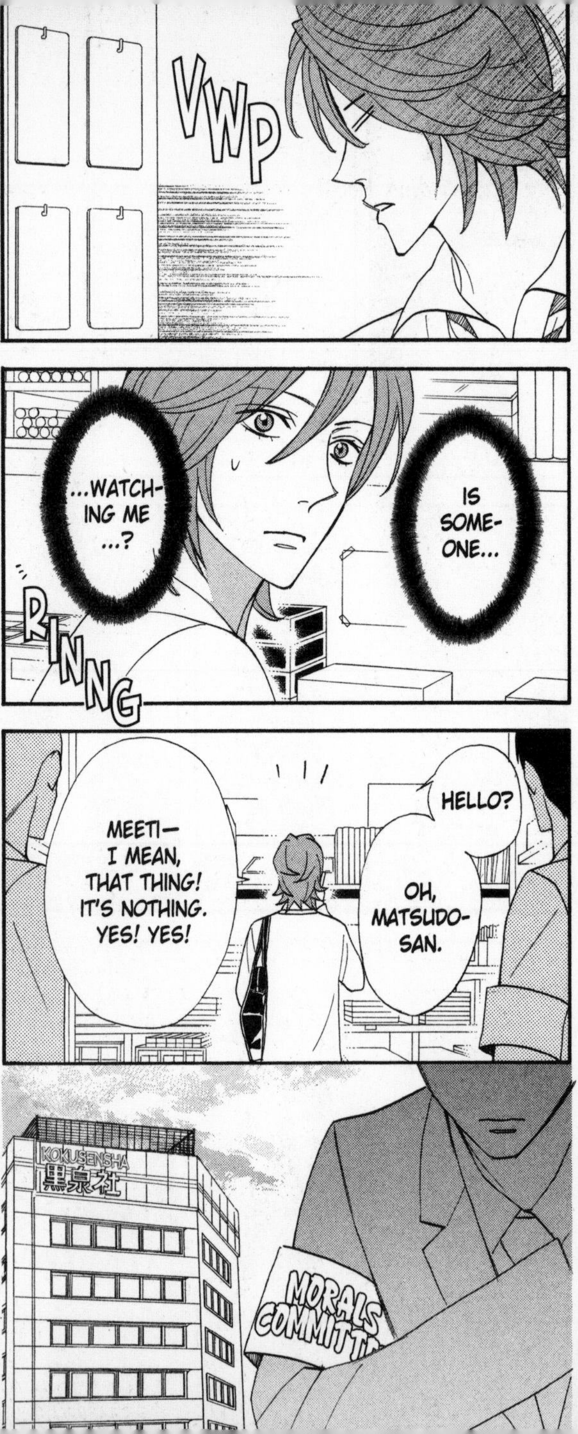
VWP
IS SOMEONE...
...WATCHING ME ...?
RINNG
HELLO?
OH, MATSUDO-SAN.
MEETI— I MEAN, THAT THING! IT'S NOTHING. YES! YES!
KOKUSENSHA
黒泉社
MORALS COMMITT

This series is about students, but I noticed that not many of the stories take place at school. That's why I tried to focus on some school-based stories for a while. As I was drawing, however, I realized that over ten years have passed since I graduated. I don't remember much from those days... I can't remember my classes or my lifestyle... I wasn't a very good student in high school... To those of you in school right now, it's better to be serious about your studies. Really.

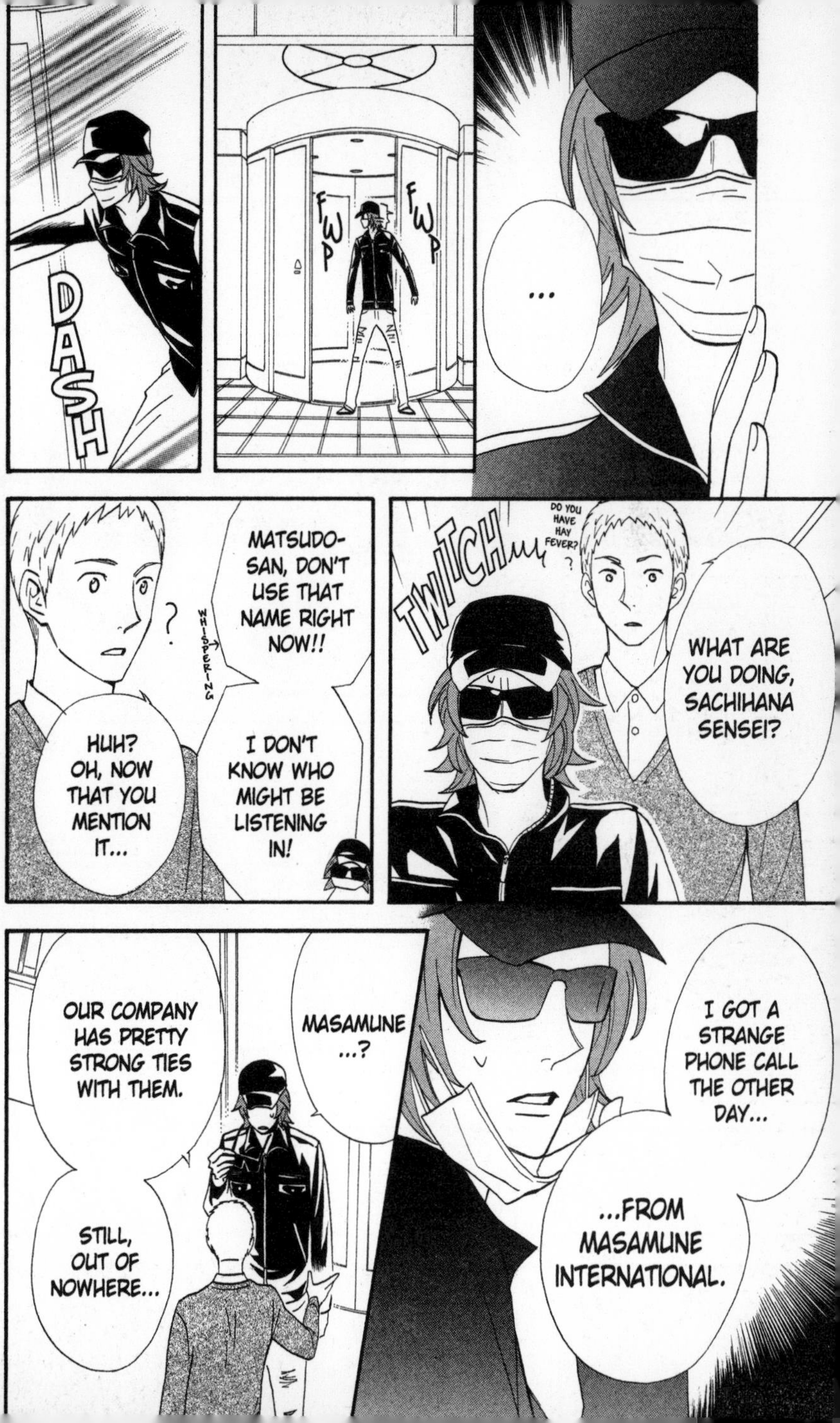
...
FWP
FWP
DASH
WHAT ARE YOU DOING, SACHIHANA SENSEI?
DO YOU HAVE HAY FEVER?
?
TWITCH
MATSUDO-SAN, DON'T USE THAT NAME RIGHT NOW!!
WHISPERING
I DON'T KNOW WHO MIGHT BE LISTENING IN!
?
HUH? OH, NOW THAT YOU MENTION IT...
I GOT A STRANGE PHONE CALL THE OTHER DAY...
...FROM MASAMUNE INTERNATIONAL.
MASAMUNE ...?
OUR COMPANY HAS PRETTY STRONG TIES WITH THEM.
STILL, OUT OF NOWHERE...

NATURALLY, I COULDN'T TELL THEM, SO I REFUSED!

...JEWEL SACHIHANA'S TRUE IDENTITY!

...

...THEY ASKED ME TO REVEAL...

SIGH

IT'S KASUGA...

NO DOUBT ABOUT IT.

I CAN'T WORK ON MY STORY-BOARDS...

NOT HERE ANY-WAY.

FWOO

WHAT'S WRONG, JUTA?

THAT ASIDE, CAN WE TALK ABOUT YOUR NEXT STORY-BOARD?

NOT BEING ABLE TO WORK ON MY STORYBOARDS HERE AT SCHOOL IS REALLY ROUGH...

IT'S NOT LIKE I CAN STAY HOME ALL THE TIME.

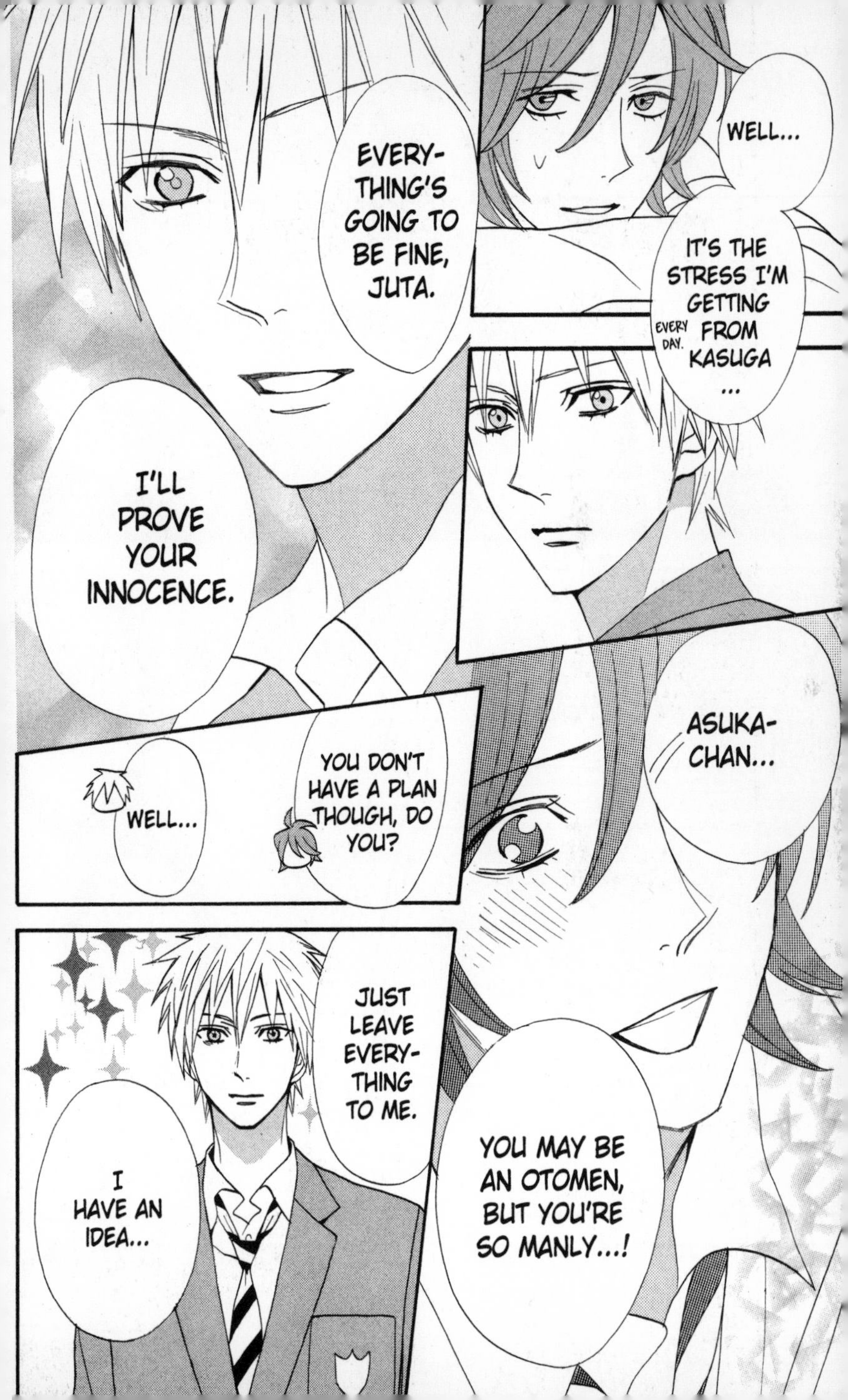
WELL...
IT'S THE STRESS I'M GETTING FROM KASUGA ... EVERY DAY.
EVERY-THING'S GOING TO BE FINE, JUTA.
I'LL PROVE YOUR INNOCENCE.
ASUKA-CHAN...
YOU MAY BE AN OTOMEN, BUT YOU'RE SO MANLY...!
YOU DON'T HAVE A PLAN THOUGH, DO YOU?
WELL...
JUST LEAVE EVERY-THING TO ME.
I HAVE AN IDEA...

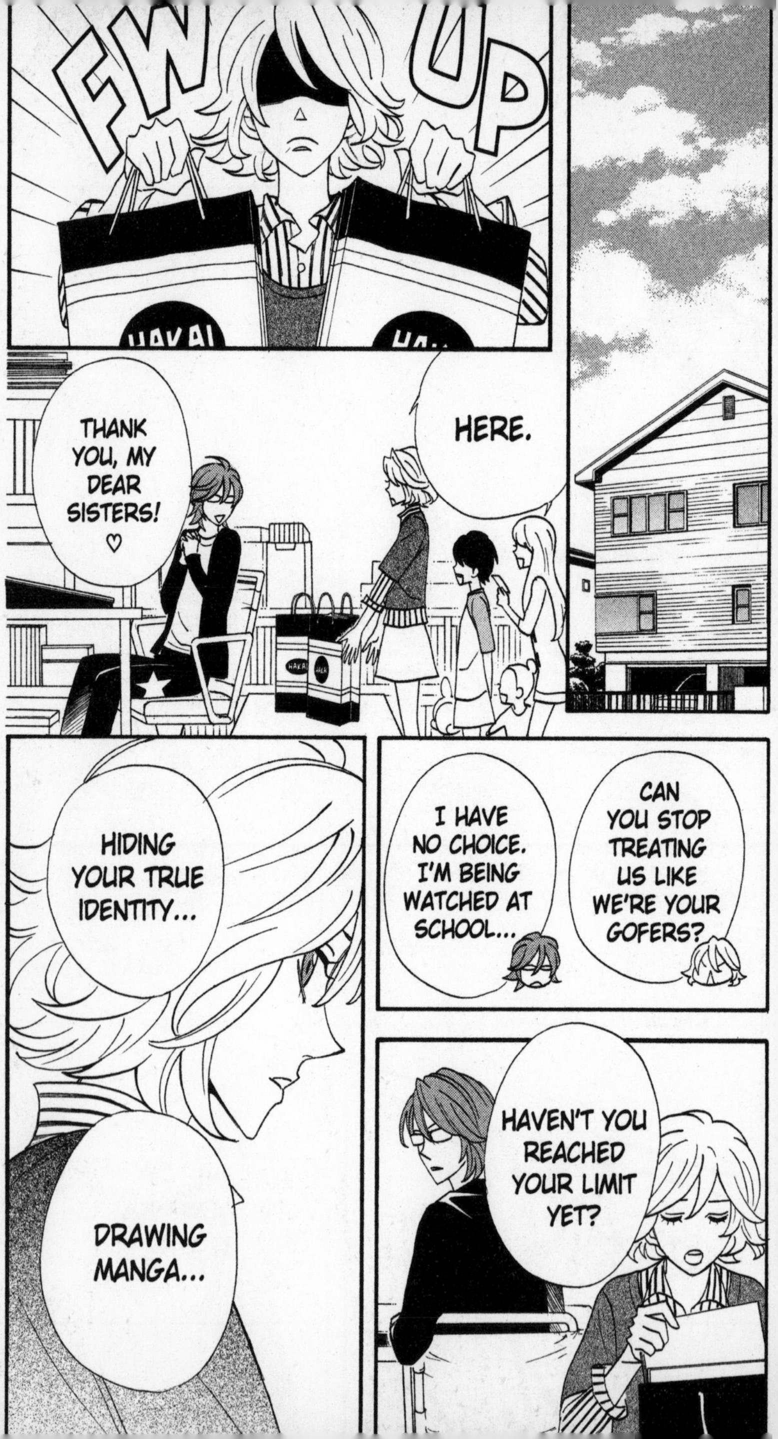
FWUP
HERE.
THANK YOU, MY DEAR SISTERS! ♡
CAN YOU STOP TREATING US LIKE WE'RE YOUR GOFERS?
I HAVE NO CHOICE. I'M BEING WATCHED AT SCHOOL...
HAVEN'T YOU REACHED YOUR LIMIT YET?
HIDING YOUR TRUE IDENTITY...
DRAWING MANGA...

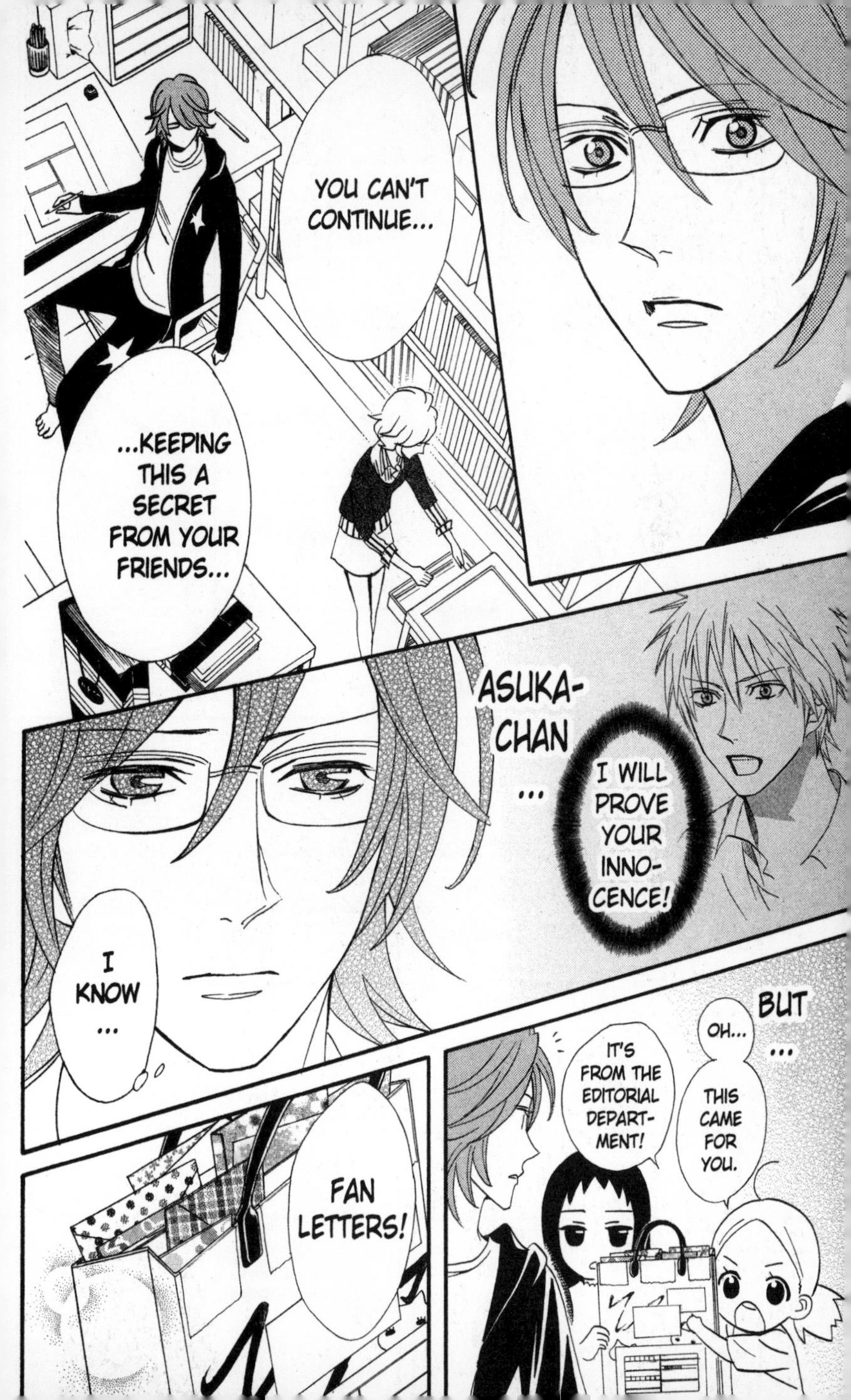
YOU CAN'T CONTINUE...
...KEEPING THIS A SECRET FROM YOUR FRIENDS...
ASUKA-CHAN...
I WILL PROVE YOUR INNOCENCE!
I KNOW...
BUT...
OH...
THIS CAME FOR YOU.
IT'S FROM THE EDITORIAL DEPARTMENT!
FAN LETTERS!

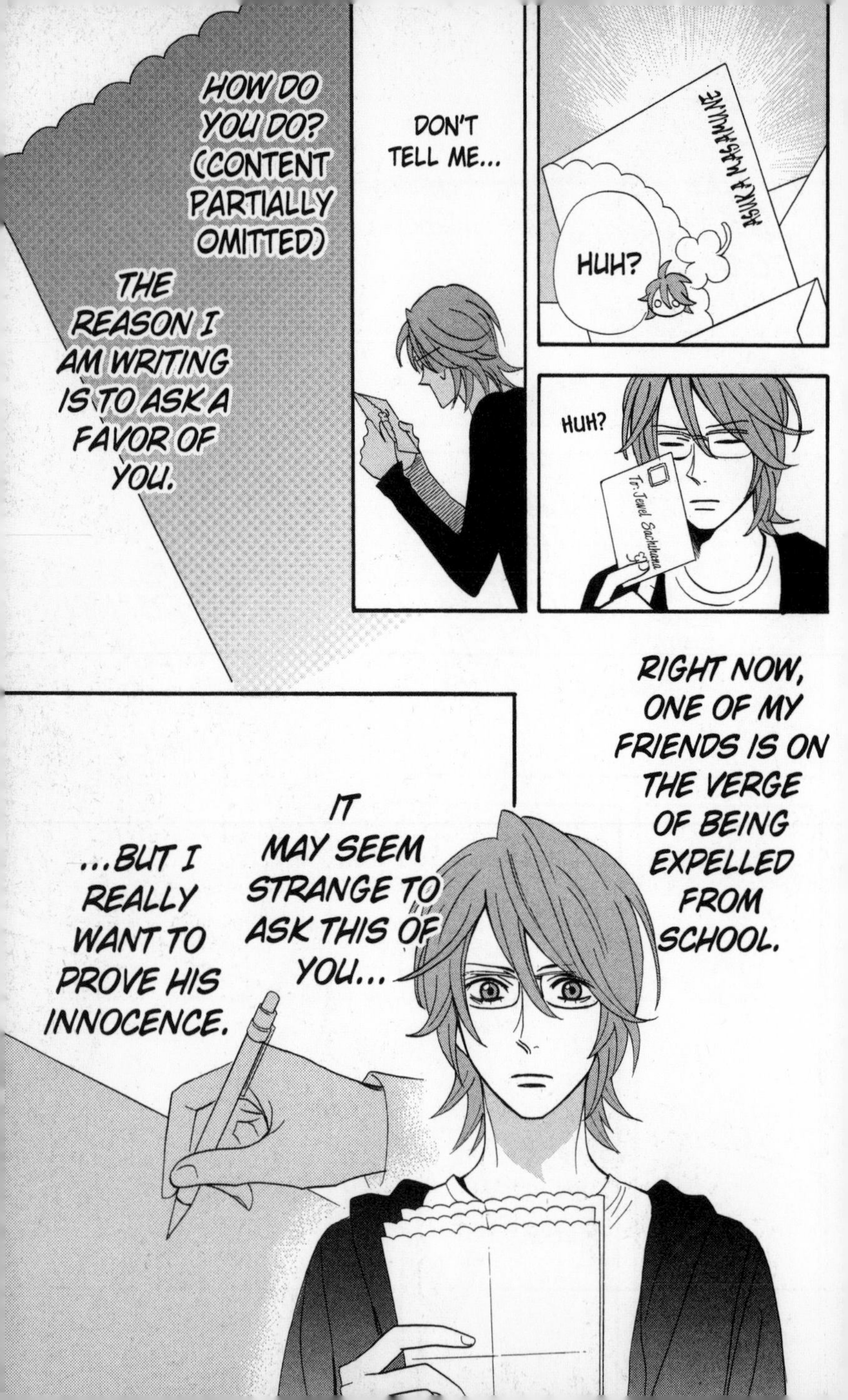
ASUKA MASAMUNE
HUH?
HUH?
To: Jewel Sachihana
DON'T TELL ME...
HOW DO YOU DO? (CONTENT PARTIALLY OMITTED)
THE REASON I AM WRITING IS TO ASK A FAVOR OF YOU.
RIGHT NOW, ONE OF MY FRIENDS IS ON THE VERGE OF BEING EXPELLED FROM SCHOOL.
IT MAY SEEM STRANGE TO ASK THIS OF YOU...
...BUT I REALLY WANT TO PROVE HIS INNOCENCE.

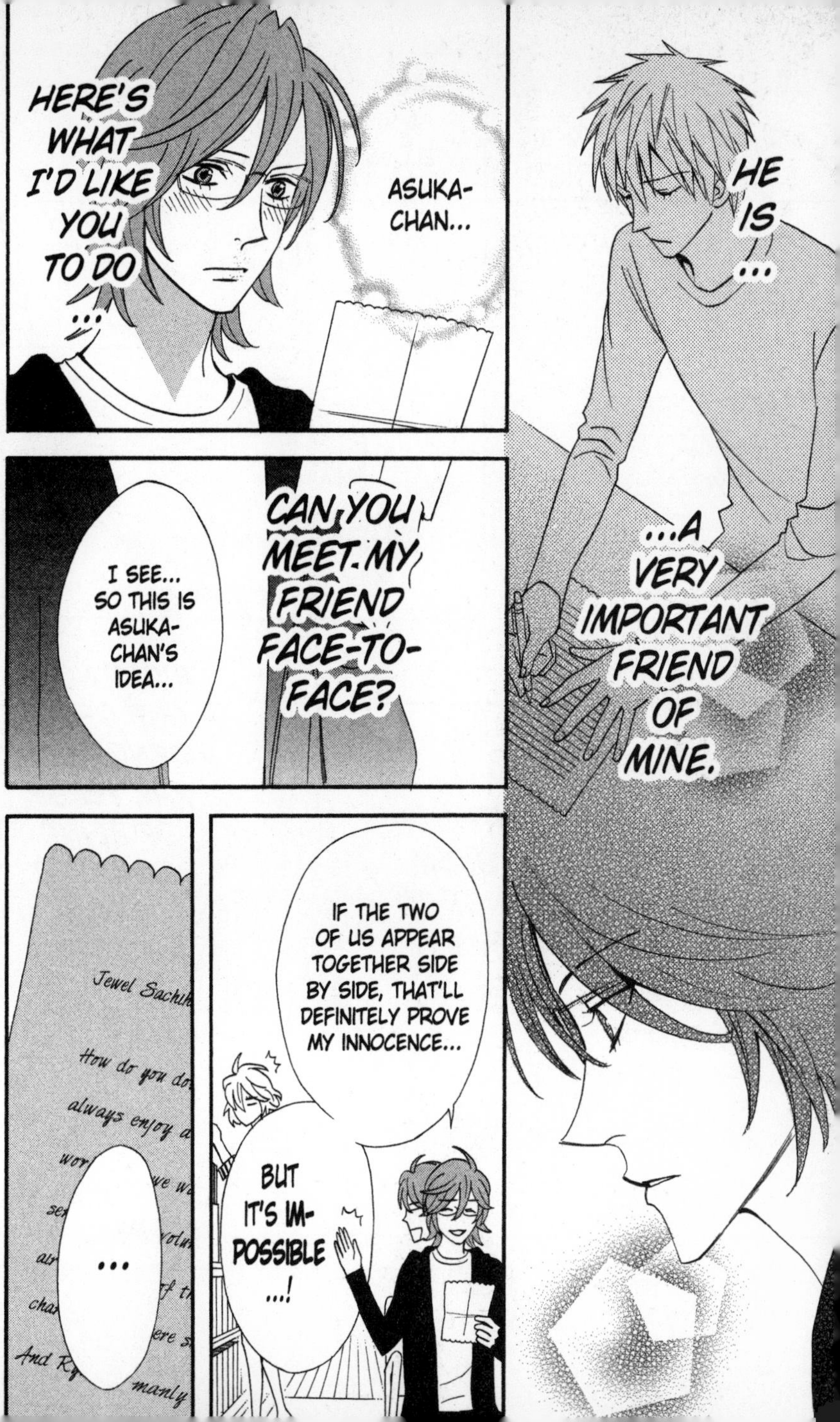
HE IS...
...A VERY IMPORTANT FRIEND OF MINE.
ASUKA-CHAN...
HERE'S WHAT I'D LIKE YOU TO DO...
CAN YOU MEET MY FRIEND FACE-TO-FACE?
I SEE... SO THIS IS ASUKA-CHAN'S IDEA...
IF THE TWO OF US APPEAR TOGETHER SIDE BY SIDE, THAT'LL DEFINITELY PROVE MY INNOCENCE...
BUT IT'S IMPOSSIBLE...!
...

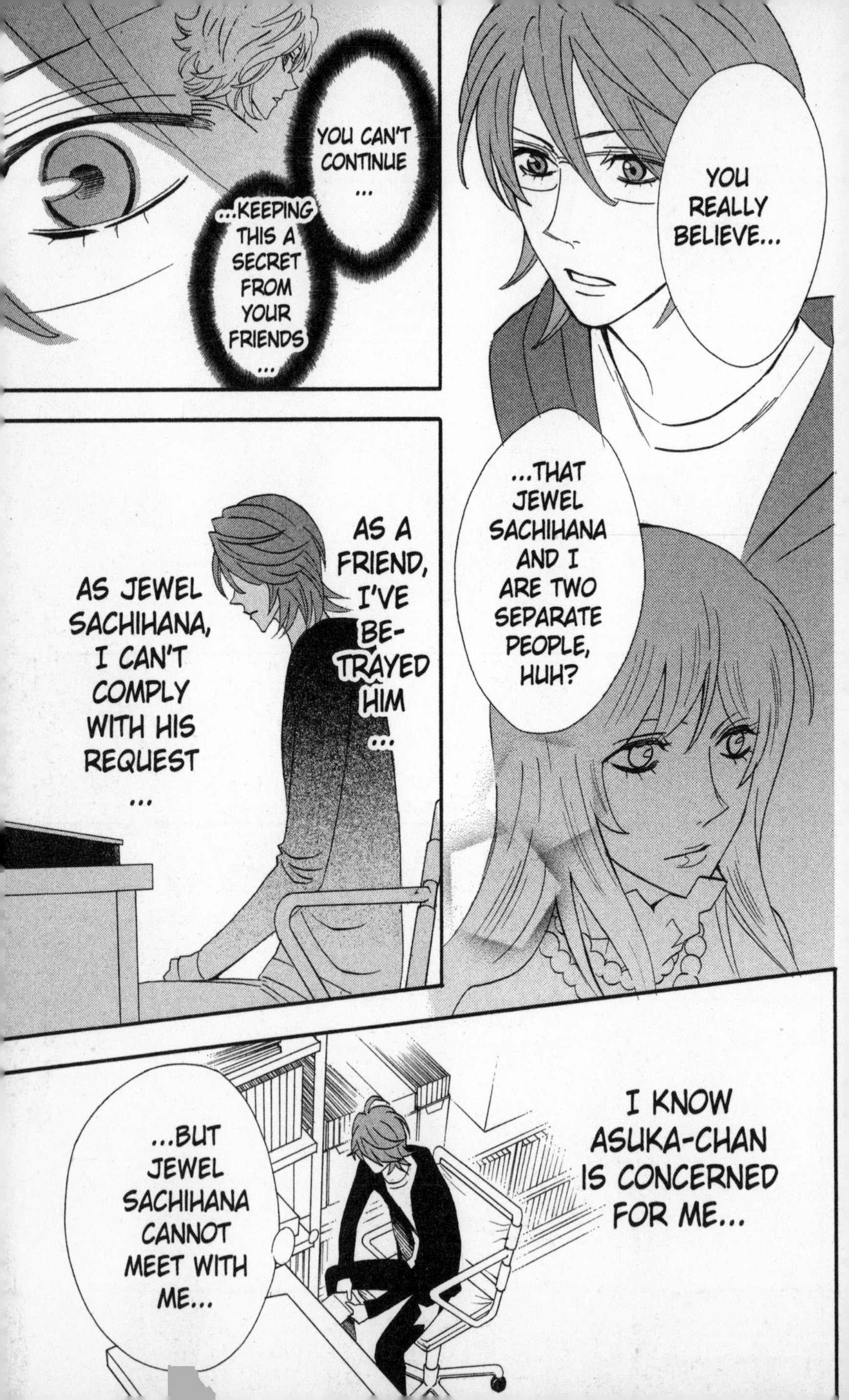
YOU REALLY BELIEVE...
...THAT JEWEL SACHIHANA AND I ARE TWO SEPARATE PEOPLE, HUH?
YOU CAN'T CONTINUE ...
...KEEPING THIS A SECRET FROM YOUR FRIENDS ...
AS A FRIEND, I'VE BE- TRAYED HIM ...
AS JEWEL SACHIHANA, I CAN'T COMPLY WITH HIS REQUEST ...
I KNOW ASUKA-CHAN IS CONCERNED FOR ME...
...BUT JEWEL SACHIHANA CANNOT MEET WITH ME...

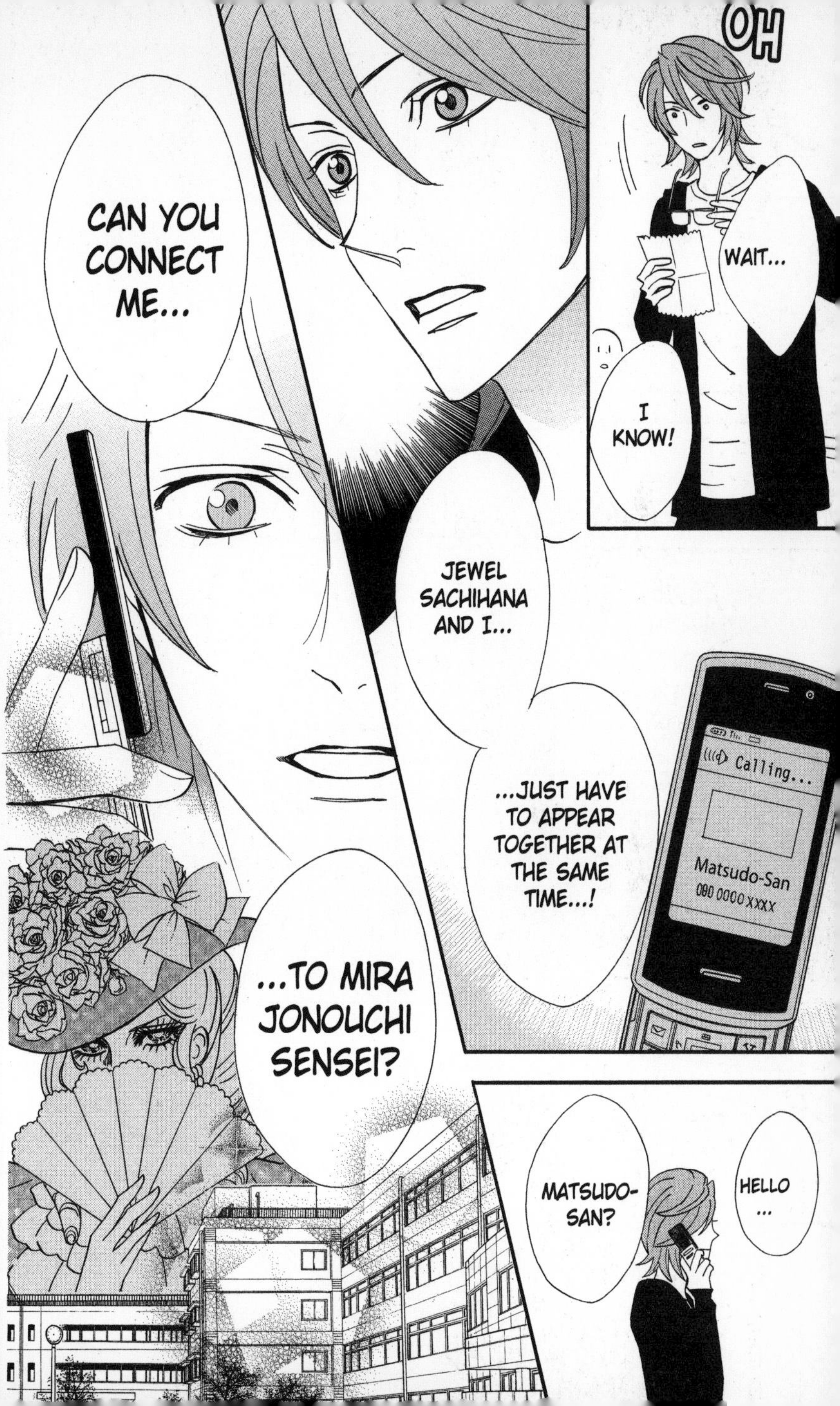
OH
WAIT...
I KNOW!
JEWEL SACHIHANA AND I...
...JUST HAVE TO APPEAR TOGETHER AT THE SAME TIME...!
Calling...
Matsudo-San
080 0000 XXXX
HELLO ...
MATSUDO-SAN?
CAN YOU CONNECT ME...
...TO MIRA JONOUCHI SENSEI?

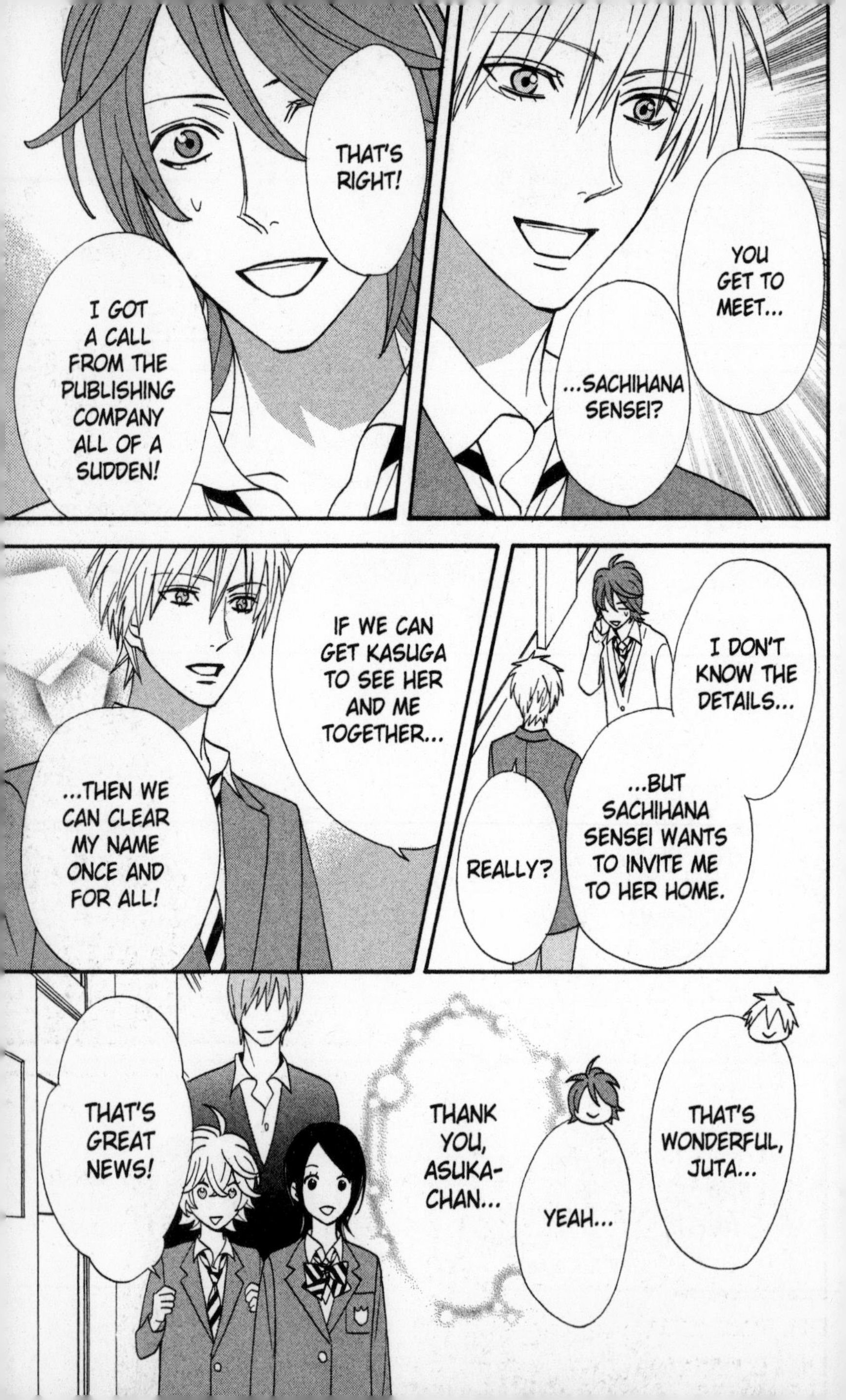
YOU GET TO MEET...
...SACHIHANA SENSEI?
THAT'S RIGHT!
I GOT A CALL FROM THE PUBLISHING COMPANY ALL OF A SUDDEN!
I DON'T KNOW THE DETAILS...
...BUT SACHIHANA SENSEI WANTS TO INVITE ME TO HER HOME.
REALLY?
IF WE CAN GET KASUGA TO SEE HER AND ME TOGETHER...
...THEN WE CAN CLEAR MY NAME ONCE AND FOR ALL!
THAT'S WONDERFUL, JUTA...
YEAH...
THANK YOU, ASUKA-CHAN...
THAT'S GREAT NEWS!

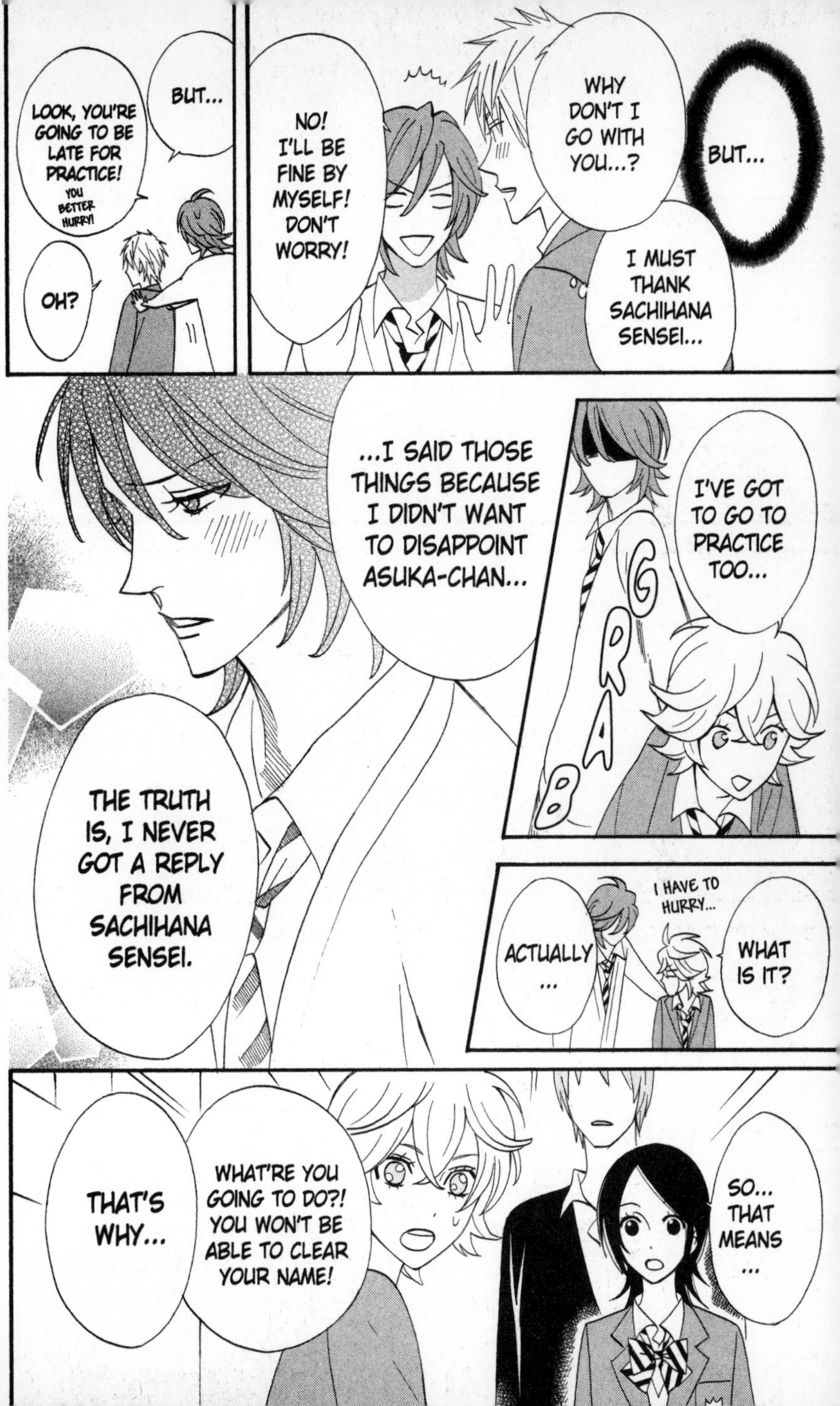
WHY DON'T I GO WITH YOU...?
BUT...
I MUST THANK SACHIHANA SENSEI...
NO! I'LL BE FINE BY MYSELF! DON'T WORRY!
BUT...
LOOK, YOU'RE GOING TO BE LATE FOR PRACTICE!
YOU BETTER HURRY!
OH?
I'VE GOT TO GO TO PRACTICE TOO...
GRAB
WHAT IS IT?
I HAVE TO HURRY...
ACTUALLY...
...I SAID THOSE THINGS BECAUSE I DIDN'T WANT TO DISAPPOINT ASUKA-CHAN...
THE TRUTH IS, I NEVER GOT A REPLY FROM SACHIHANA SENSEI.
SO... THAT MEANS...
WHAT'RE YOU GOING TO DO?! YOU WON'T BE ABLE TO CLEAR YOUR NAME!
THAT'S WHY...

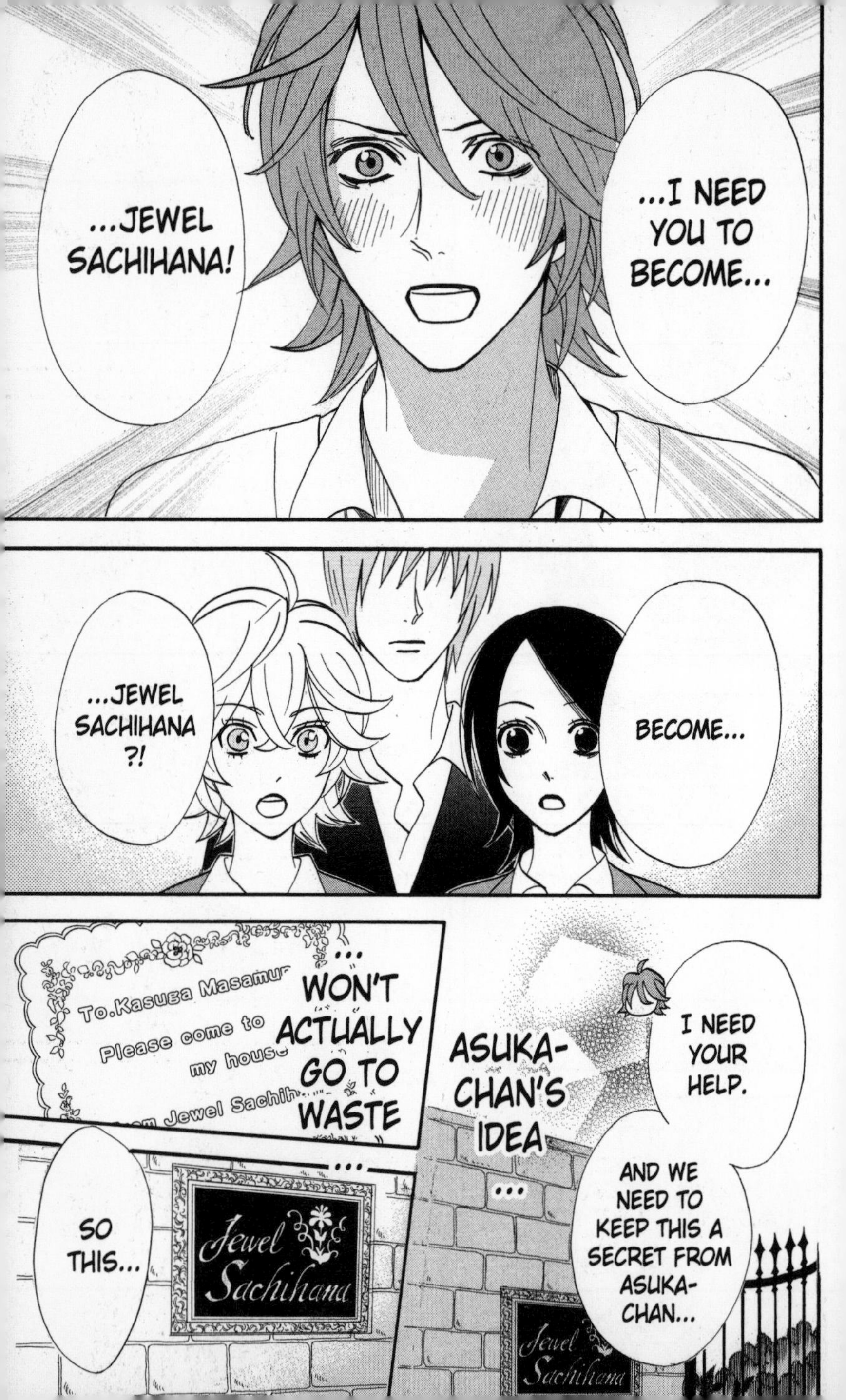
...I NEED YOU TO BECOME...
...JEWEL SACHIHANA!
BECOME...
...JEWEL SACHIHANA ?!
I NEED YOUR HELP.
AND WE NEED TO KEEP THIS A SECRET FROM ASUKA-CHAN...
ASUKA-CHAN'S IDEA ...
... WON'T ACTUALLY GO TO WASTE ...
To.Kasuga Masamu
Please come to
my house
Jewel Sachih
Jewel Sachihana
SO THIS...
Jewel Sachihana

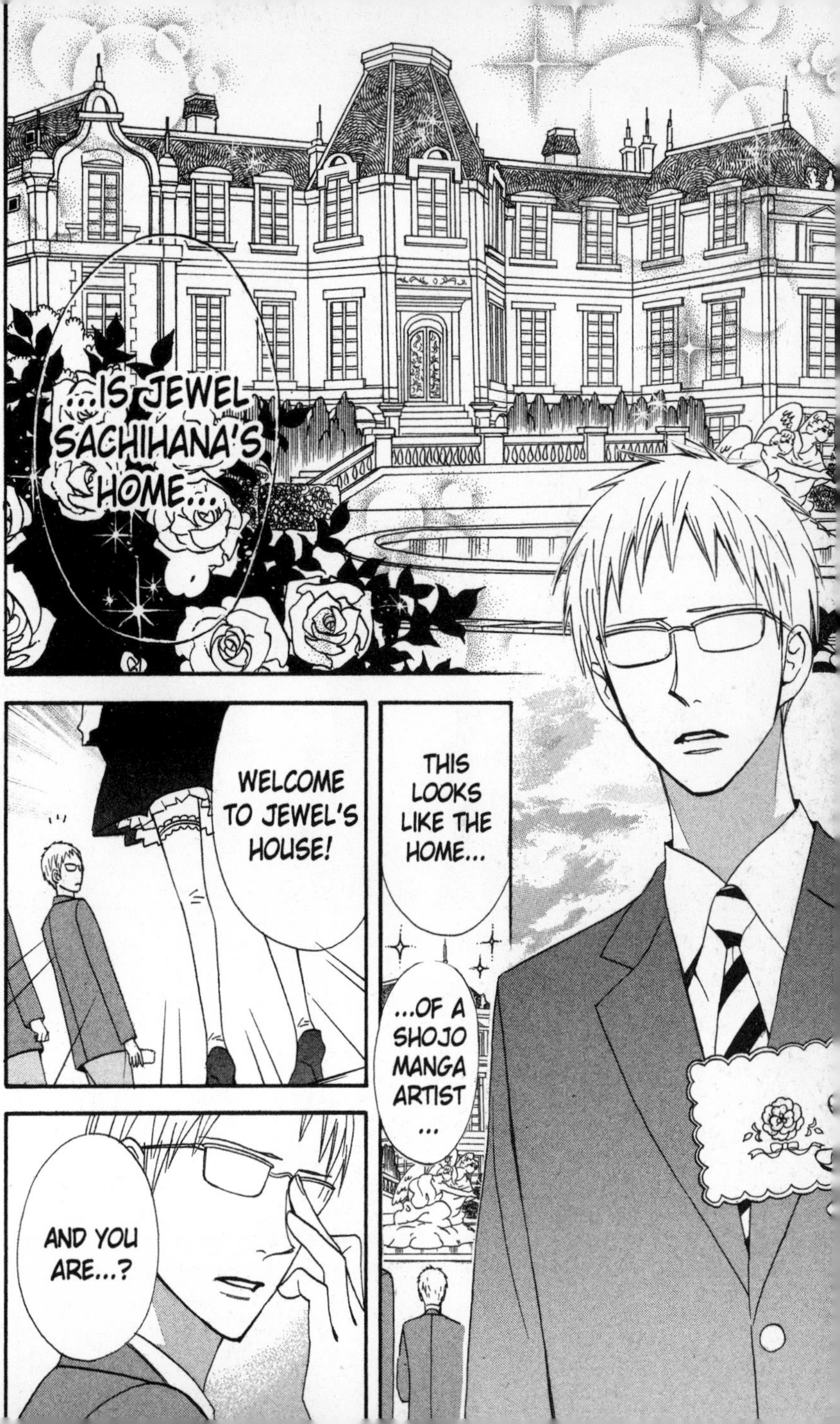

...IS JEWEL SACHIHANA'S HOME...
THIS LOOKS LIKE THE HOME...
...OF A SHOJO MANGA ARTIST ...
WELCOME TO JEWEL'S HOUSE!
AND YOU ARE...?

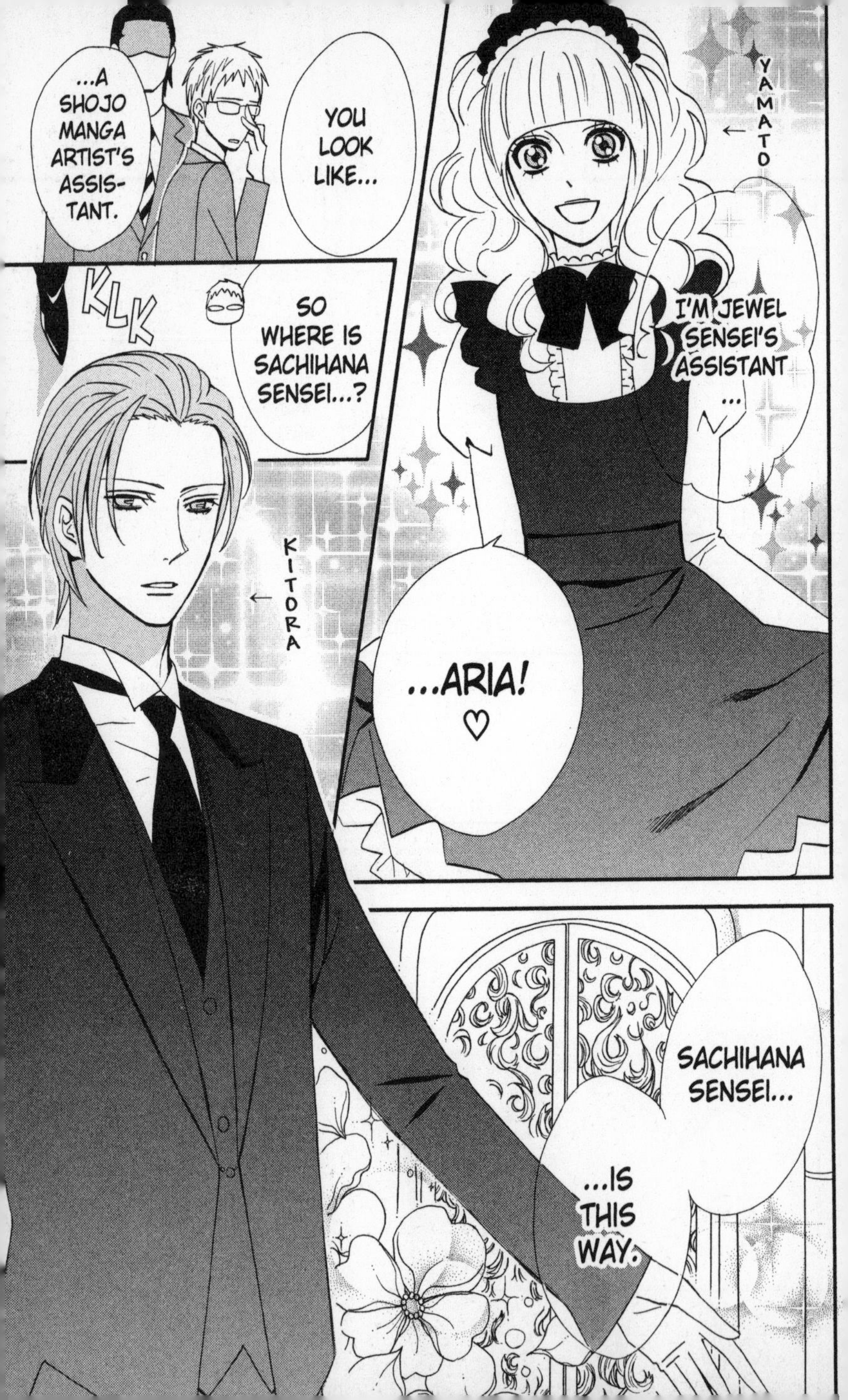
YAMATO
I'M JEWEL SENSEI'S ASSISTANT ...
...ARIA! ♡
YOU LOOK LIKE...
...A SHOJO MANGA ARTIST'S ASSIS-TANT.
KLK
SO WHERE IS SACHIHANA SENSEI...?
KITORA
SACHIHANA SENSEI...
...IS THIS WAY.

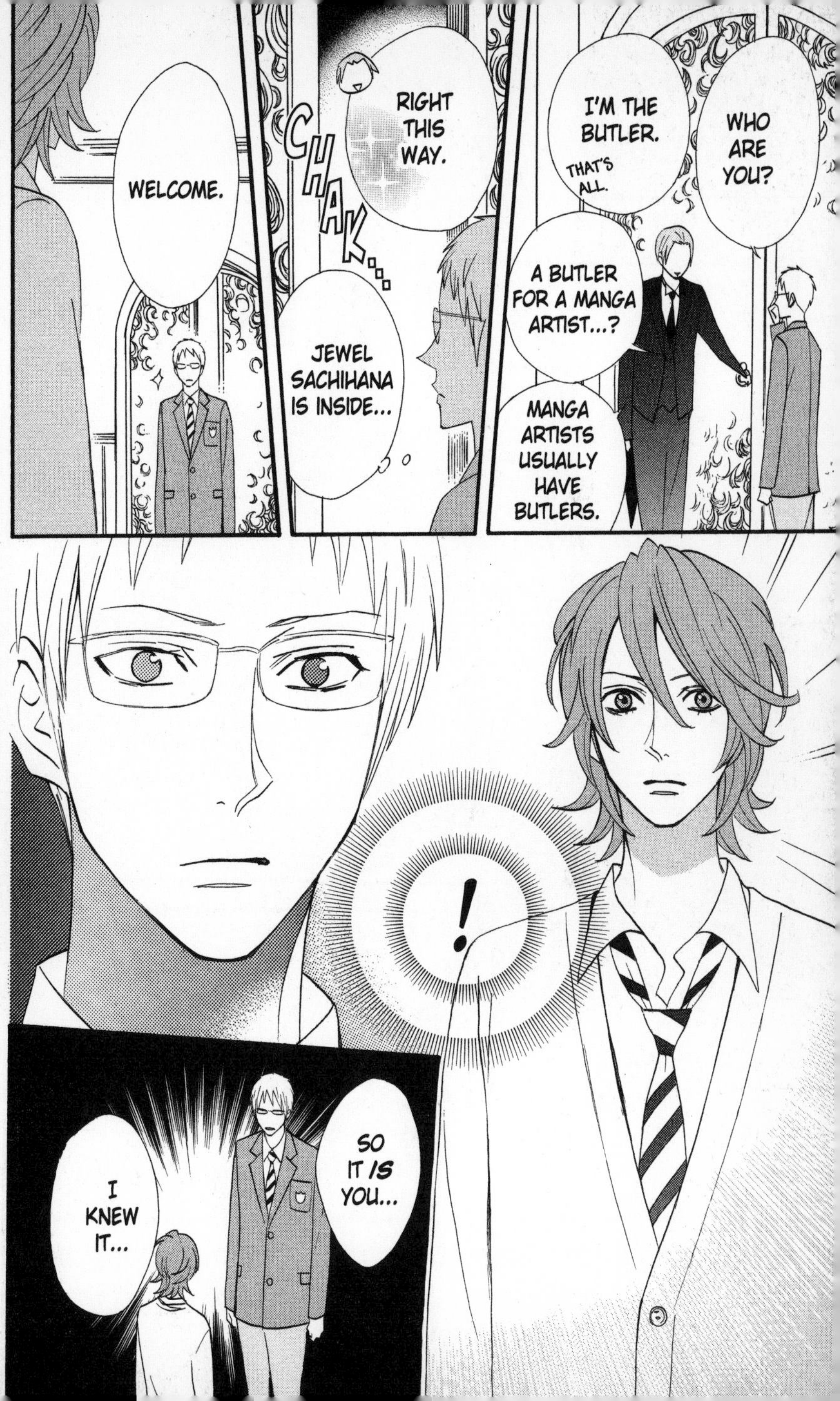
WHO ARE YOU?
I'M THE BUTLER.
THAT'S ALL.
A BUTLER FOR A MANGA ARTIST...?
MANGA ARTISTS USUALLY HAVE BUTLERS.
RIGHT THIS WAY.
CHAK...
JEWEL SACHIHANA IS INSIDE...
WELCOME.
!
SO IT *IS* YOU...
I KNEW IT...

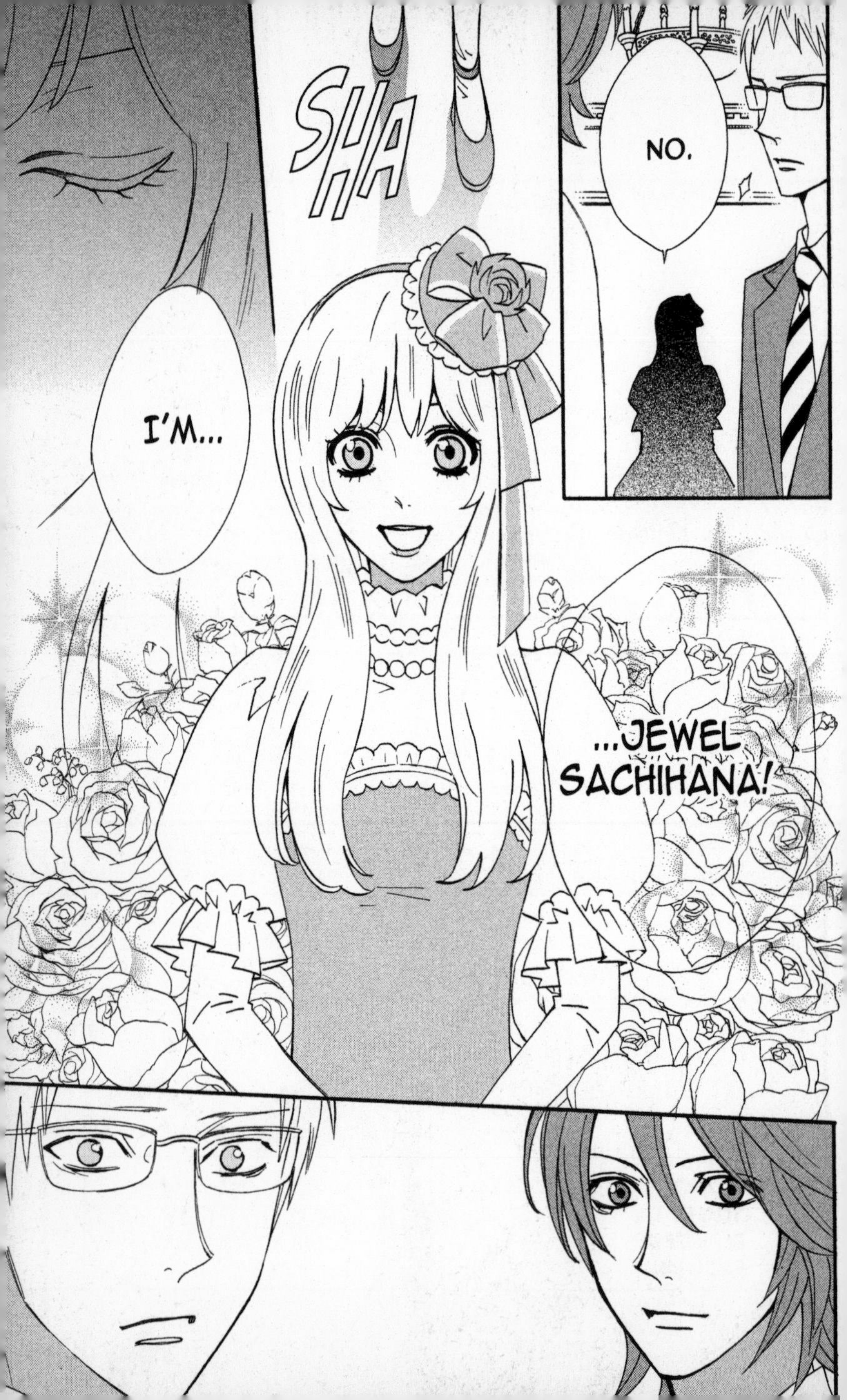
NO.
SHA
I'M...
...JEWEL SACHIHANA!

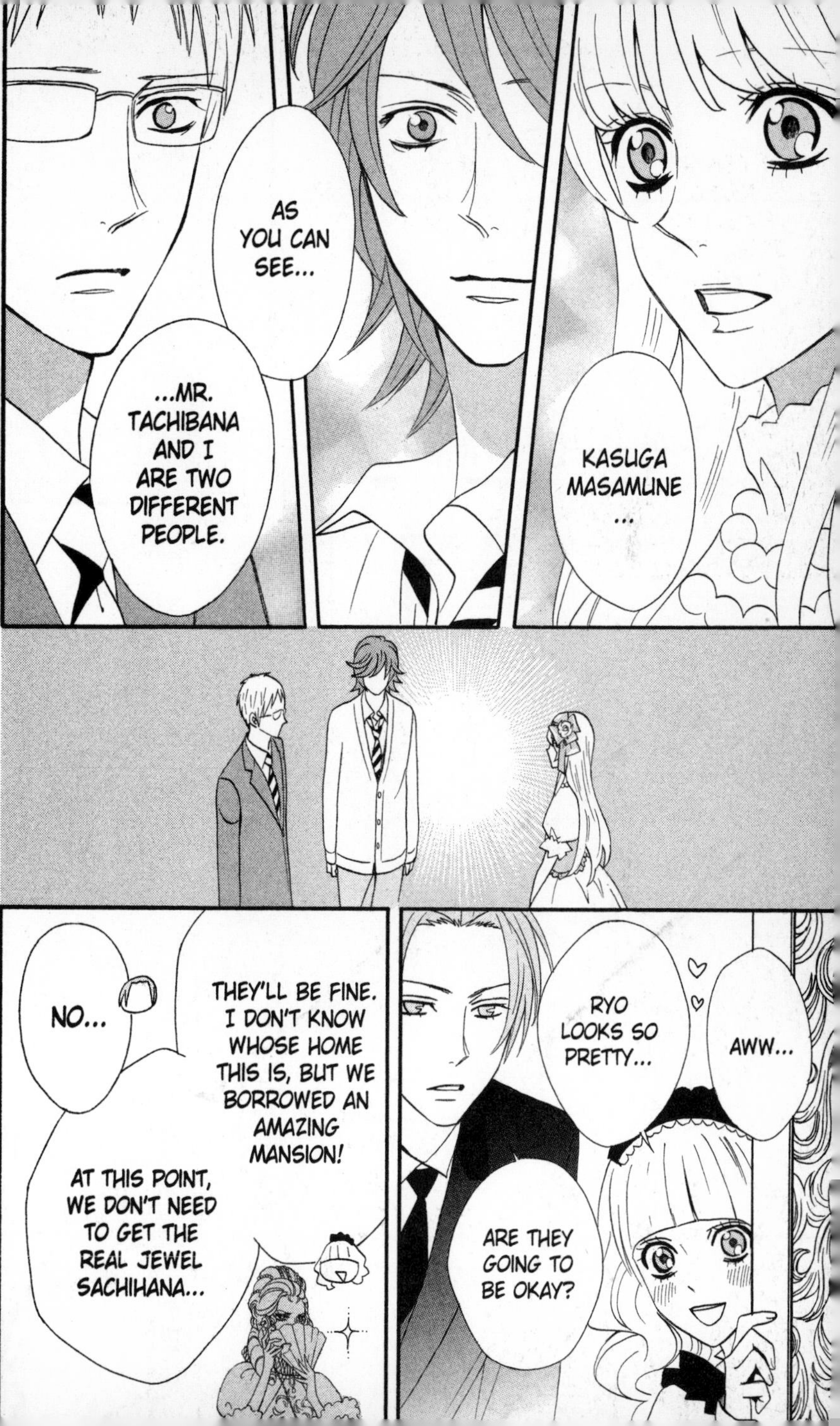
KASUGA MASAMUNE ...
AS YOU CAN SEE...
...MR. TACHIBANA AND I ARE TWO DIFFERENT PEOPLE.
AWW...
RYO LOOKS SO PRETTY...
ARE THEY GOING TO BE OKAY?
THEY'LL BE FINE. I DON'T KNOW WHOSE HOME THIS IS, BUT WE BORROWED AN AMAZING MANSION!
NO...
AT THIS POINT, WE DON'T NEED TO GET THE REAL JEWEL SACHIHANA...

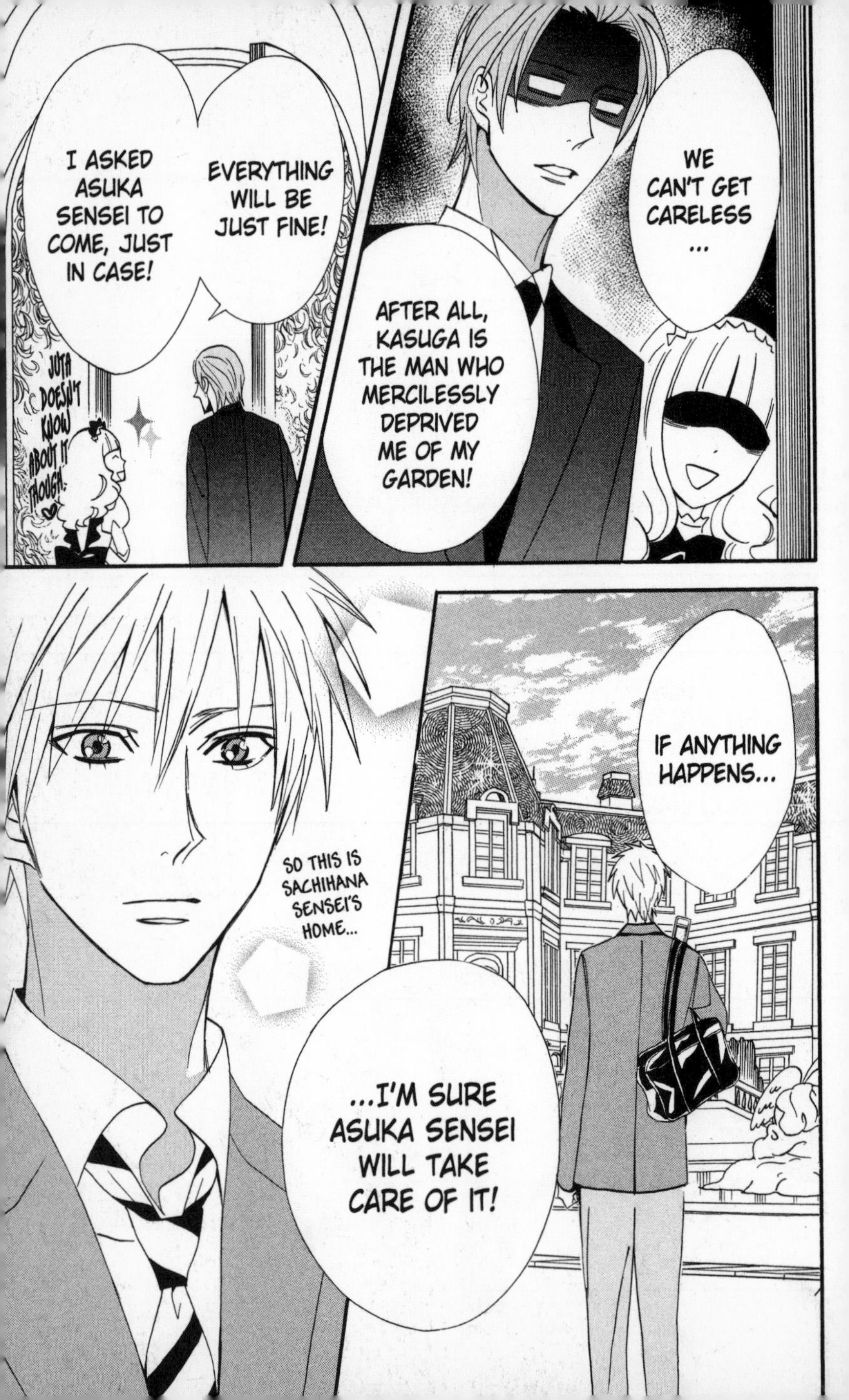
WE CAN'T GET CARELESS ...
AFTER ALL, KASUGA IS THE MAN WHO MERCILESSLY DEPRIVED ME OF MY GARDEN!
EVERYTHING WILL BE JUST FINE!
I ASKED ASUKA SENSEI TO COME, JUST IN CASE!
JUTA DOESN'T KNOW ABOUT IT THOUGH.
IF ANYTHING HAPPENS...
...I'M SURE ASUKA SENSEI WILL TAKE CARE OF IT!
SO THIS IS SACHIHANA SENSEI'S HOME...

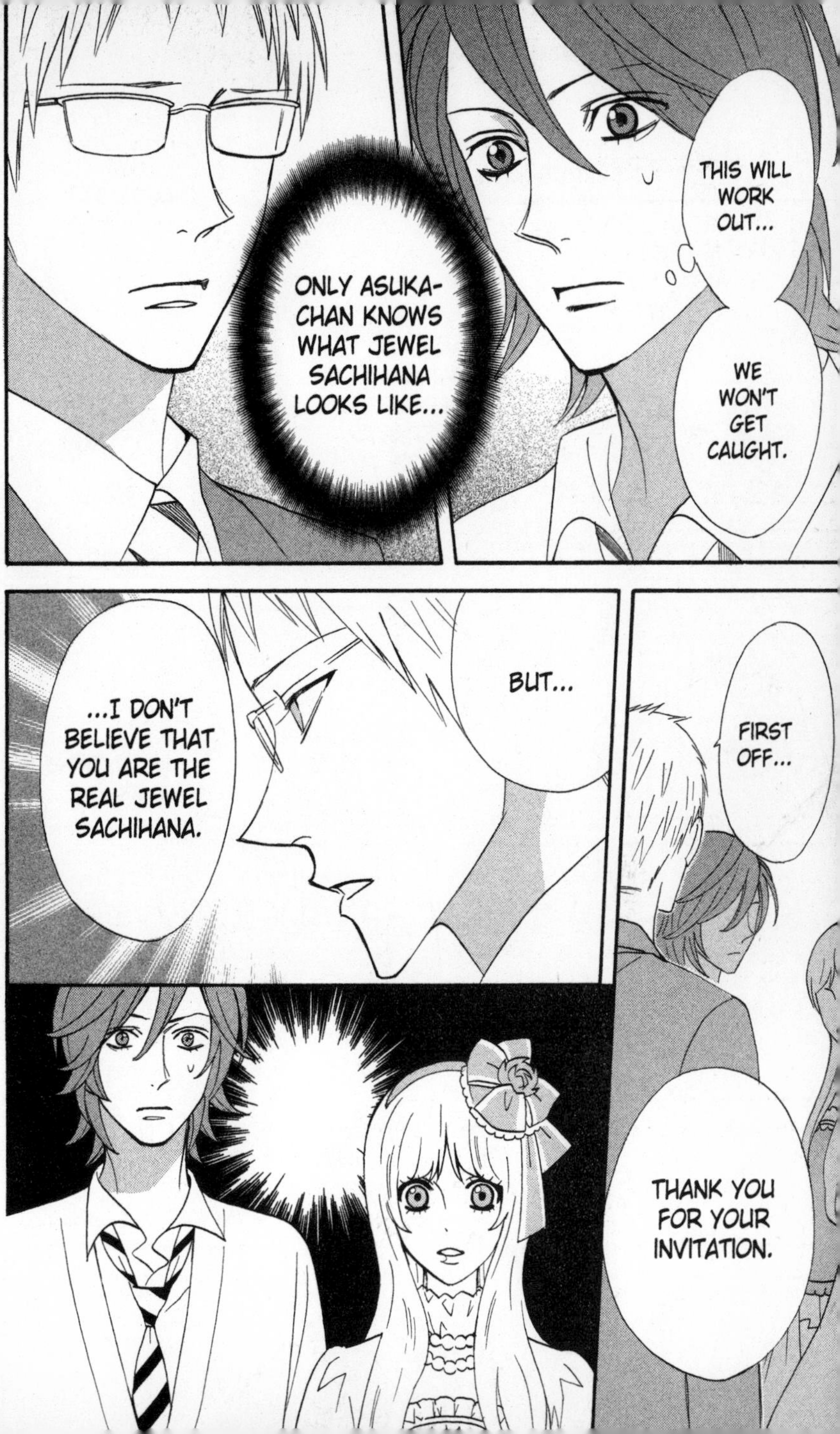
THIS WILL WORK OUT...
WE WON'T GET CAUGHT.
ONLY ASUKA-CHAN KNOWS WHAT JEWEL SACHIHANA LOOKS LIKE...
FIRST OFF...
THANK YOU FOR YOUR INVITATION.
BUT...
...I DON'T BELIEVE THAT YOU ARE THE REAL JEWEL SACHIHANA.

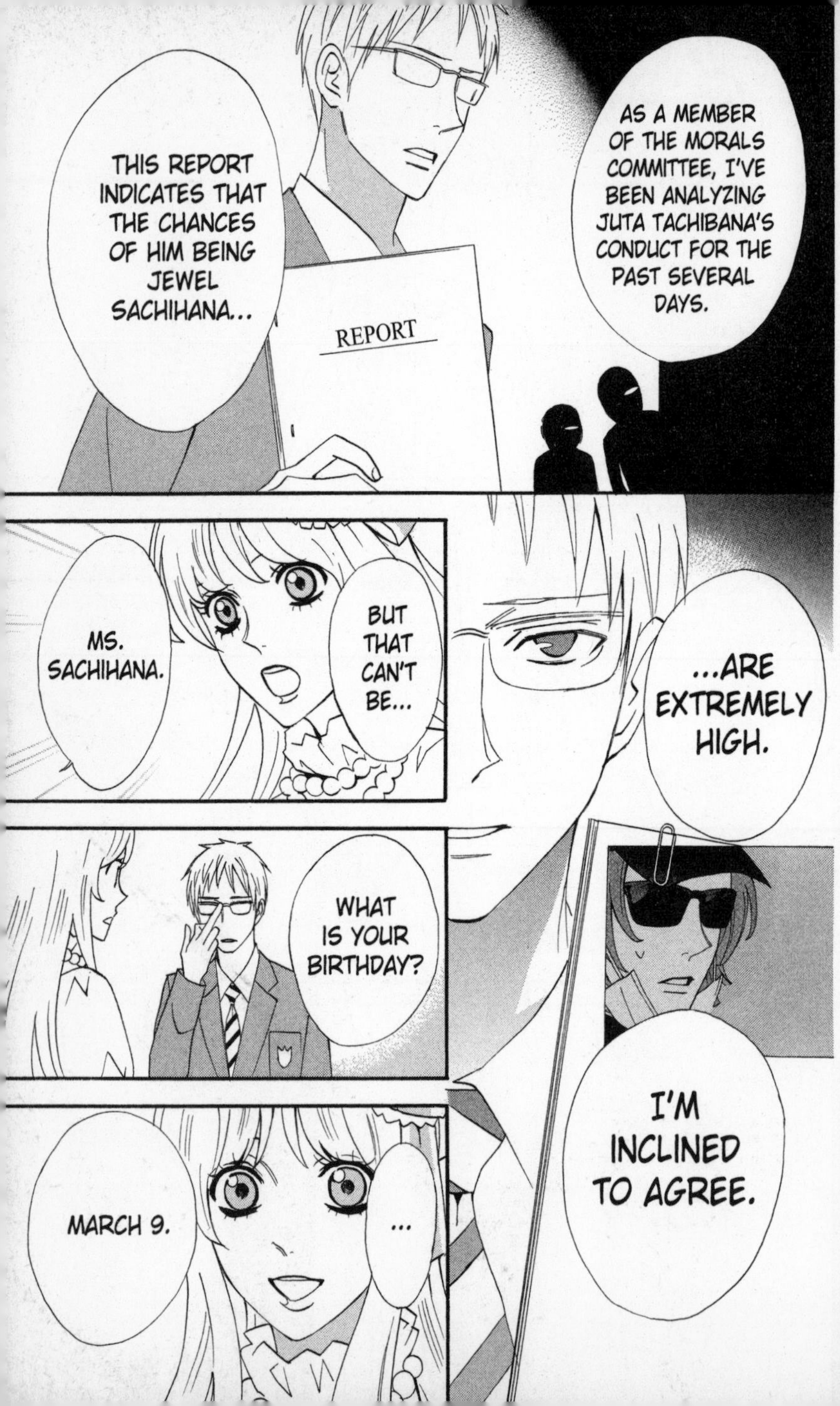
AS A MEMBER OF THE MORALS COMMITTEE, I'VE BEEN ANALYZING JUTA TACHIBANA'S CONDUCT FOR THE PAST SEVERAL DAYS.
THIS REPORT INDICATES THAT THE CHANCES OF HIM BEING JEWEL SACHIHANA...
REPORT
...ARE EXTREMELY HIGH.
I'M INCLINED TO AGREE.
BUT THAT CAN'T BE...
MS. SACHIHANA.
WHAT IS YOUR BIRTHDAY?
...
MARCH 9.

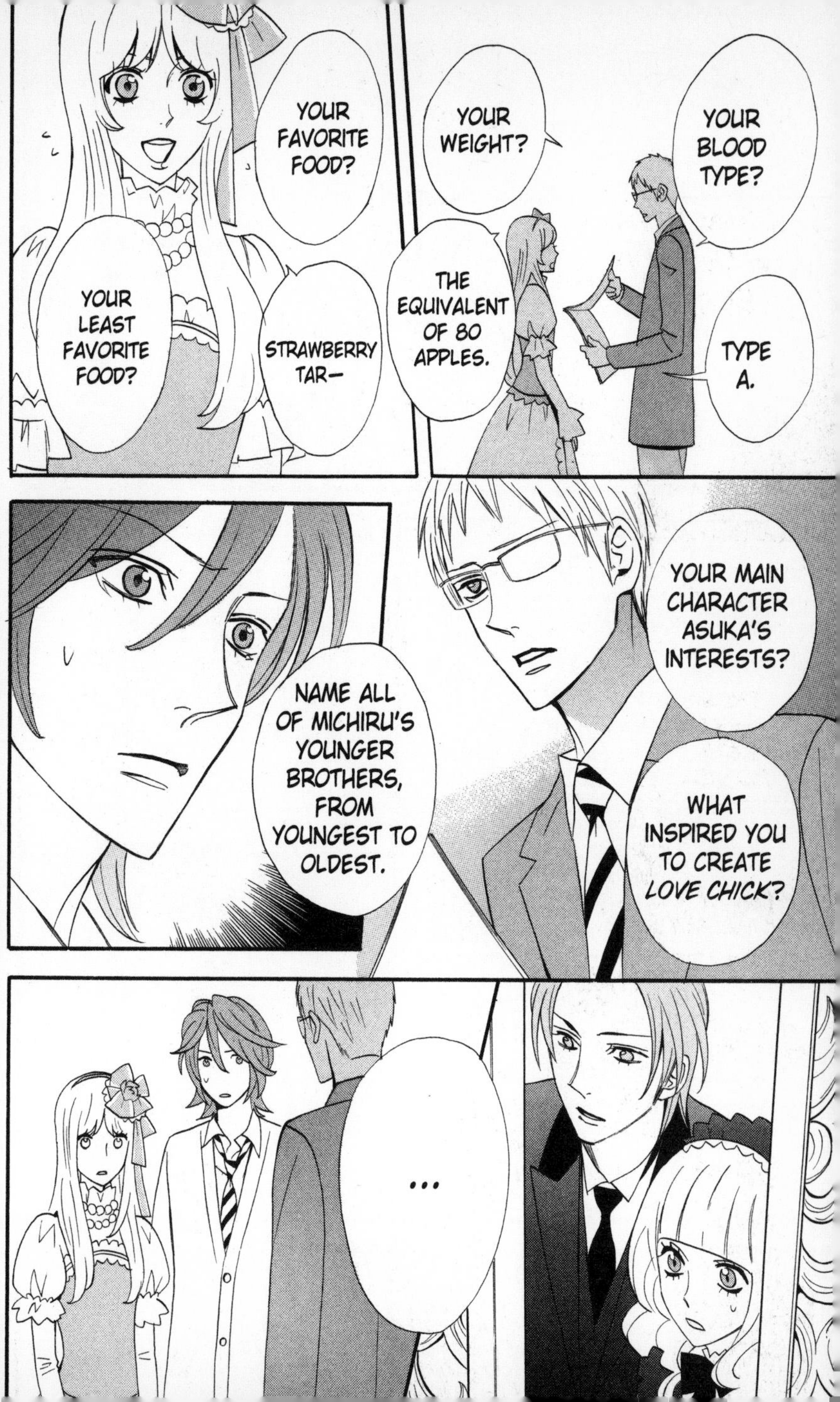
YOUR BLOOD TYPE?
TYPE A.
YOUR WEIGHT?
THE EQUIVALENT OF 80 APPLES.
YOUR FAVORITE FOOD?
STRAWBERRY TAR—
YOUR LEAST FAVORITE FOOD?
YOUR MAIN CHARACTER ASUKA'S INTERESTS?
WHAT INSPIRED YOU TO CREATE *LOVE CHICK*?
NAME ALL OF MICHIRU'S YOUNGER BROTHERS, FROM YOUNGEST TO OLDEST.
...

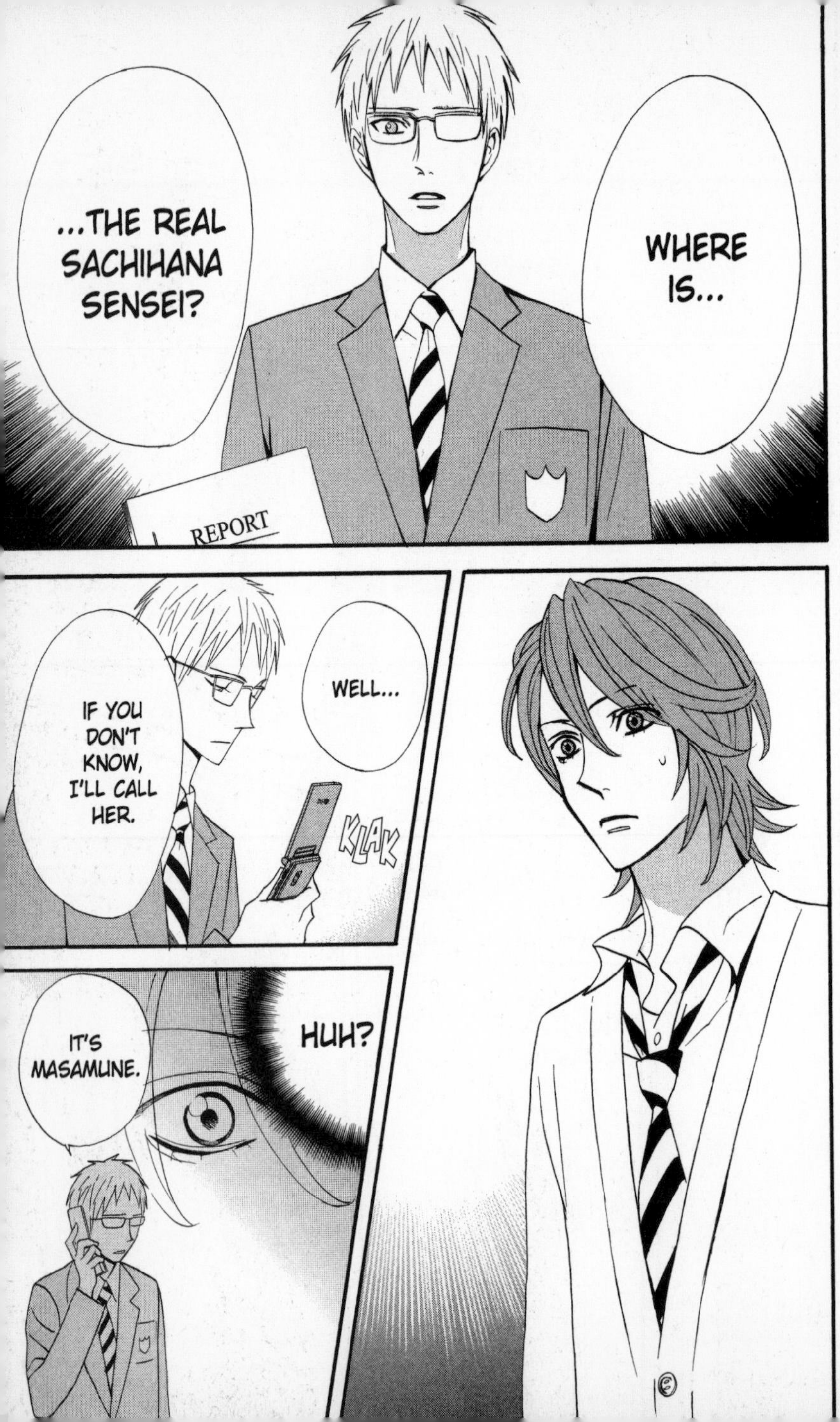
WHERE IS...
...THE REAL SACHIHANA SENSEI?
REPORT
WELL...
IF YOU DON'T KNOW, I'LL CALL HER.
KLAK
HUH?
IT'S MASAMUNE.

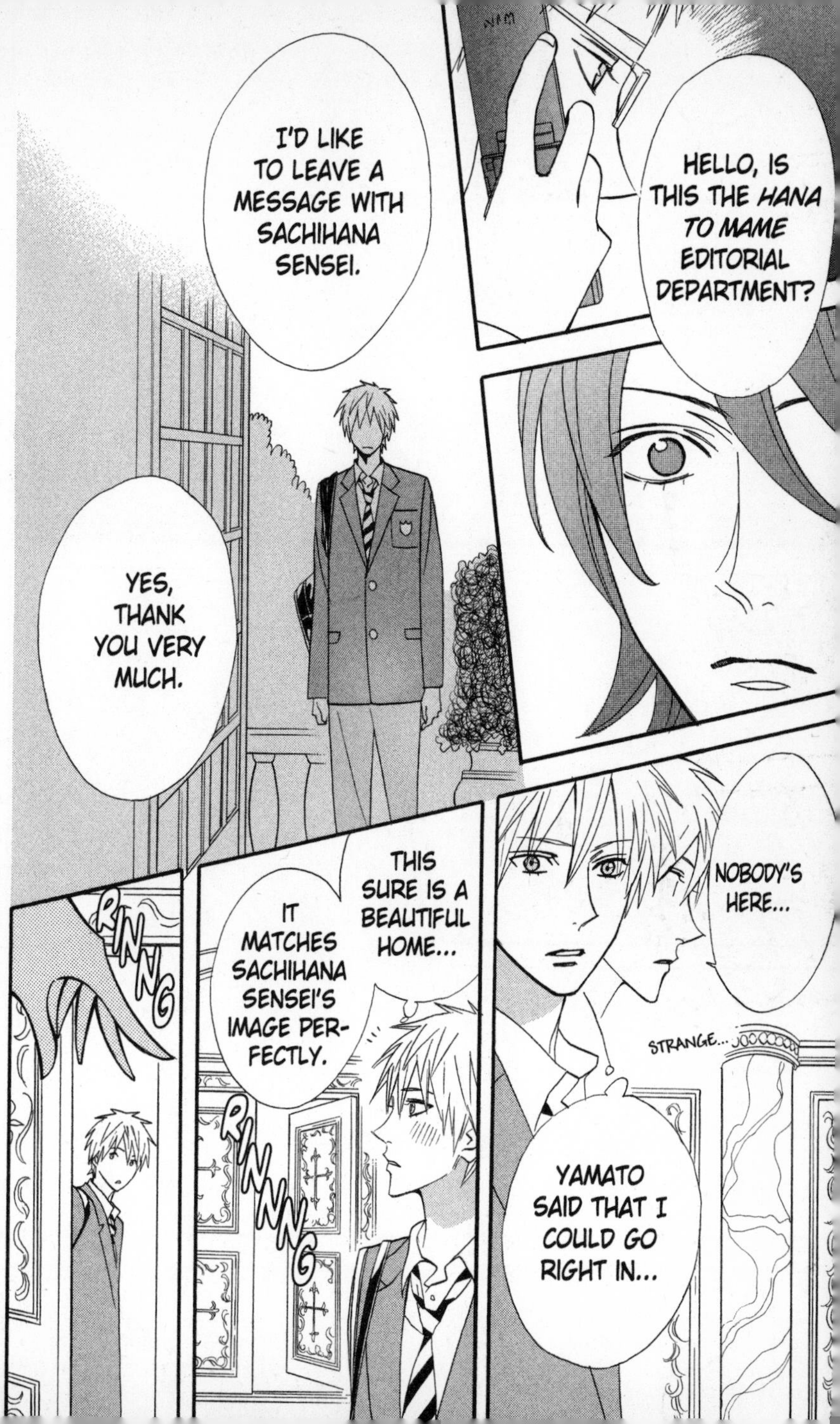
HELLO, IS THIS THE *HANA TO MAME* EDITORIAL DEPARTMENT?
I'D LIKE TO LEAVE A MESSAGE WITH SACHIHANA SENSEI.
YES, THANK YOU VERY MUCH.
NOBODY'S HERE...
STRANGE...
YAMATO SAID THAT I COULD GO RIGHT IN...
THIS SURE IS A BEAUTIFUL HOME...
IT MATCHES SACHIHANA SENSEI'S IMAGE PER-FECTLY.
RINNNG
RINNG

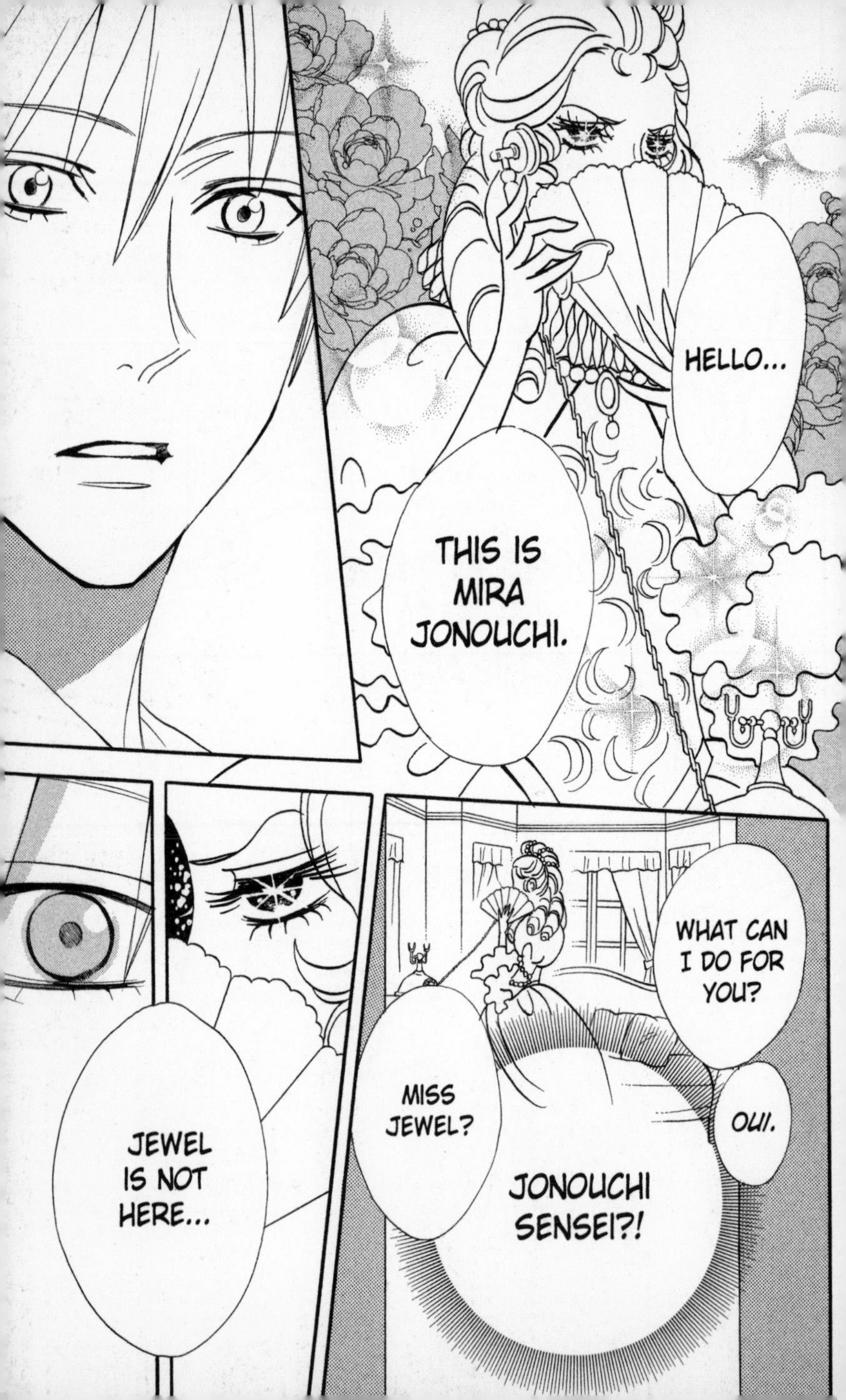
HELLO...
THIS IS MIRA JONOUCHI.
WHAT CAN I DO FOR YOU?
MISS JEWEL?
OUI.
JONOUCHI SENSEI?!
JEWEL IS NOT HERE...

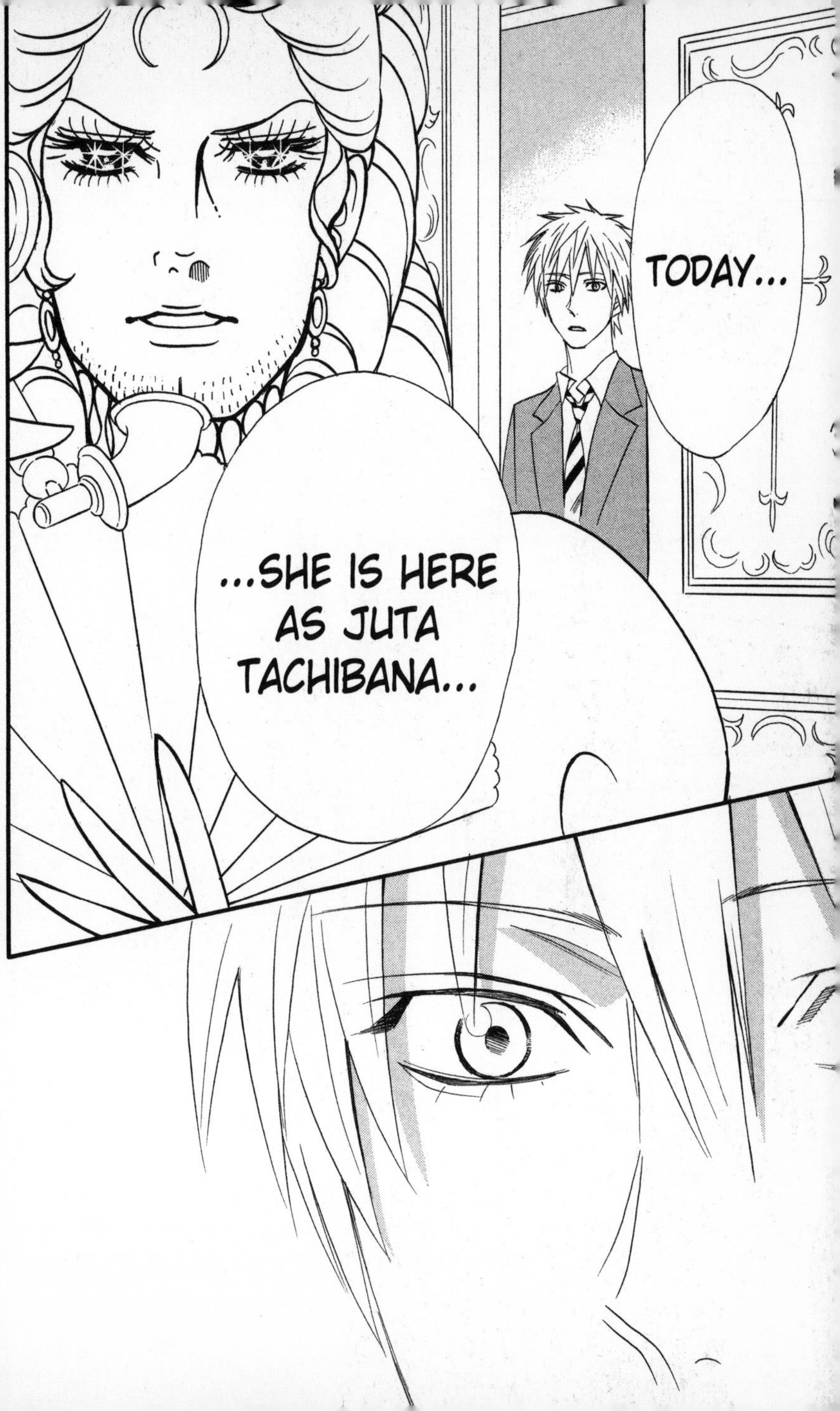
TODAY...
...SHE IS HERE AS JUTA TACHIBANA...

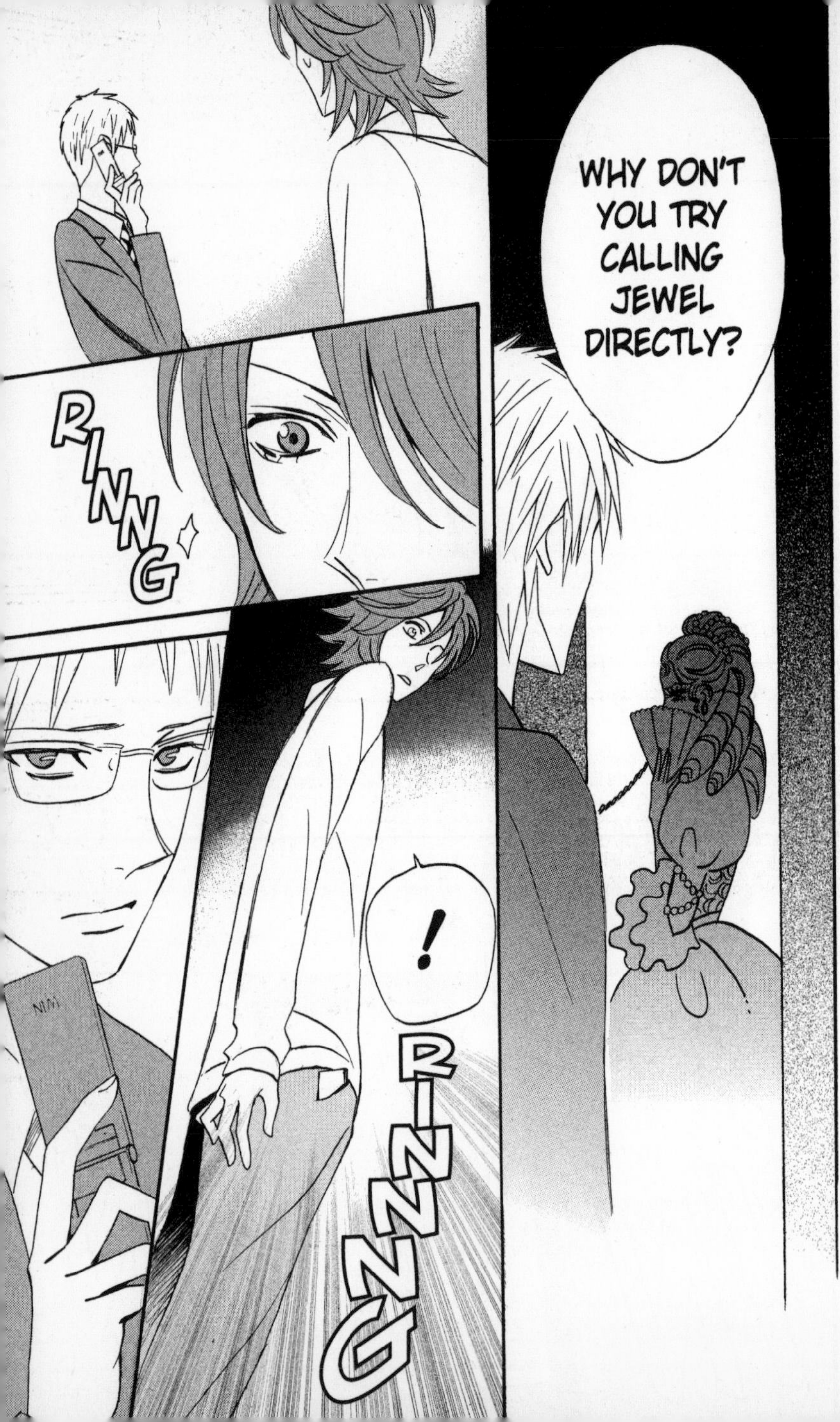
WHY DON'T YOU TRY CALLING JEWEL DIRECTLY?
RINNG
!
RINNNG

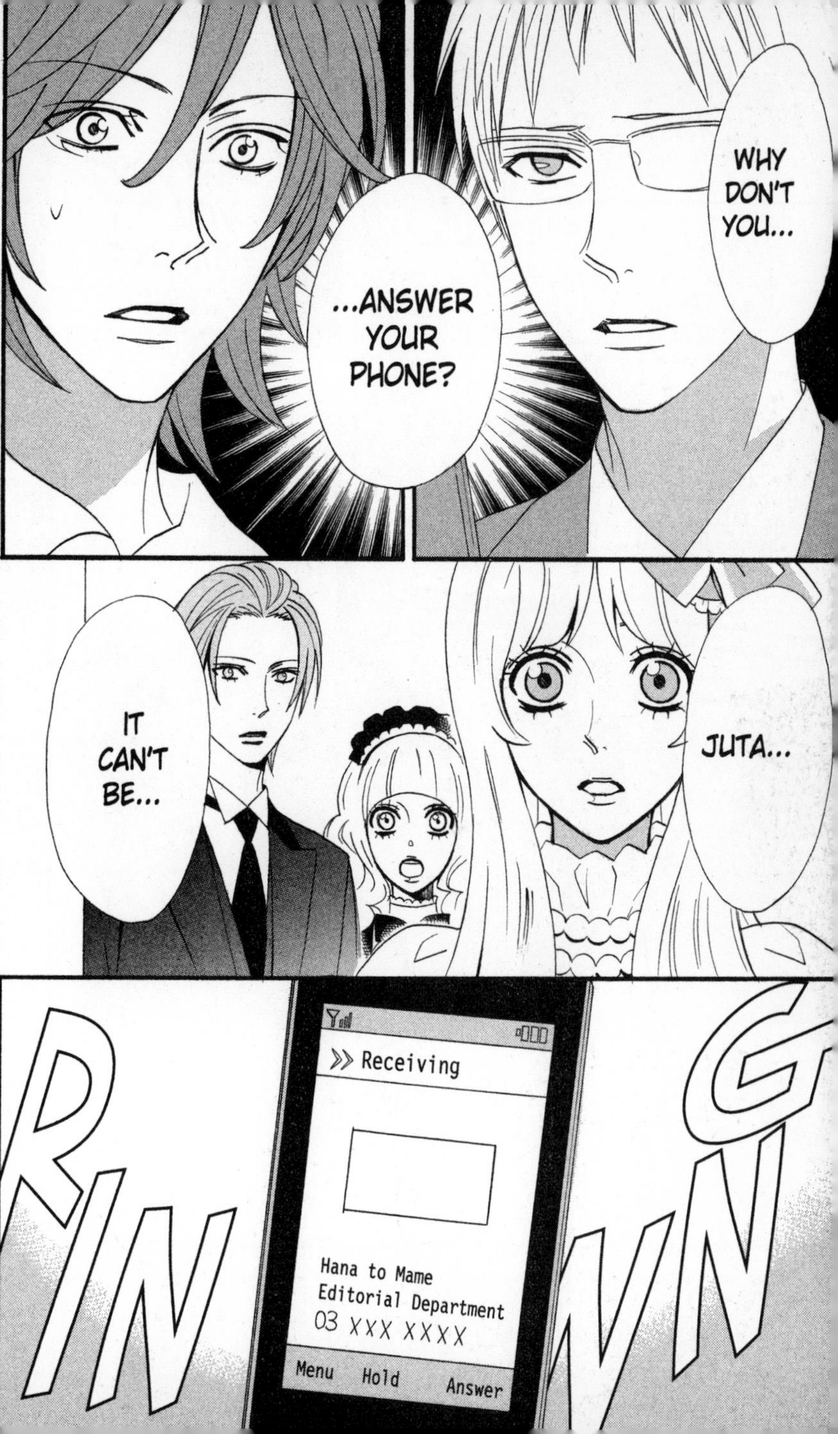
WHY DON'T YOU...
...ANSWER YOUR PHONE?
JUTA...
IT CAN'T BE...
RINNNG
Receiving
Hana to Mame
Editorial Department
03 XXX XXXX
Menu
Hold
Answer

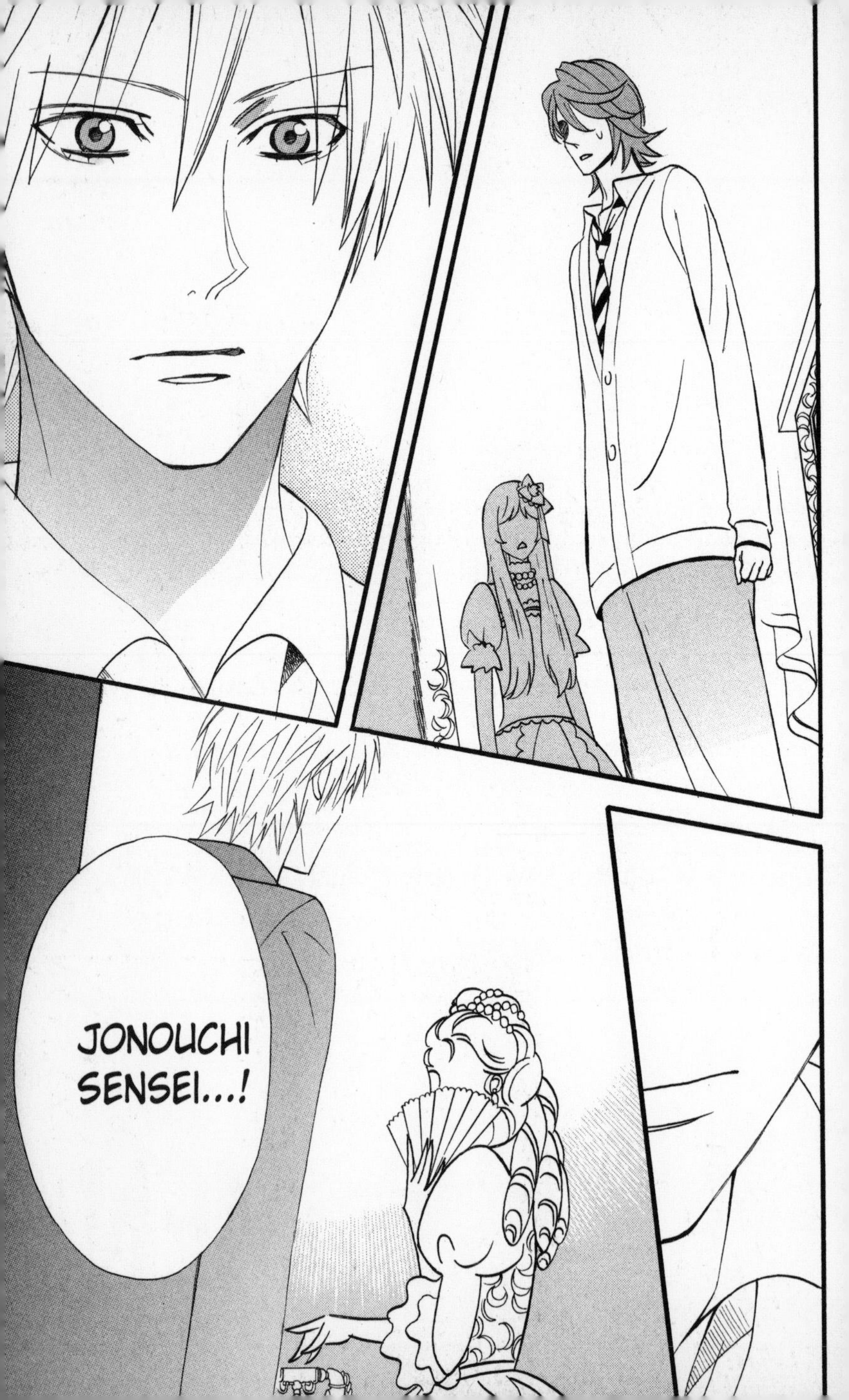
JONOUCHI SENSEI...!

OTOMEN

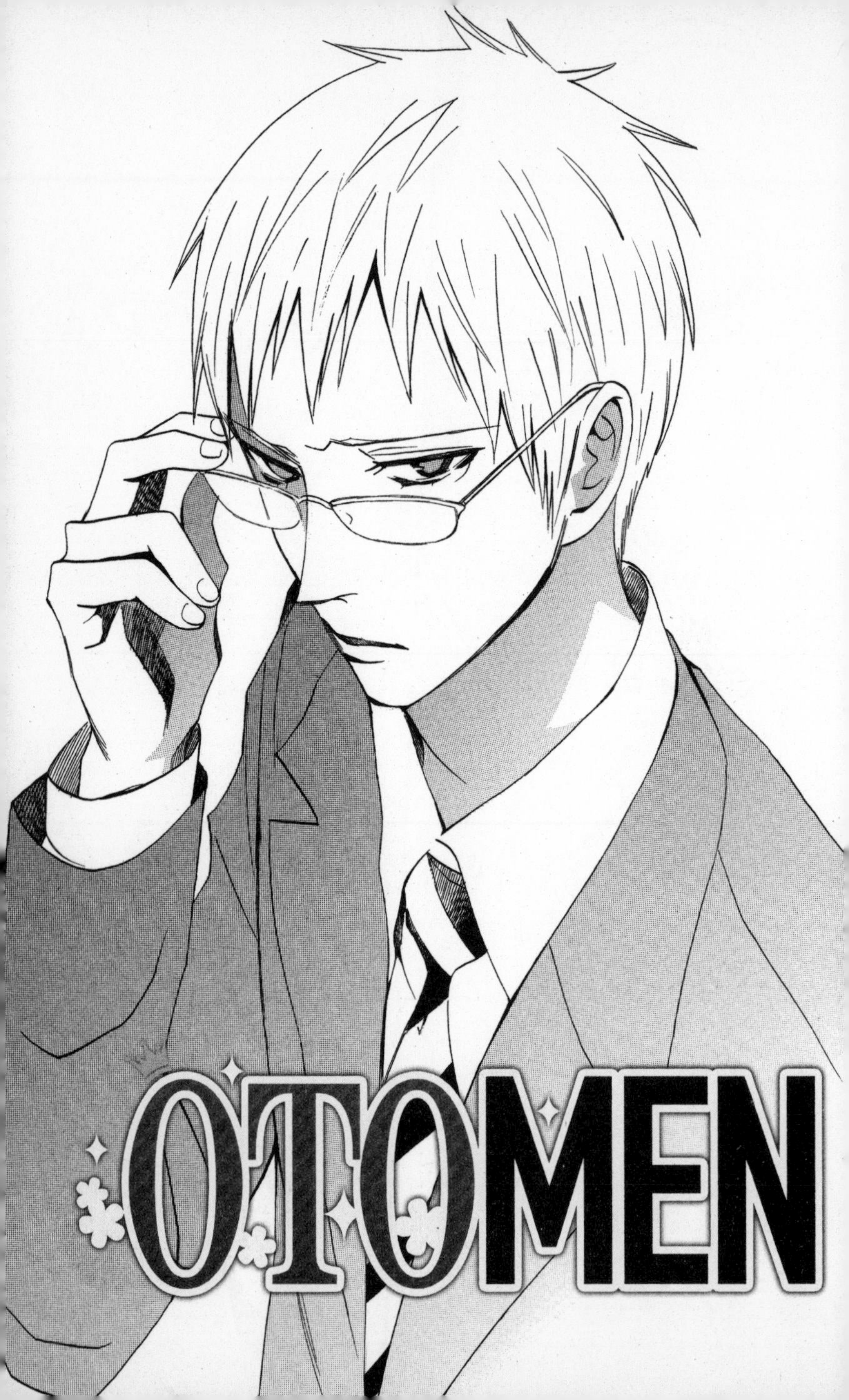
OTOMEN

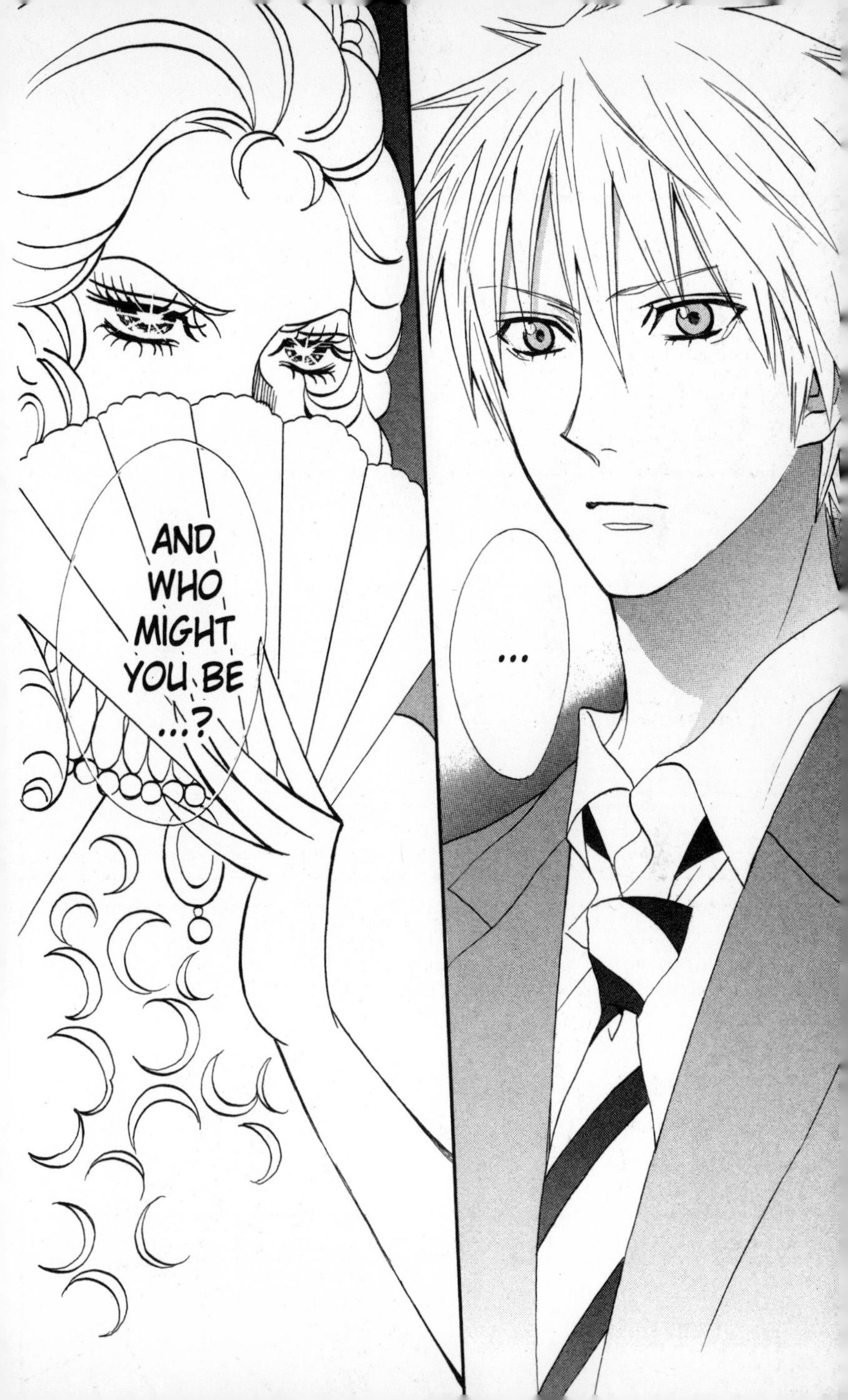
...
AND WHO MIGHT YOU BE ...?

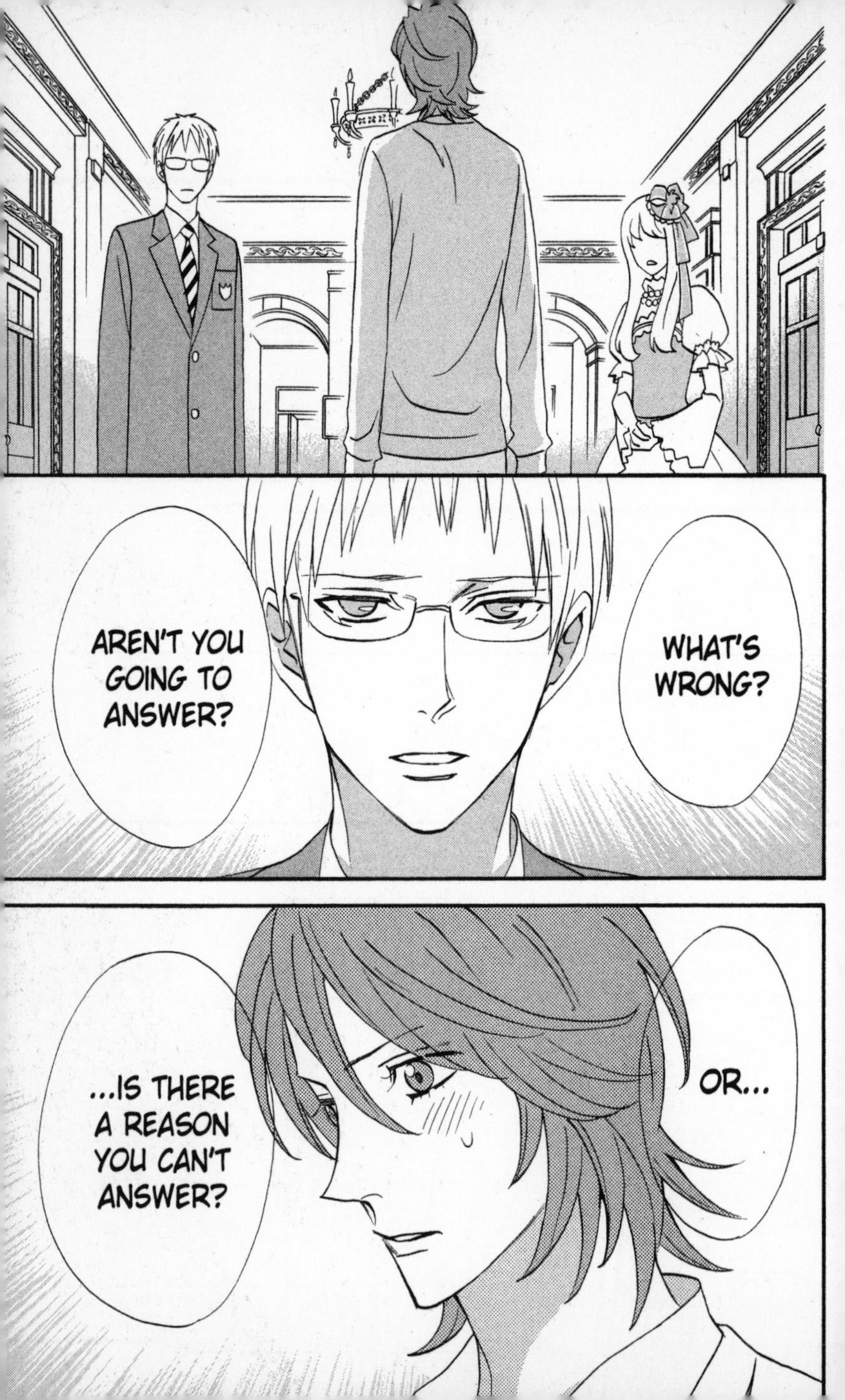
WHAT'S WRONG?
AREN'T YOU GOING TO ANSWER?
OR...
...IS THERE A REASON YOU CAN'T ANSWER?

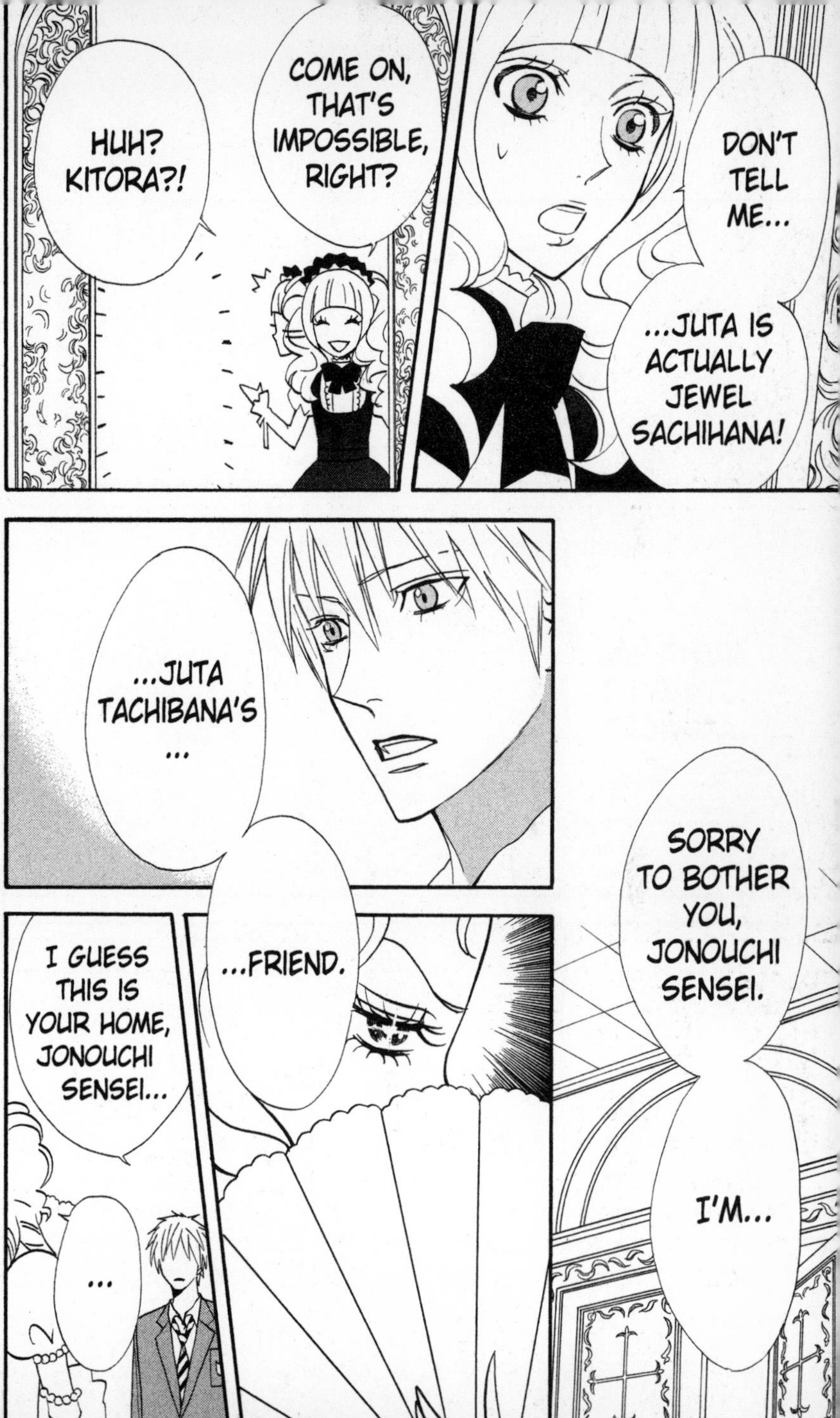
DON'T TELL ME...
...JUTA IS ACTUALLY JEWEL SACHIHANA!
COME ON, THAT'S IMPOSSIBLE, RIGHT?
HUH? KITORA?!
SORRY TO BOTHER YOU, JONOUCHI SENSEI.
I'M...
...JUTA TACHIBANA'S ...
...FRIEND.
I GUESS THIS IS YOUR HOME, JONOUCHI SENSEI...
...

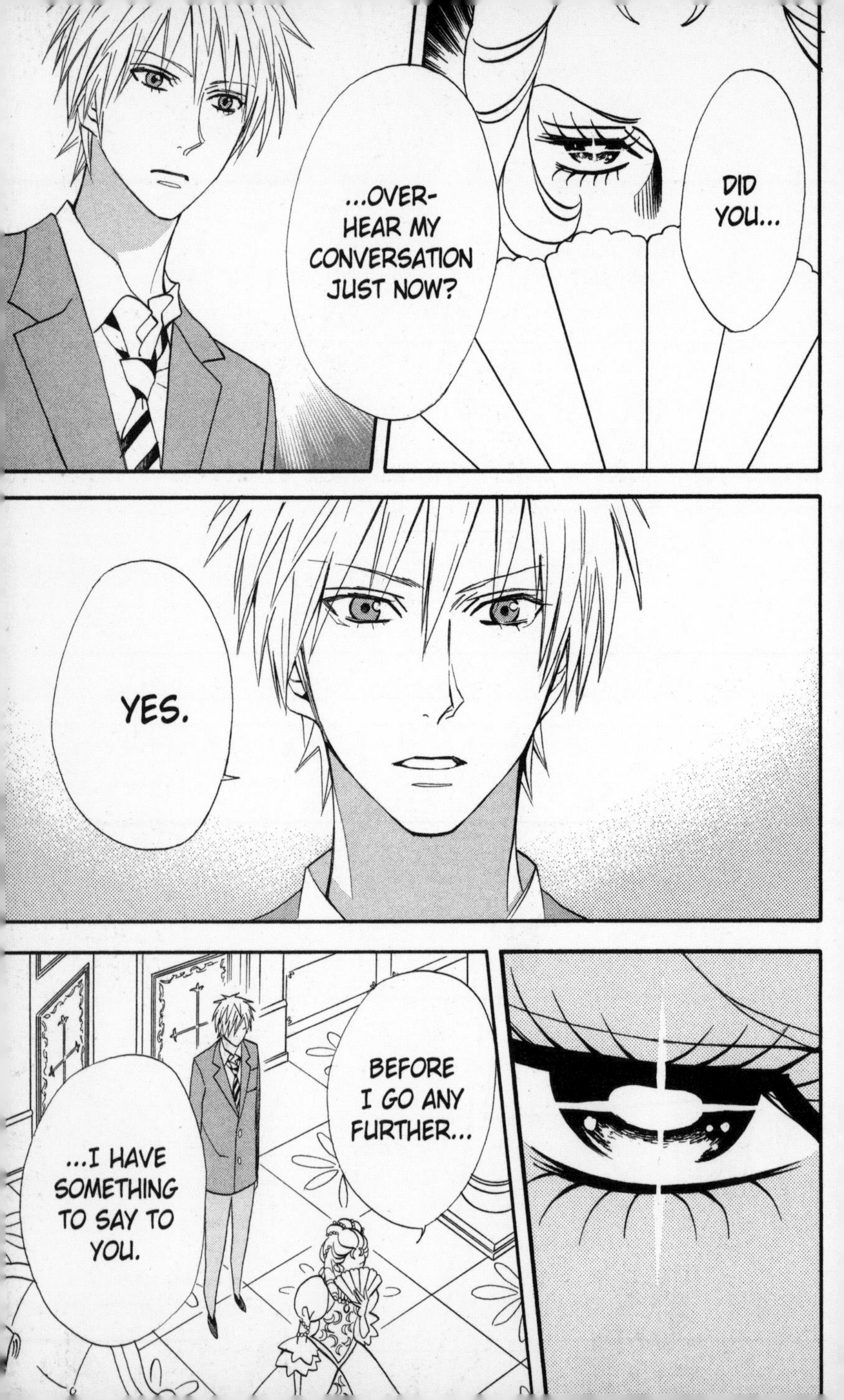
DID YOU...
...OVER-HEAR MY CONVERSATION JUST NOW?
YES.
BEFORE I GO ANY FURTHER...
...I HAVE SOMETHING TO SAY TO YOU.

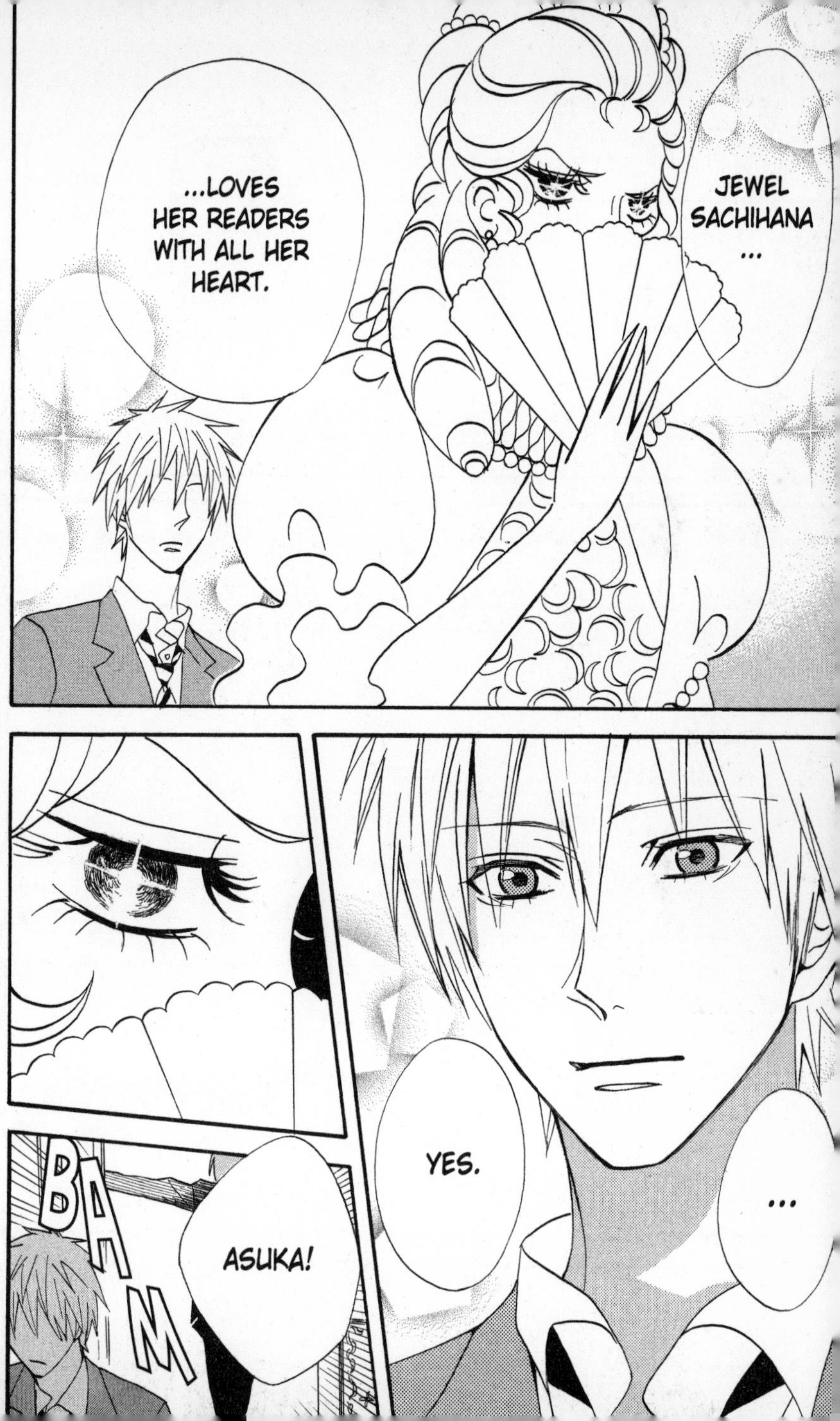
JEWEL SACHIHANA ...
...LOVES HER READERS WITH ALL HER HEART.
...
YES.
BAM
ASUKA!

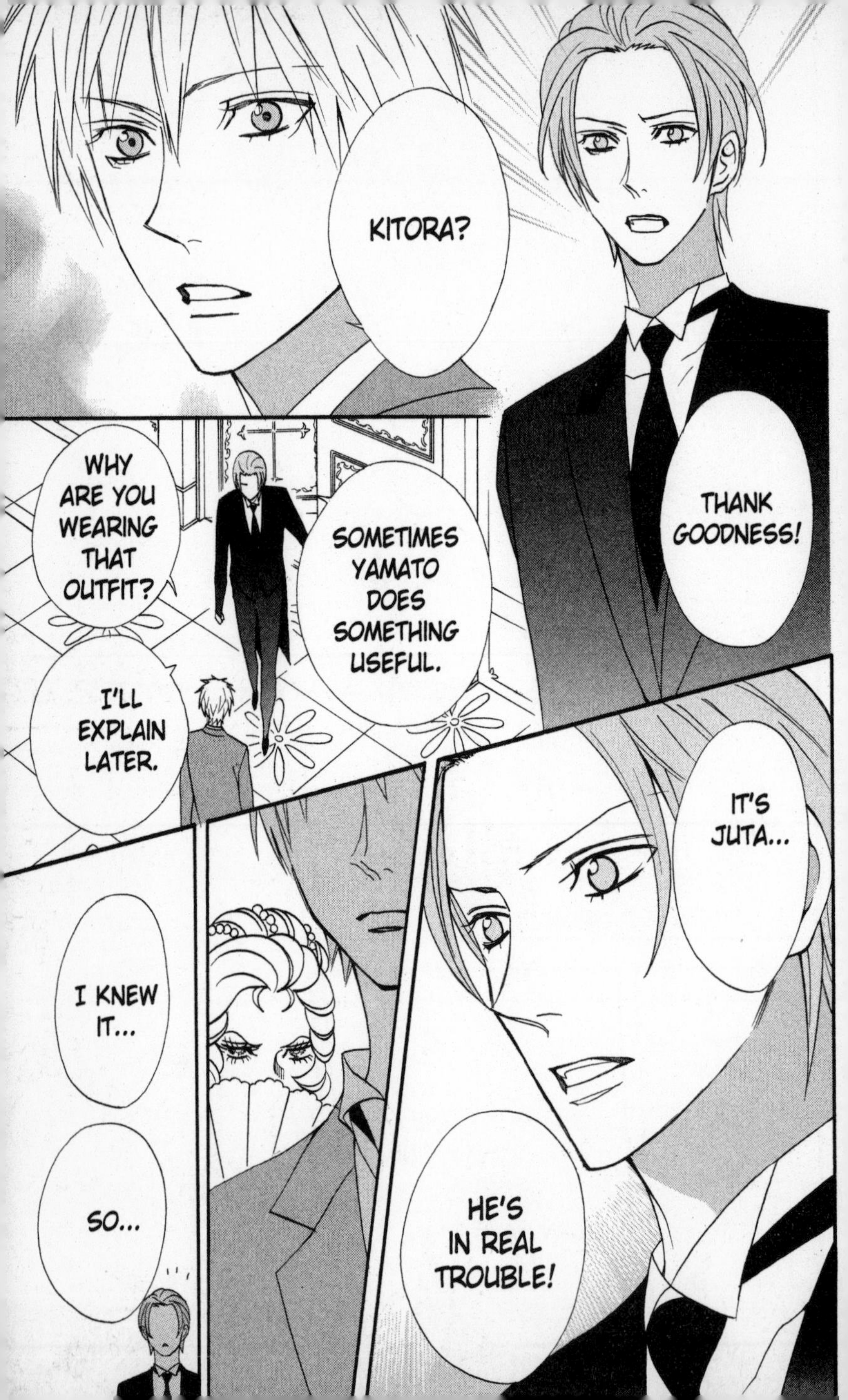
THANK GOODNESS!
KITORA?
SOMETIMES YAMATO DOES SOMETHING USEFUL.
WHY ARE YOU WEARING THAT OUTFIT?
I'LL EXPLAIN LATER.
IT'S JUTA...
HE'S IN REAL TROUBLE!
I KNEW IT...
SO...

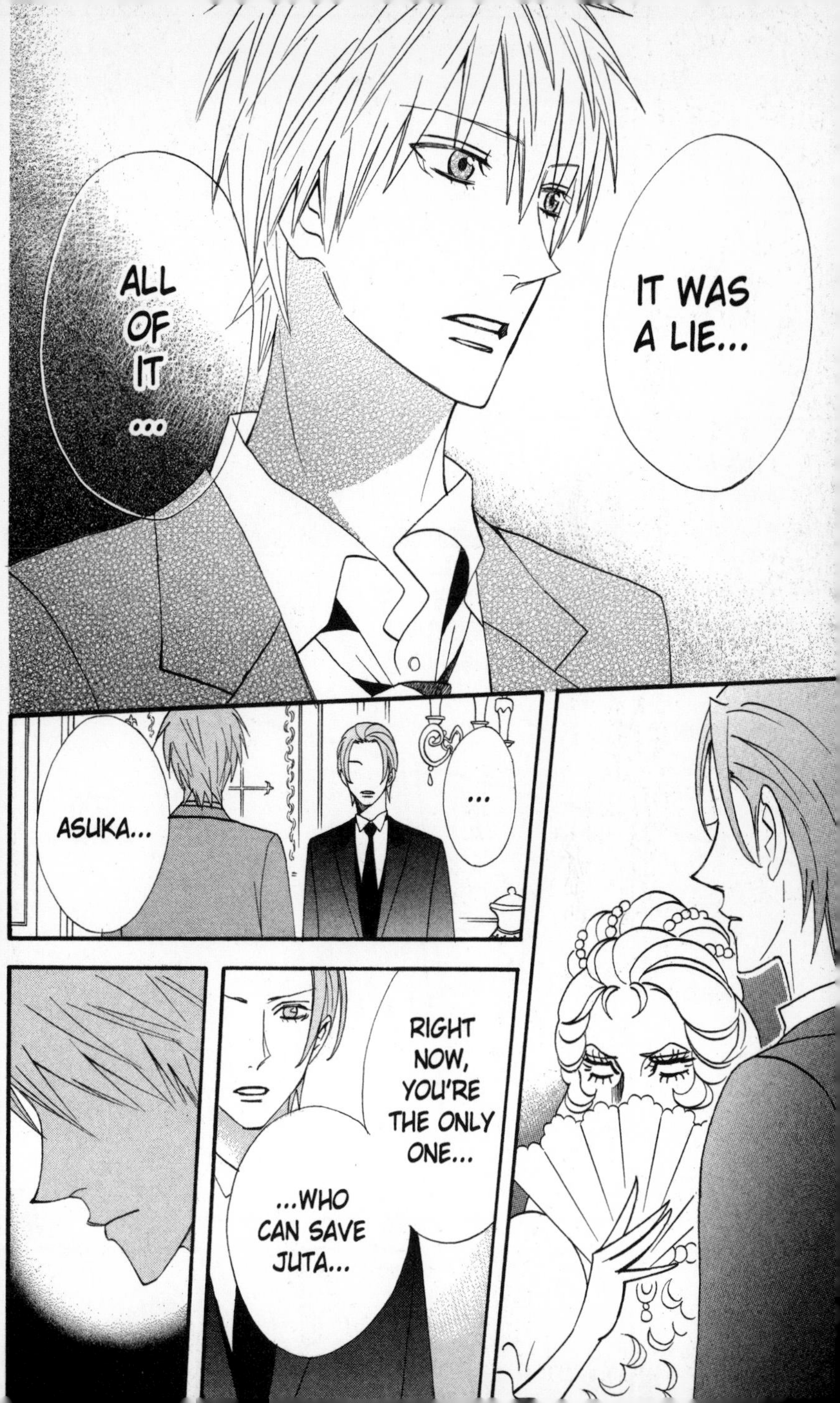
IT WAS A LIE...
ALL OF IT ...
...
ASUKA...
RIGHT NOW, YOU'RE THE ONLY ONE...
...WHO CAN SAVE JUTA...

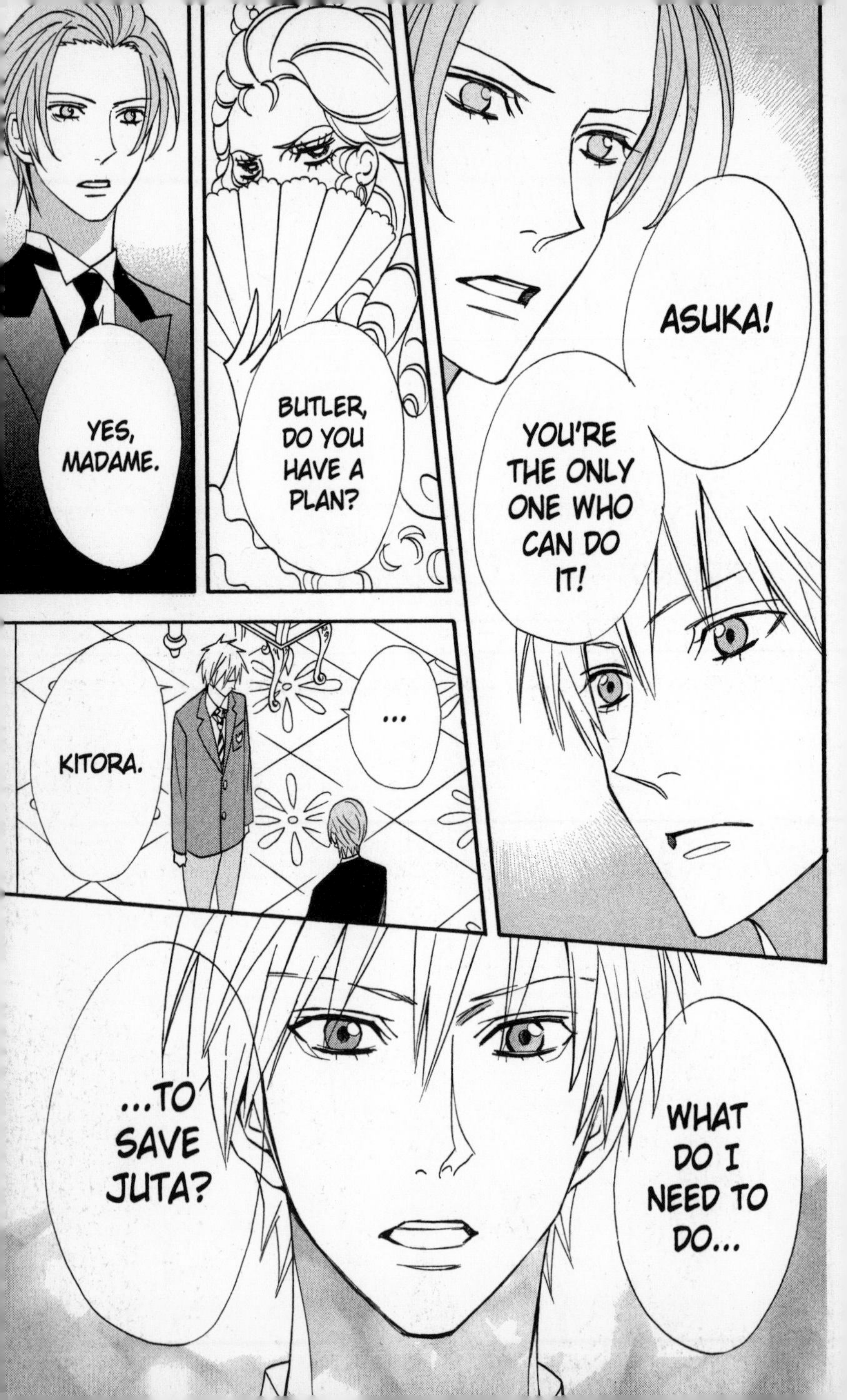
ASUKA!
YOU'RE THE ONLY ONE WHO CAN DO IT!
BUTLER, DO YOU HAVE A PLAN?
YES, MADAME.
...
KITORA.
WHAT DO I NEED TO DO...
...TO SAVE JUTA?

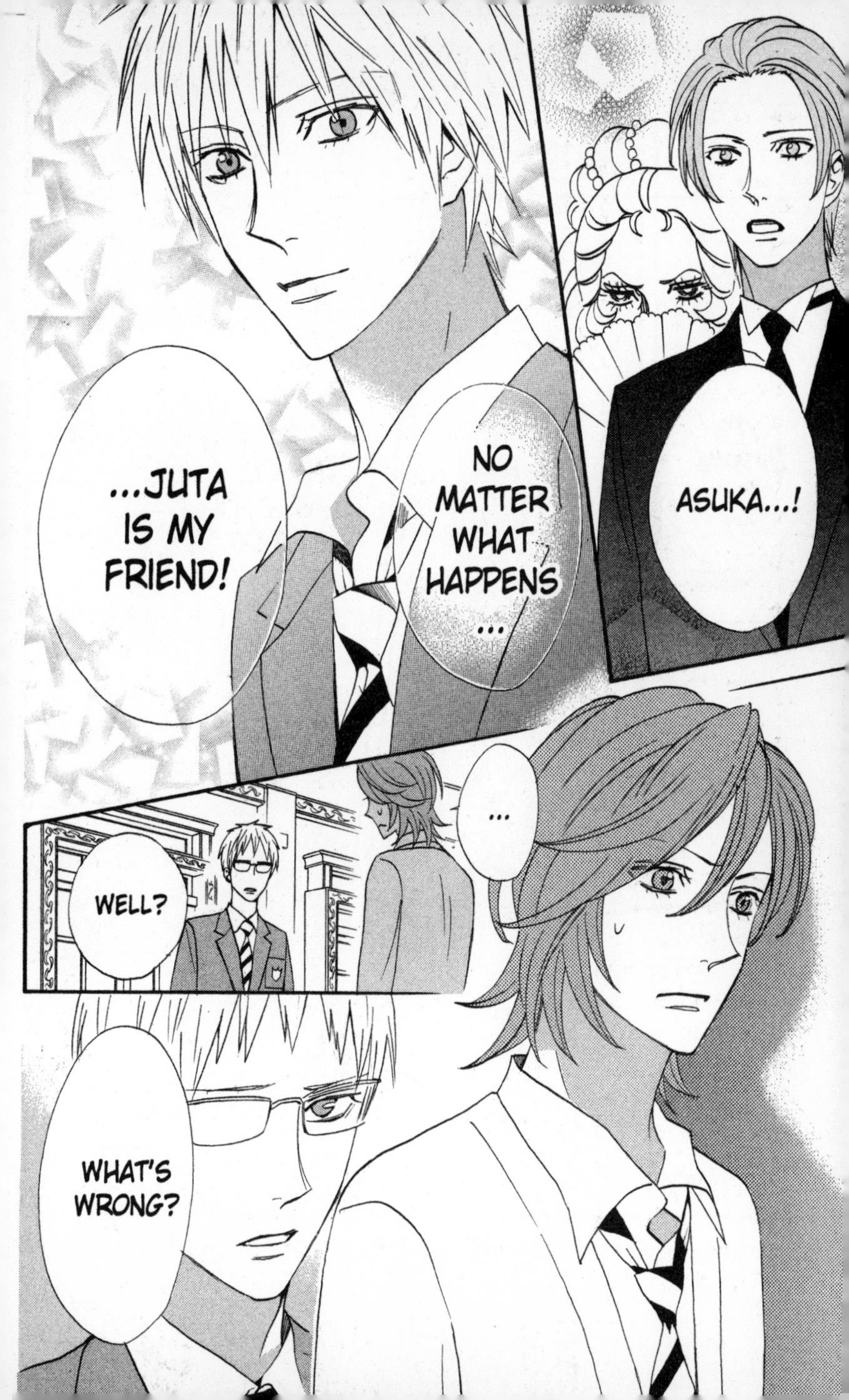
ASUKA...!
NO MATTER WHAT HAPPENS...
...JUTA IS MY FRIEND!
...
WELL?
WHAT'S WRONG?

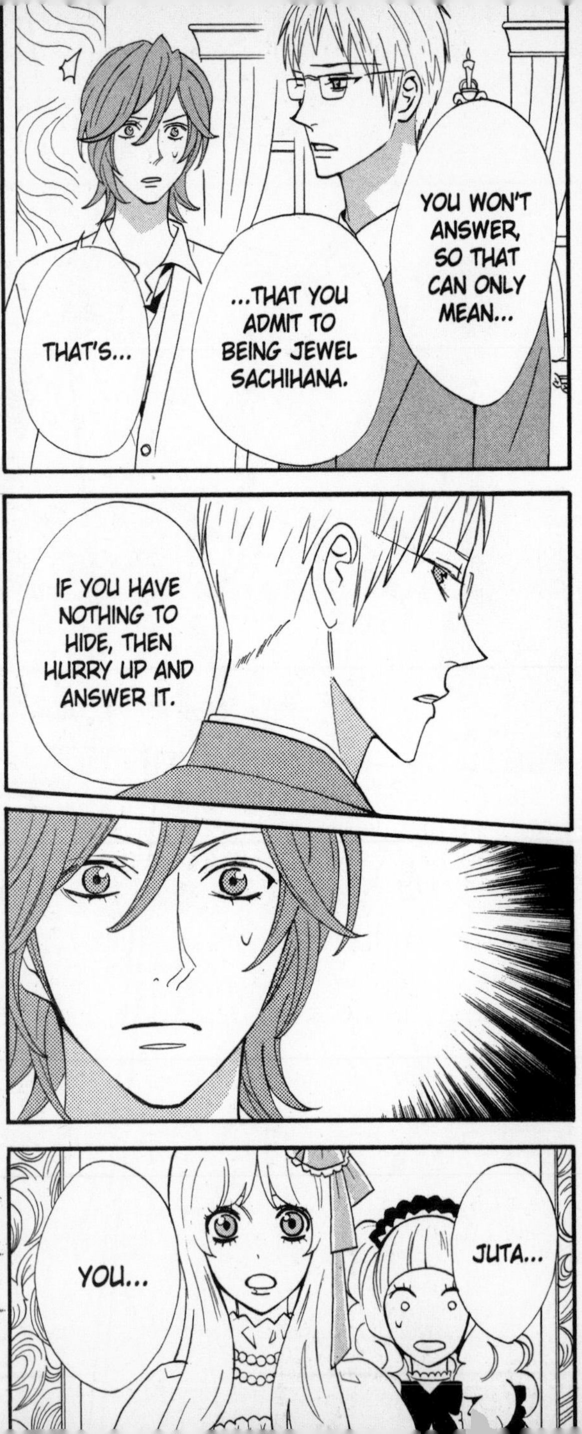
YOU WON'T ANSWER, SO THAT CAN ONLY MEAN...
...THAT YOU ADMIT TO BEING JEWEL SACHIHANA.
THAT'S...
IF YOU HAVE NOTHING TO HIDE, THEN HURRY UP AND ANSWER IT.
JUTA...
YOU...

Every time I draw a story, I feel apologetic about it. Be it manga or life, you're always learning something until the day you die.
The other day, I went to the shooting of the *Otomen* TV drama and was really impressed by the sight of all those pros gathered together to make *Otomen*.
It made me want to work hard on my manga.

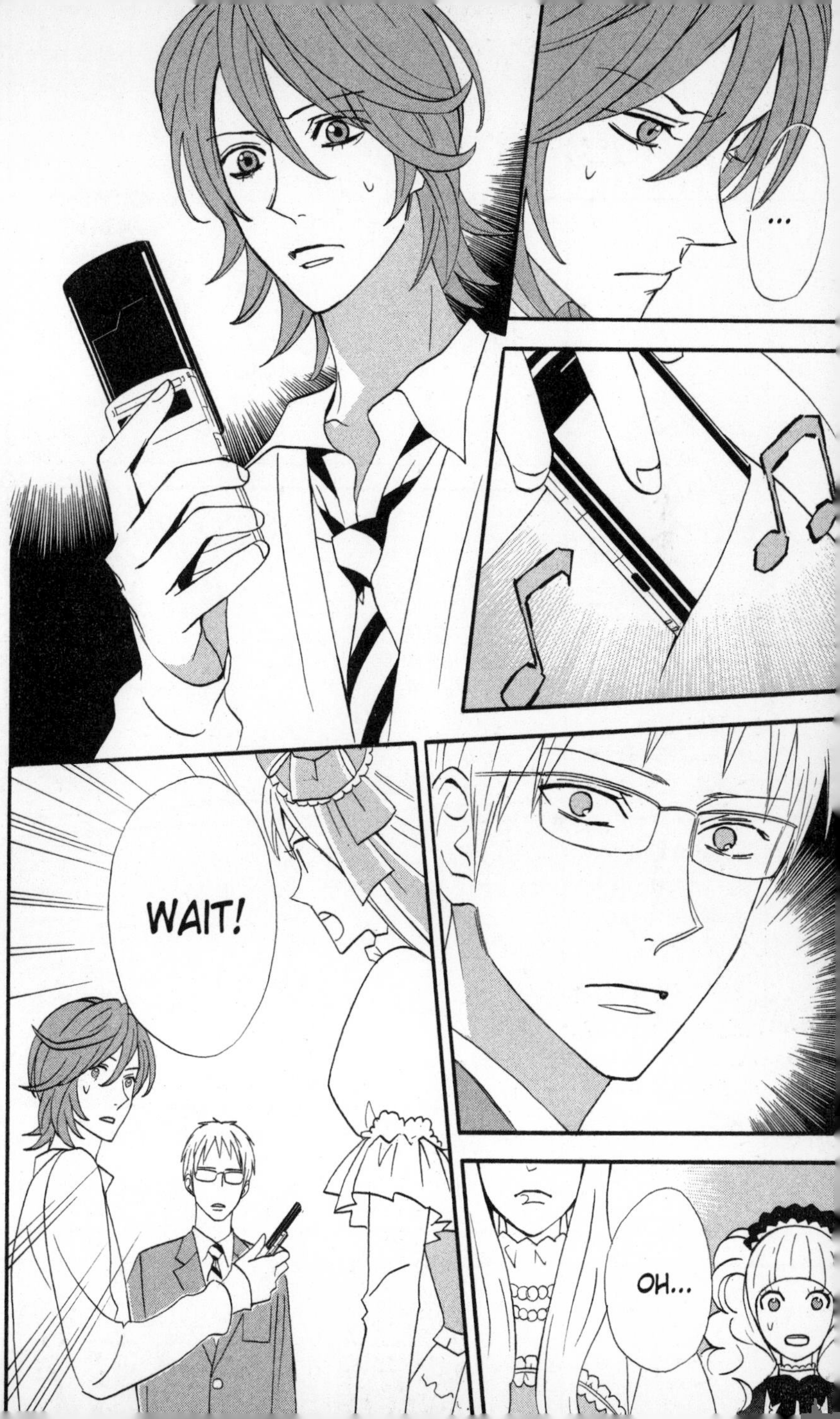
...
WAIT!
OH...

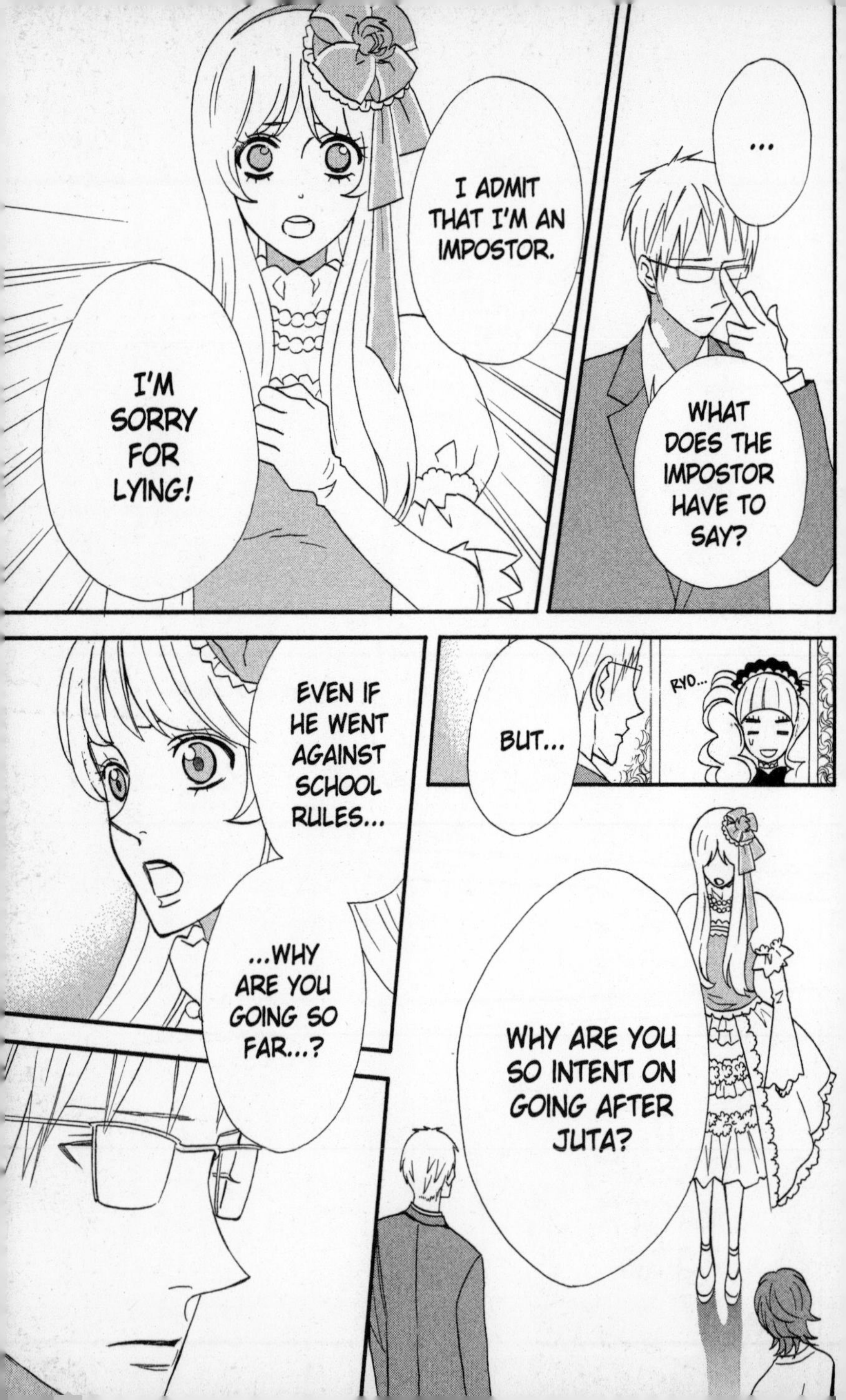
...
WHAT DOES THE IMPOSTOR HAVE TO SAY?
I ADMIT THAT I'M AN IMPOSTOR.
I'M SORRY FOR LYING!
RYO...
BUT...
EVEN IF HE WENT AGAINST SCHOOL RULES...
...WHY ARE YOU GOING SO FAR...?
WHY ARE YOU SO INTENT ON GOING AFTER JUTA?

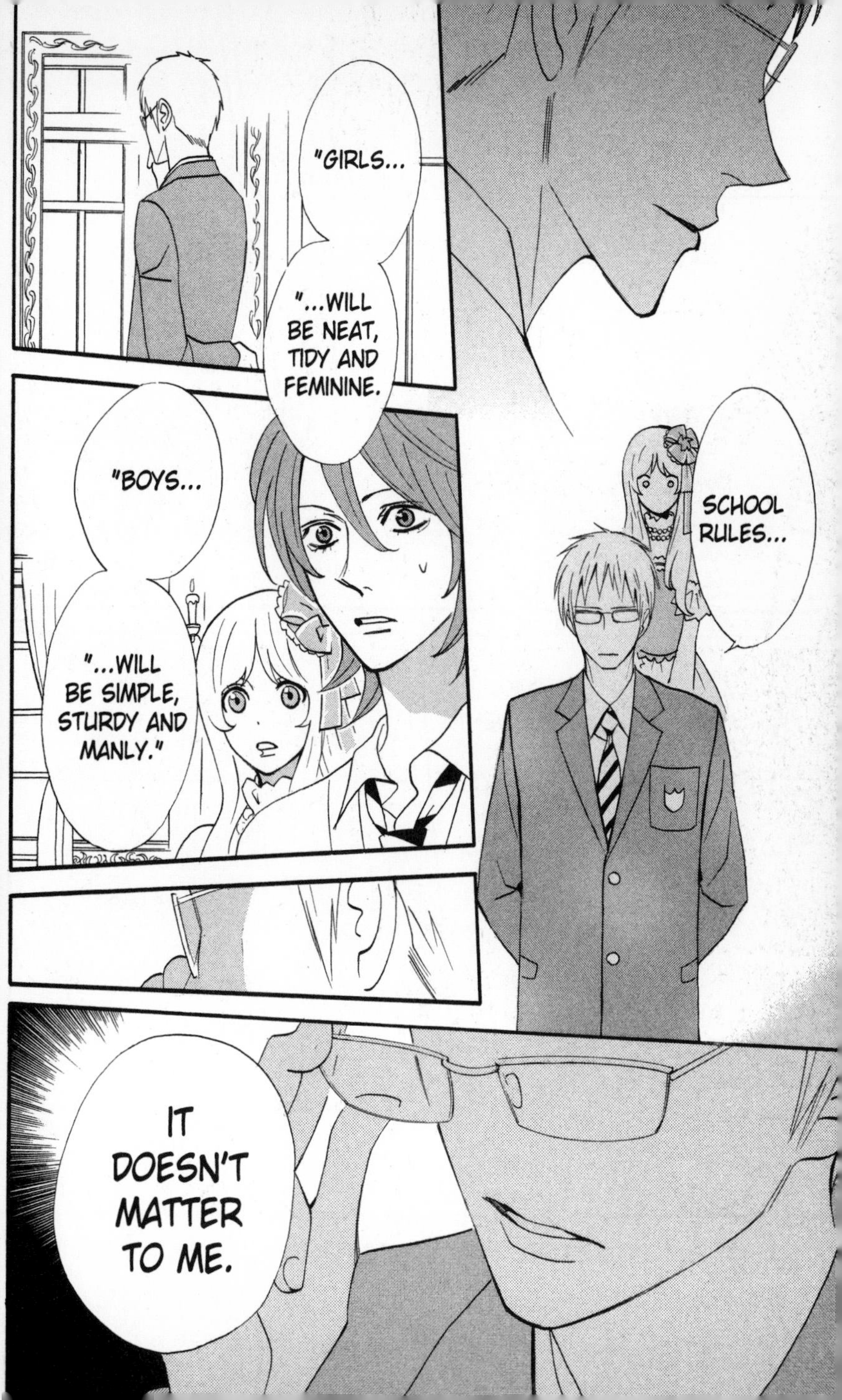
SCHOOL RULES...
"GIRLS...
"...WILL BE NEAT, TIDY AND FEMININE.
"BOYS...
"...WILL BE SIMPLE, STURDY AND MANLY."
IT DOESN'T MATTER TO ME.

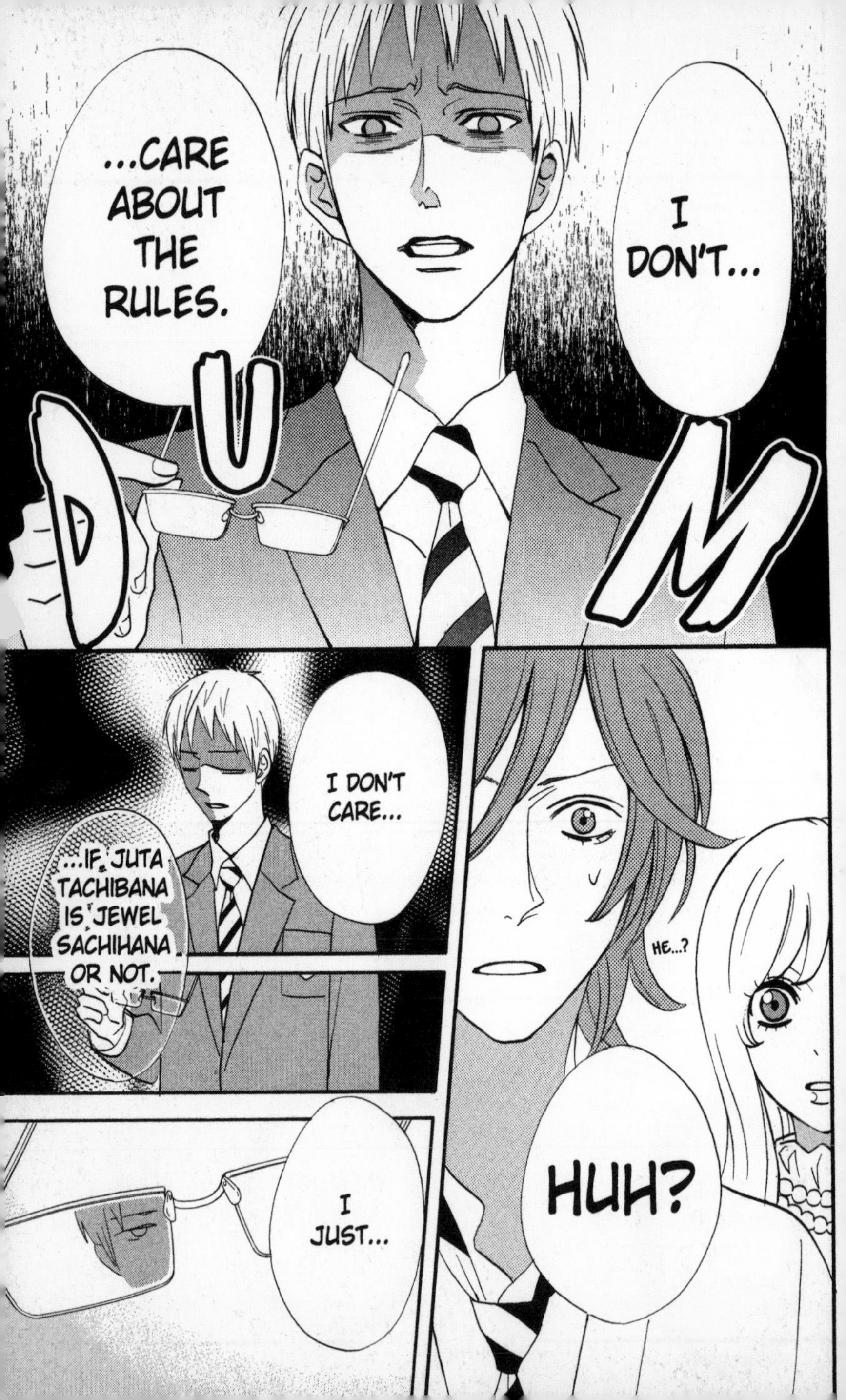

I DON'T...
...CARE ABOUT THE RULES.
DUM
HE...?
HUH?
I DON'T CARE...
...IF JUTA TACHIBANA IS JEWEL SACHIHANA OR NOT.
I JUST...

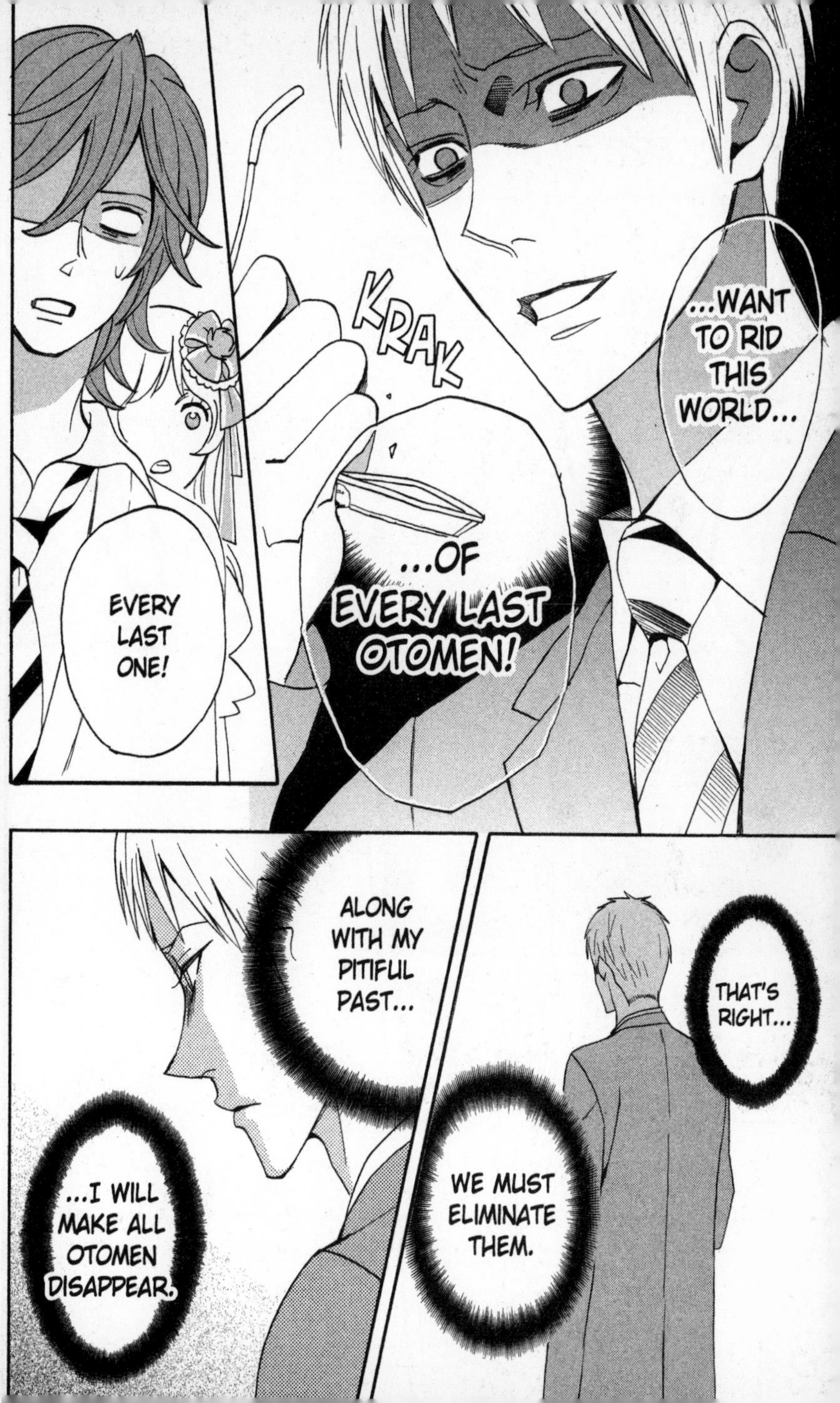
...WANT TO RID THIS WORLD...
KRAK
...OF EVERY LAST OTOMEN!
EVERY LAST ONE!
THAT'S RIGHT...
WE MUST ELIMINATE THEM.
ALONG WITH MY PITIFUL PAST...
...I WILL MAKE ALL OTOMEN DISAPPEAR.

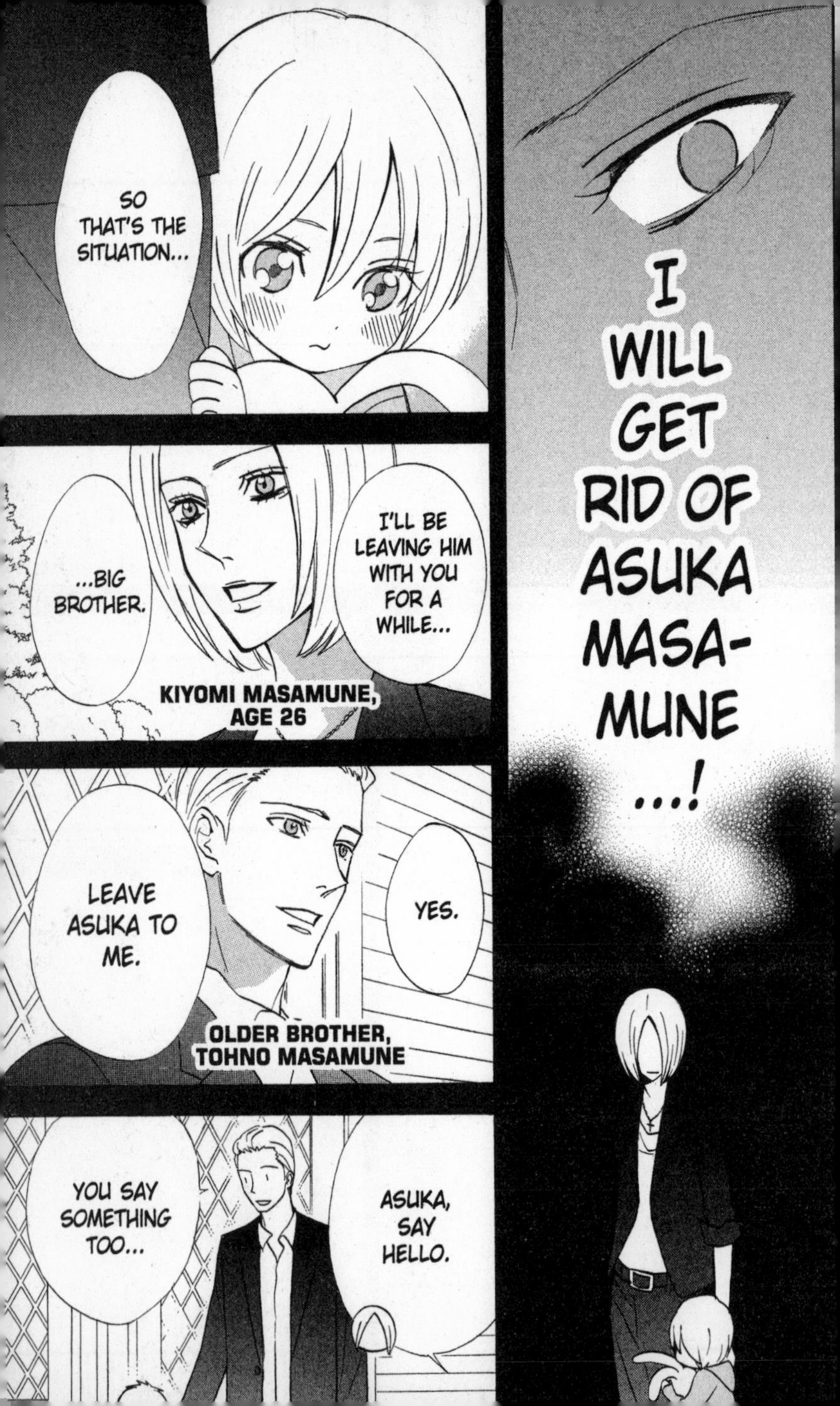
I WILL GET RID OF ASUKA MASAMUNE ...!
SO THAT'S THE SITUATION...
I'LL BE LEAVING HIM WITH YOU FOR A WHILE...
...BIG BROTHER.
KIYOMI MASAMUNE, AGE 26
YES.
LEAVE ASUKA TO ME.
OLDER BROTHER, TOHNO MASAMUNE
ASUKA, SAY HELLO.
YOU SAY SOMETHING TOO...

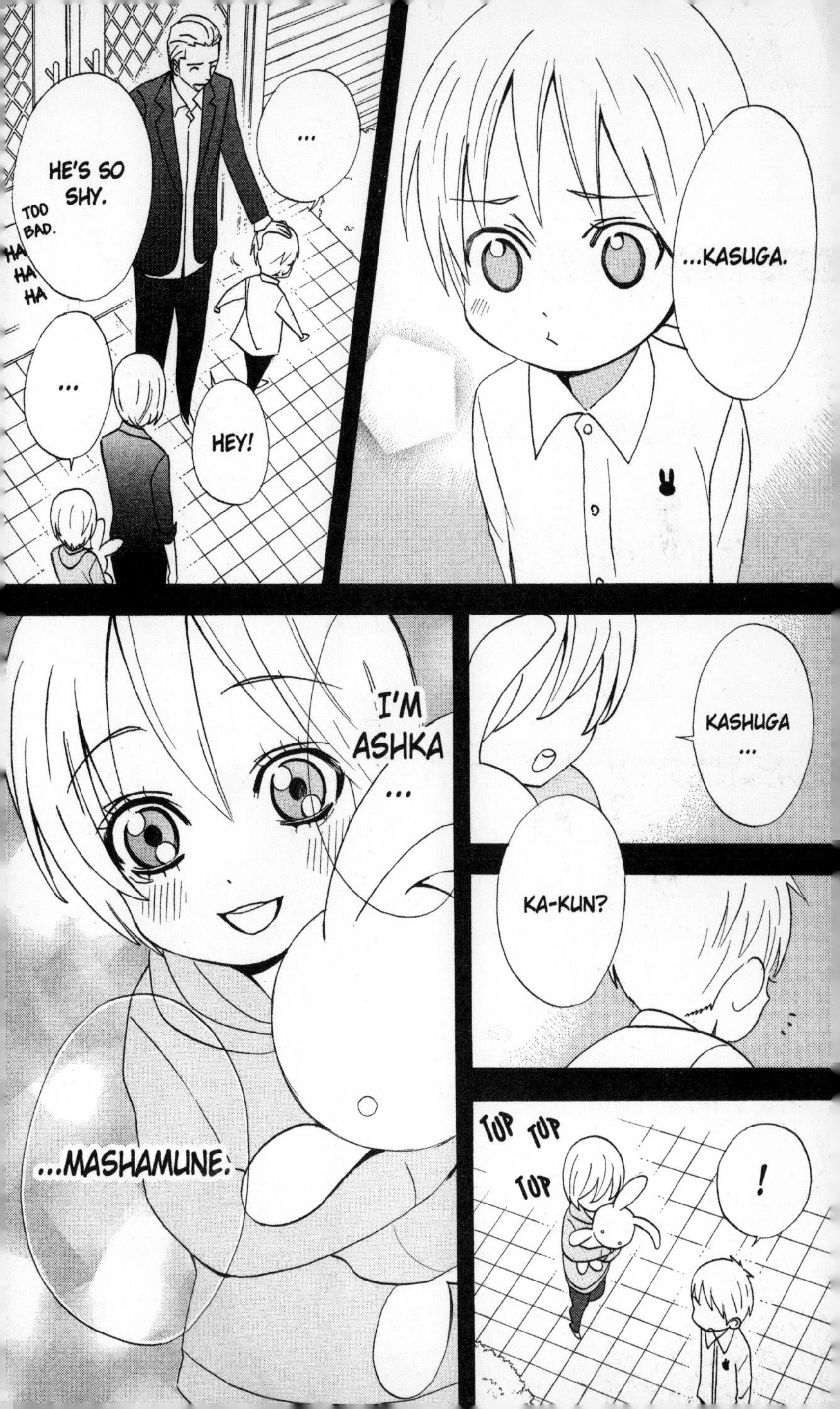
...KASUGA.
...
HE'S SO SHY.
TOO BAD.
HA HA HA
HEY!
...
KASHUGA ...
KA-KUN?
!
TUP TUP
TUP
I'M ASHKA ...
...MASHAMUNE.

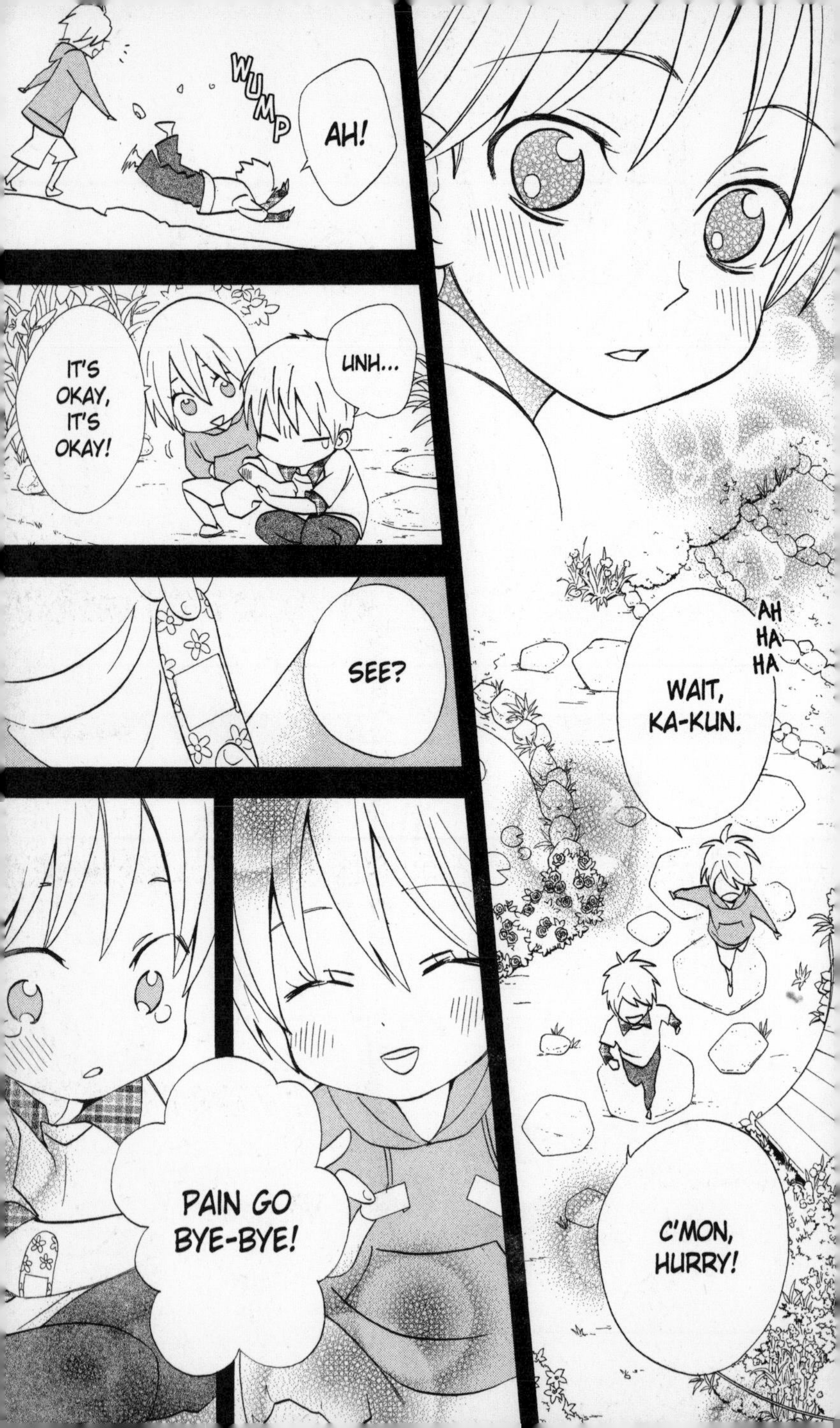
AH HA HA
WAIT, KA-KUN.
C'MON, HURRY!
WUMP
AH!
UNH...
IT'S OKAY, IT'S OKAY!
SEE?
PAIN GO BYE-BYE!

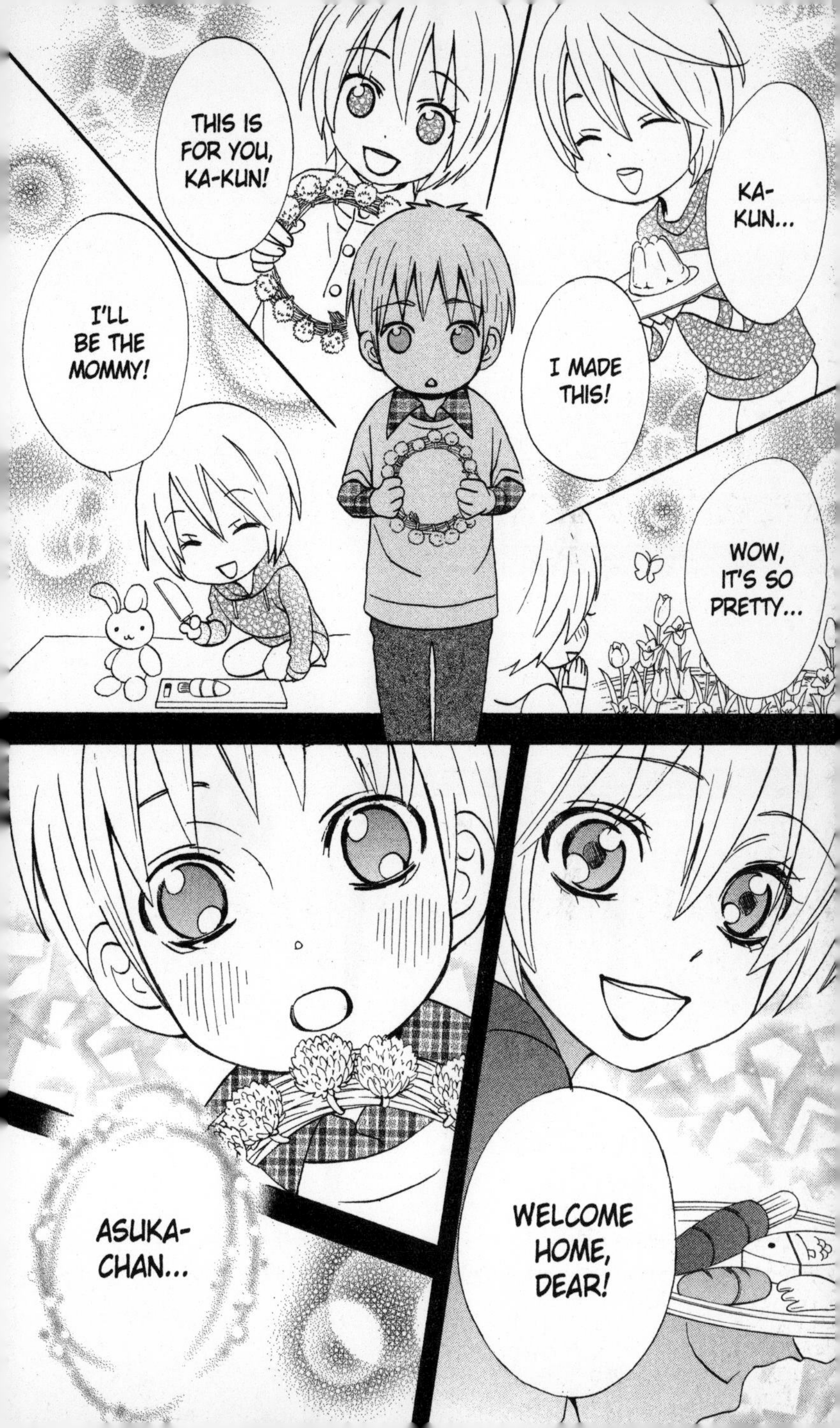
KA-KUN...
I MADE THIS!
THIS IS FOR YOU, KA-KUN!
WOW, IT'S SO PRETTY...
I'LL BE THE MOMMY!
WELCOME HOME, DEAR!
ASUKA-CHAN...

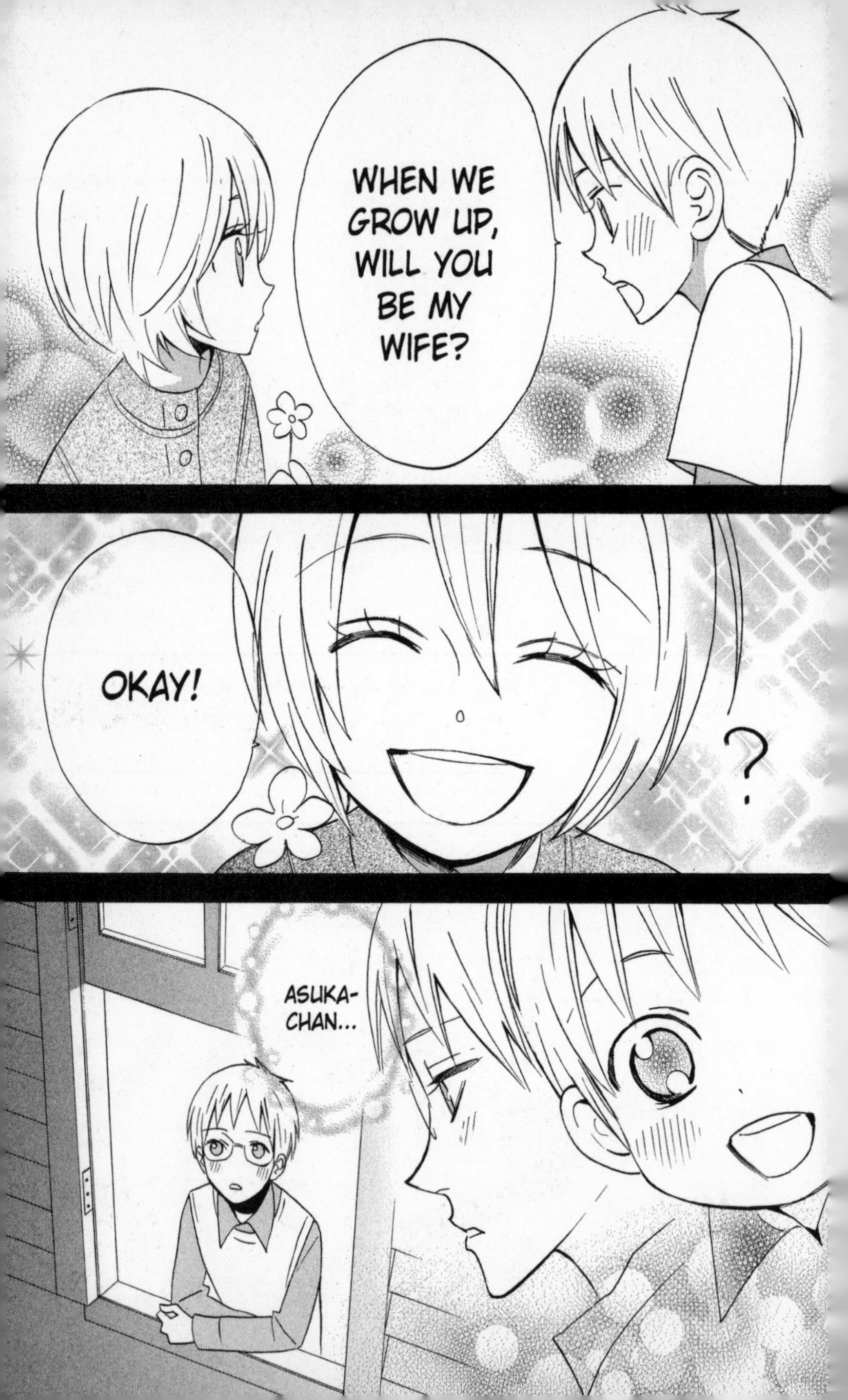
WHEN WE GROW UP, WILL YOU BE MY WIFE?
OKAY!
?
ASUKA-CHAN...

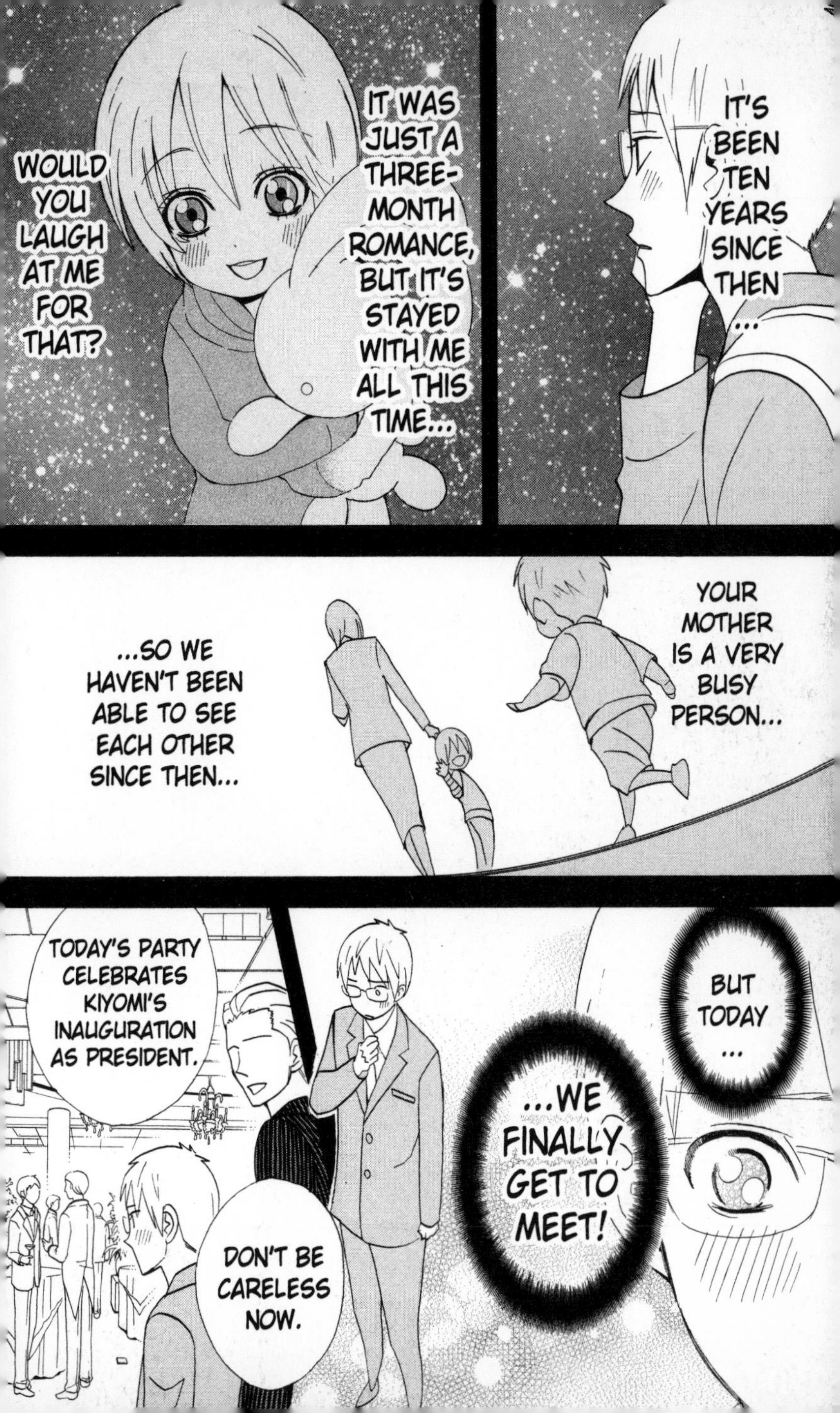
IT'S BEEN TEN YEARS SINCE THEN...
IT WAS JUST A THREE-MONTH ROMANCE, BUT IT'S STAYED WITH ME ALL THIS TIME...
WOULD YOU LAUGH AT ME FOR THAT?
YOUR MOTHER IS A VERY BUSY PERSON...
...SO WE HAVEN'T BEEN ABLE TO SEE EACH OTHER SINCE THEN...
BUT TODAY...
...WE FINALLY GET TO MEET!
TODAY'S PARTY CELEBRATES KIYOMI'S INAUGURATION AS PRESIDENT.
DON'T BE CARELESS NOW.

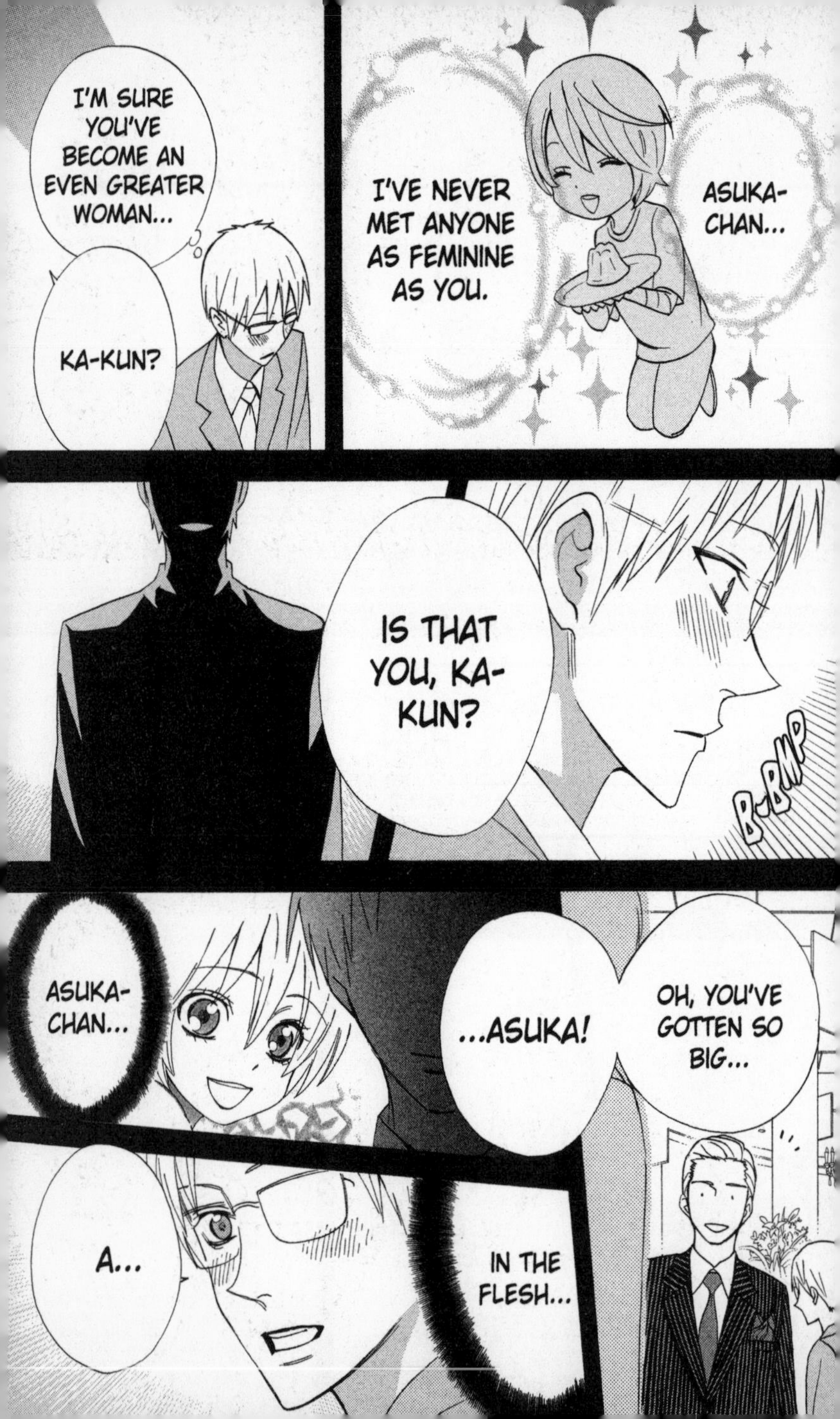
ASUKA-CHAN...
I'VE NEVER MET ANYONE AS FEMININE AS YOU.
I'M SURE YOU'VE BECOME AN EVEN GREATER WOMAN...
KA-KUN?
IS THAT YOU, KA-KUN?
B-BMP
OH, YOU'VE GOTTEN SO BIG...
...ASUKA!
ASUKA-CHAN...
IN THE FLESH...
A...

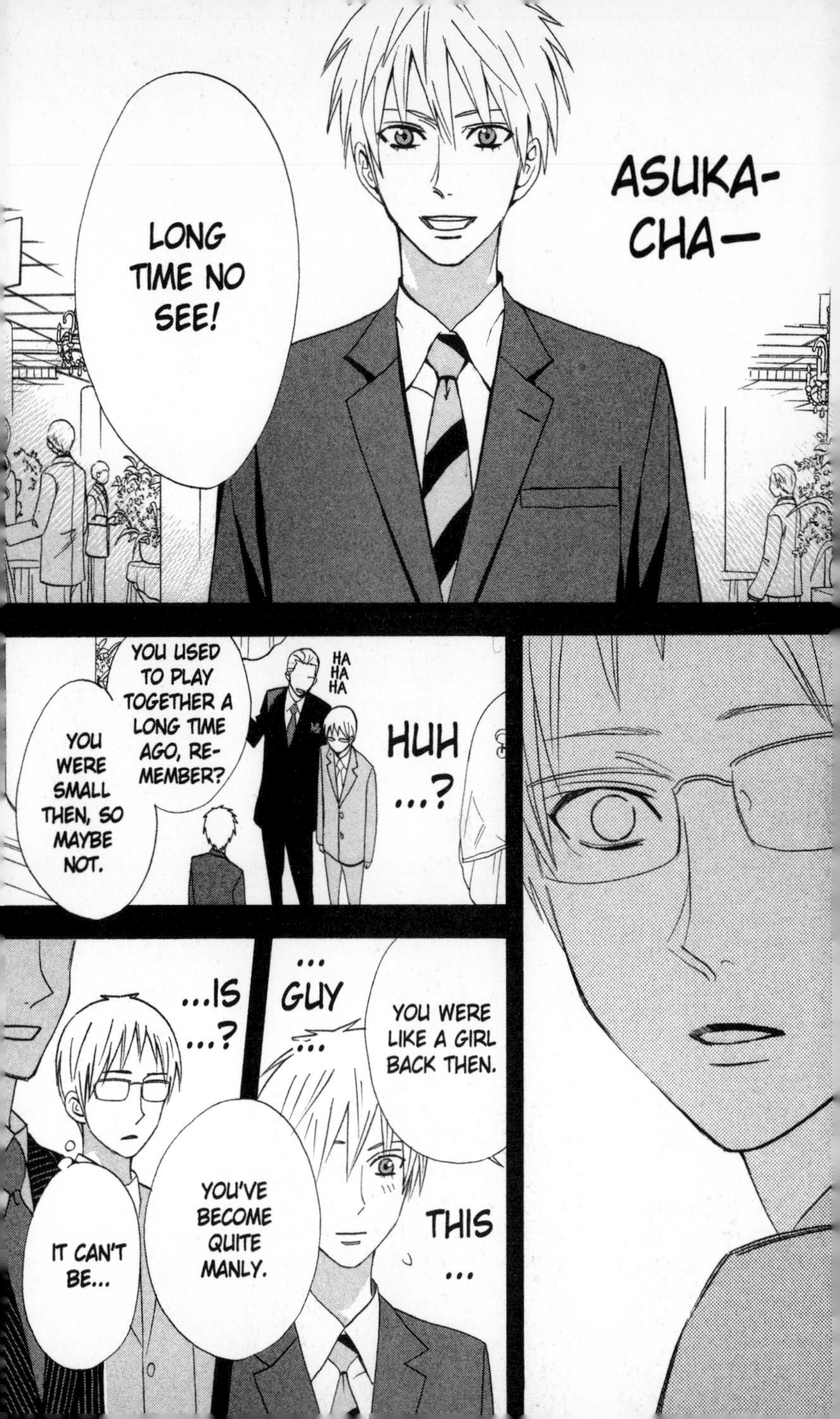

ASUKA-CHA—
LONG TIME NO SEE!
HUH ...?
HA HA HA
YOU USED TO PLAY TOGETHER A LONG TIME AGO, RE-MEMBER?
YOU WERE SMALL THEN, SO MAYBE NOT.
YOU WERE LIKE A GIRL BACK THEN.
... GUY ...
THIS ...
YOU'VE BECOME QUITE MANLY.
...IS ...?
IT CAN'T BE...

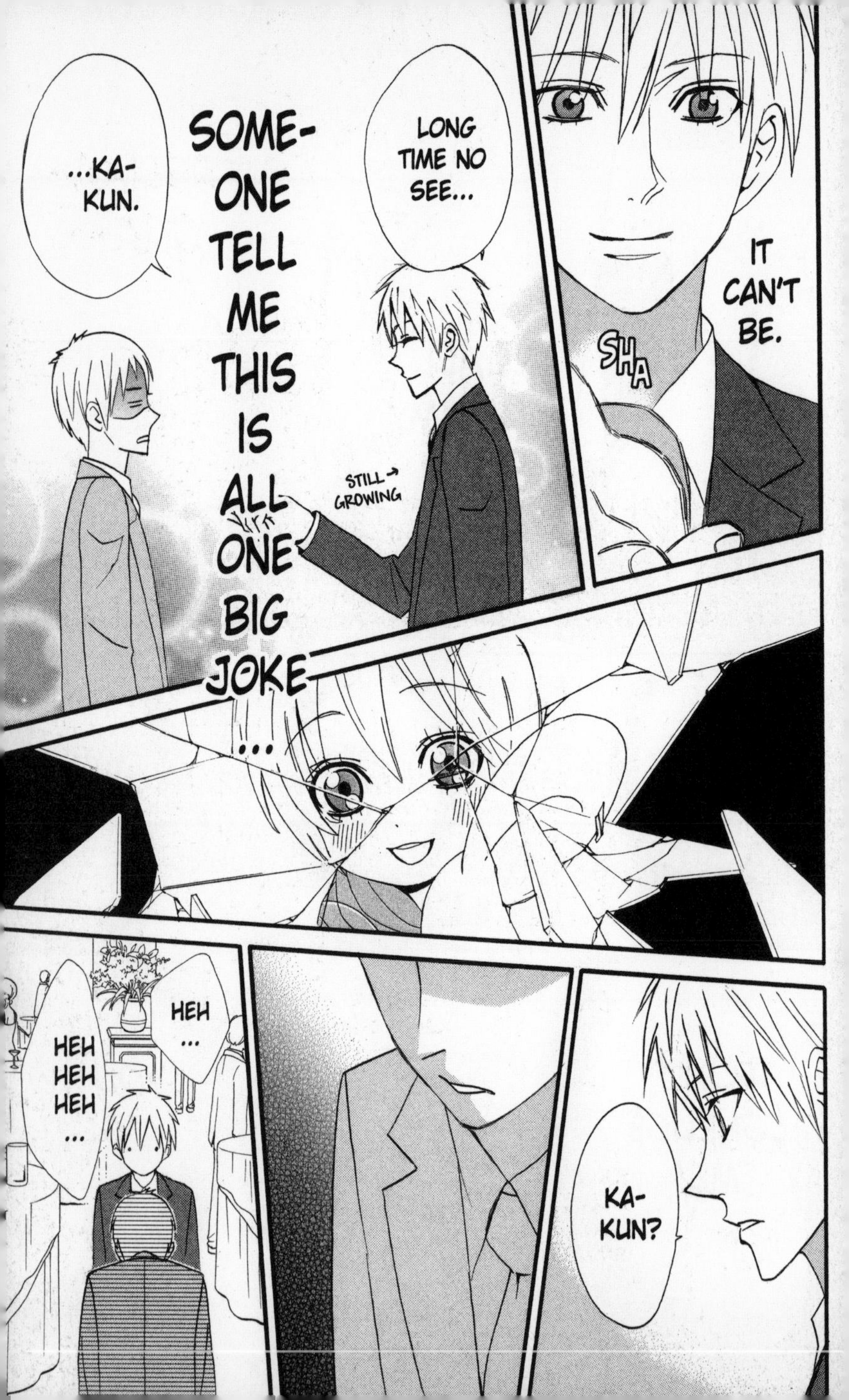
IT CAN'T BE.
SHA
LONG TIME NO SEE...
SOME-ONE TELL ME THIS IS ALL ONE BIG JOKE...
STILL→ GROWING
...KA-KUN.
KA-KUN?
HEH...
HEH HEH HEH...

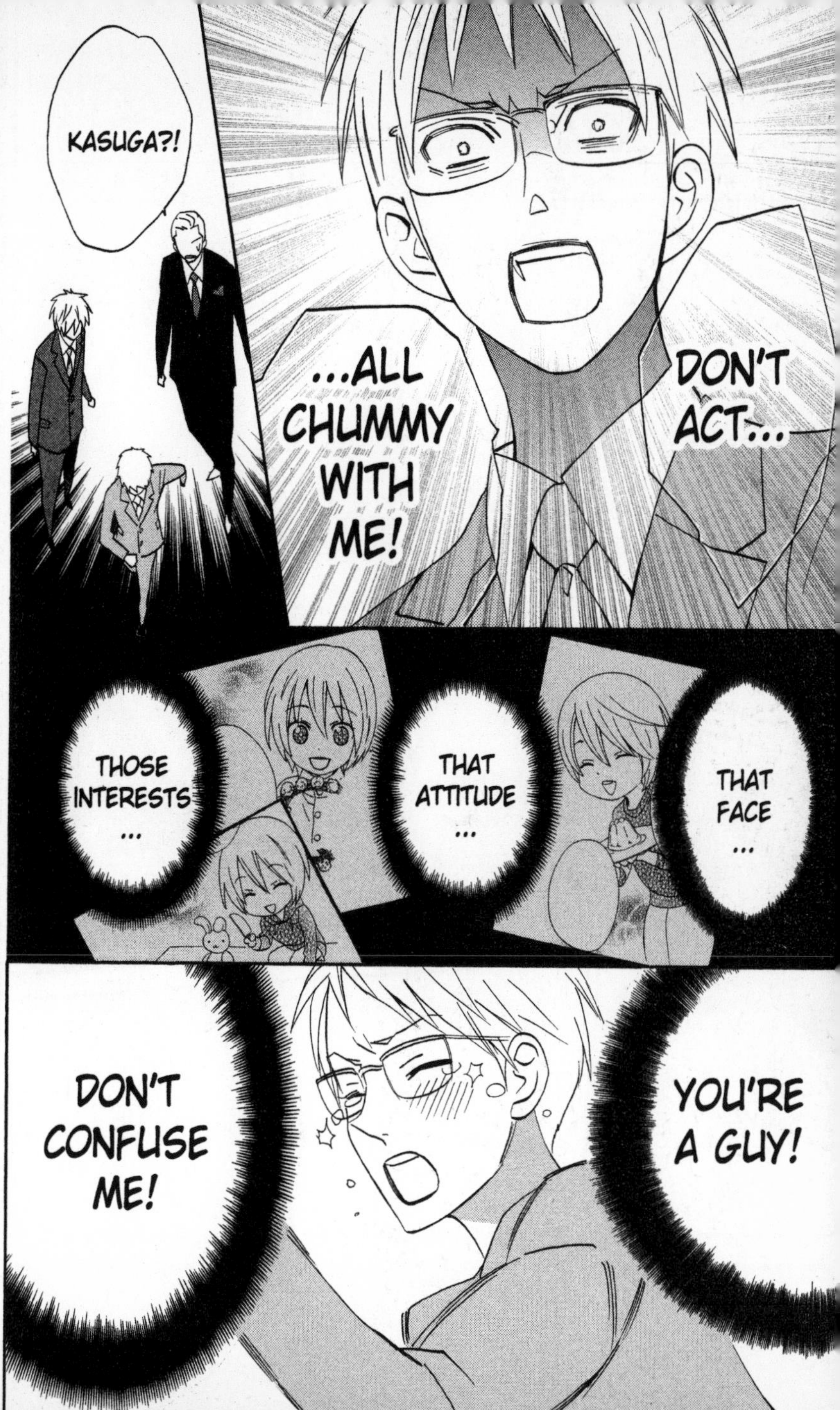
DON'T ACT...
...ALL CHUMMY WITH ME!
KASUGA?!
THAT FACE ...
THAT ATTITUDE ...
THOSE INTERESTS ...
YOU'RE A GUY!
DON'T CONFUSE ME!

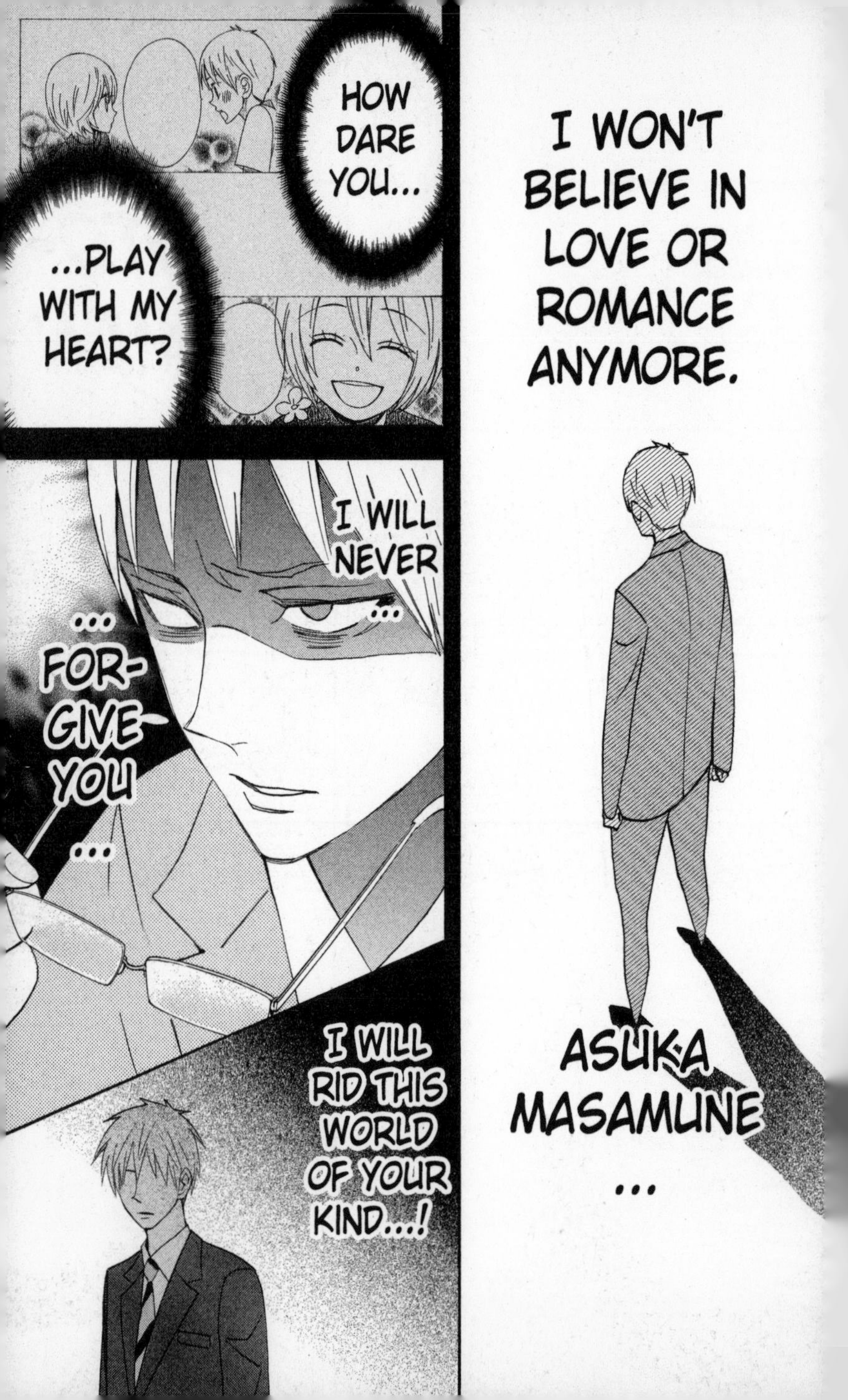
HOW DARE YOU...
...PLAY WITH MY HEART?
I WILL NEVER...
...FOR-GIVE YOU...
I WILL RID THIS WORLD OF YOUR KIND...!
I WON'T BELIEVE IN LOVE OR ROMANCE ANYMORE.
ASUKA MASAMUNE...

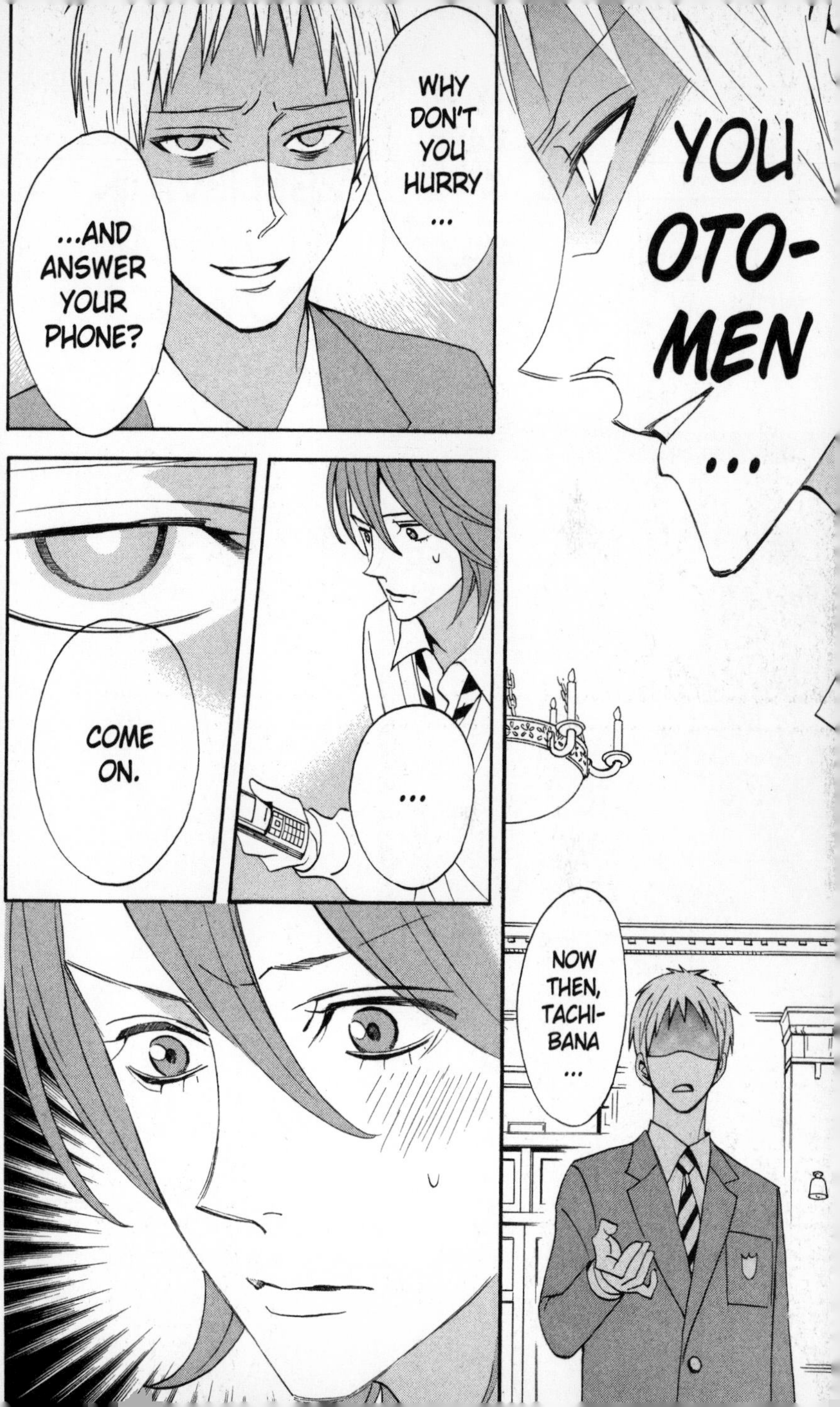
YOU OTO-MEN ...
WHY DON'T YOU HURRY ...
...AND ANSWER YOUR PHONE?
...
COME ON.
NOW THEN, TACHI-BANA ...

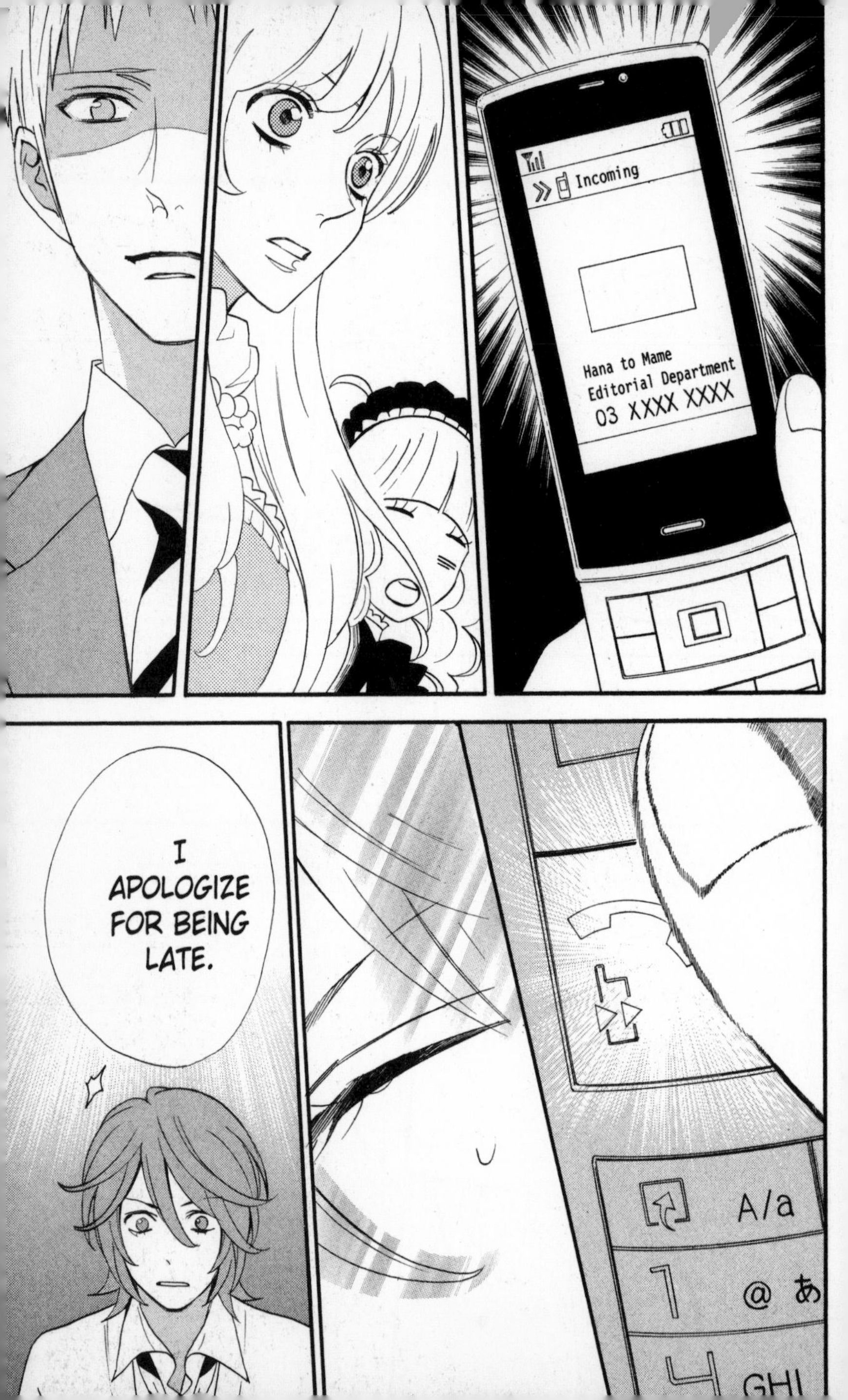
Incoming
Hana to Mame
Editorial Department
03 XXXX XXXX
A/a
1 @ あ
4 GHI
I APOLOGIZE FOR BEING LATE.

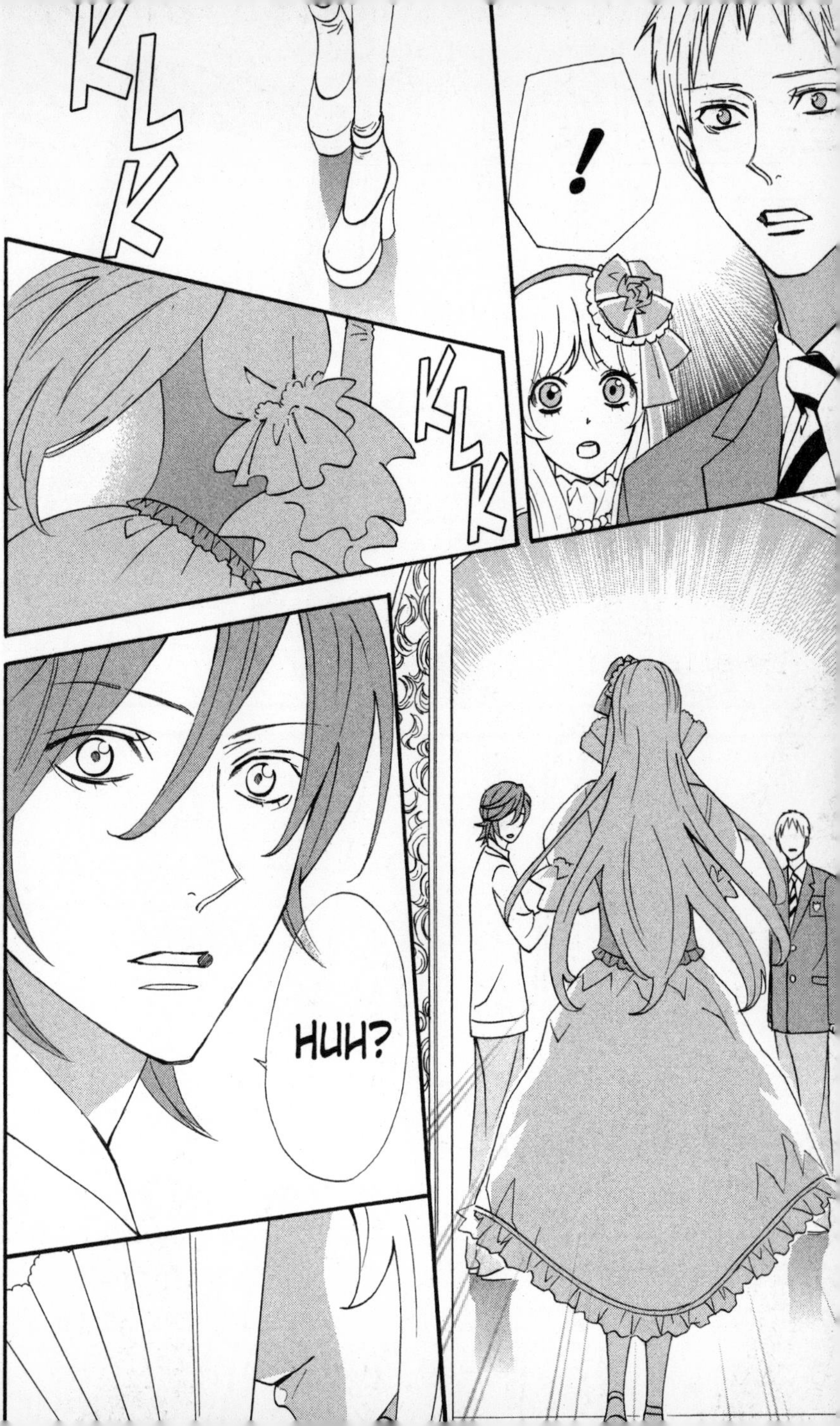
!
KLKK
KLKK
HUH?

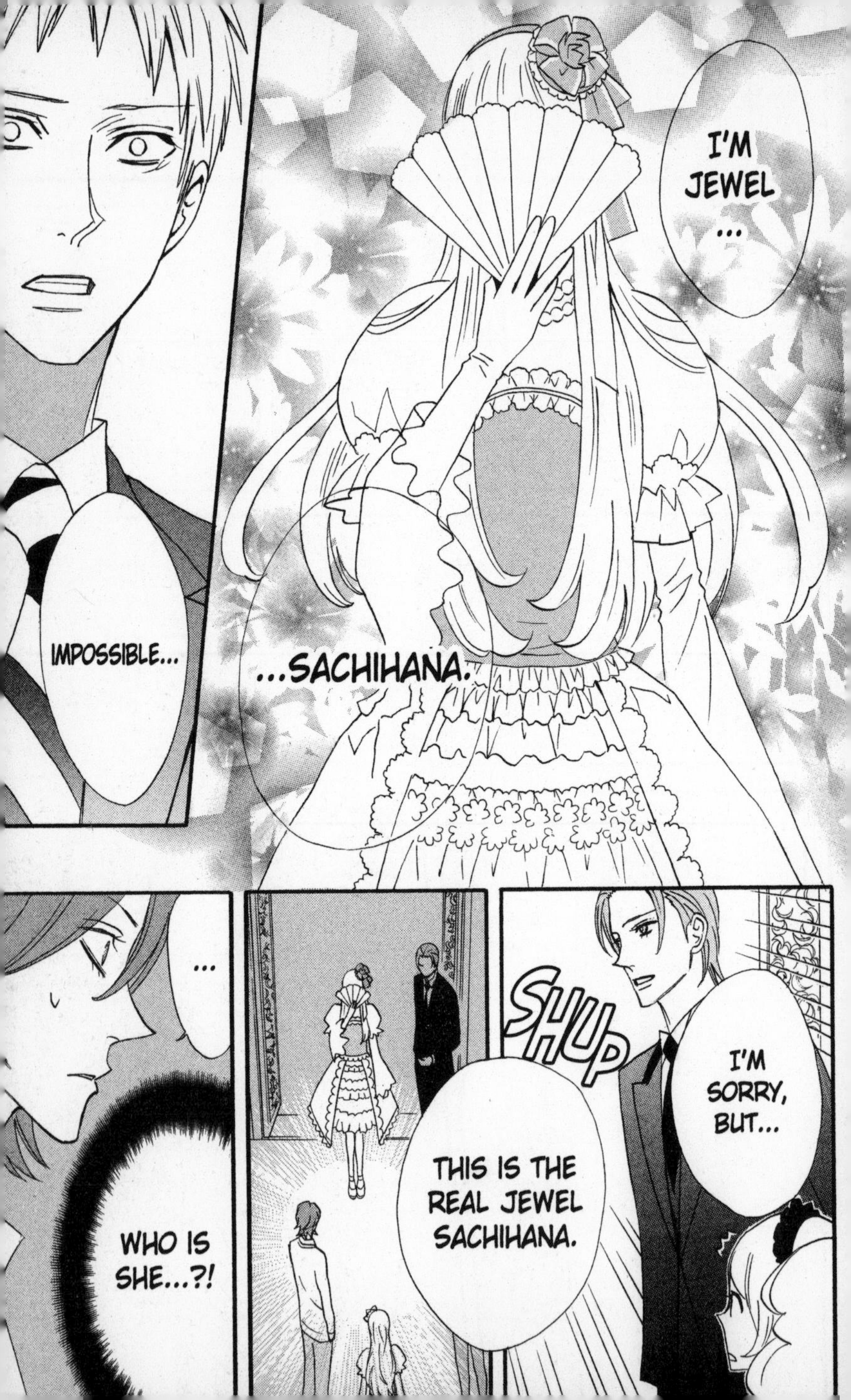
I'M JEWEL ...
...SACHIHANA.
IMPOSSIBLE...
SHUP
I'M SORRY, BUT...
THIS IS THE REAL JEWEL SACHIHANA.
...
WHO IS SHE...?!

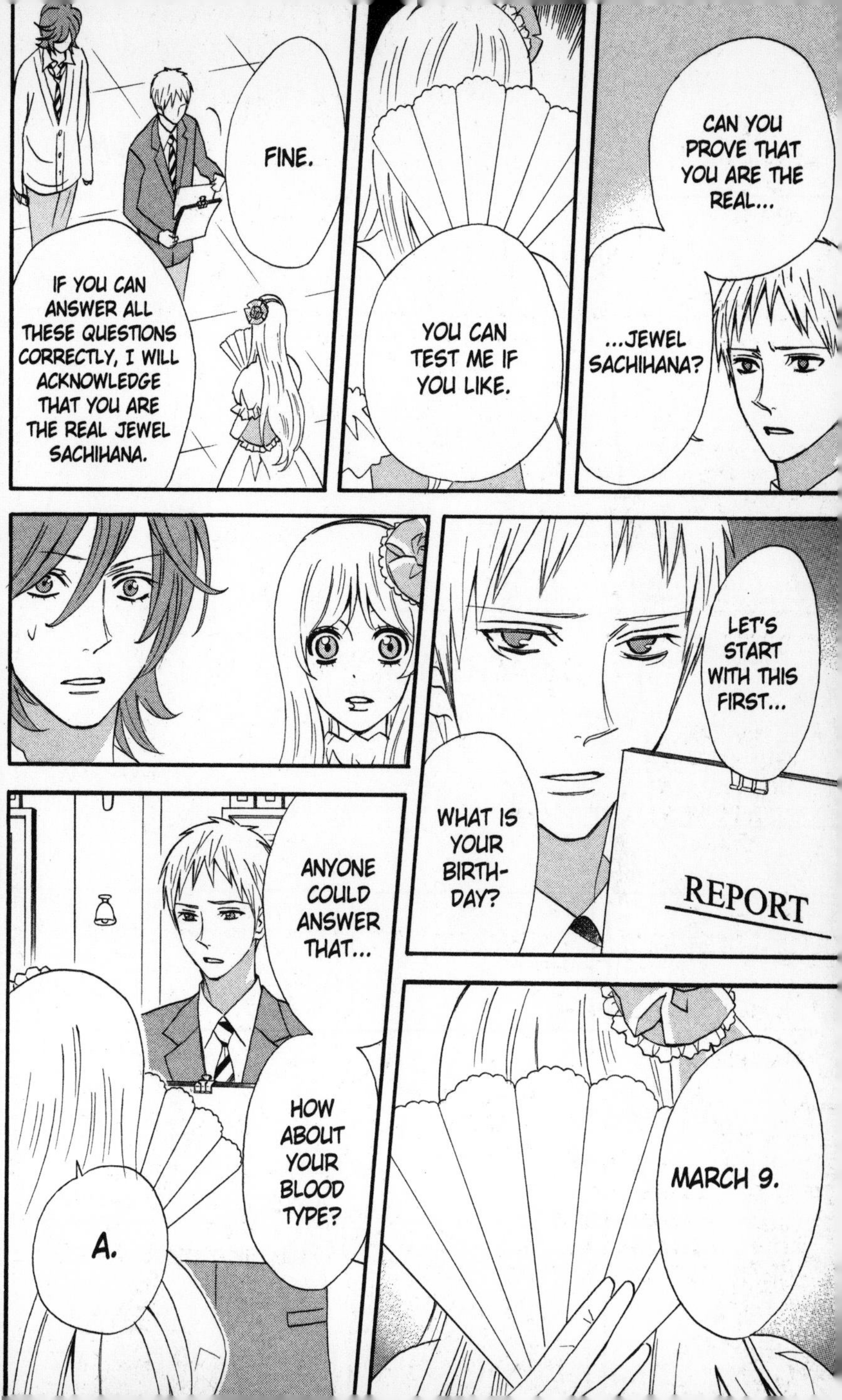
CAN YOU PROVE THAT YOU ARE THE REAL...
...JEWEL SACHIHANA?
YOU CAN TEST ME IF YOU LIKE.
FINE.
IF YOU CAN ANSWER ALL THESE QUESTIONS CORRECTLY, I WILL ACKNOWLEDGE THAT YOU ARE THE REAL JEWEL SACHIHANA.
LET'S START WITH THIS FIRST...
WHAT IS YOUR BIRTH-DAY?
REPORT
MARCH 9.
ANYONE COULD ANSWER THAT...
HOW ABOUT YOUR BLOOD TYPE?
A.

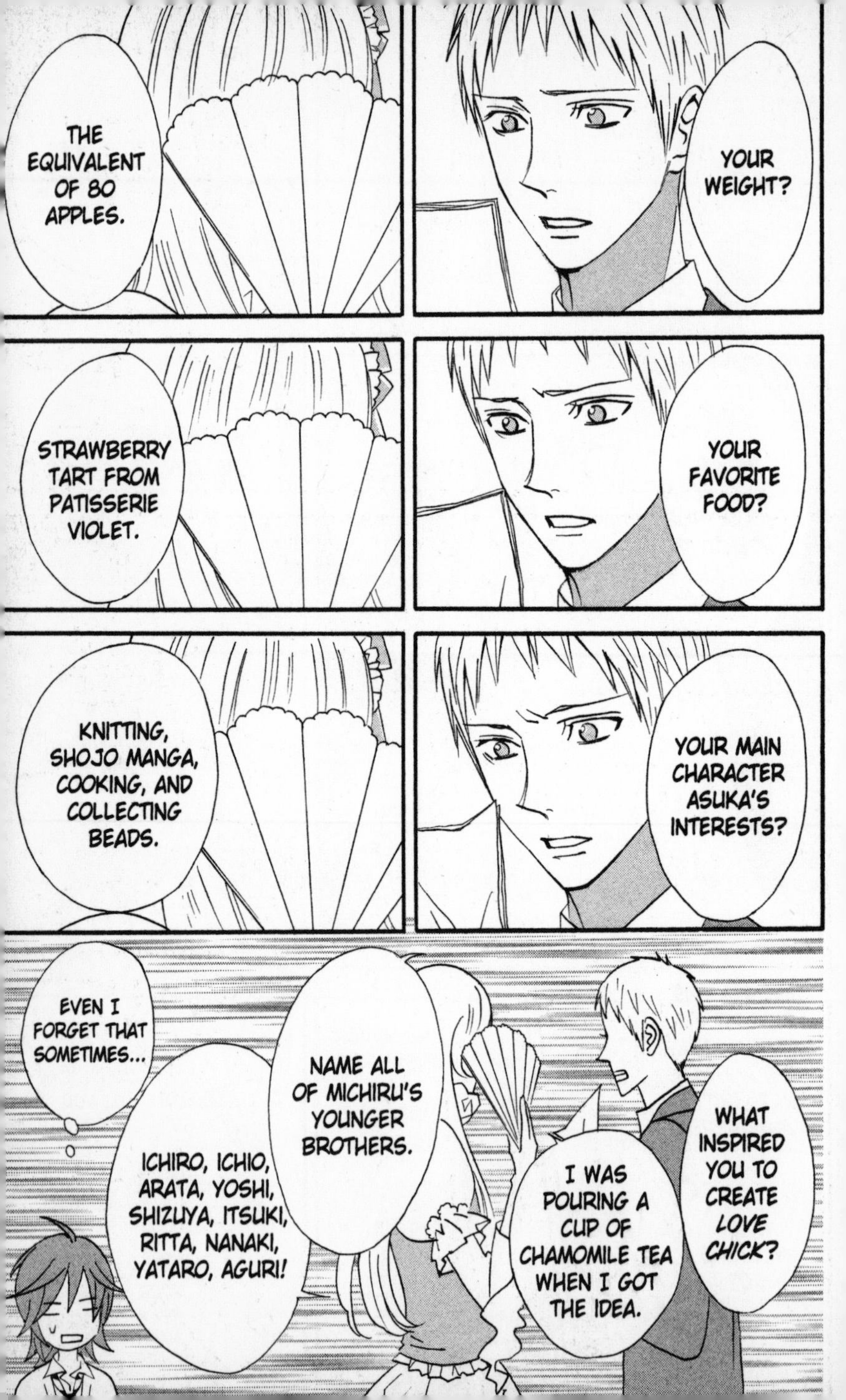

YOUR WEIGHT?
THE EQUIVALENT OF 80 APPLES.
YOUR FAVORITE FOOD?
STRAWBERRY TART FROM PATISSERIE VIOLET.
YOUR MAIN CHARACTER ASUKA'S INTERESTS?
KNITTING, SHOJO MANGA, COOKING, AND COLLECTING BEADS.
WHAT INSPIRED YOU TO CREATE *LOVE CHICK*?
I WAS POURING A CUP OF CHAMOMILE TEA WHEN I GOT THE IDEA.
NAME ALL OF MICHIRU'S YOUNGER BROTHERS.
ICHIRO, ICHIO, ARATA, YOSHI, SHIZUYA, ITSUKI, RITTA, NANAKI, YATARO, AGURI!
EVEN I FORGET THAT SOMETIMES...

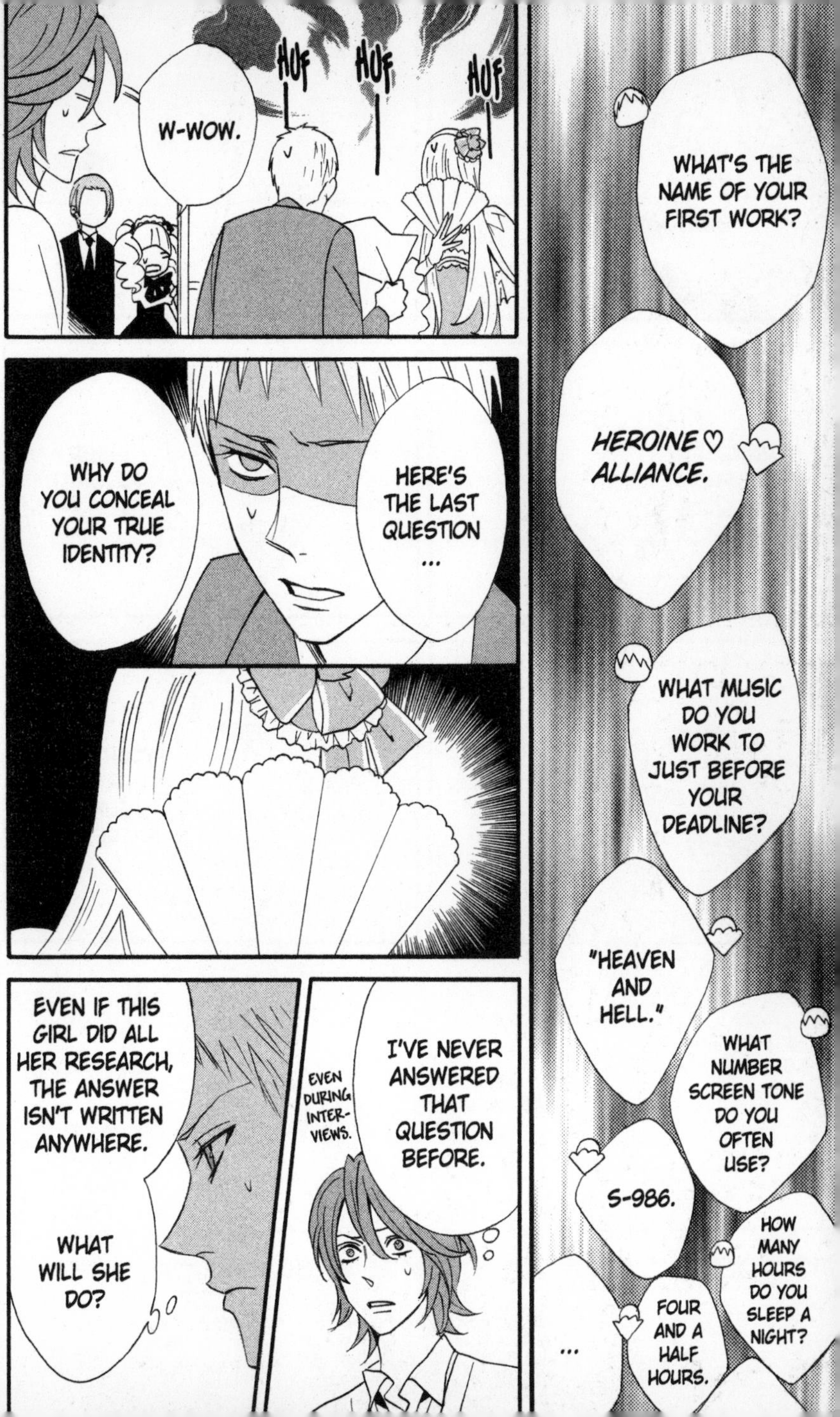
WHAT'S THE NAME OF YOUR FIRST WORK?
HEROINE ♡ ALLIANCE.
WHAT MUSIC DO YOU WORK TO JUST BEFORE YOUR DEADLINE?
"HEAVEN AND HELL."
WHAT NUMBER SCREEN TONE DO YOU OFTEN USE?
S-986.
HOW MANY HOURS DO YOU SLEEP A NIGHT?
FOUR AND A HALF HOURS.
...
HUF
HUF
HUF
W-WOW.
HERE'S THE LAST QUESTION ...
WHY DO YOU CONCEAL YOUR TRUE IDENTITY?
I'VE NEVER ANSWERED THAT QUESTION BEFORE.
EVEN DURING INTER-VIEWS.
EVEN IF THIS GIRL DID ALL HER RESEARCH, THE ANSWER ISN'T WRITTEN ANYWHERE.
WHAT WILL SHE DO?

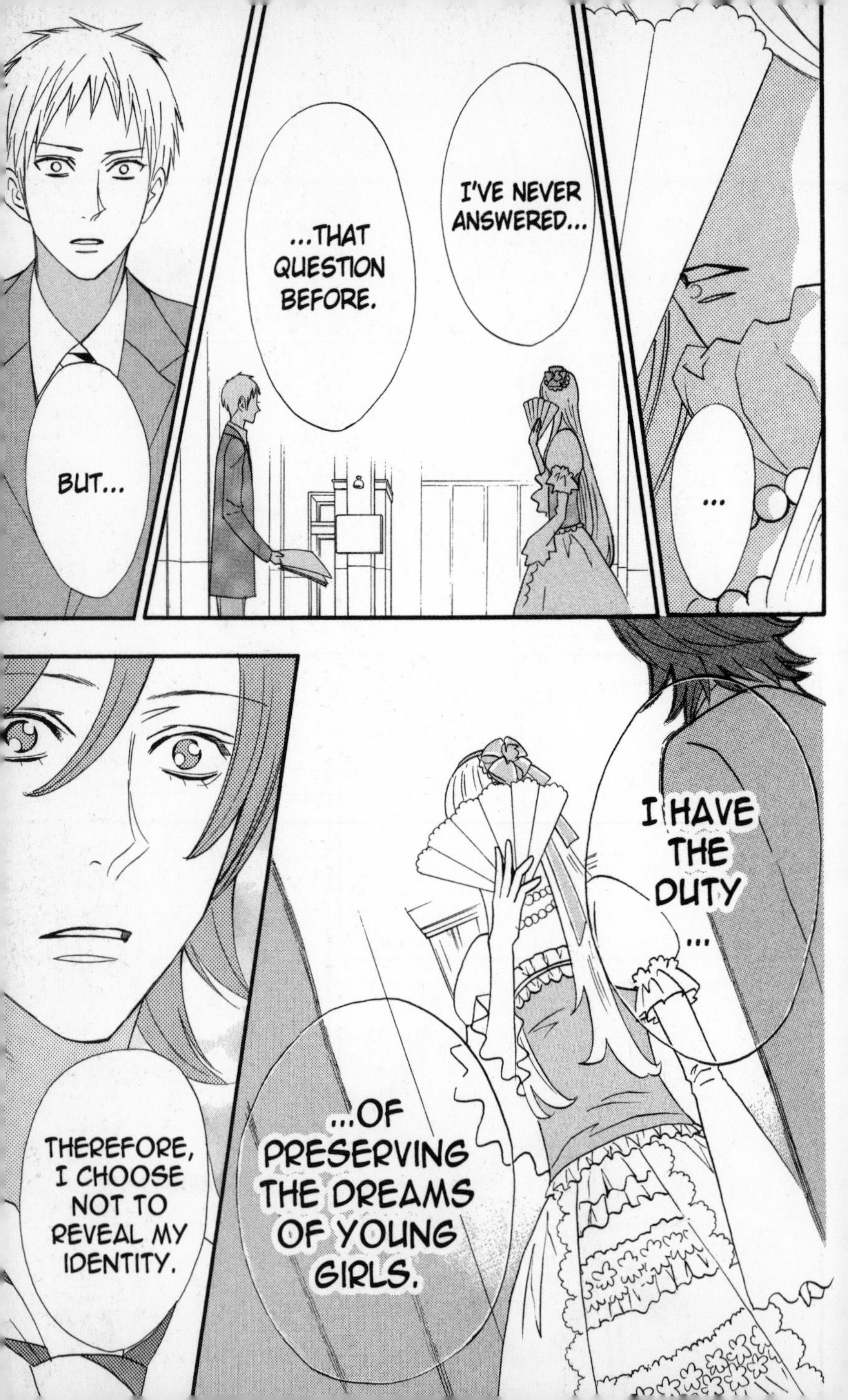
...
I'VE NEVER ANSWERED...
...THAT QUESTION BEFORE.
BUT...
I HAVE THE DUTY ...
...OF PRESERVING THE DREAMS OF YOUNG GIRLS.
THEREFORE, I CHOOSE NOT TO REVEAL MY IDENTITY.

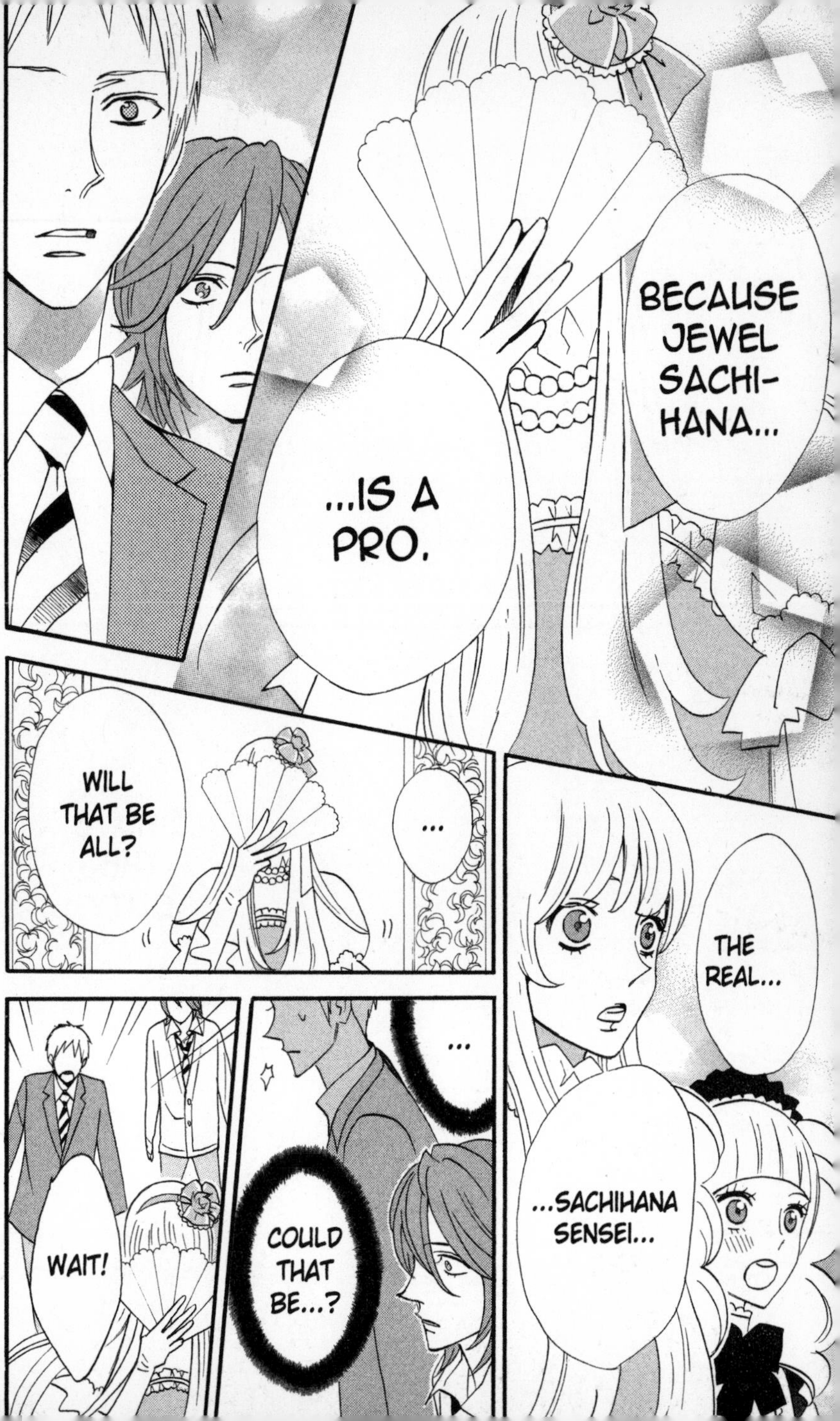
BECAUSE JEWEL SACHI-HANA...
...IS A PRO.
THE REAL...
...SACHIHANA SENSEI...
...
WILL THAT BE ALL?
...
COULD THAT BE...?
WAIT!

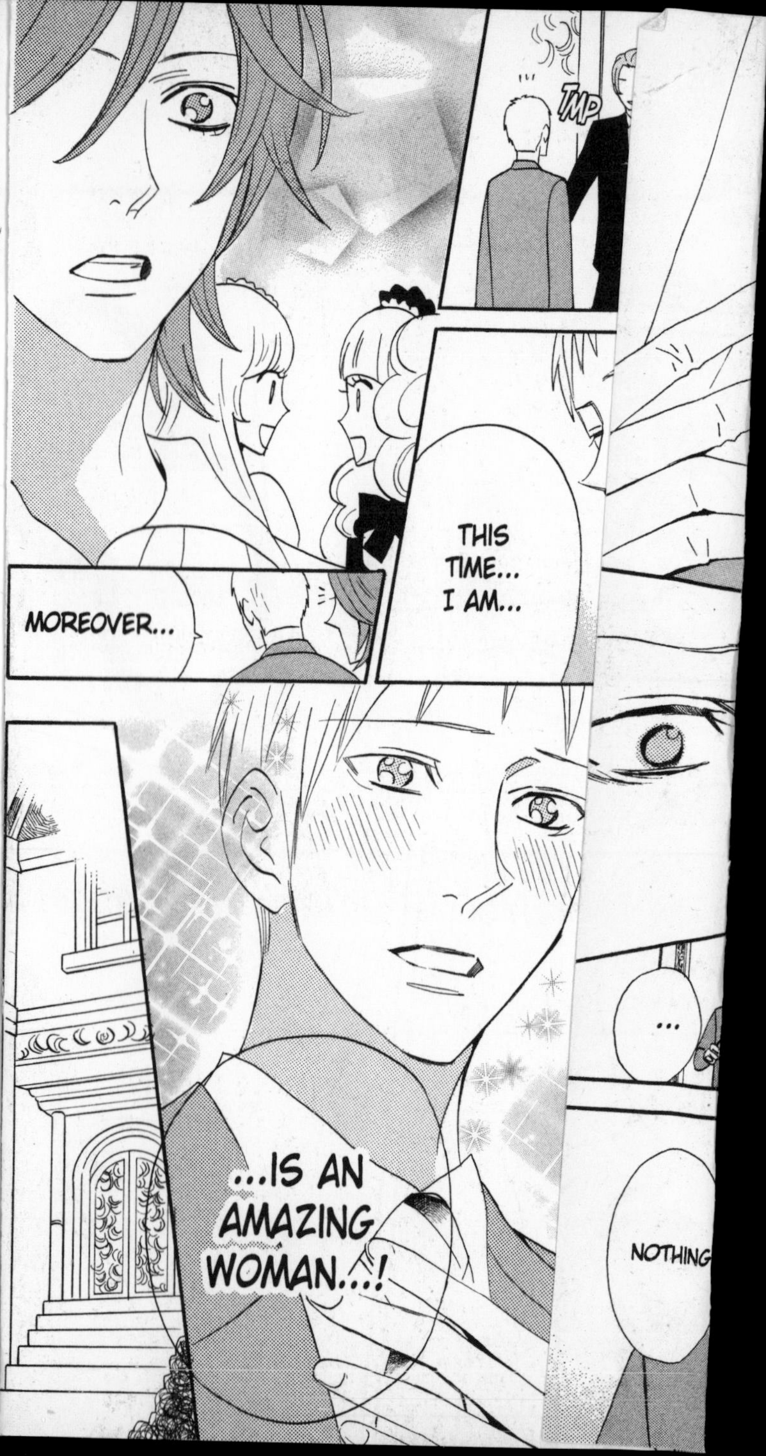
TMP
THIS TIME... I AM...
MOREOVER...
...IS AN AMAZING WOMAN...!
...
NOTHING

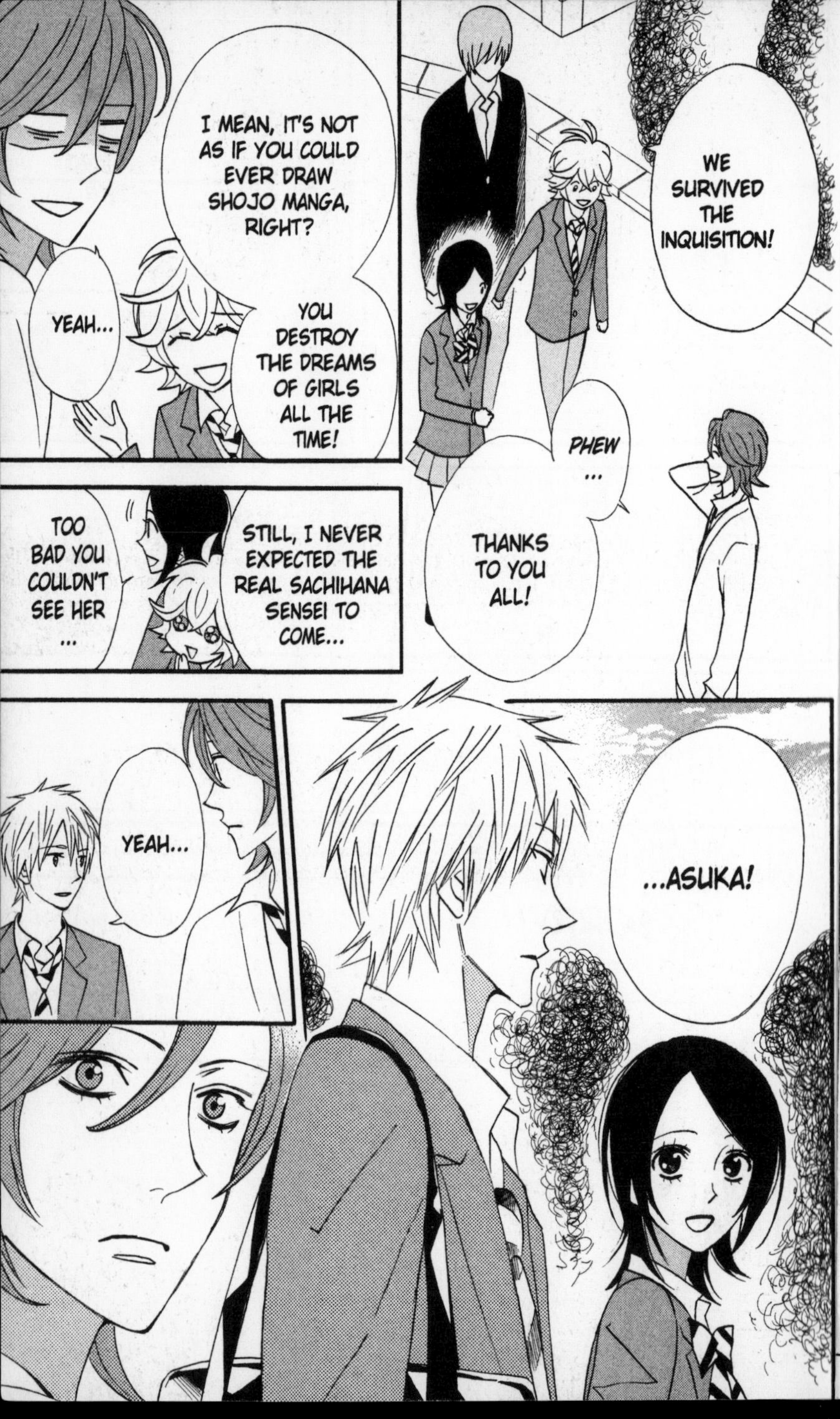
WE SURVIVED THE INQUISITION!
PHEW ...
THANKS TO YOU ALL!
I MEAN, IT'S NOT AS IF YOU COULD EVER DRAW SHOJO MANGA, RIGHT?
YOU DESTROY THE DREAMS OF GIRLS ALL THE TIME!
YEAH...
STILL, I NEVER EXPECTED THE REAL SACHIHANA SENSEI TO COME...
TOO BAD YOU COULDN'T SEE HER ...
...ASUKA!
YEAH...

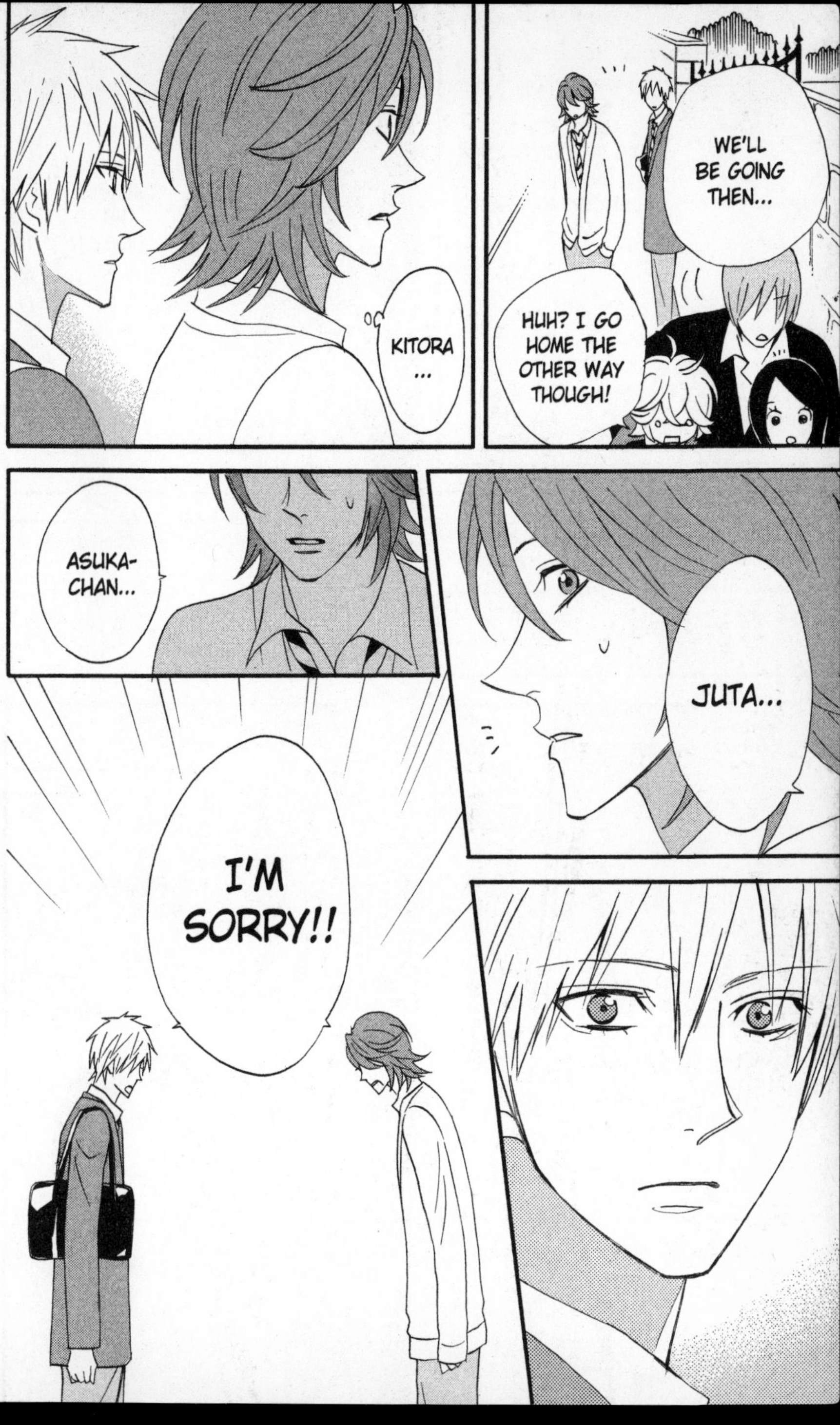
WE'LL BE GOING THEN...
HUH? I GO HOME THE OTHER WAY THOUGH!
KITORA ...
JUTA...
ASUKA-CHAN...
I'M SORRY!!

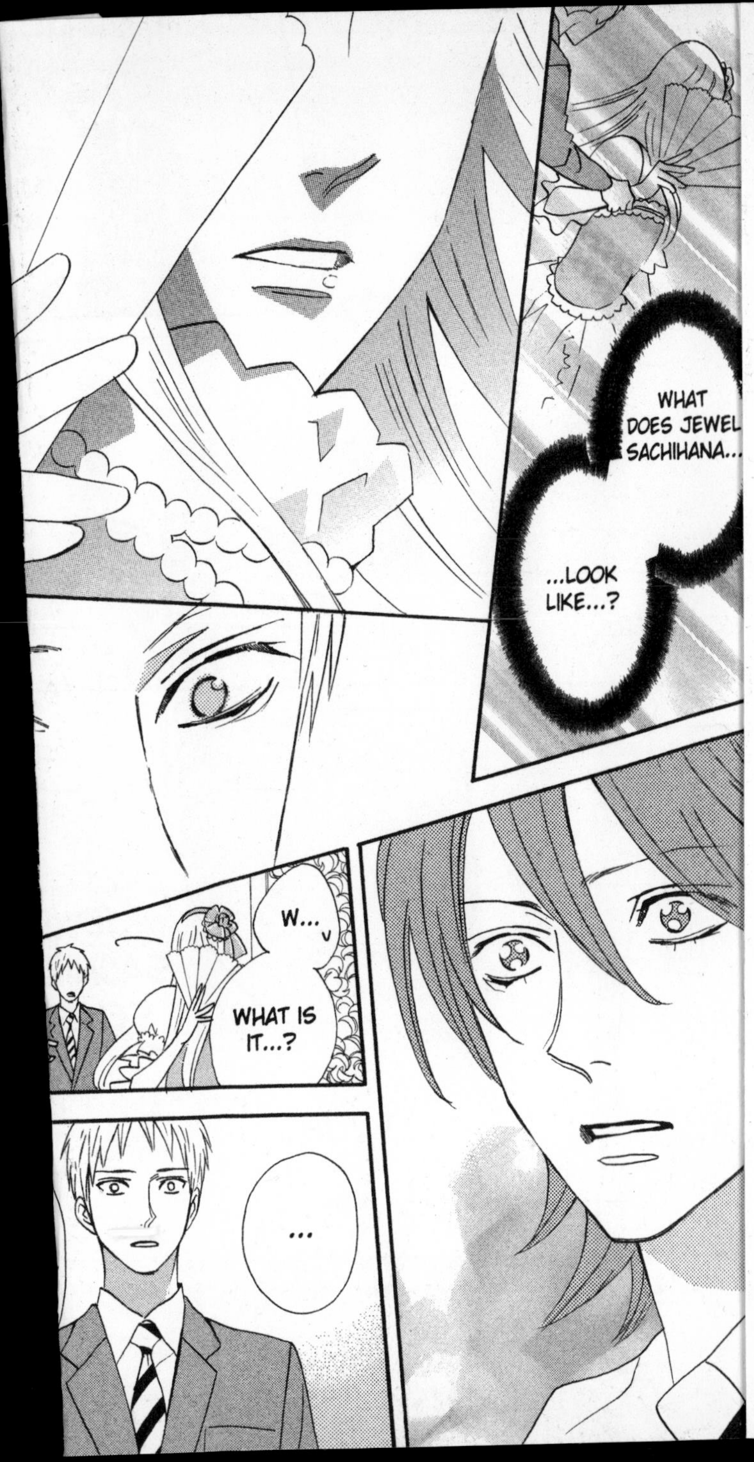
WHAT DOES JEWEL SACHIHANA...
...LOOK LIKE...?
W...
WHAT IS IT...?
...

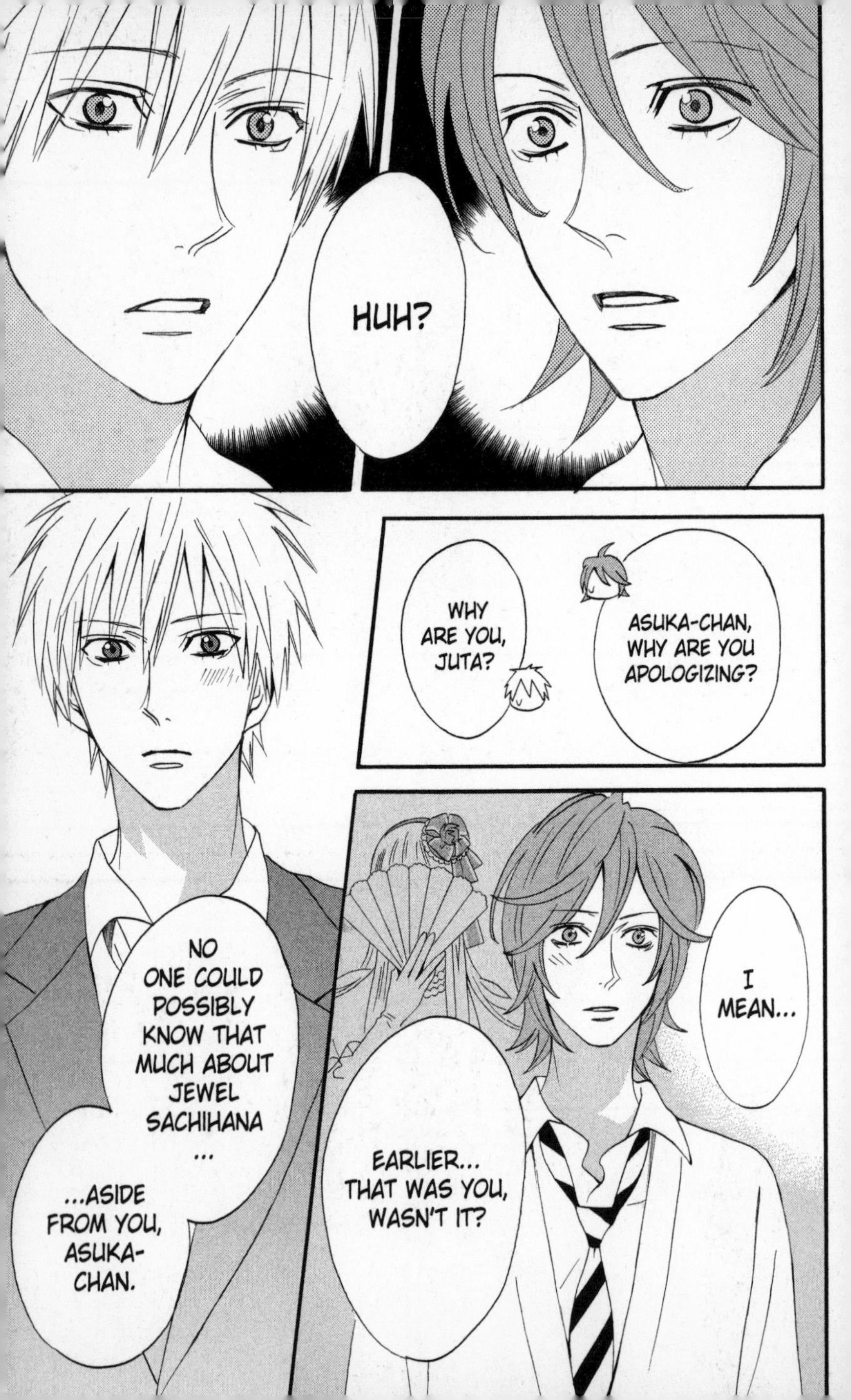
HUH?
ASUKA-CHAN, WHY ARE YOU APOLOGIZING?
WHY ARE YOU, JUTA?
I MEAN...
EARLIER... THAT WAS YOU, WASN'T IT?
NO ONE COULD POSSIBLY KNOW THAT MUCH ABOUT JEWEL SACHIHANA ...
...ASIDE FROM YOU, ASUKA-CHAN.

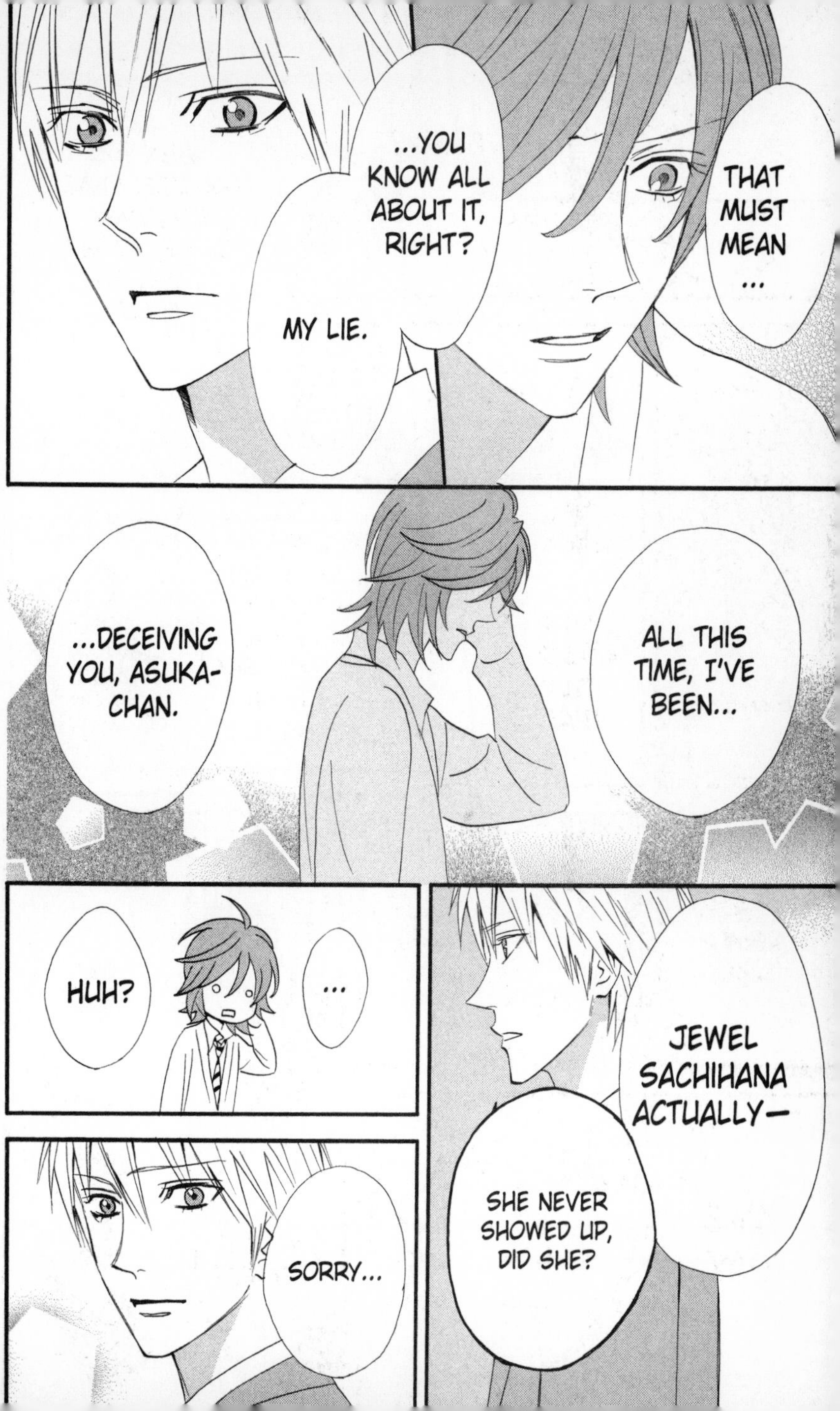
THAT MUST MEAN ...
...YOU KNOW ALL ABOUT IT, RIGHT?
MY LIE.
ALL THIS TIME, I'VE BEEN...
...DECEIVING YOU, ASUKA-CHAN.
JEWEL SACHIHANA ACTUALLY—
SHE NEVER SHOWED UP, DID SHE?
...
HUH?
SORRY...

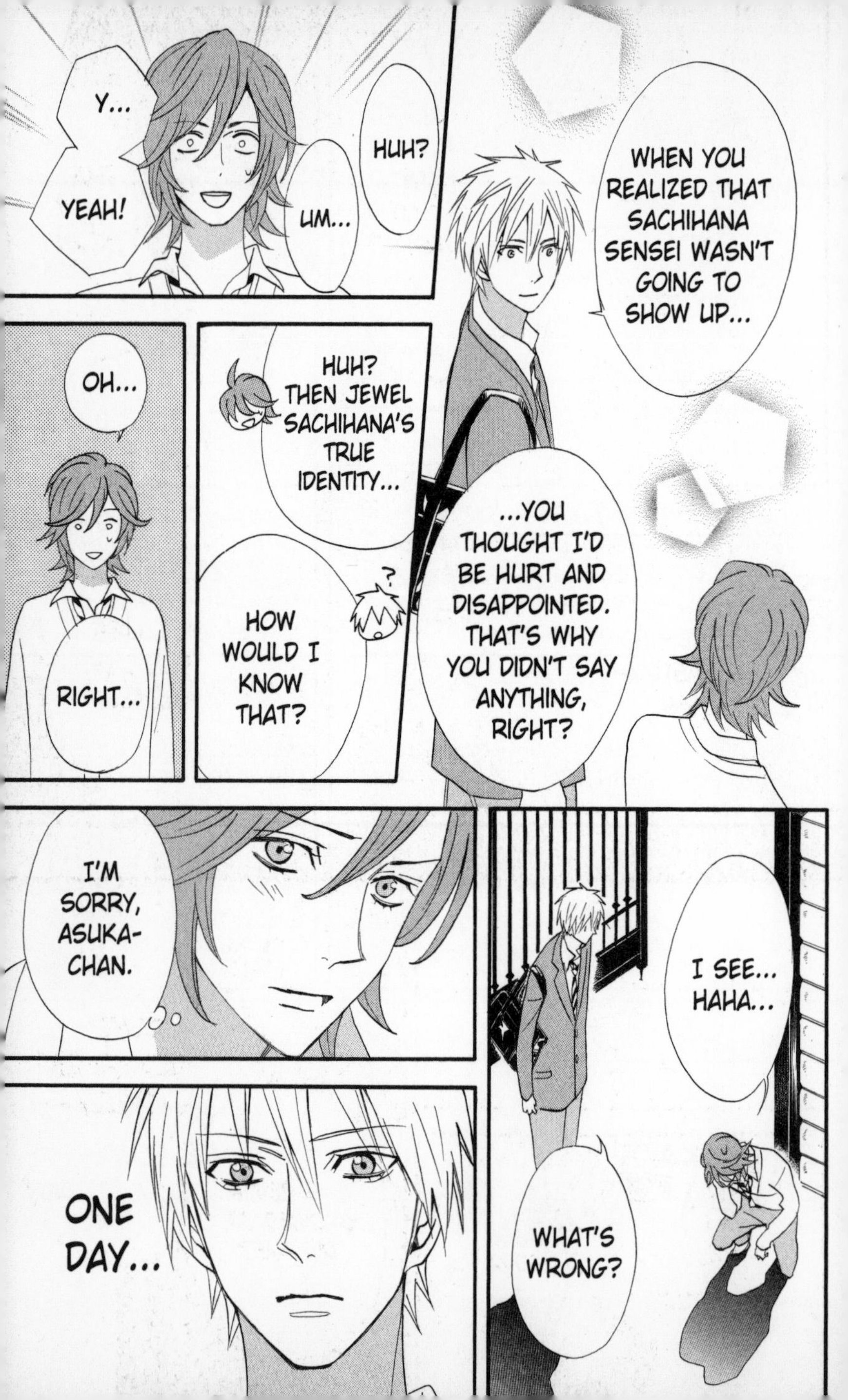
WHEN YOU REALIZED THAT SACHIHANA SENSEI WASN'T GOING TO SHOW UP...
...YOU THOUGHT I'D BE HURT AND DISAPPOINTED. THAT'S WHY YOU DIDN'T SAY ANYTHING, RIGHT?
HUH?
UM...
Y...
YEAH!
HUH? THEN JEWEL SACHIHANA'S TRUE IDENTITY...
HOW WOULD I KNOW THAT?
?
OH...
RIGHT...
I SEE... HAHA...
WHAT'S WRONG?
I'M SORRY, ASUKA-CHAN.
ONE DAY...

RIGHT NOW, I CAN'T...

I DON'T KNOW WHAT THE TRUTH IS...

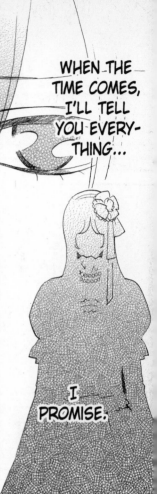

WHEN THE TIME COMES, I'LL TELL YOU EVERYTHING...

I PROMISE.

...BUT IF THERE'S SOMETHING YOU DON'T WANT TO TELL ME...

...I WON'T ASK, JUTA.

...OKAY?

BUT TELL ME SOMEDAY...

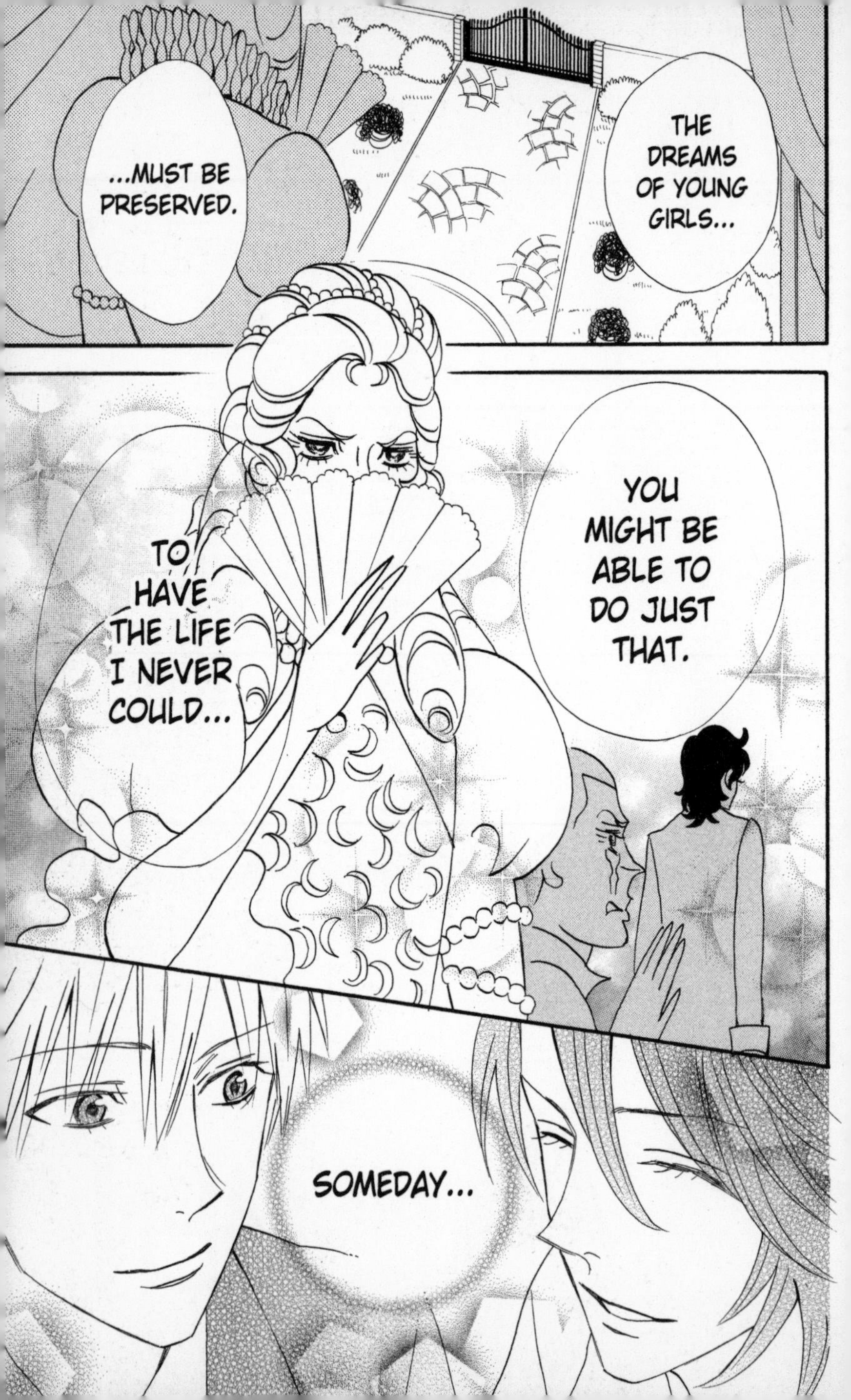
THE DREAMS OF YOUNG GIRLS...
...MUST BE PRESERVED.
YOU MIGHT BE ABLE TO DO JUST THAT.
TO HAVE THE LIFE I NEVER COULD...
SOMEDAY...

OTOMEN

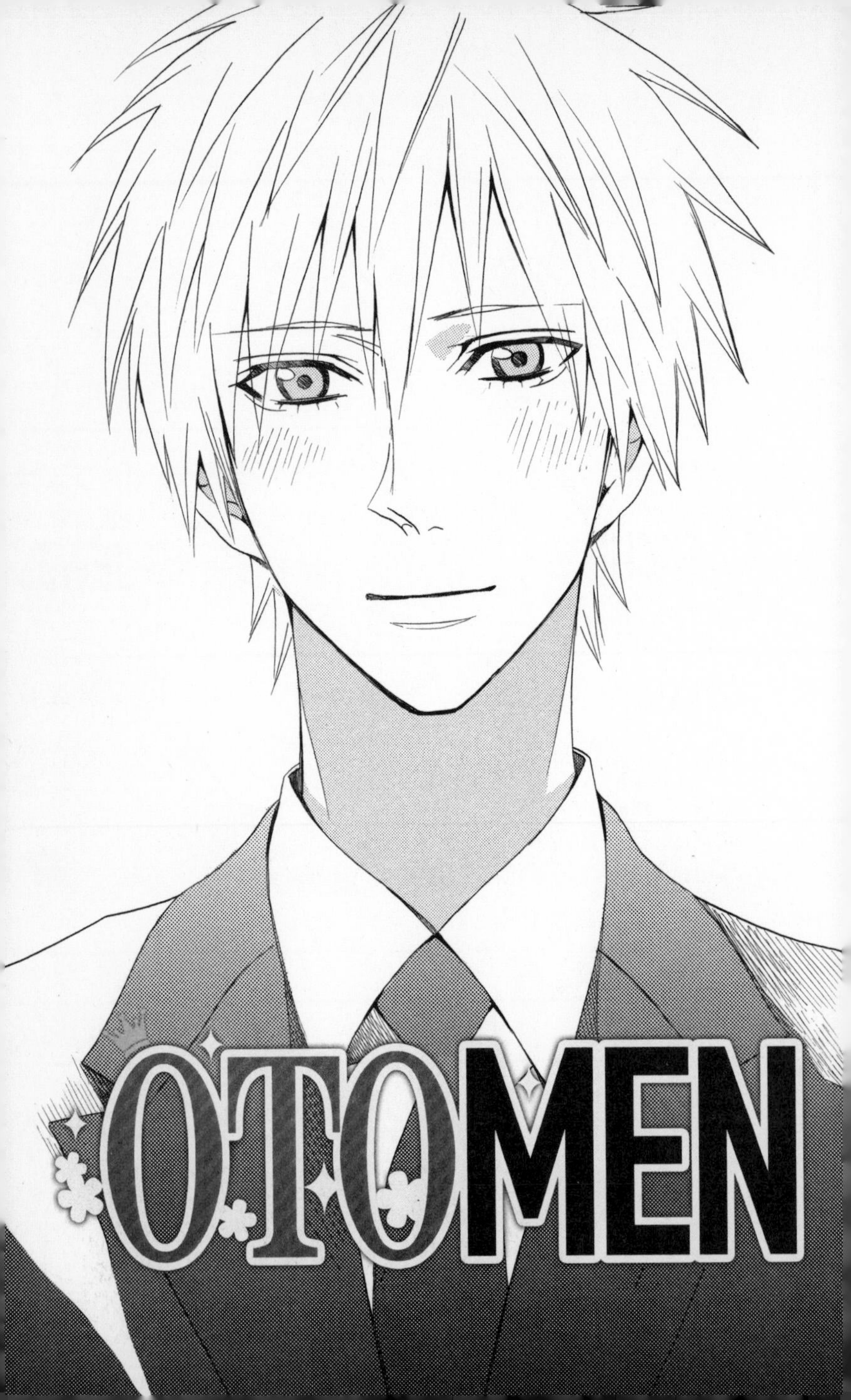
OTOMEN

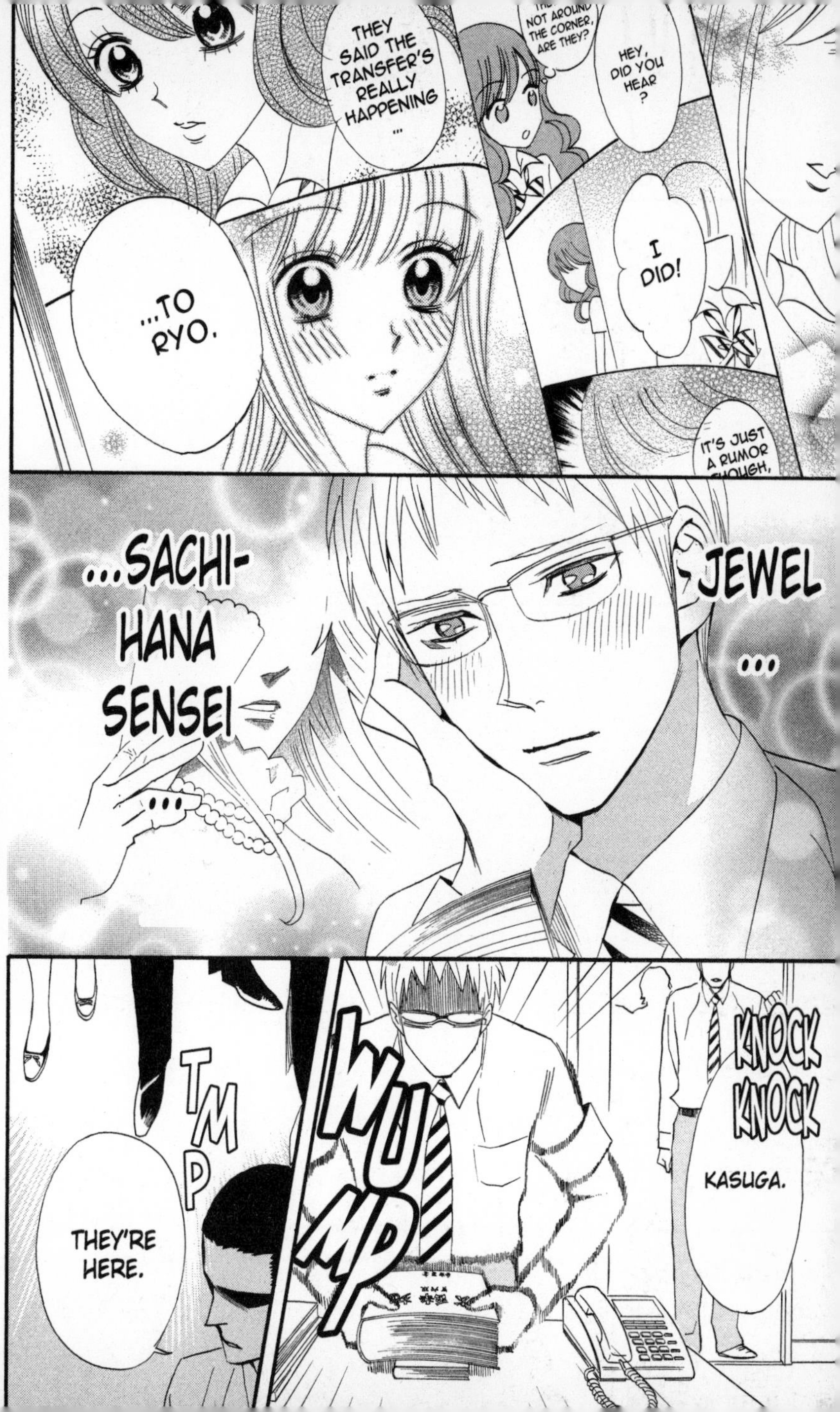
HEY, DID YOU HEAR?
I DID!
IT'S JUST A RUMOR THOUGH,
NOT AROUND THE CORNER, ARE THEY?
THEY SAID THE TRANSFER'S REALLY HAPPENING...
...TO RYO.
JEWEL...
...SACHI-HANA SENSEI...
KNOCK KNOCK
KASUGA.
WUMP
TMP
THEY'RE HERE.

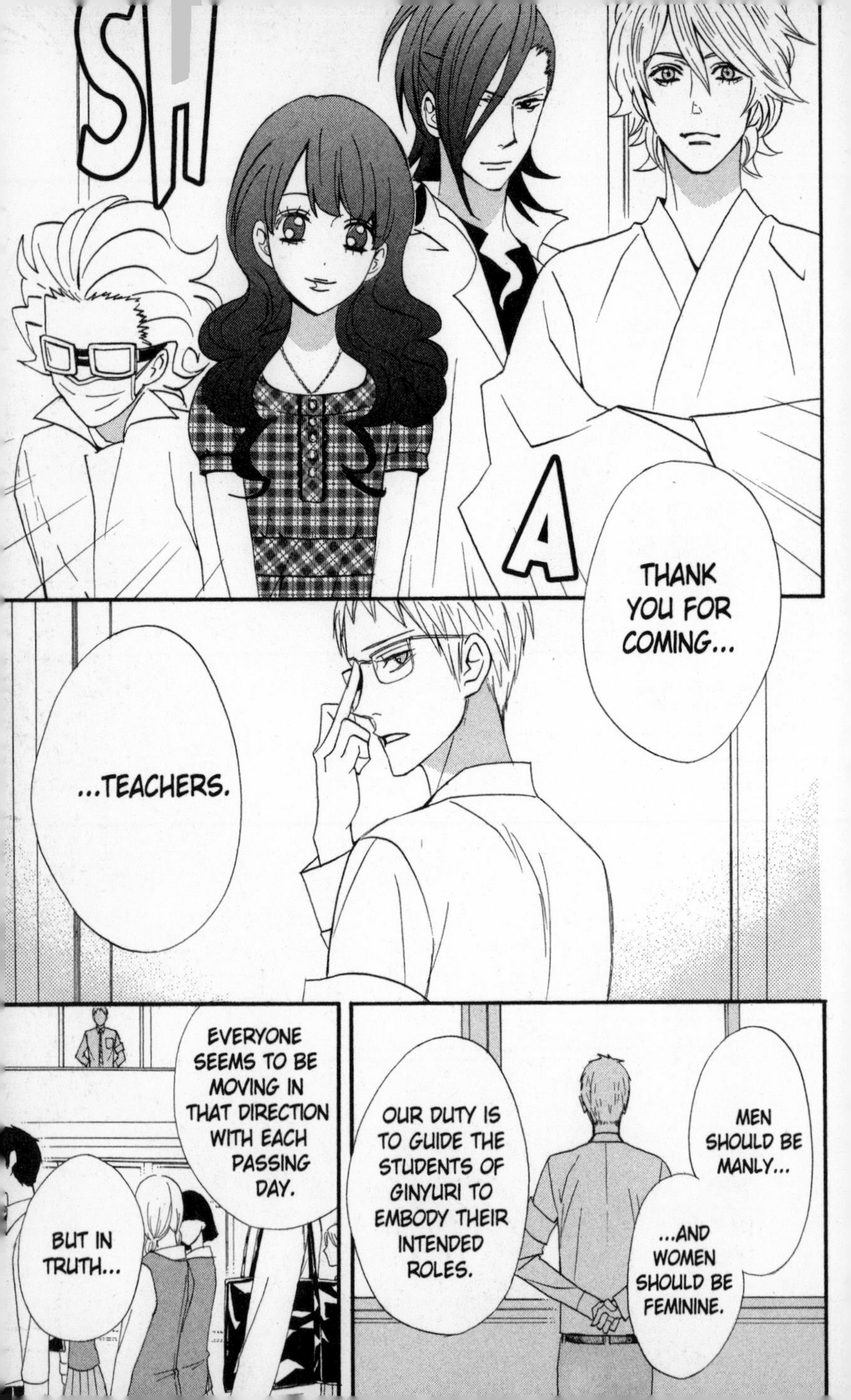
SH
A
THANK YOU FOR COMING...
...TEACHERS.
MEN SHOULD BE MANLY...
...AND WOMEN SHOULD BE FEMININE.
OUR DUTY IS TO GUIDE THE STUDENTS OF GINYURI TO EMBODY THEIR INTENDED ROLES.
EVERYONE SEEMS TO BE MOVING IN THAT DIRECTION WITH EACH PASSING DAY.
BUT IN TRUTH...

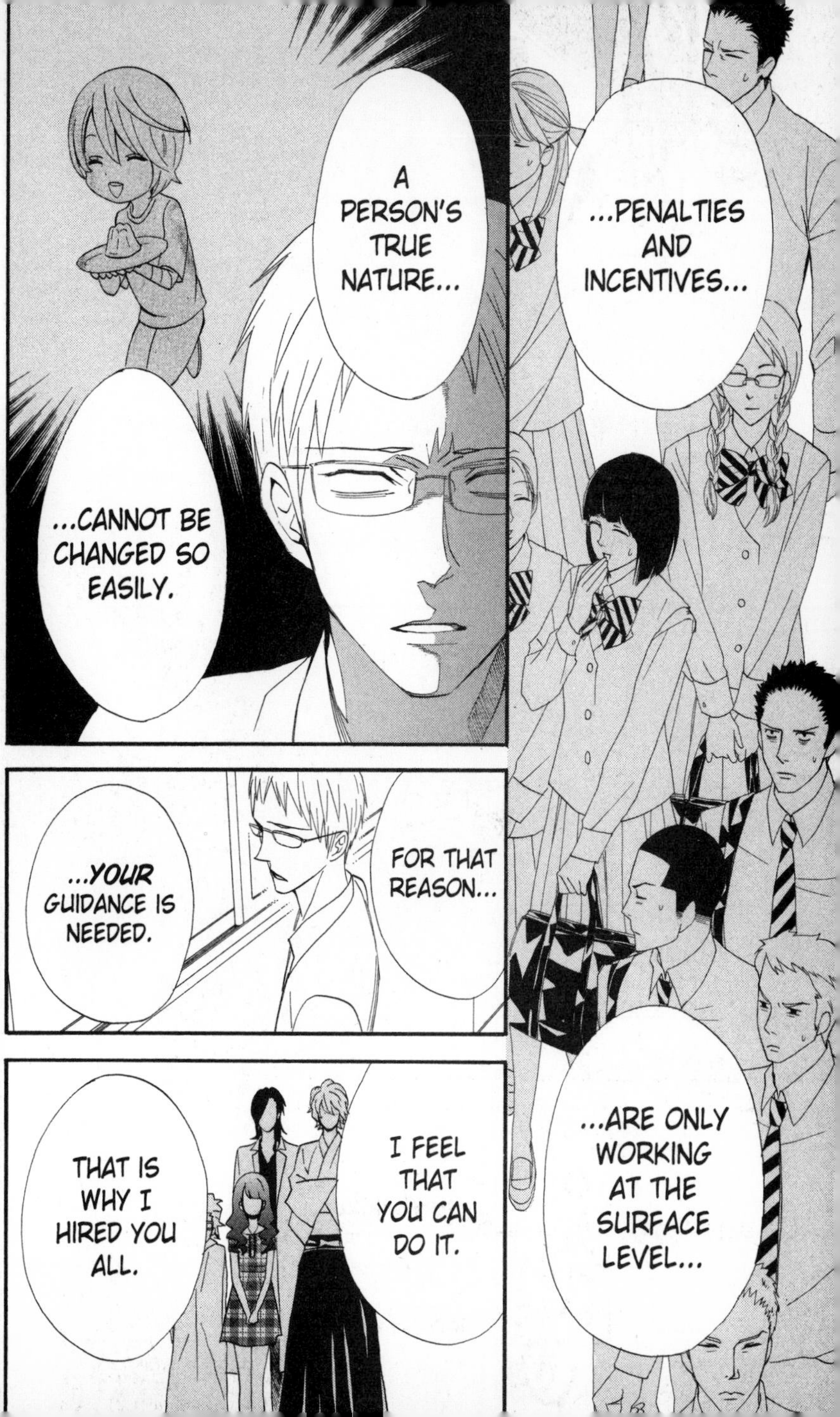
...PENALTIES AND INCENTIVES...
...ARE ONLY WORKING AT THE SURFACE LEVEL...
A PERSON'S TRUE NATURE...
...CANNOT BE CHANGED SO EASILY.
FOR THAT REASON...
...*YOUR* GUIDANCE IS NEEDED.
I FEEL THAT YOU CAN DO IT.
THAT IS WHY I HIRED YOU ALL.

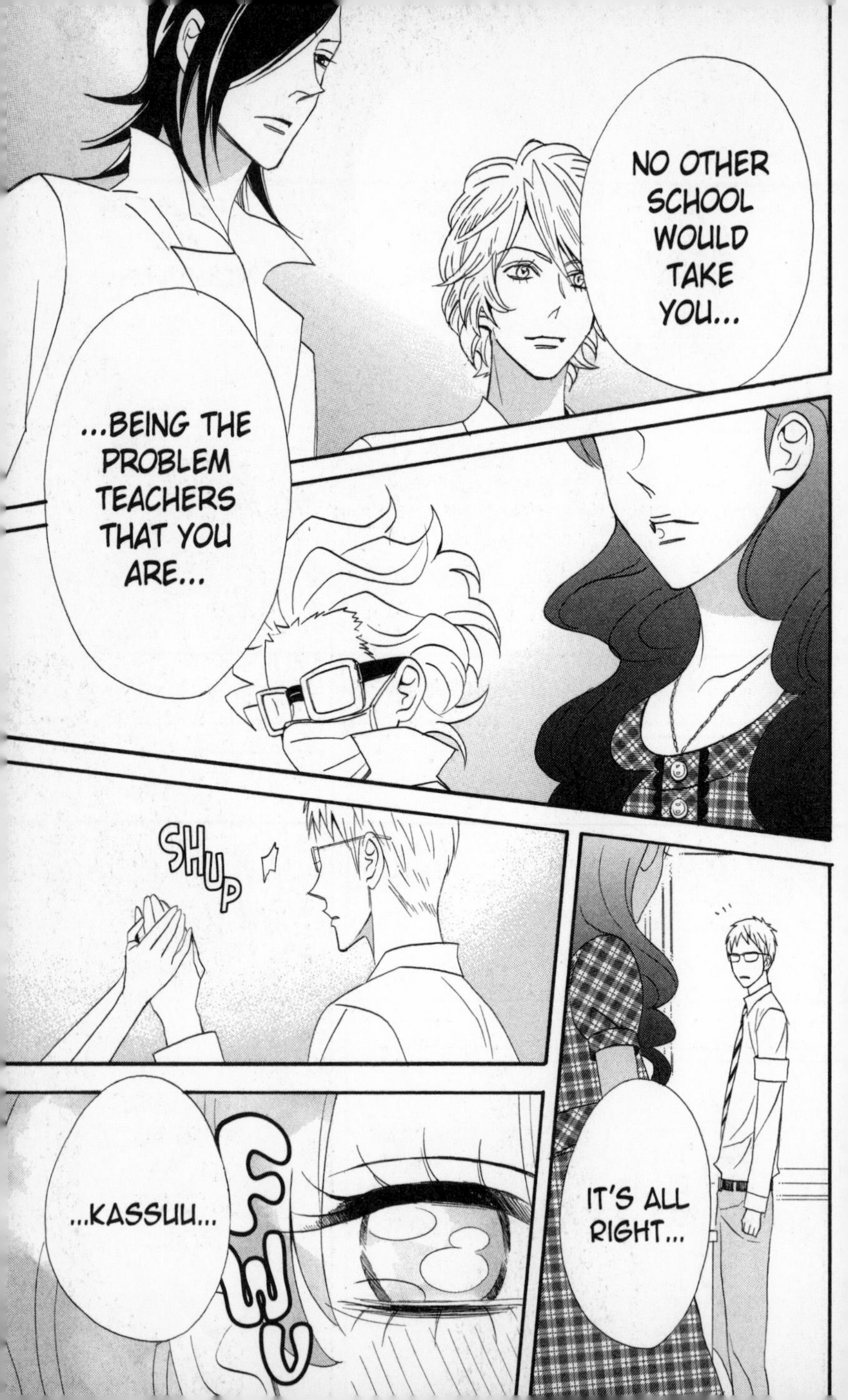
NO OTHER SCHOOL WOULD TAKE YOU...
...BEING THE PROBLEM TEACHERS THAT YOU ARE...
IT'S ALL RIGHT...
SHUP
...KASSUU...

...BUT I, OTOWA, WILL TRY MY VERY BEST!

I DON'T KNOW IF I'LL BE ABLE TO DO IT WELL...

GOT IT!

...

KASSUU...?

I HOPE SO.

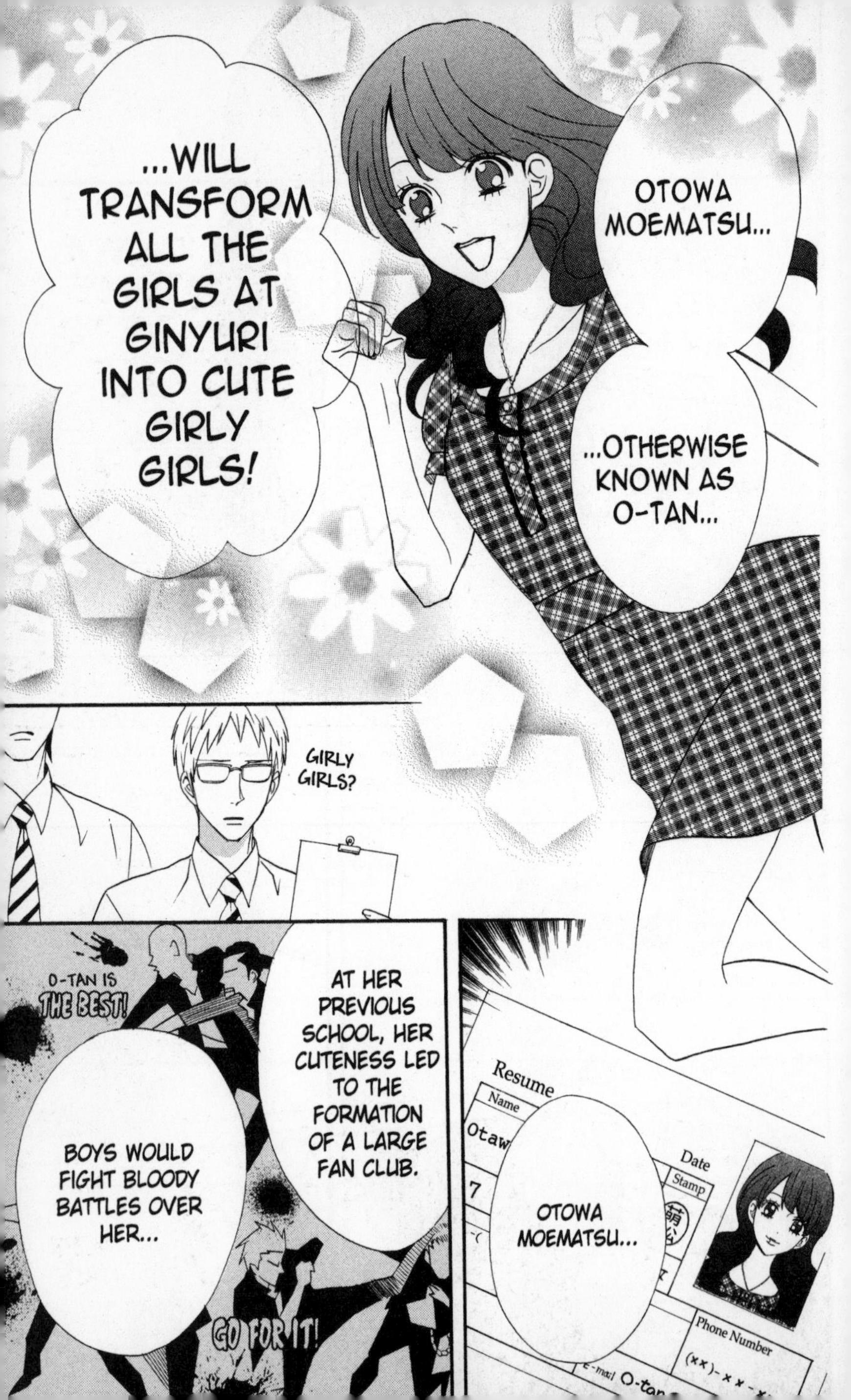
OTOWA MOEMATSU...
...OTHERWISE KNOWN AS O-TAN...
...WILL TRANSFORM ALL THE GIRLS AT GINYURI INTO CUTE GIRLY GIRLS!
GIRLY GIRLS?
Resume
Name
Date
Stamp
Phone Number
OTOWA MOEMATSU...
AT HER PREVIOUS SCHOOL, HER CUTENESS LED TO THE FORMATION OF A LARGE FAN CLUB.
O-TAN IS THE BEST!
BOYS WOULD FIGHT BLOODY BATTLES OVER HER...
GO FOR IT!

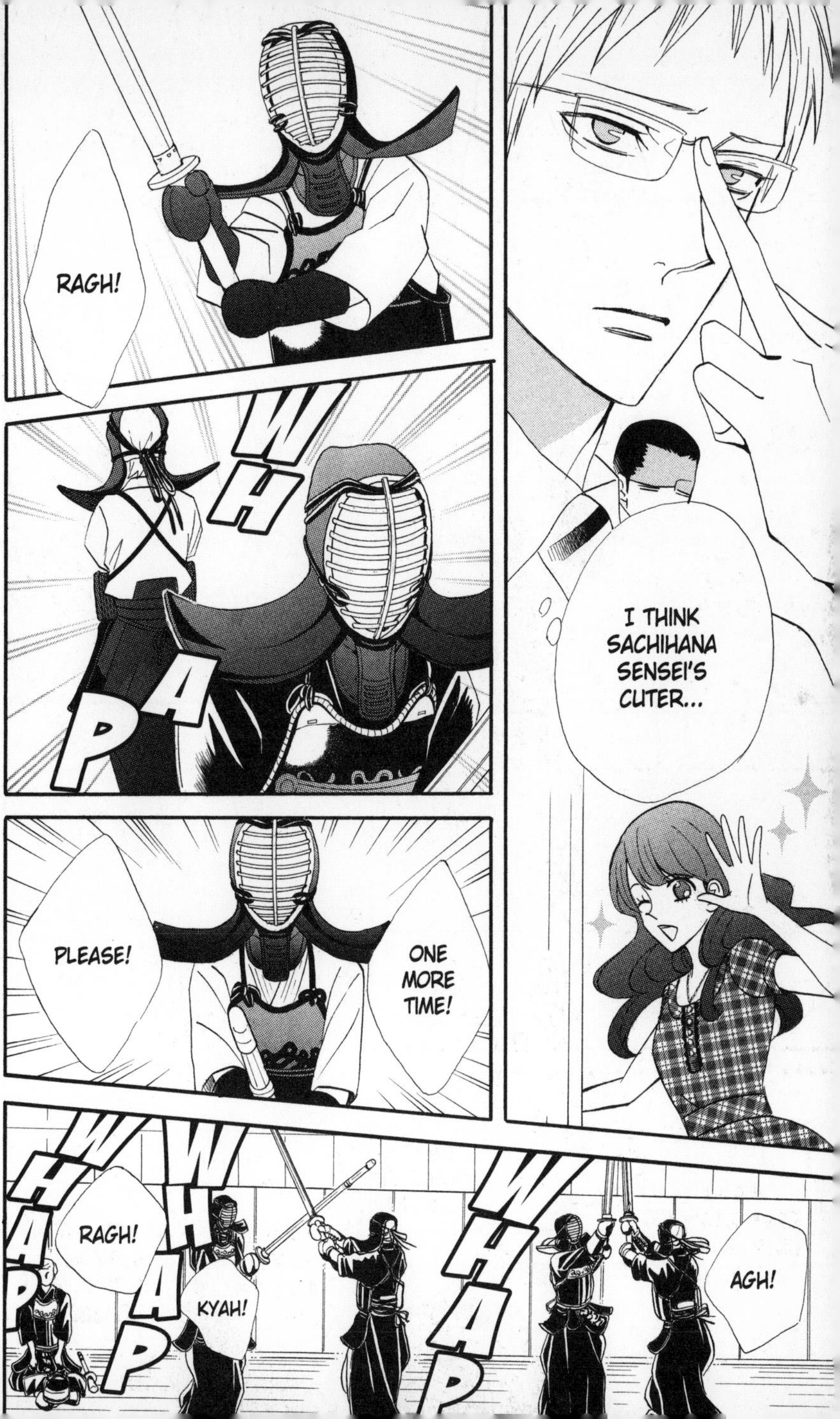
I THINK SACHIHANA SENSEI'S CUTER...
RAGH!
WHAP
ONE MORE TIME!
PLEASE!
AGH!
WHAP
WHAP
KYAH!
RAGH!
WHAP

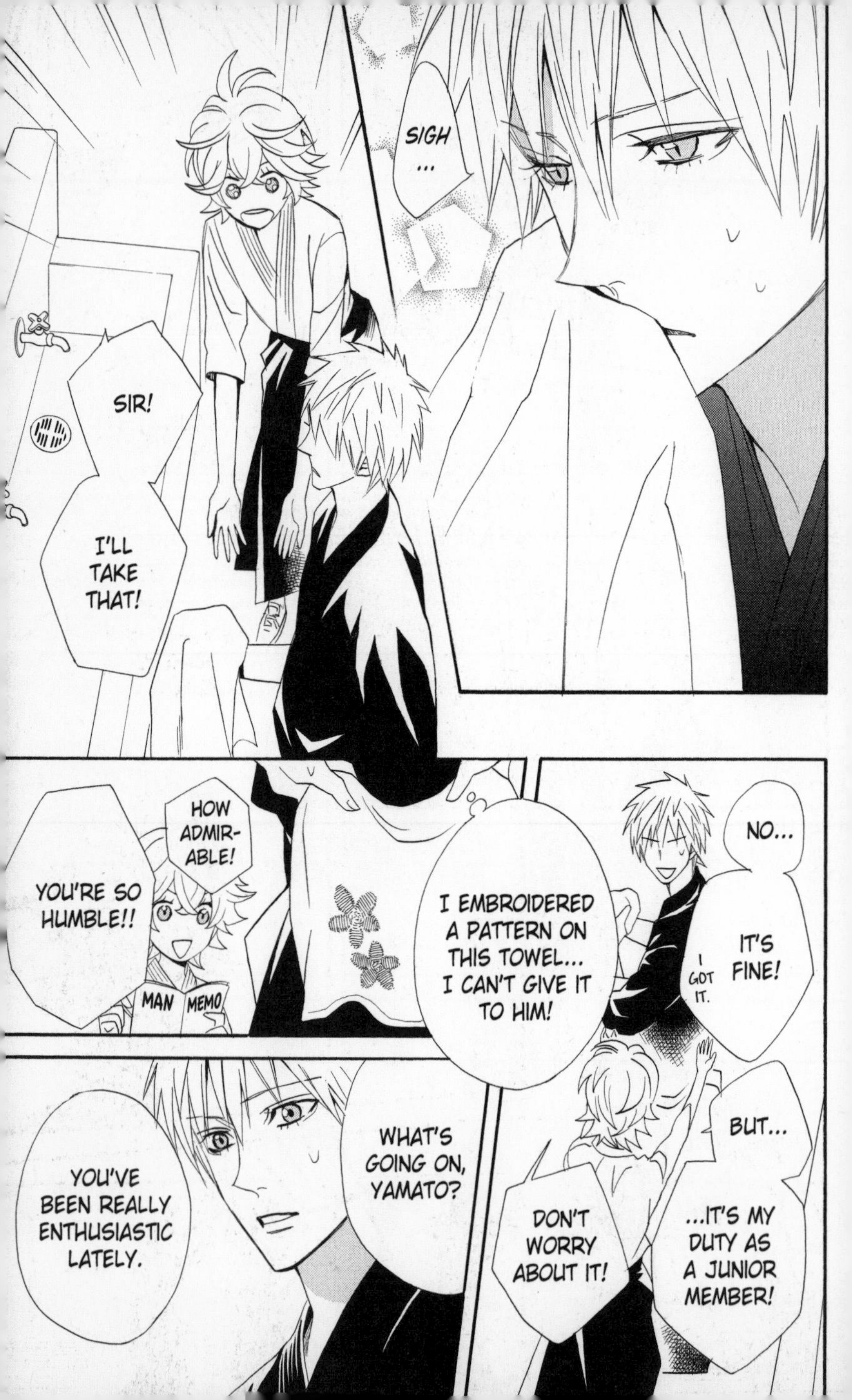
SIGH ...
SIR!
I'LL TAKE THAT!
NO...
IT'S FINE!
I GOT IT.
I EMBROIDERED A PATTERN ON THIS TOWEL... I CAN'T GIVE IT TO HIM!
HOW ADMIRABLE!
YOU'RE SO HUMBLE!!
MAN MEMO
BUT...
...IT'S MY DUTY AS A JUNIOR MEMBER!
DON'T WORRY ABOUT IT!
WHAT'S GOING ON, YAMATO?
YOU'VE BEEN REALLY ENTHUSIASTIC LATELY.

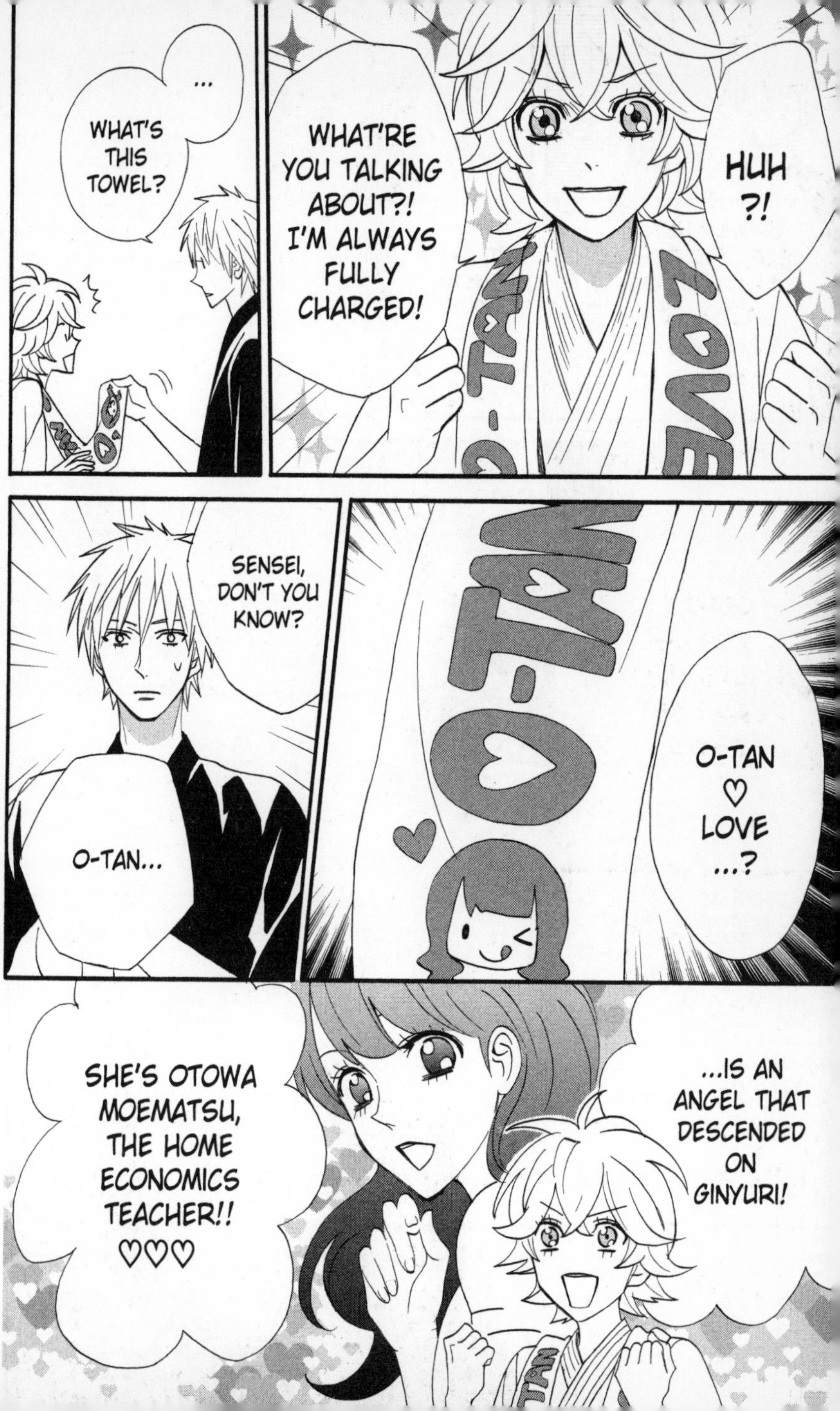
HUH ?!
WHAT'RE YOU TALKING ABOUT?! I'M ALWAYS FULLY CHARGED!
...
WHAT'S THIS TOWEL?
O-TAN ♡ LOVE ...?
SENSEI, DON'T YOU KNOW?
O-TAN...
...IS AN ANGEL THAT DESCENDED ON GINYURI!
SHE'S OTOWA MOEMATSU, THE HOME ECONOMICS TEACHER!! ♡♡♡

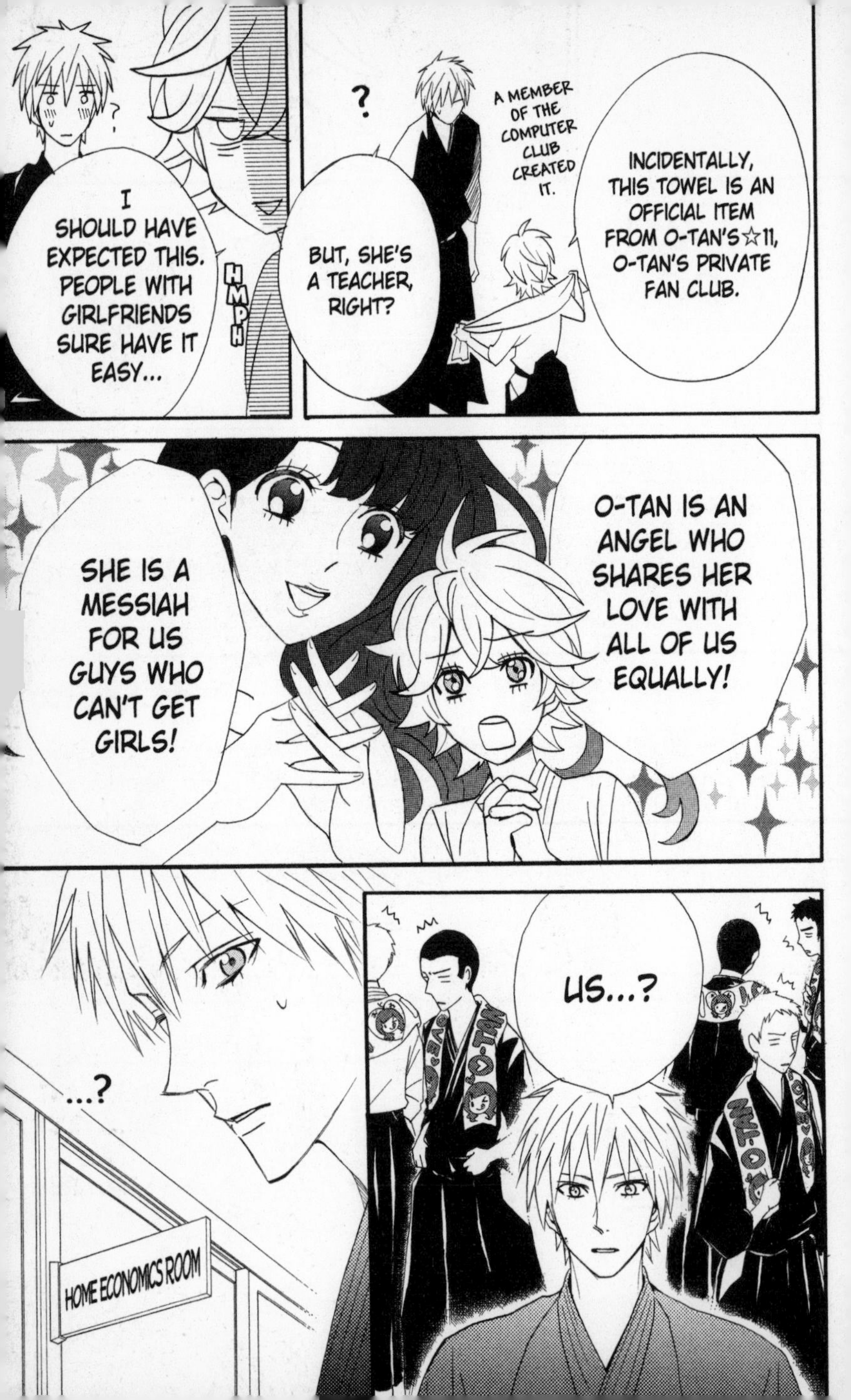
INCIDENTALLY, THIS TOWEL IS AN OFFICIAL ITEM FROM O-TAN'S☆11, O-TAN'S PRIVATE FAN CLUB.
A MEMBER OF THE COMPUTER CLUB CREATED IT.
?
BUT, SHE'S A TEACHER, RIGHT?
HMPH
I SHOULD HAVE EXPECTED THIS. PEOPLE WITH GIRLFRIENDS SURE HAVE IT EASY...
?
O-TAN IS AN ANGEL WHO SHARES HER LOVE WITH ALL OF US EQUALLY!
SHE IS A MESSIAH FOR US GUYS WHO CAN'T GET GIRLS!
US...?
...?
HOME ECONOMICS ROOM

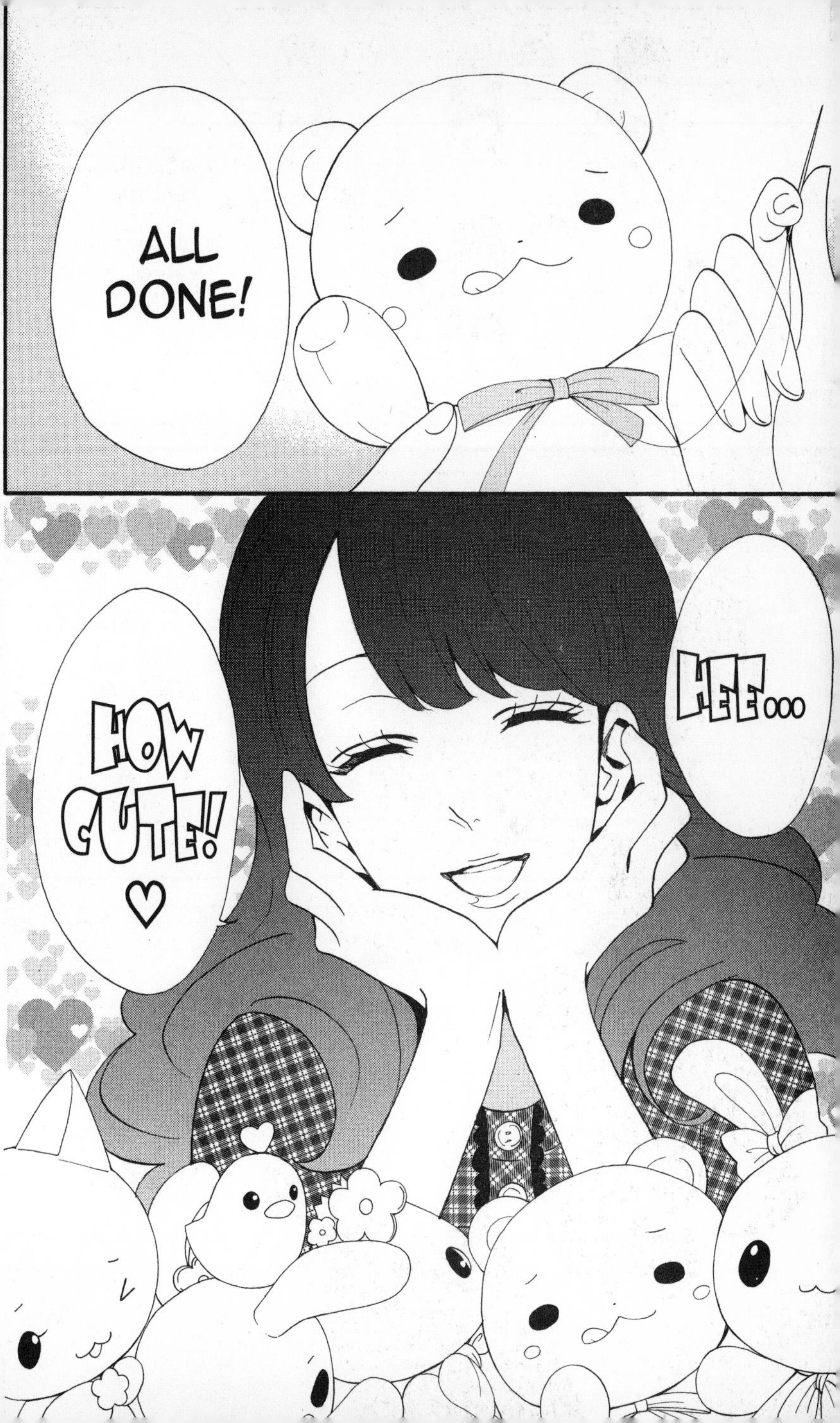
ALL DONE!
HEE...
HOW CUTE! ♡

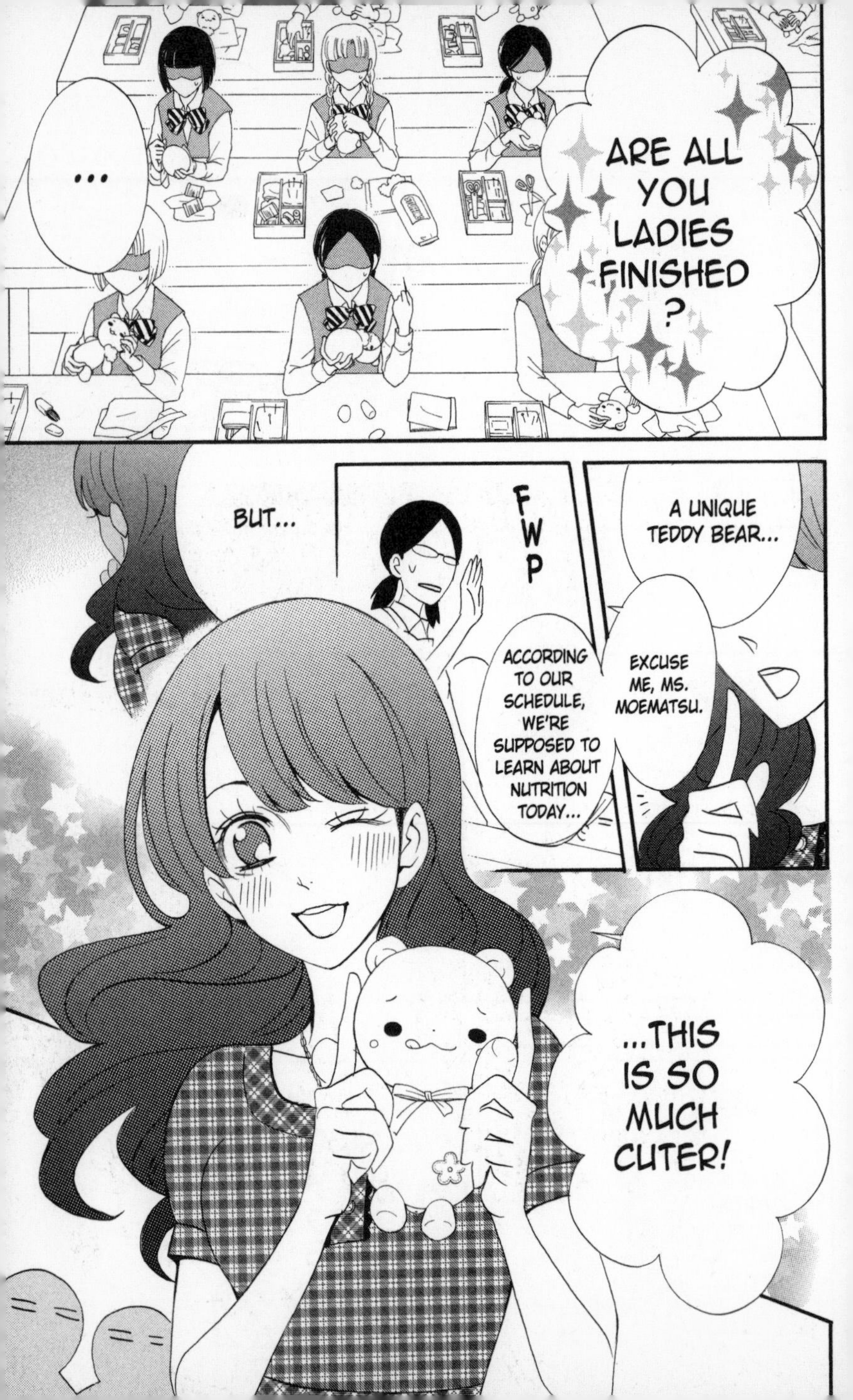
ARE ALL YOU LADIES FINISHED?
...
A UNIQUE TEDDY BEAR...
EXCUSE ME, MS. MOEMATSU.
FWP
ACCORDING TO OUR SCHEDULE, WE'RE SUPPOSED TO LEARN ABOUT NUTRITION TODAY...
BUT...
...THIS IS SO MUCH CUTER!

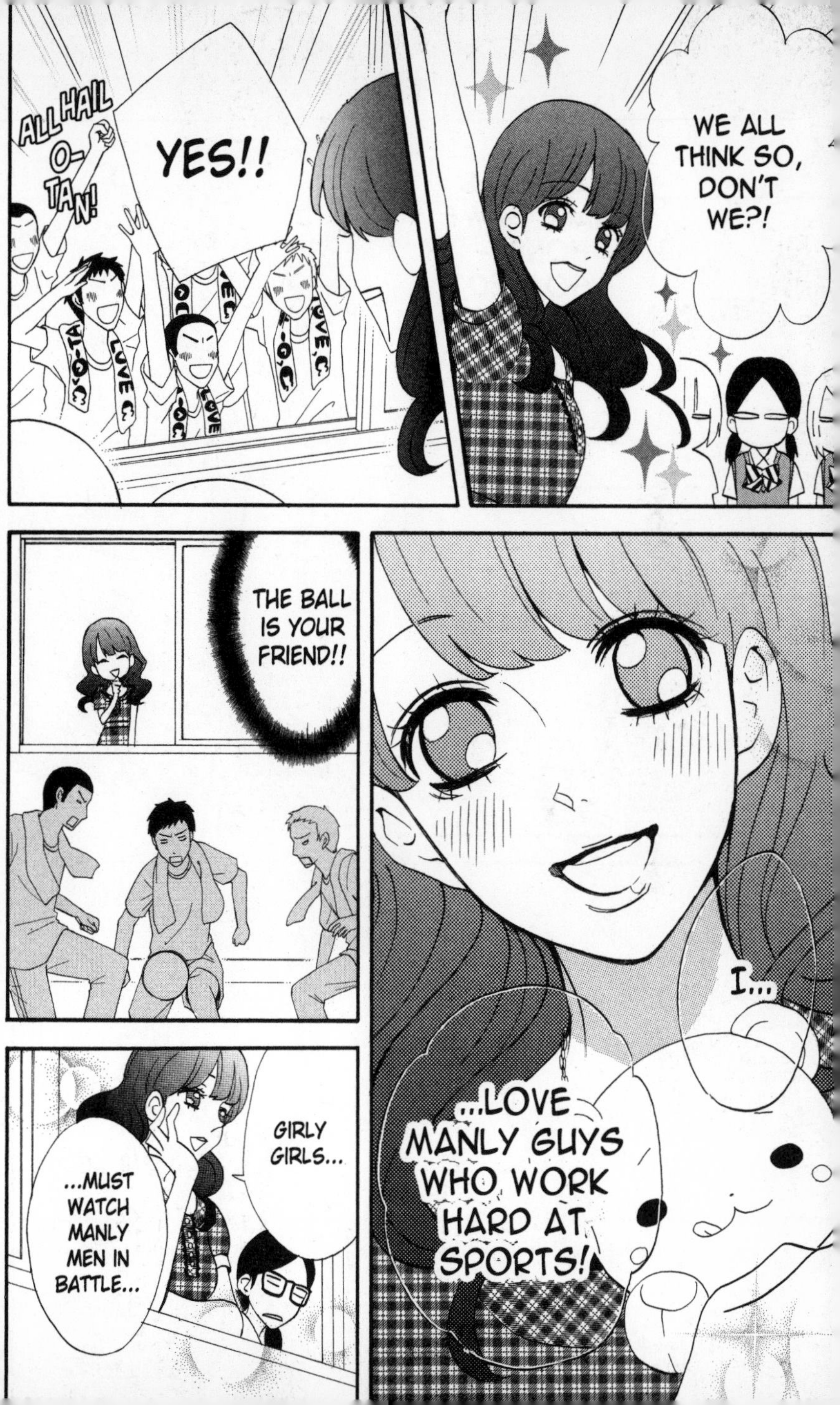
WE ALL THINK SO, DON'T WE?!
YES!!
ALL HAIL O-TAN!
I...
...LOVE MANLY GUYS WHO WORK HARD AT SPORTS!
THE BALL IS YOUR FRIEND!!
GIRLY GIRLS...
...MUST WATCH MANLY MEN IN BATTLE...

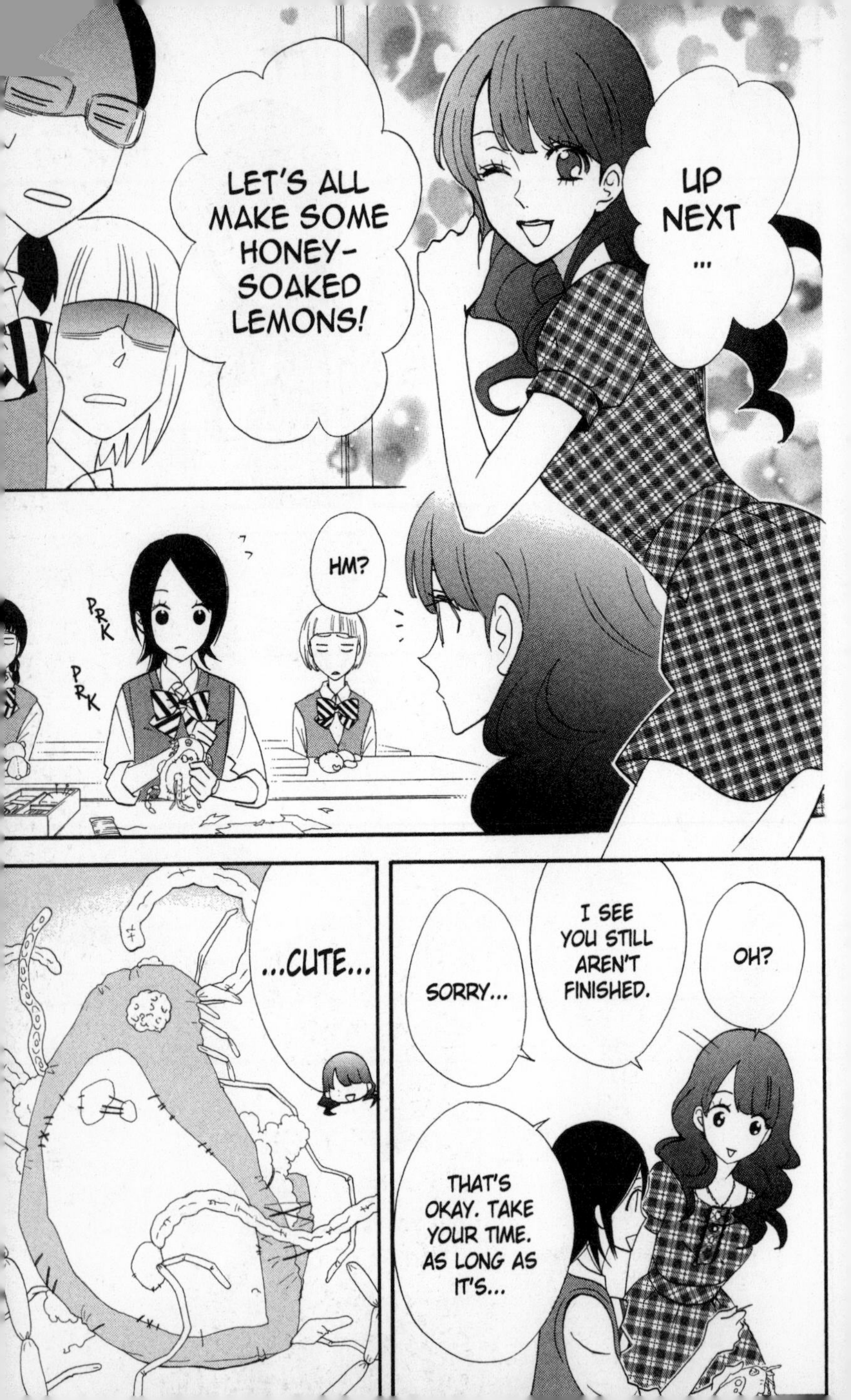
UP NEXT ...
LET'S ALL MAKE SOME HONEY-SOAKED LEMONS!
HM?
PRK PRK
OH?
I SEE YOU STILL AREN'T FINISHED.
SORRY...
THAT'S OKAY. TAKE YOUR TIME. AS LONG AS IT'S...
...CUTE...

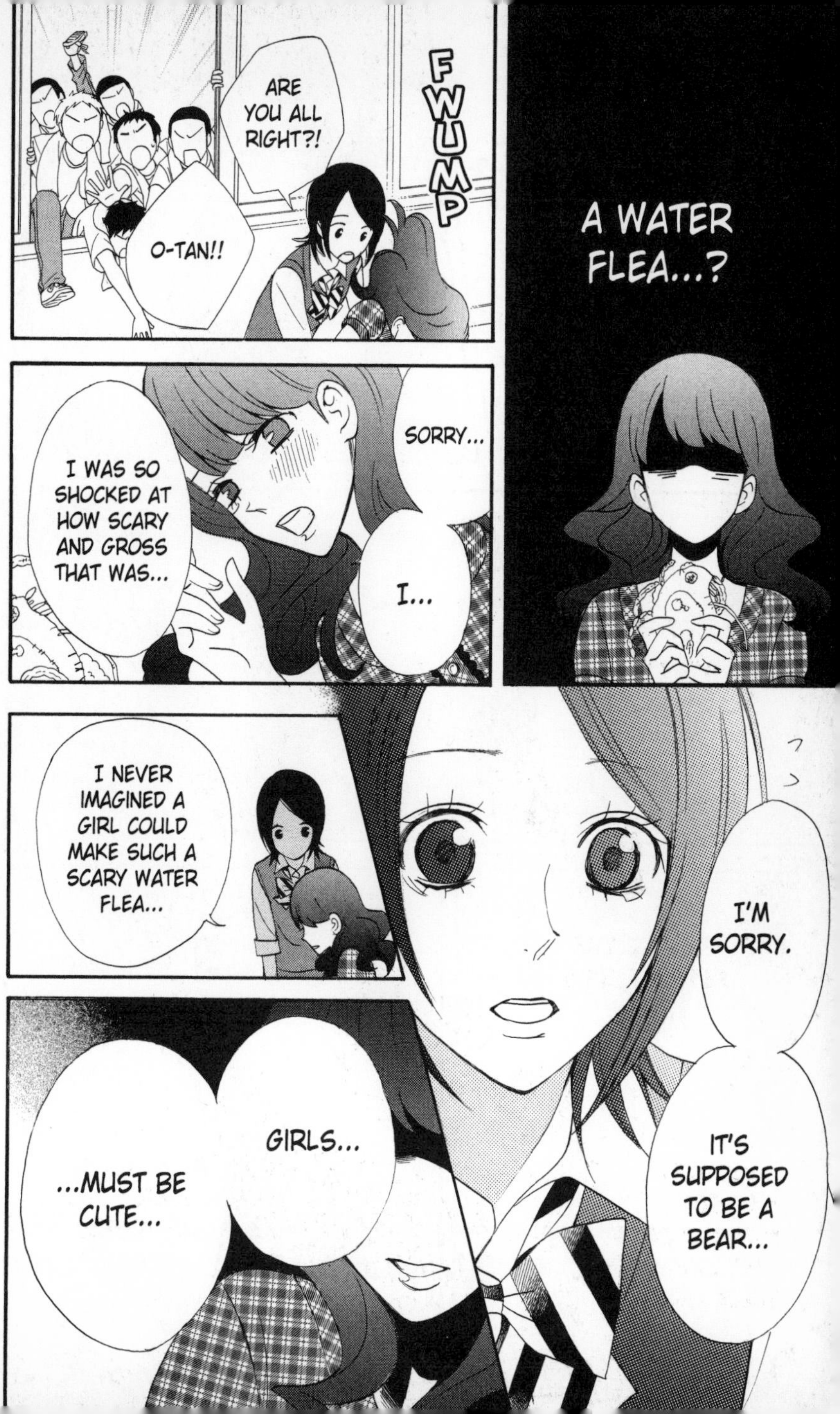
A WATER FLEA...?
FWUMP
ARE YOU ALL RIGHT?!
O-TAN!!
SORRY...
I...
I WAS SO SHOCKED AT HOW SCARY AND GROSS THAT WAS...
I'M SORRY.
IT'S SUPPOSED TO BE A BEAR...
I NEVER IMAGINED A GIRL COULD MAKE SUCH A SCARY WATER FLEA...
GIRLS...
...MUST BE CUTE...

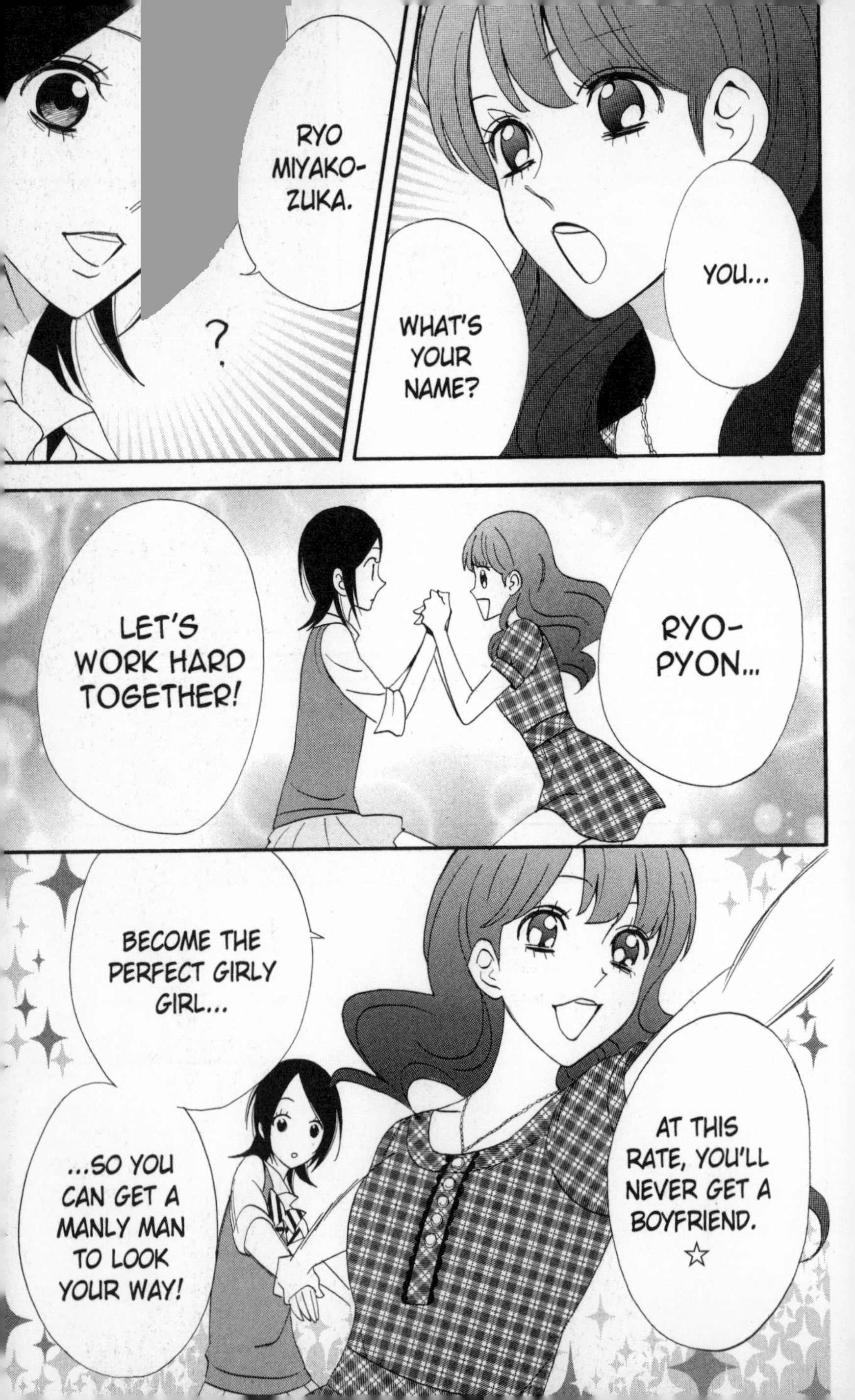
YOU...
WHAT'S YOUR NAME?
RYO MIYAKO-ZUKA.
?
RYO-PYON...
LET'S WORK HARD TOGETHER!
AT THIS RATE, YOU'LL NEVER GET A BOYFRIEND. ☆
BECOME THE PERFECT GIRLY GIRL...
...SO YOU CAN GET A MANLY MAN TO LOOK YOUR WAY!

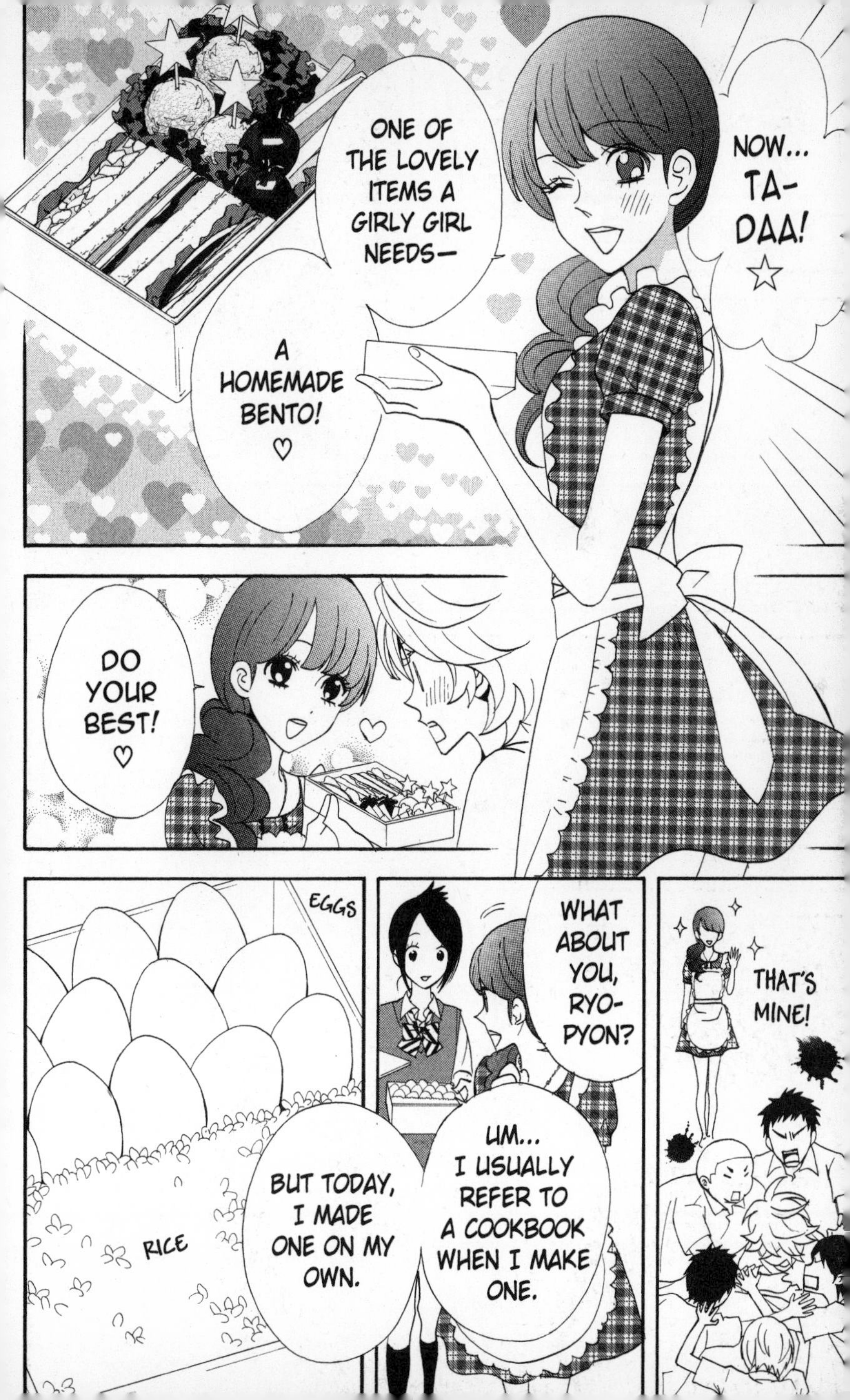
NOW... TA-DAA! ☆
ONE OF THE LOVELY ITEMS A GIRLY GIRL NEEDS—
A HOMEMADE BENTO! ♡
DO YOUR BEST! ♡
THAT'S MINE!
WHAT ABOUT YOU, RYO-PYON?
UM... I USUALLY REFER TO A COOKBOOK WHEN I MAKE ONE.
BUT TODAY, I MADE ONE ON MY OWN.
EGGS
RICE

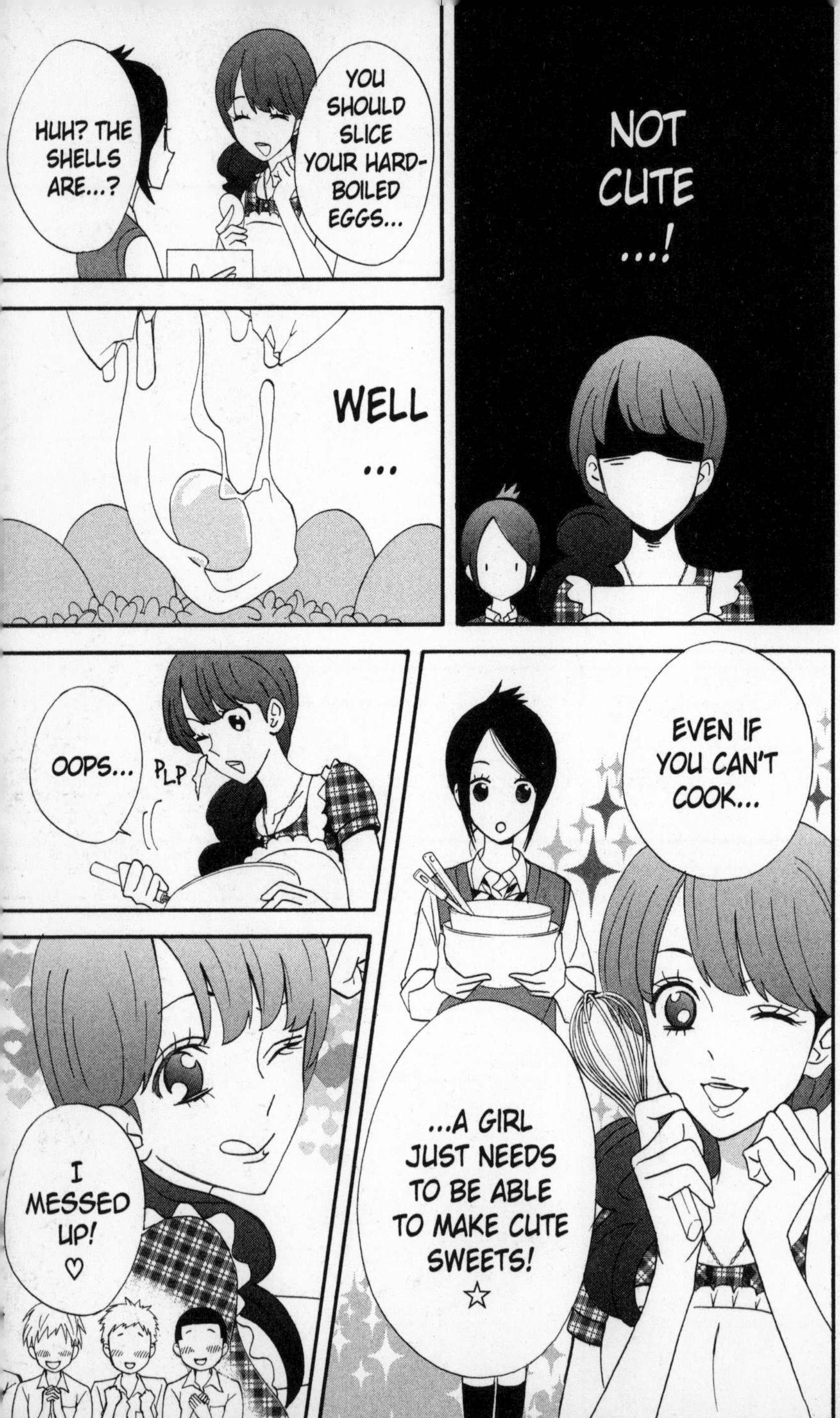
NOT CUTE ...!
YOU SHOULD SLICE YOUR HARD-BOILED EGGS...
HUH? THE SHELLS ARE...?
WELL ...
EVEN IF YOU CAN'T COOK...
...A GIRL JUST NEEDS TO BE ABLE TO MAKE CUTE SWEETS! ☆
OOPS...
PLP
I MESSED UP! ♡

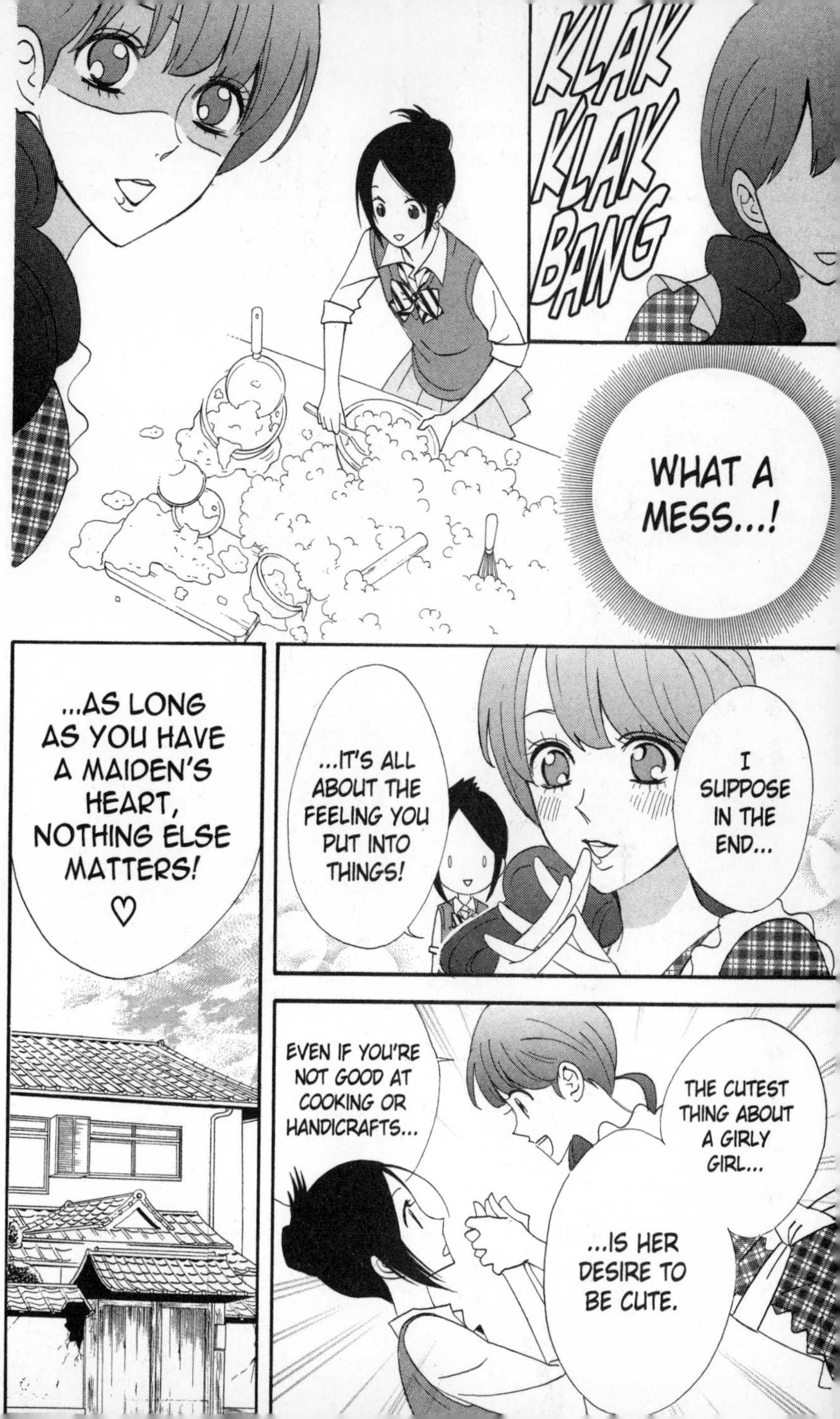
KLAK KLAK BANG
WHAT A MESS...!
I SUPPOSE IN THE END...
...IT'S ALL ABOUT THE FEELING YOU PUT INTO THINGS!
THE CUTEST THING ABOUT A GIRLY GIRL...
...IS HER DESIRE TO BE CUTE.
EVEN IF YOU'RE NOT GOOD AT COOKING OR HANDICRAFTS...
...AS LONG AS YOU HAVE A MAIDEN'S HEART, NOTHING ELSE MATTERS! ♡

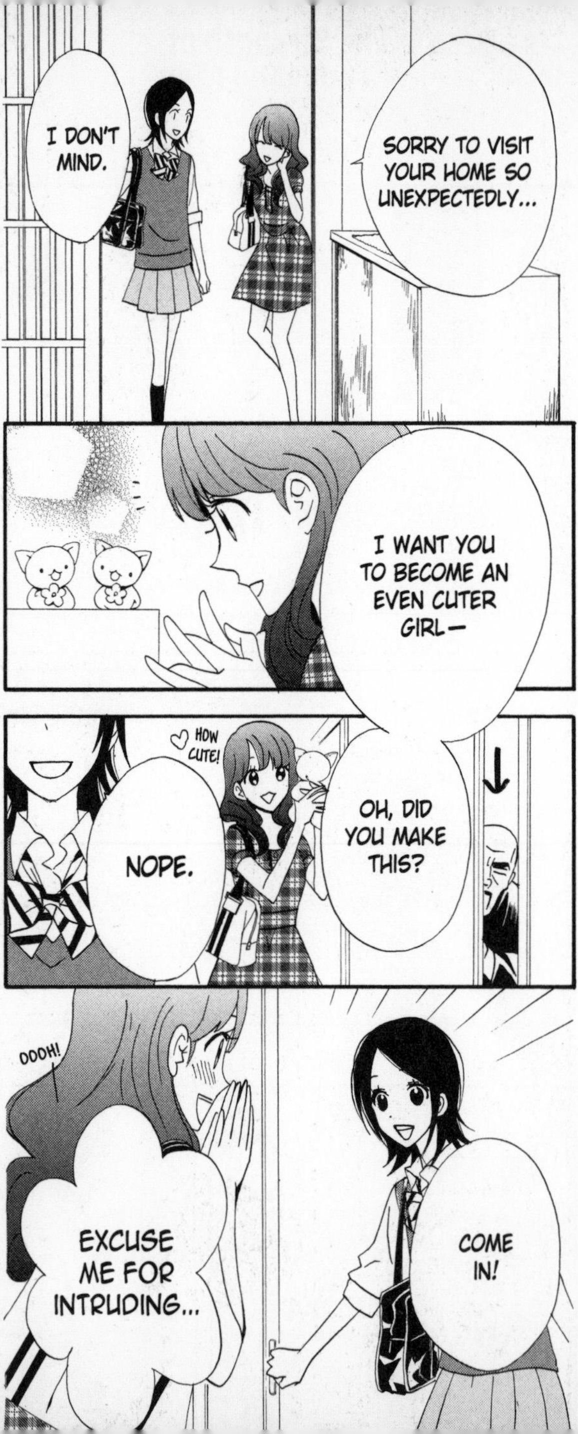
SORRY TO VISIT YOUR HOME SO UNEXPECTEDLY...
I DON'T MIND.
I WANT YOU TO BECOME AN EVEN CUTER GIRL—
OH, DID YOU MAKE THIS?
HOW CUTE!
NOPE.
COME IN!
OOOH!
EXCUSE ME FOR INTRUDING...

Production Assistance

Shimada-san
Takowa-san
Kuwana-san
Kaneko-san
Tanaka-san
Nakazawa-san
Sakurai-san
Kawashima-san
Sayaka-san
Yoneyan
Nishizawa-san

Special Thanks:

Abe-san
All the Readers

Thank you for reading.
It'd be great to see you in the next volume.

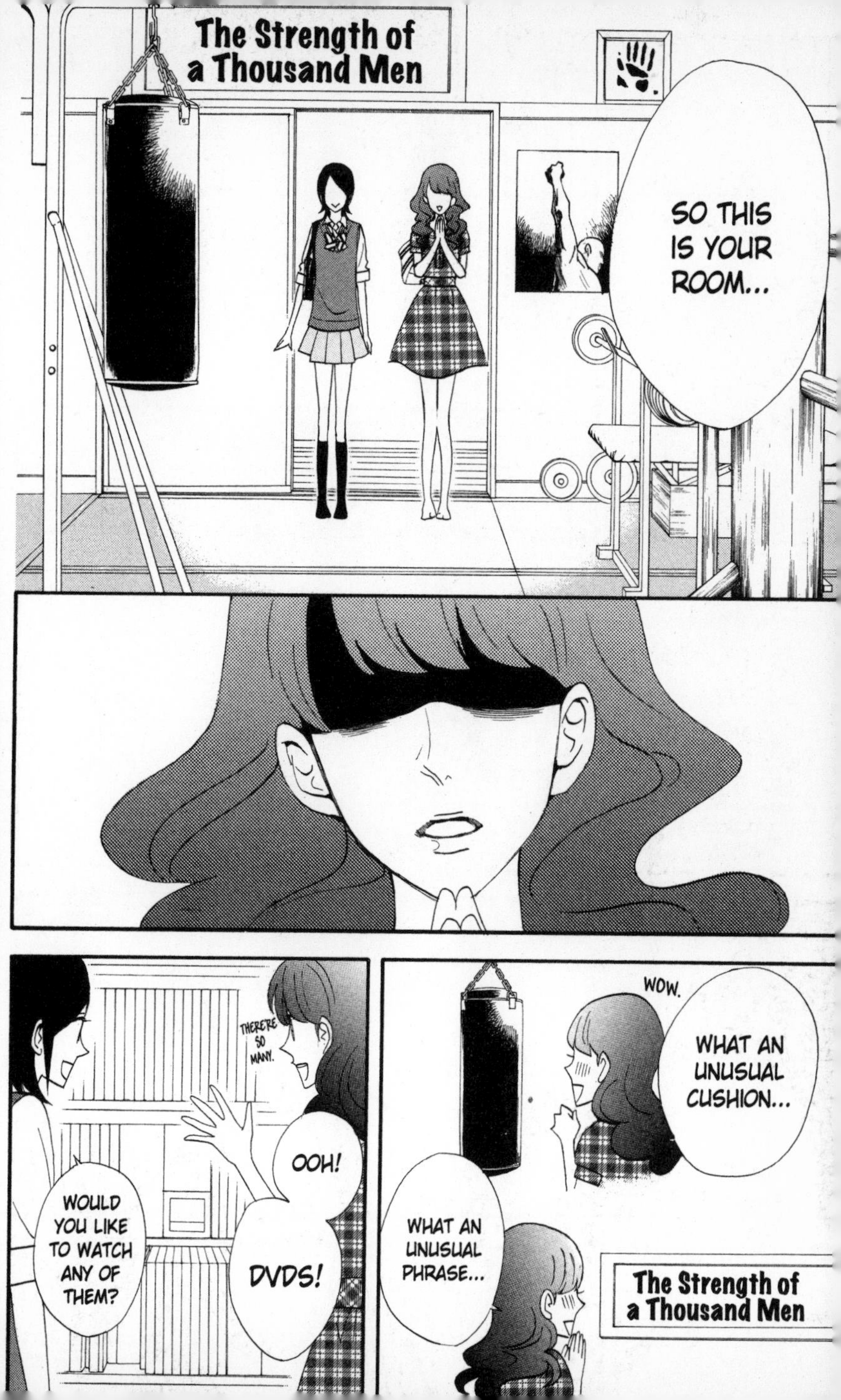
The Strength of a Thousand Men
SO THIS IS YOUR ROOM...
WOW.
WHAT AN UNUSUAL CUSHION...
WHAT AN UNUSUAL PHRASE...
The Strength of a Thousand Men
THERE'RE SO MANY.
OOH!
DVDS!
WOULD YOU LIKE TO WATCH ANY OF THEM?

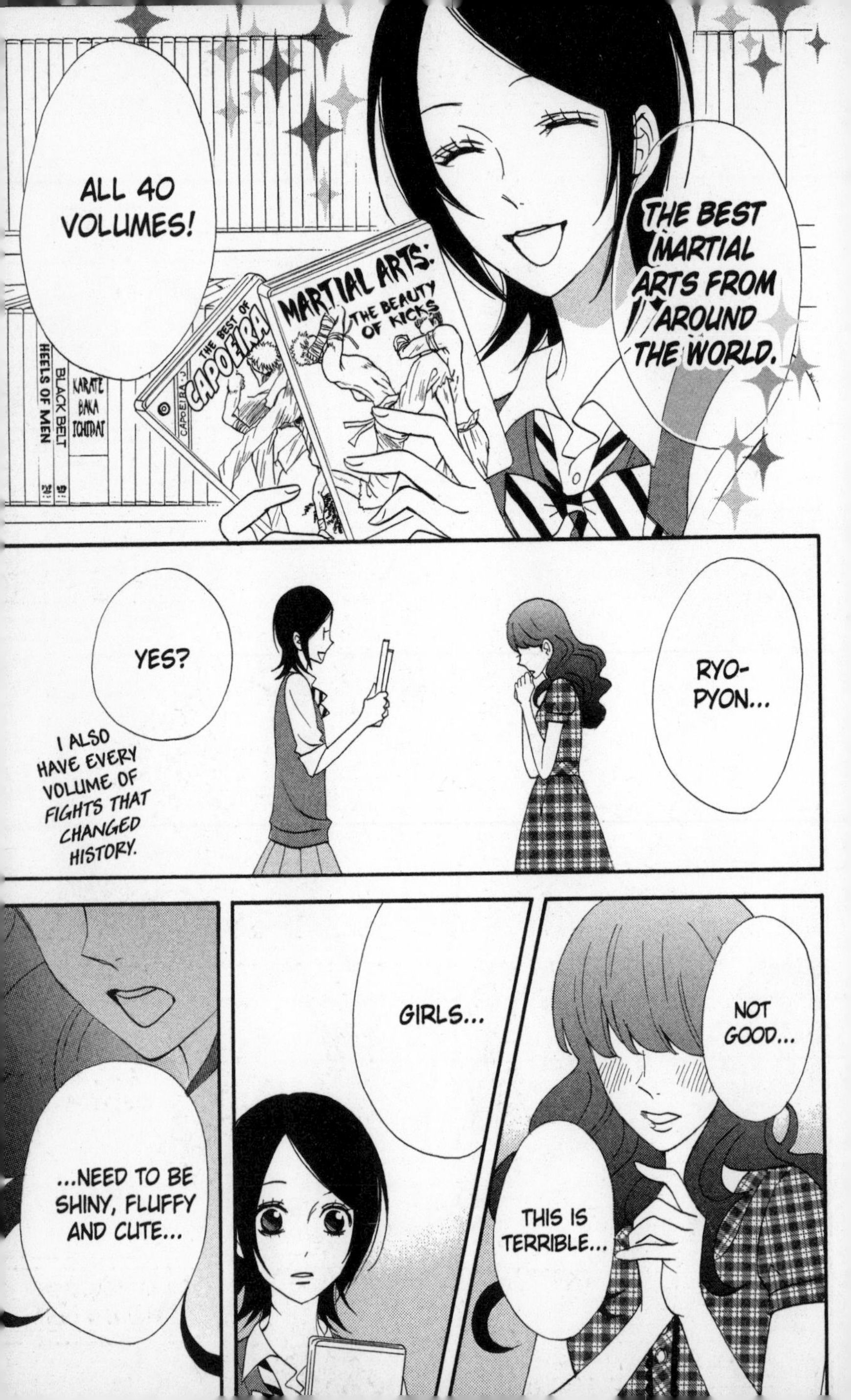
THE BEST MARTIAL ARTS FROM AROUND THE WORLD.
MARTIAL ARTS: THE BEAUTY OF KICKS
THE BEST OF CAPOEIRA
CAPOEIRA
KARATE BAKA ICHIDAI
BLACK BELT
HEELS OF MEN
ALL 40 VOLUMES!
RYO-PYON...
YES?
I ALSO HAVE EVERY VOLUME OF FIGHTS THAT CHANGED HISTORY.
NOT GOOD...
THIS IS TERRIBLE...
GIRLS...
...NEED TO BE SHINY, FLUFFY AND CUTE...

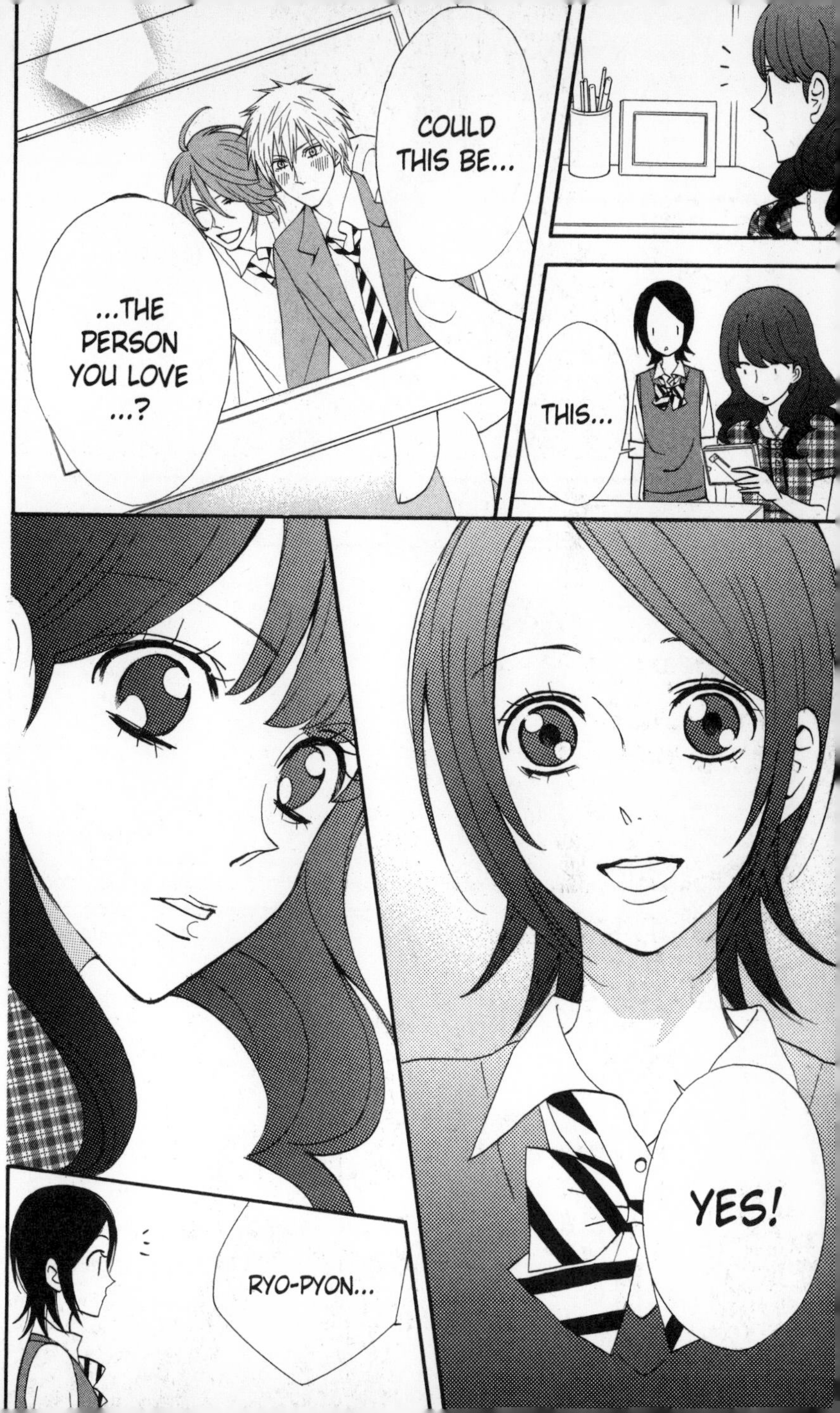
THIS...
COULD THIS BE...
...THE PERSON YOU LOVE ...?
YES!
RYO-PYON...

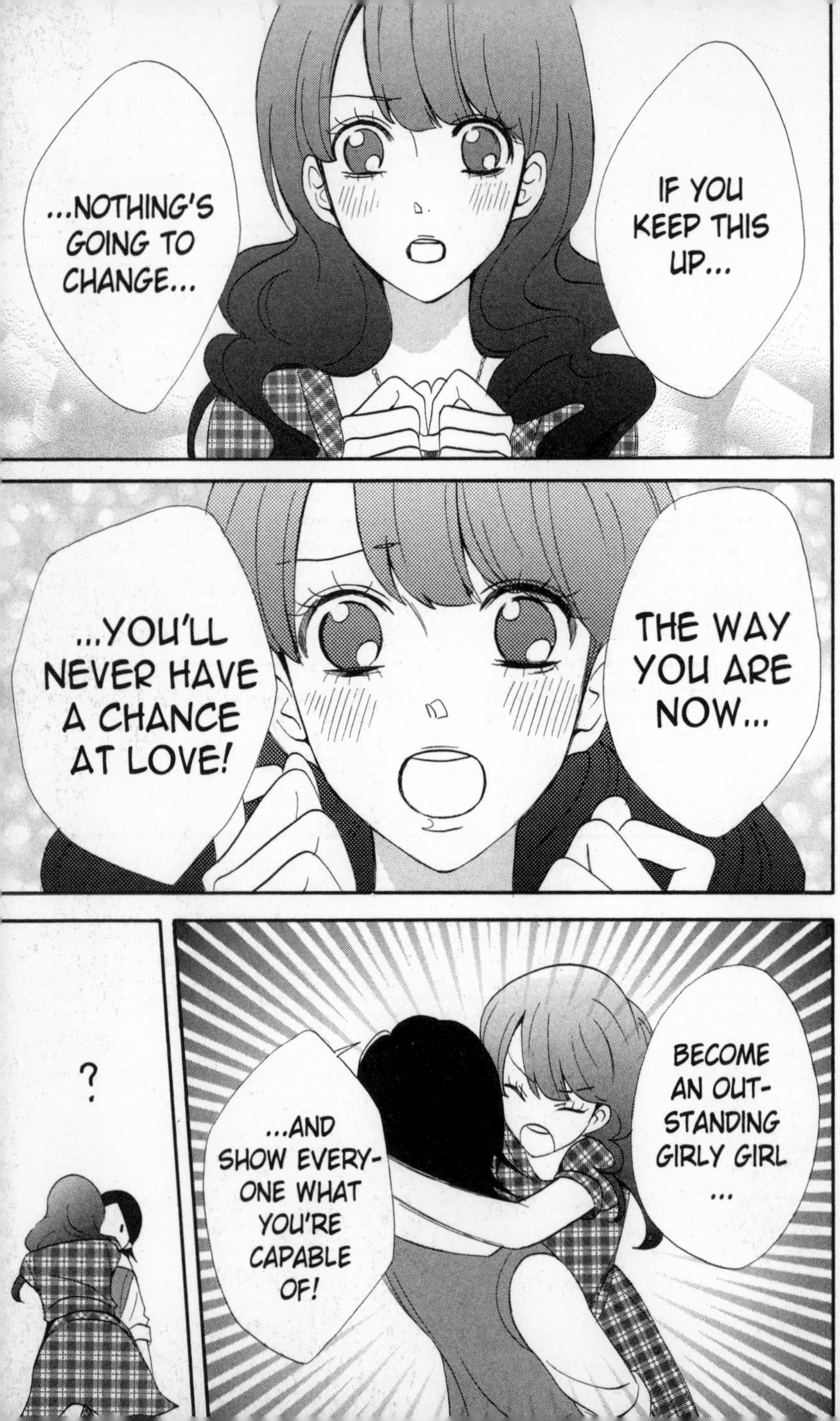
IF YOU KEEP THIS UP...
...NOTHING'S GOING TO CHANGE...
THE WAY YOU ARE NOW...
...YOU'LL NEVER HAVE A CHANCE AT LOVE!
BECOME AN OUT-STANDING GIRLY GIRL ...
...AND SHOW EVERY-ONE WHAT YOU'RE CAPABLE OF!
?

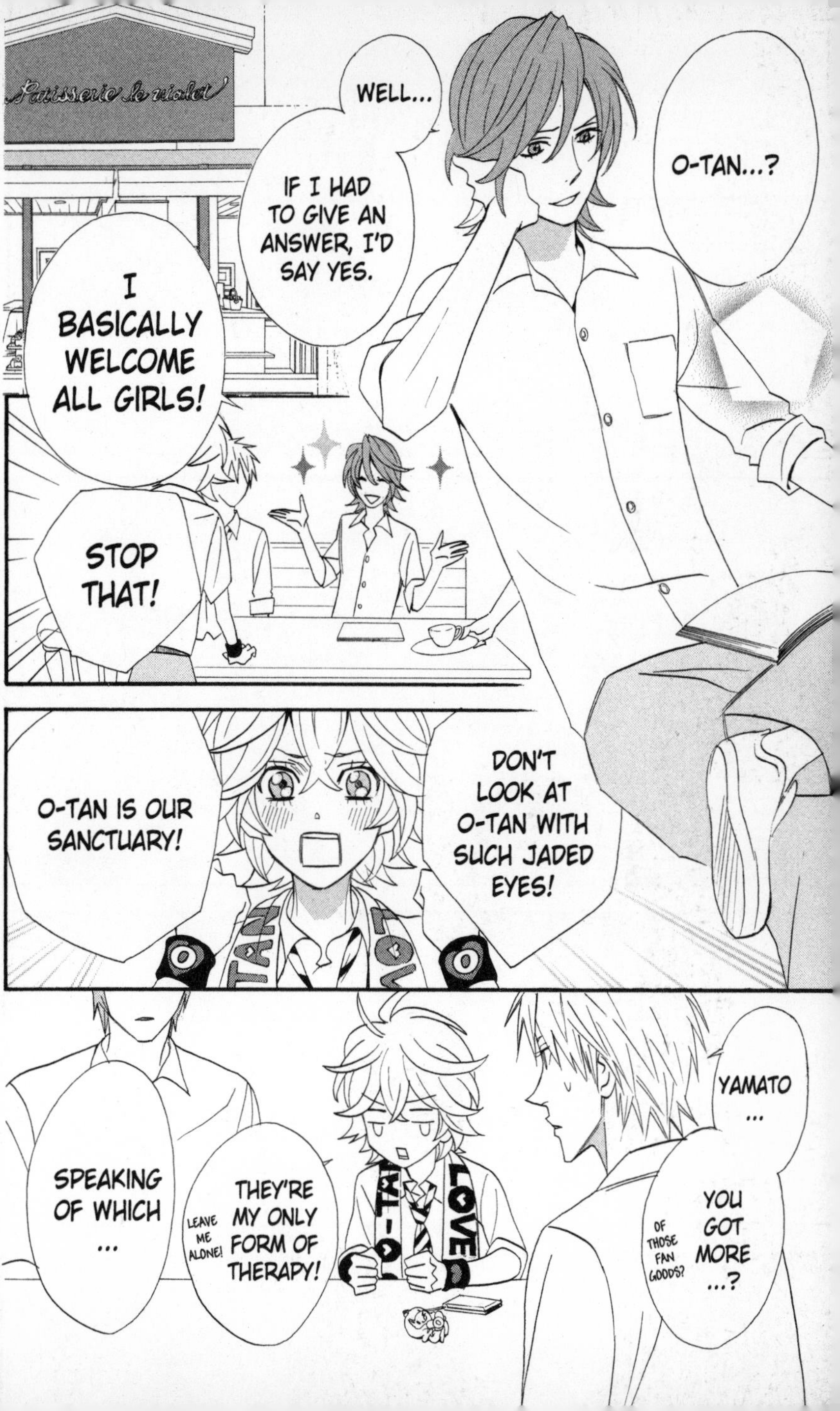
O-TAN...?
WELL...
IF I HAD TO GIVE AN ANSWER, I'D SAY YES.
Patisserie le violet
I BASICALLY WELCOME ALL GIRLS!
STOP THAT!
DON'T LOOK AT O-TAN WITH SUCH JADED EYES!
O-TAN IS OUR SANCTUARY!
YAMATO...
YOU GOT MORE...?
OF THOSE FAN GOODS?
THEY'RE MY ONLY FORM OF THERAPY!
LEAVE ME ALONE!
SPEAKING OF WHICH...

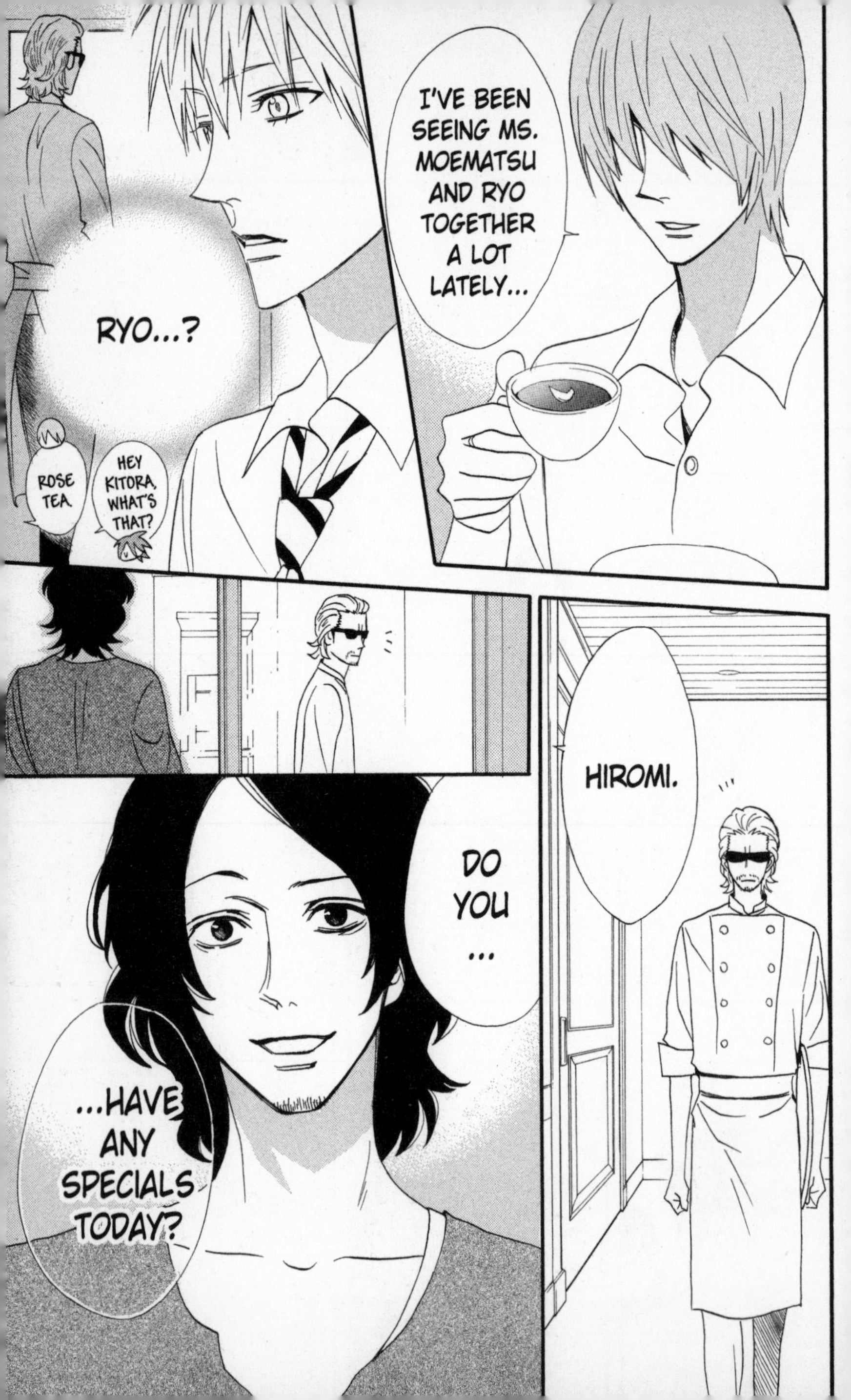
I'VE BEEN SEEING MS. MOEMATSU AND RYO TOGETHER A LOT LATELY...
RYO...?
HEY KITORA, WHAT'S THAT?
ROSE TEA.
HIROMI.
DO YOU ...
...HAVE ANY SPECIALS TODAY?

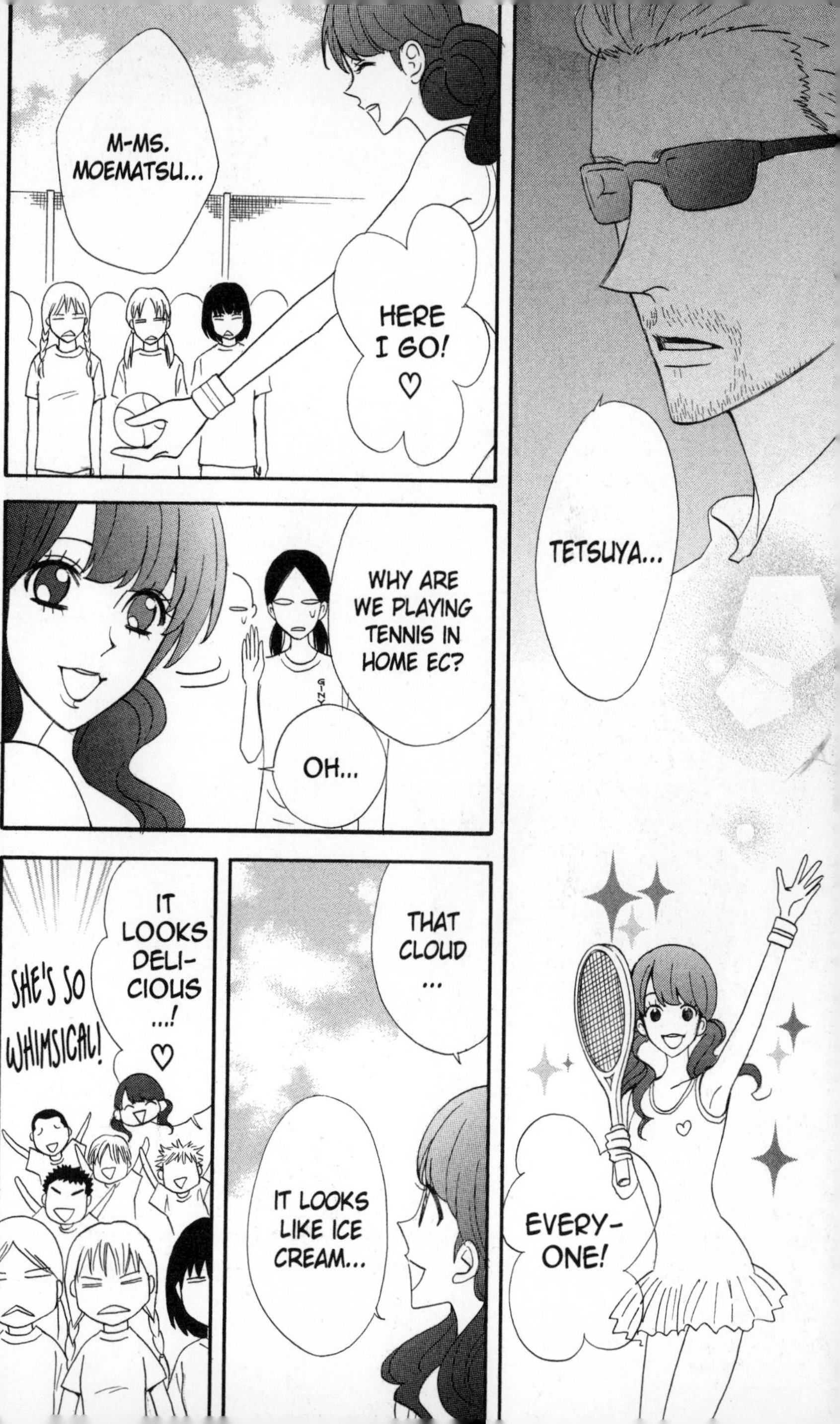
TETSUYA...
EVERY-ONE!
HERE I GO! ♥
M-MS. MOEMATSU...
WHY ARE WE PLAYING TENNIS IN HOME EC?
OH...
THAT CLOUD...
IT LOOKS LIKE ICE CREAM...
IT LOOKS DELICIOUS...! ♥
SHE'S SO WHIMSICAL!

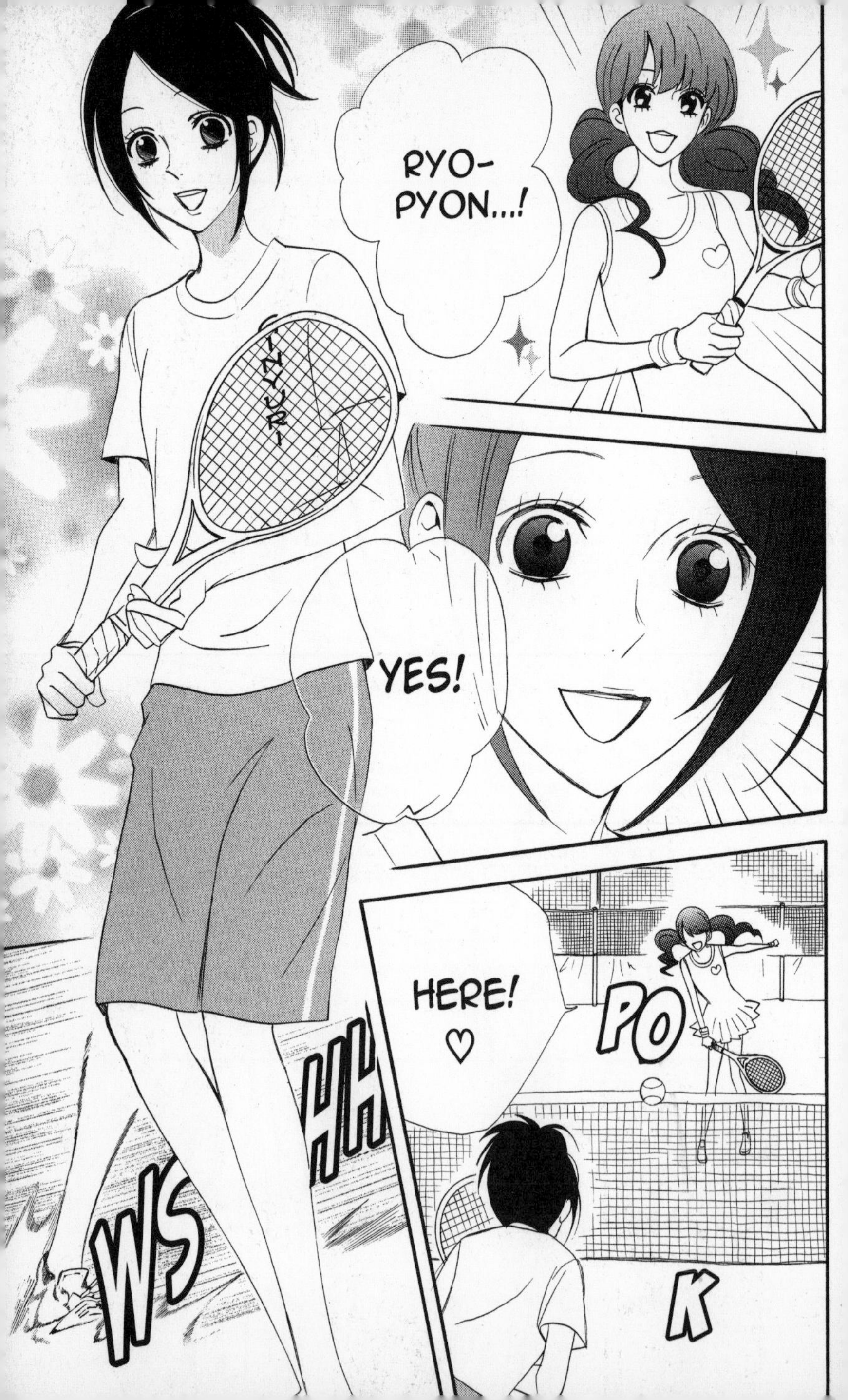
RYO-PYON...!
YES!
HERE! ♡
POK
WSHH
INYURI

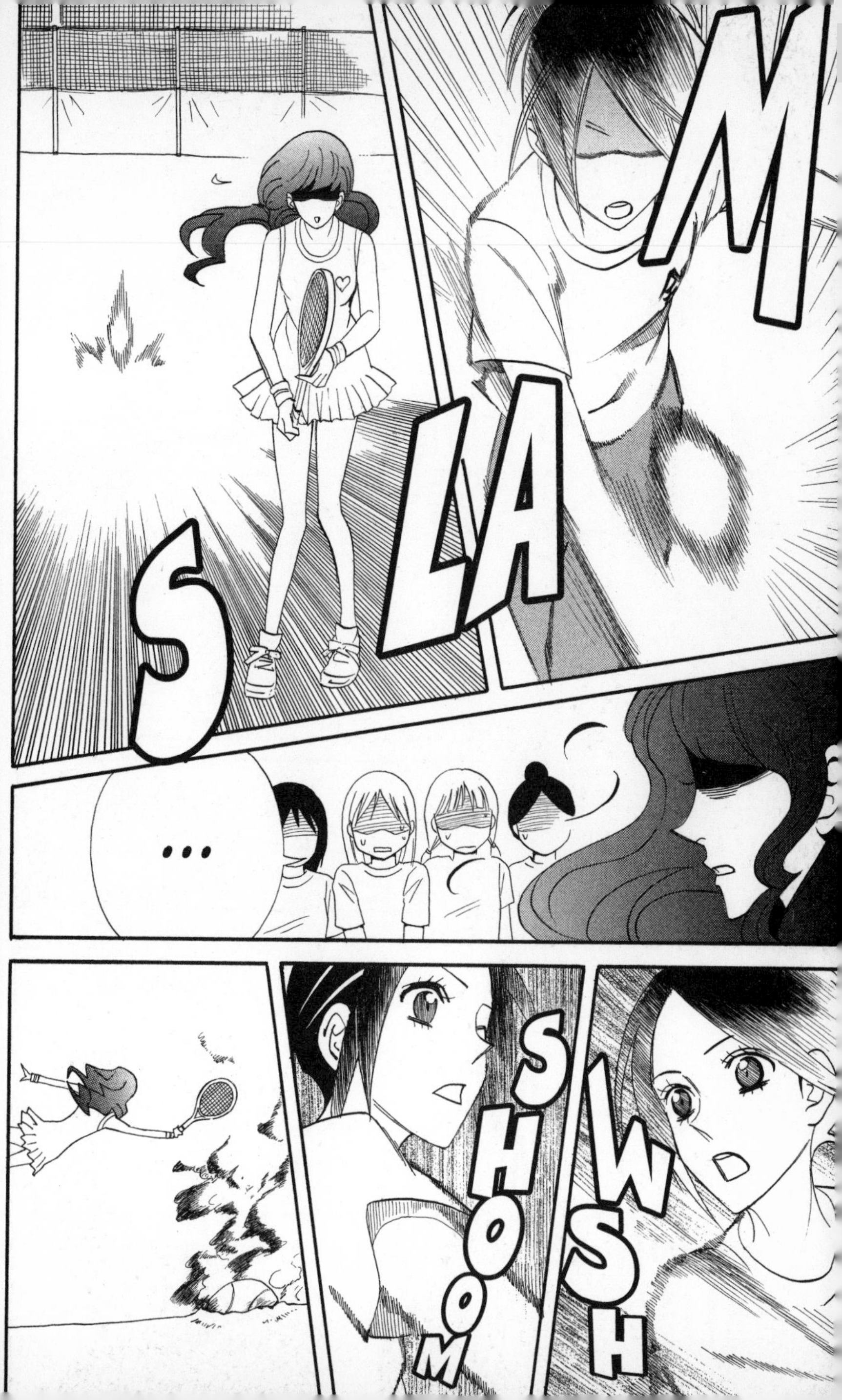

SLAM
...
WSH
SHOOOM

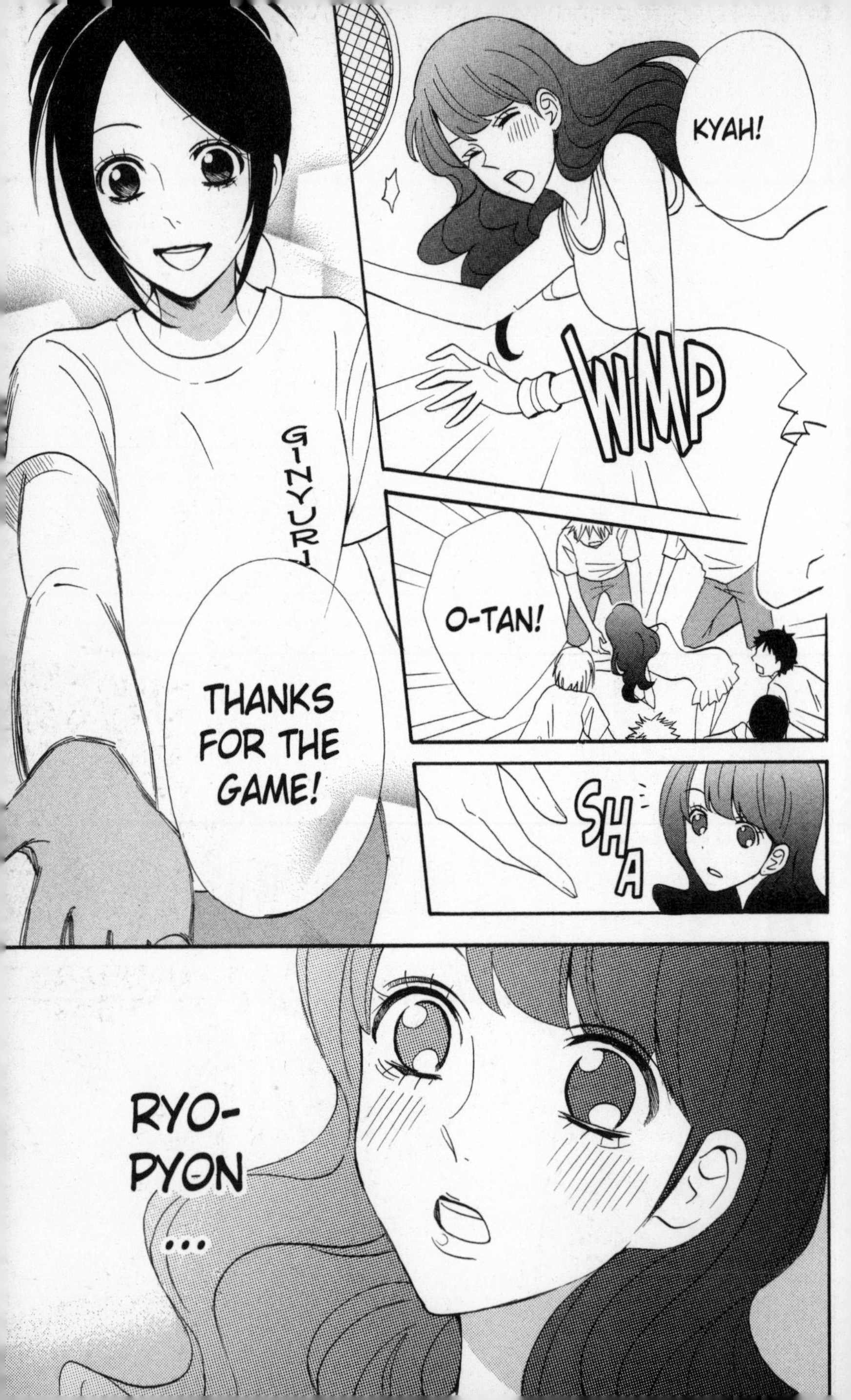
KYAH!
WMP
O-TAN!
SHA
GINYUR
THANKS FOR THE GAME!
RYO-PYON
...

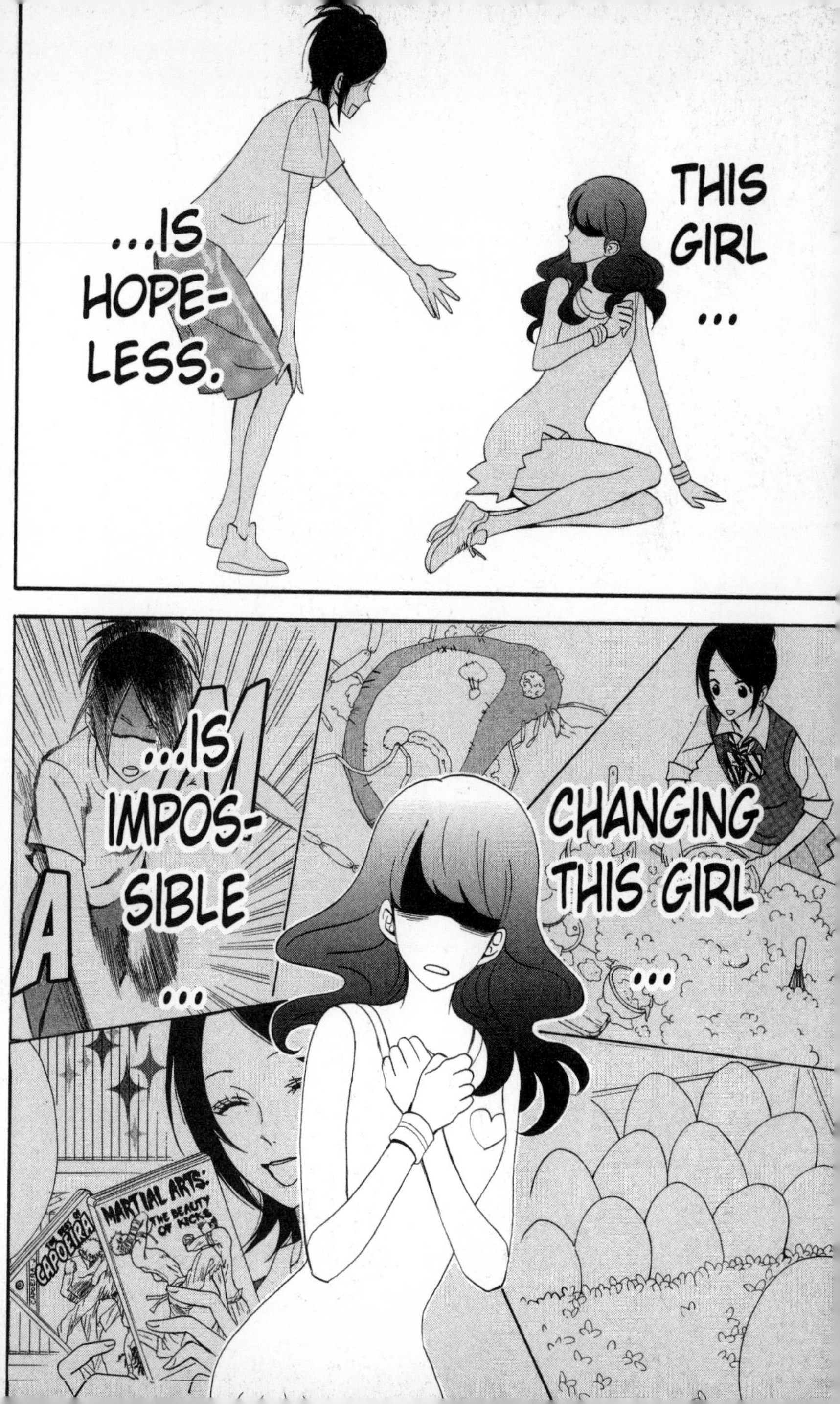
THIS GIRL ...
...IS HOPE-LESS.
CHANGING THIS GIRL ...
...IS IMPOS-SIBLE ...
MARTIAL ARTS:
THE BEAUTY OF KICKS
CAPOEIRA

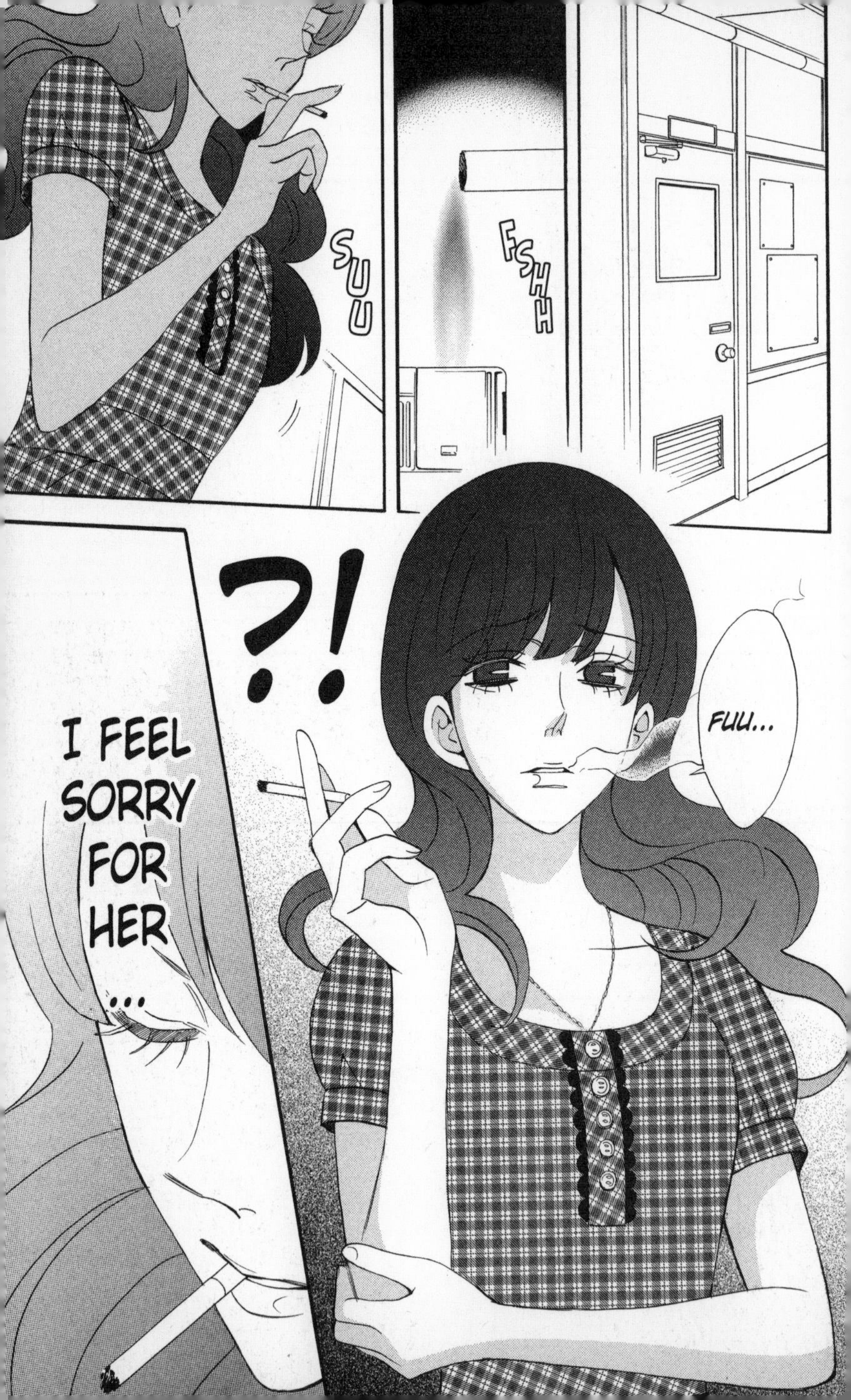
FSHH
SUUU
FUU...
?!
I FEEL SORRY FOR HER...

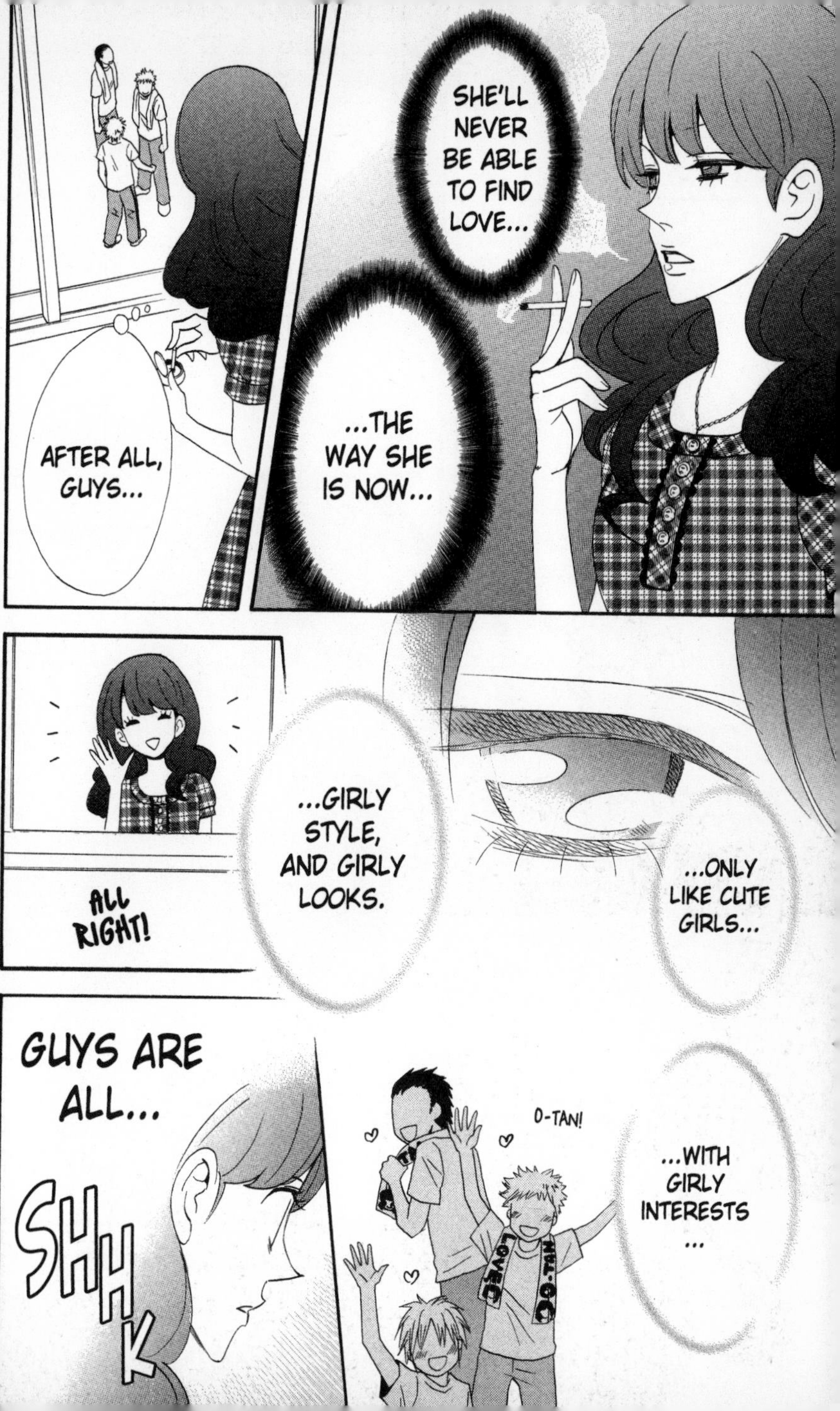
SHE'LL NEVER BE ABLE TO FIND LOVE...
...THE WAY SHE IS NOW...
AFTER ALL, GUYS...
...ONLY LIKE CUTE GIRLS...
...GIRLY STYLE, AND GIRLY LOOKS.
ALL RIGHT!
...WITH GIRLY INTERESTS ...
O-TAN!
GUYS ARE ALL...
SHHK

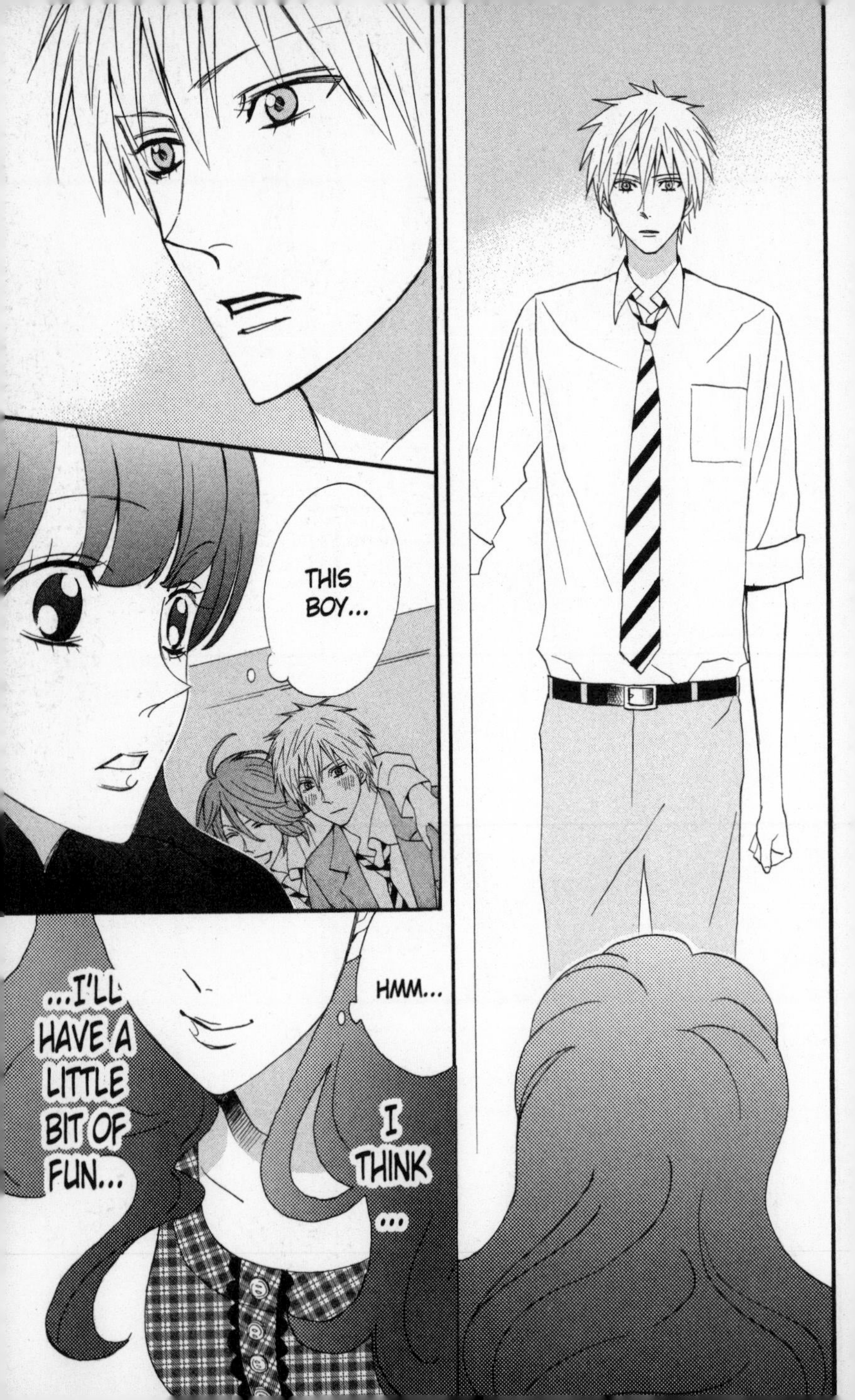
THIS BOY...
HMM...
I THINK ...
...I'LL HAVE A LITTLE BIT OF FUN...

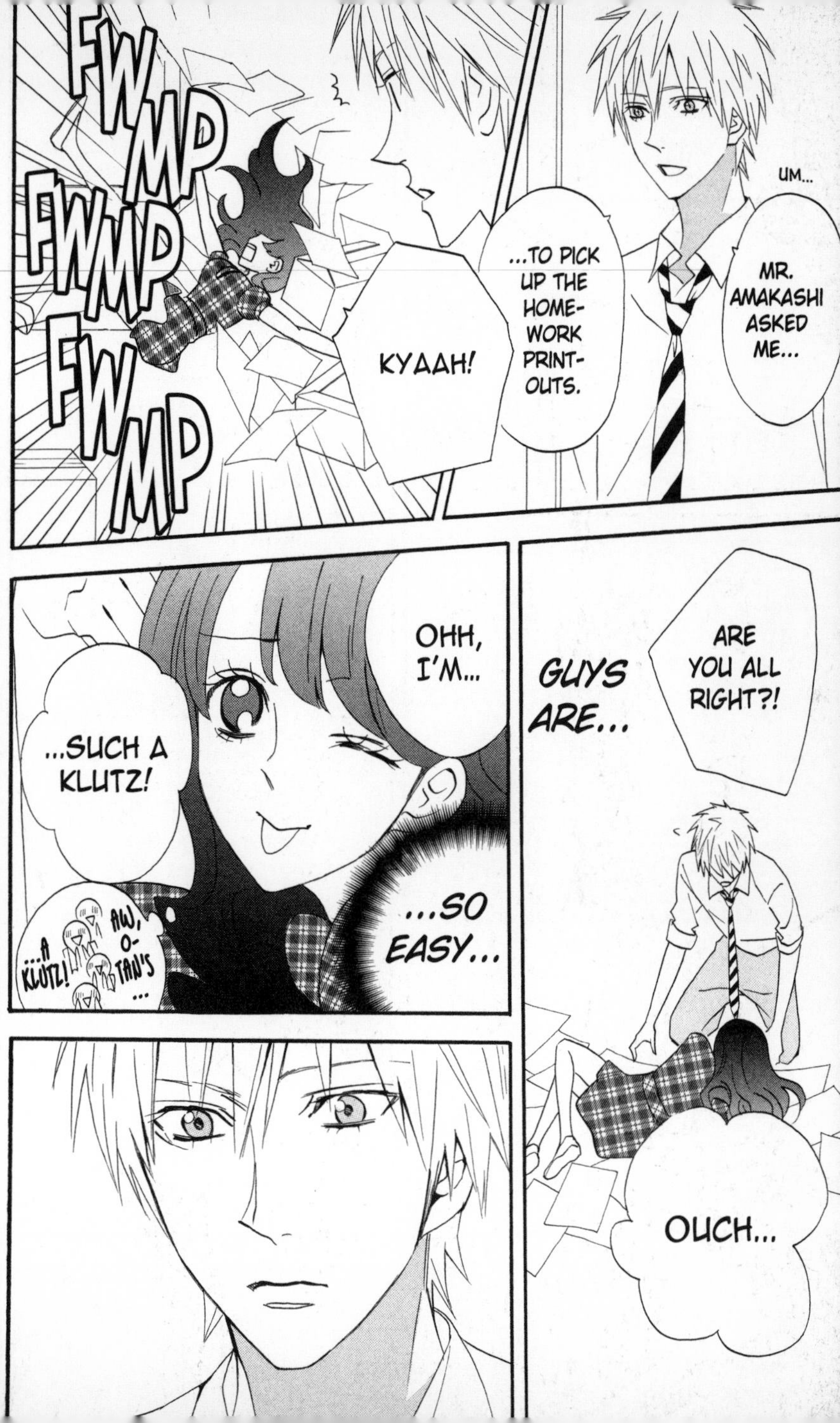
UM...
MR. AMAKASHI ASKED ME...
...TO PICK UP THE HOME-WORK PRINT-OUTS.
KYAAH!
FWMP
FWMP
FWMP
ARE YOU ALL RIGHT?!
GUYS ARE...
OUCH...
OHH, I'M...
...SUCH A KLUTZ!
...SO EASY...
AW, O-TAN'S ...
...A KLUTZ!

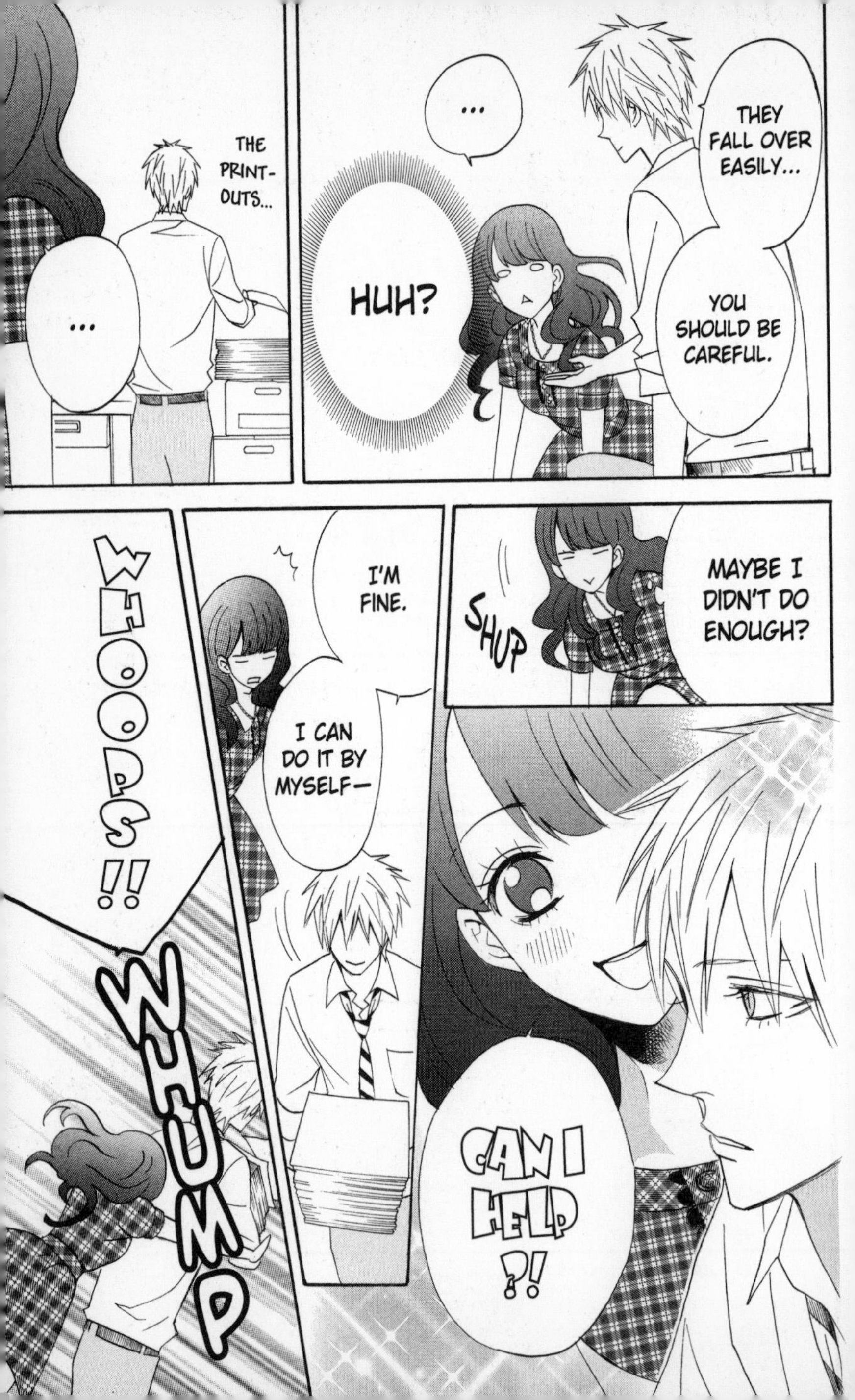
THEY FALL OVER EASILY...
...
YOU SHOULD BE CAREFUL.
HUH?
THE PRINT-OUTS...
...
MAYBE I DIDN'T DO ENOUGH?
SHUP
CAN I HELP?!
I'M FINE.
I CAN DO IT BY MYSELF—
WHOOPS!!
WHUMP

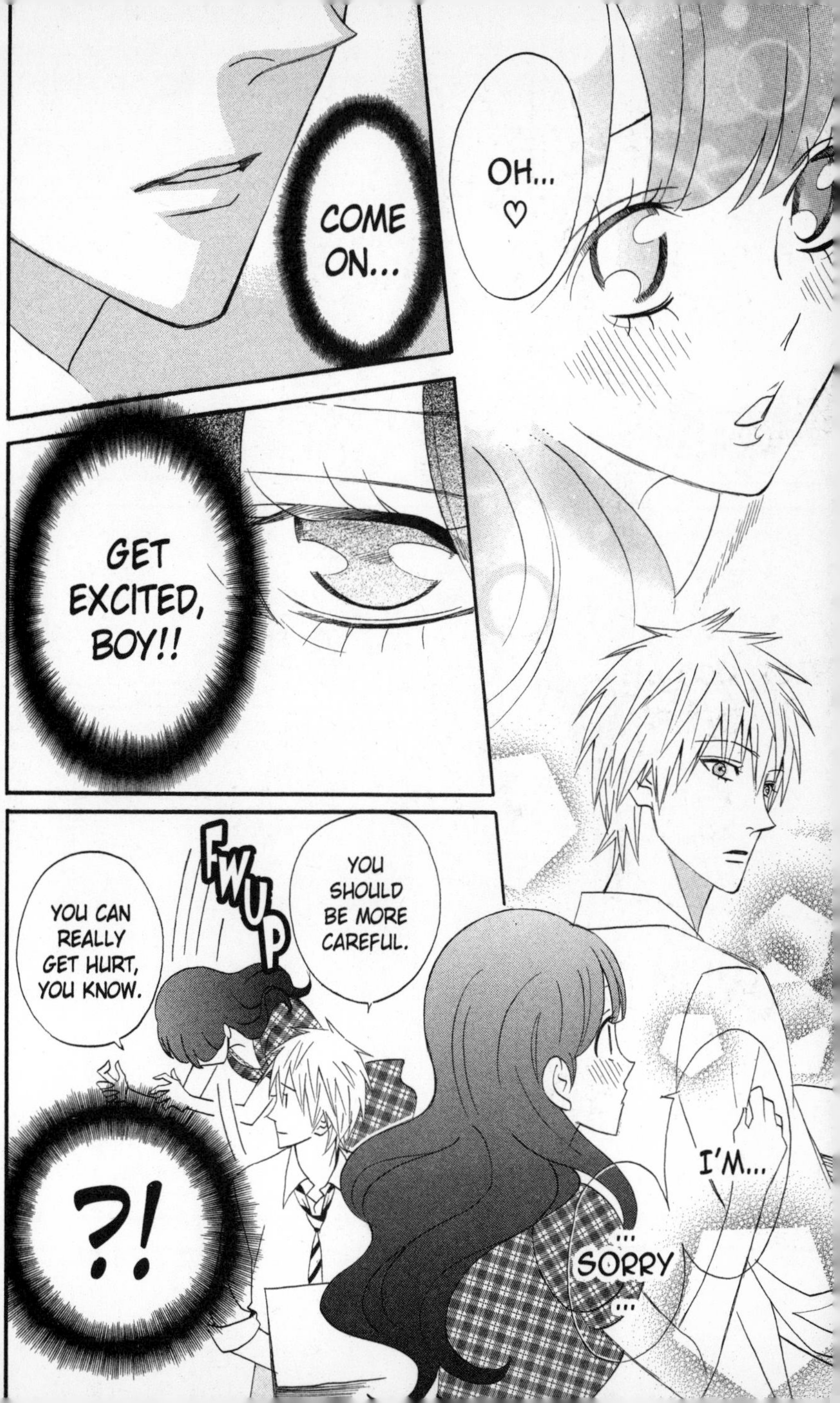
OH... ♡
I'M...
... SORRY ...
COME ON...
GET EXCITED, BOY!!
YOU SHOULD BE MORE CAREFUL.
FWUP
YOU CAN REALLY GET HURT, YOU KNOW.
?!

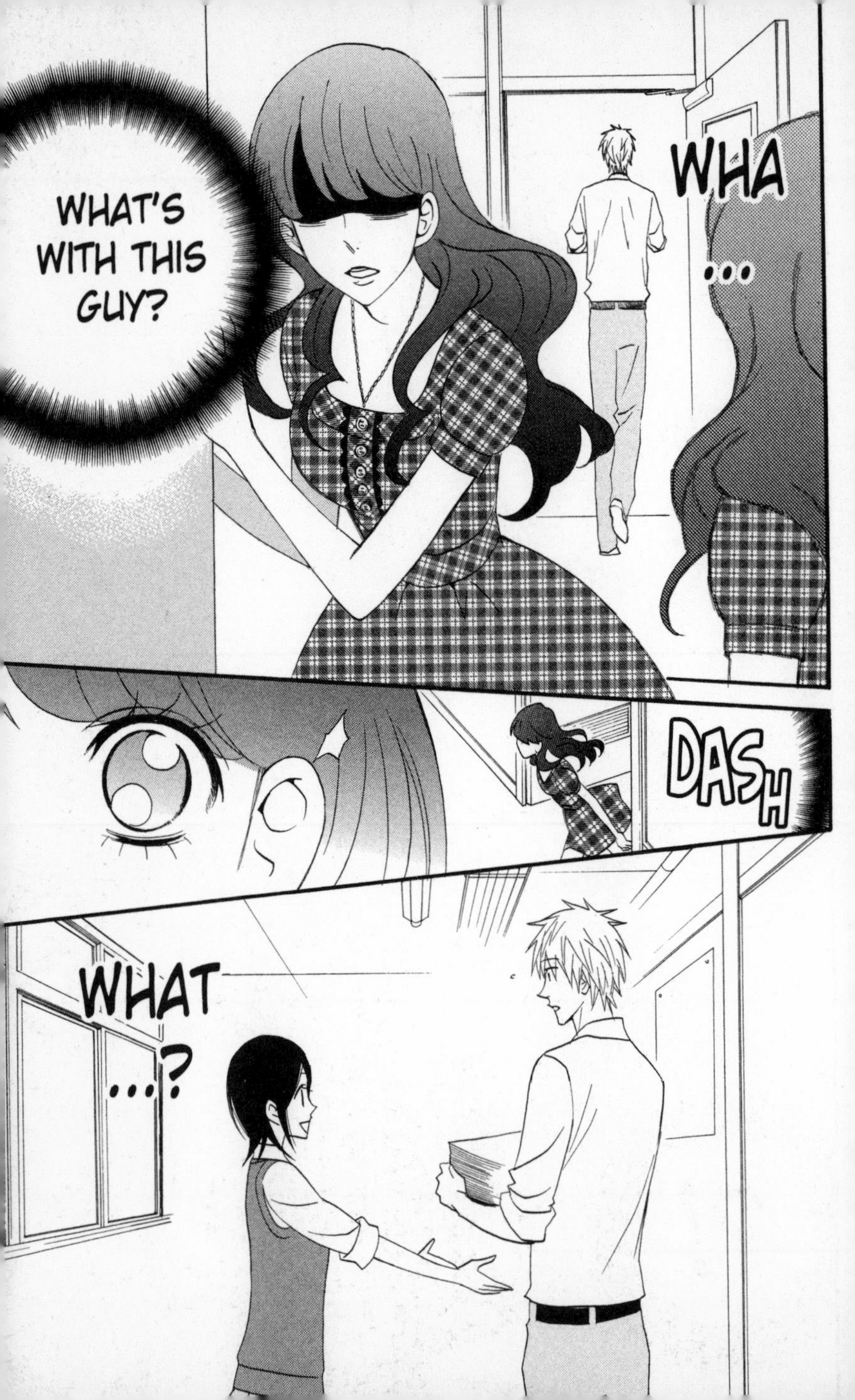
WHA...
WHAT'S WITH THIS GUY?
DASH
WHAT...?

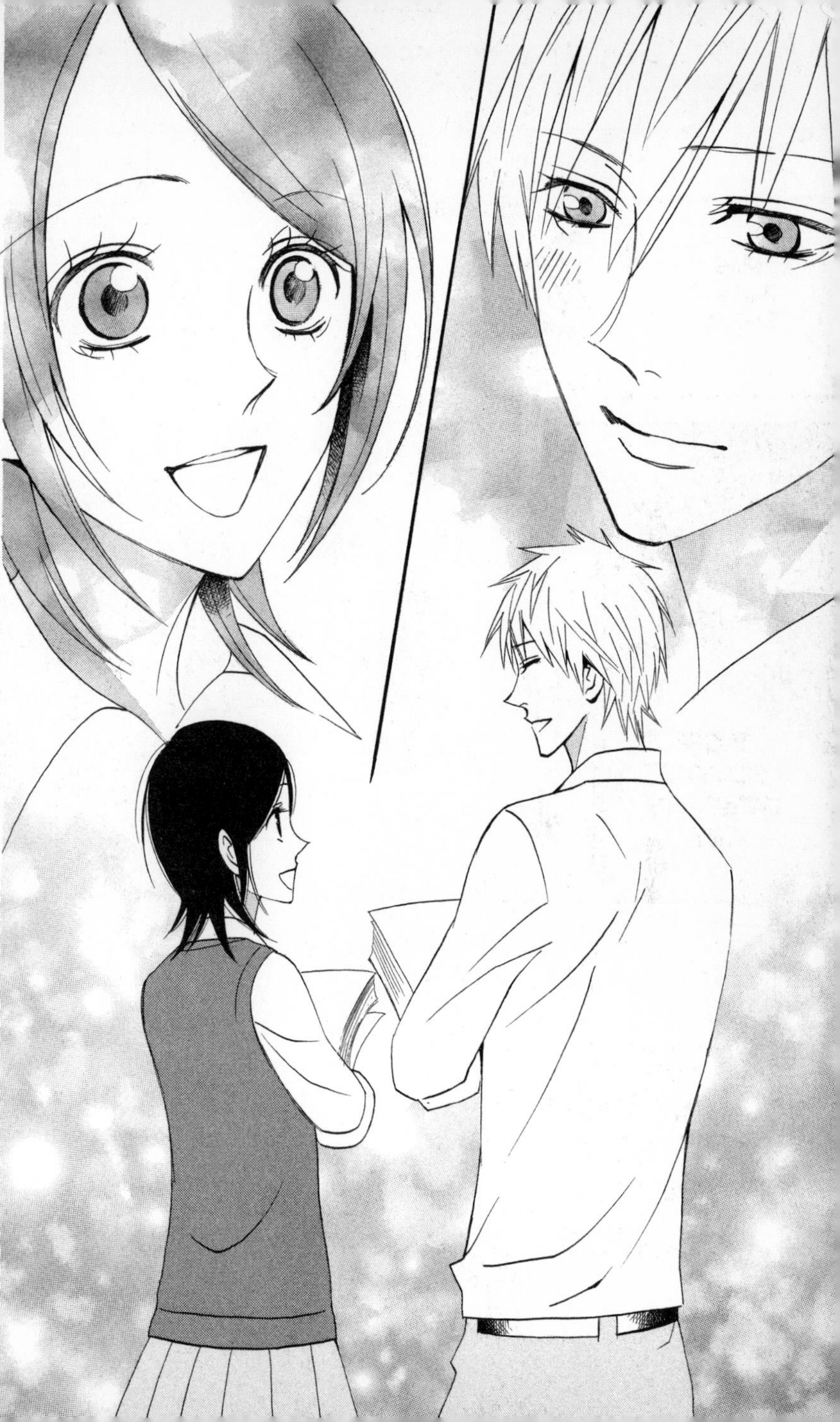

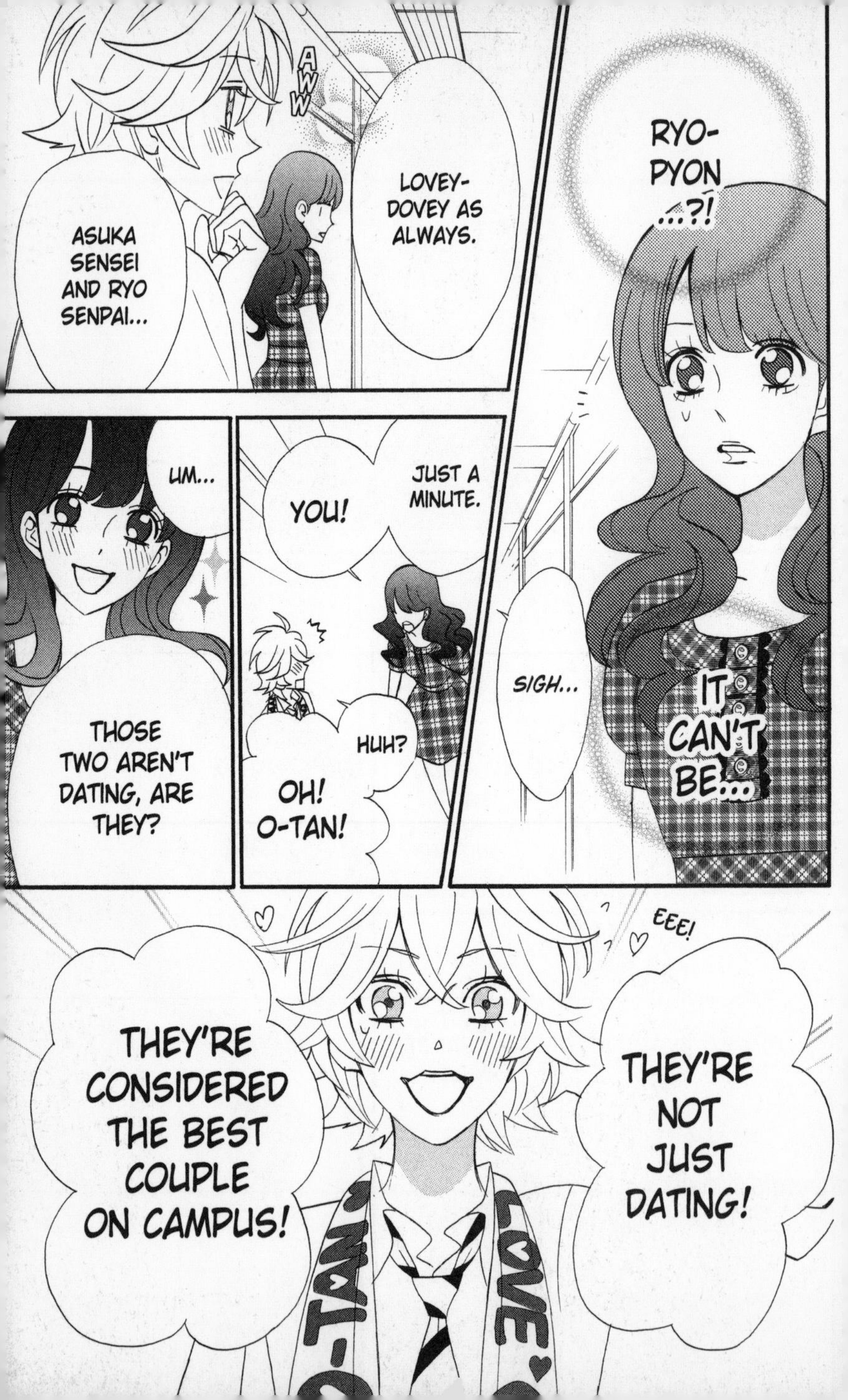
RYO-PYON ...?!
SIGH...
IT CAN'T BE...
AWW
LOVEY-DOVEY AS ALWAYS.
ASUKA SENSEI AND RYO SENPAI...
JUST A MINUTE.
YOU!
HUH?
OH! O-TAN!
UM...
THOSE TWO AREN'T DATING, ARE THEY?
EEE!
THEY'RE NOT JUST DATING!
THEY'RE CONSIDERED THE BEST COUPLE ON CAMPUS!

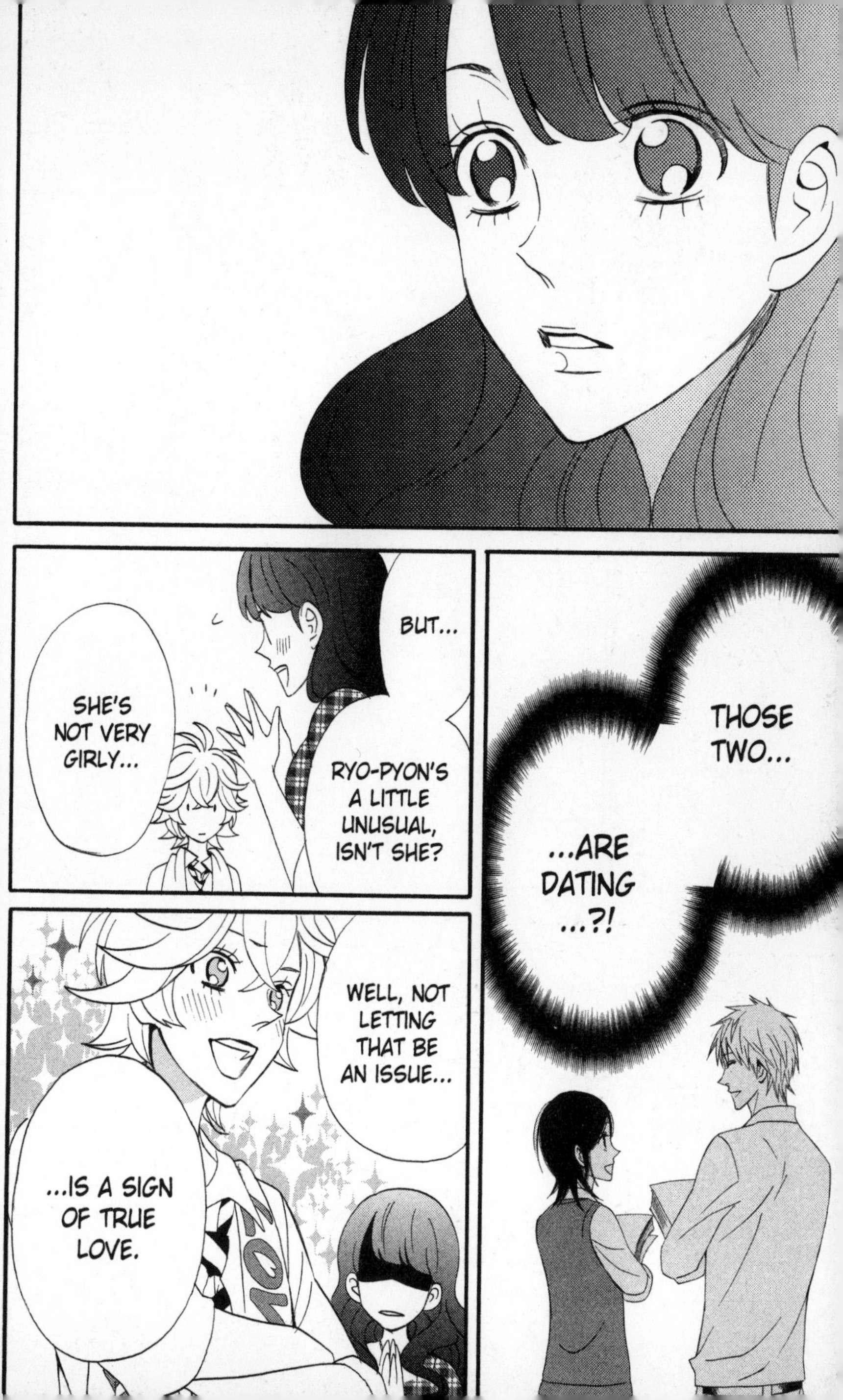
THOSE TWO...
...ARE DATING ...?!
BUT...
RYO-PYON'S A LITTLE UNUSUAL, ISN'T SHE?
SHE'S NOT VERY GIRLY...
WELL, NOT LETTING THAT BE AN ISSUE...
...IS A SIGN OF TRUE LOVE.

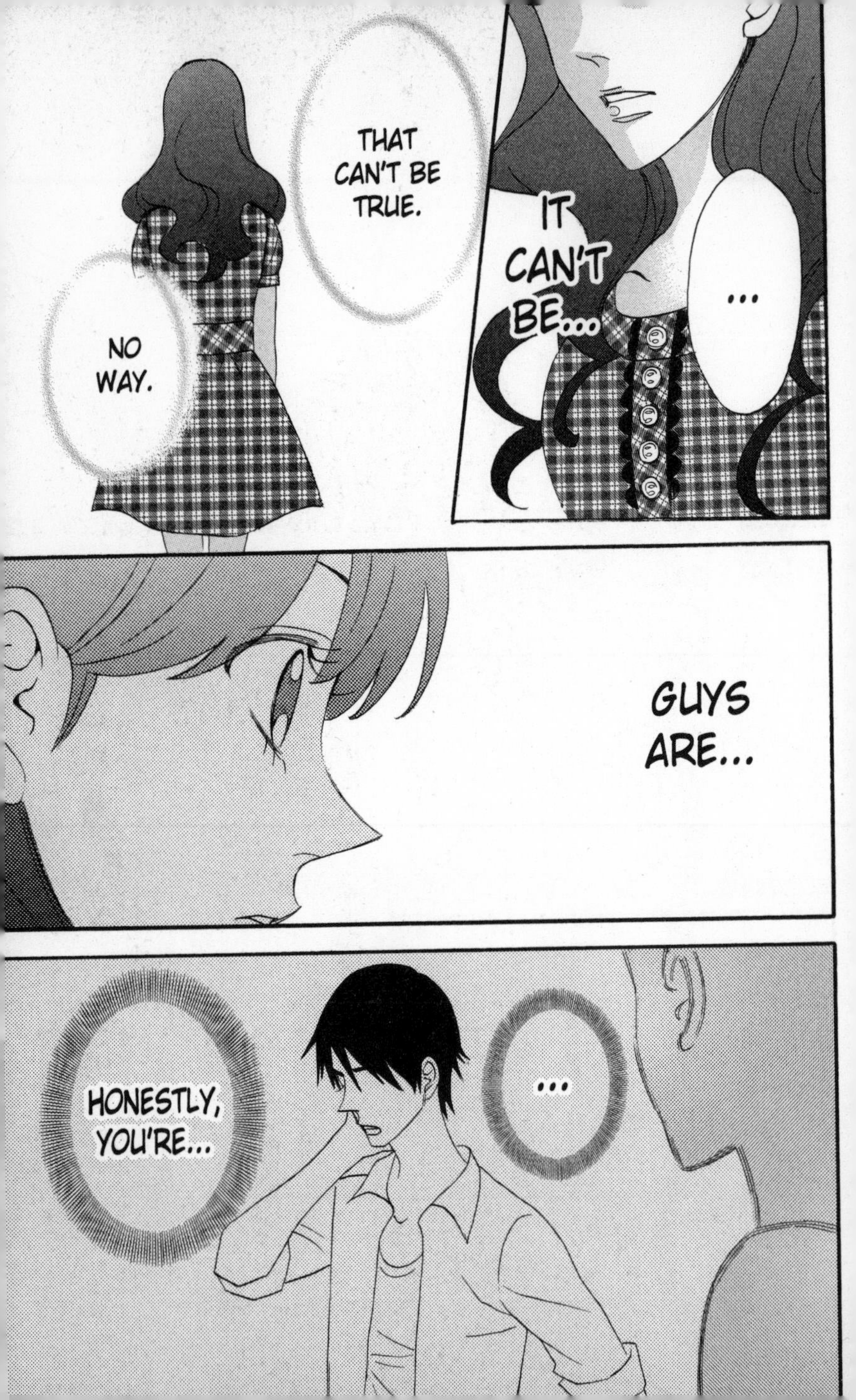
...
IT CAN'T BE...
THAT CAN'T BE TRUE.
NO WAY.
GUYS ARE...
...
HONESTLY, YOU'RE...

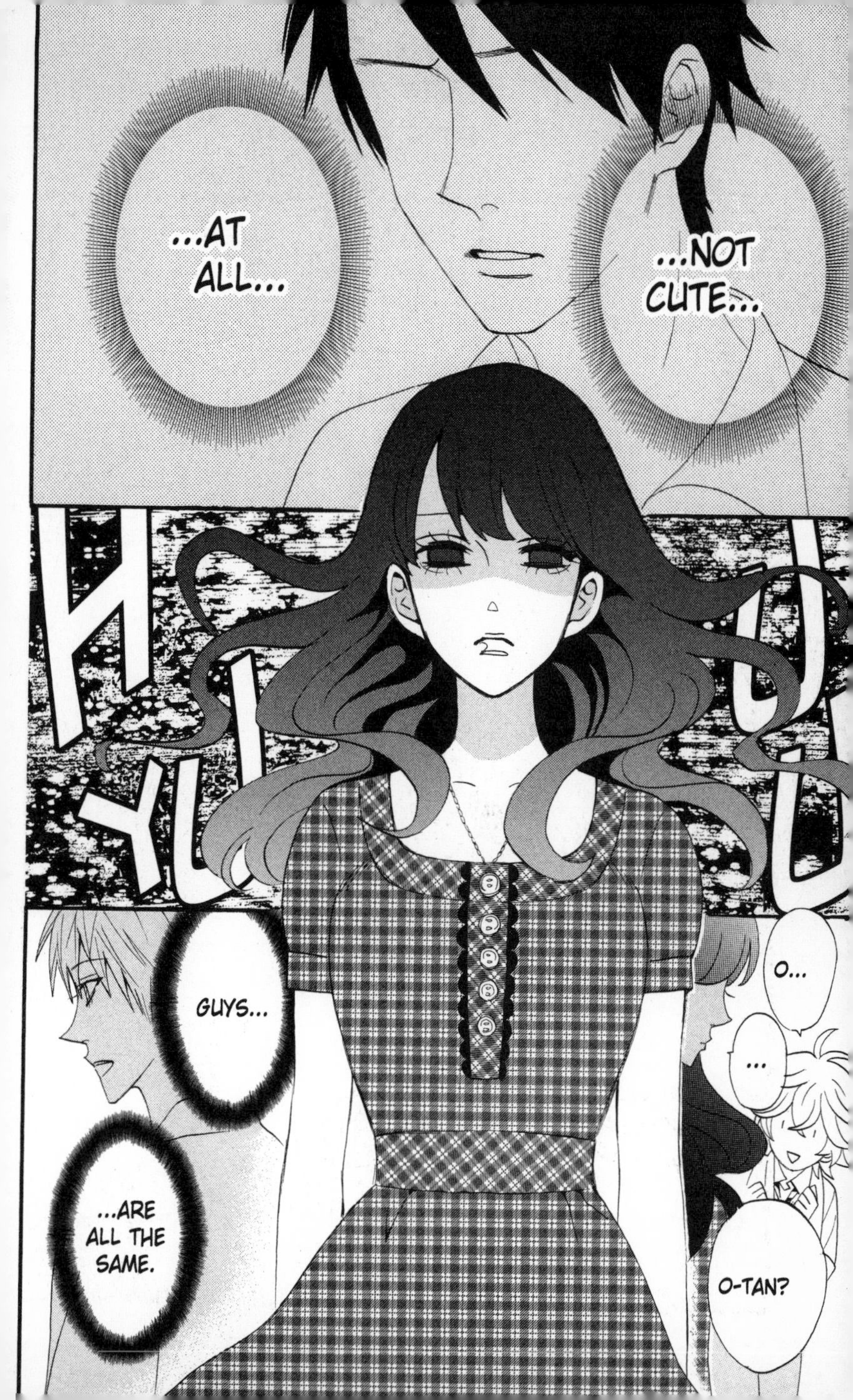
...NOT CUTE...
...AT ALL...
O...
...
O-TAN?
GUYS...
...ARE ALL THE SAME.

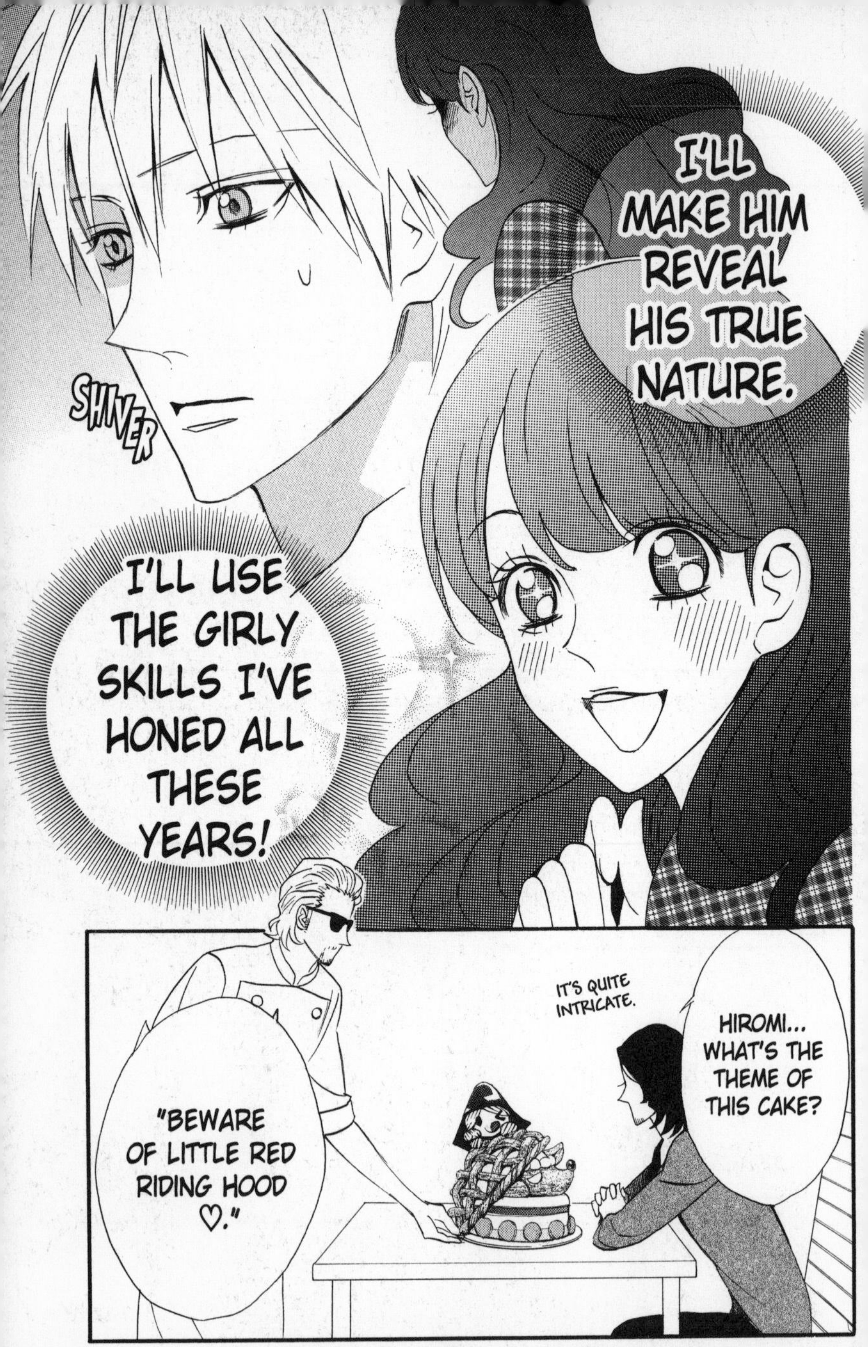
I'LL MAKE HIM REVEAL HIS TRUE NATURE.
SHIVER
I'LL USE THE GIRLY SKILLS I'VE HONED ALL THESE YEARS!
HIROMI... WHAT'S THE THEME OF THIS CAKE?
IT'S QUITE INTRICATE.
"BEWARE OF LITTLE RED RIDING HOOD ♡."

OTOMEN 9 / THE END

BONUS MANGA

OTOMANGA

MEN

Otomen in Manga Strips

STRIPS

AYA KANNO

FREAK*DUST
JUST FALL IN LOVE
ABSOLUTELY LOVE IT!!
FREAK*DUST JUST FALL IN LOVE

1

RYO...
FWOO
FWOOOO
RYO...
RYO...
FWOOOOO
OH! JUTA...
CAN YOU DO SOMETHING ABOUT YOUR HABIT OF CROCHETING THINGS WHEN YOU GET EXCITED?
PLEASE TAKE THIS
I CAN'T TAKE ANY MORE.

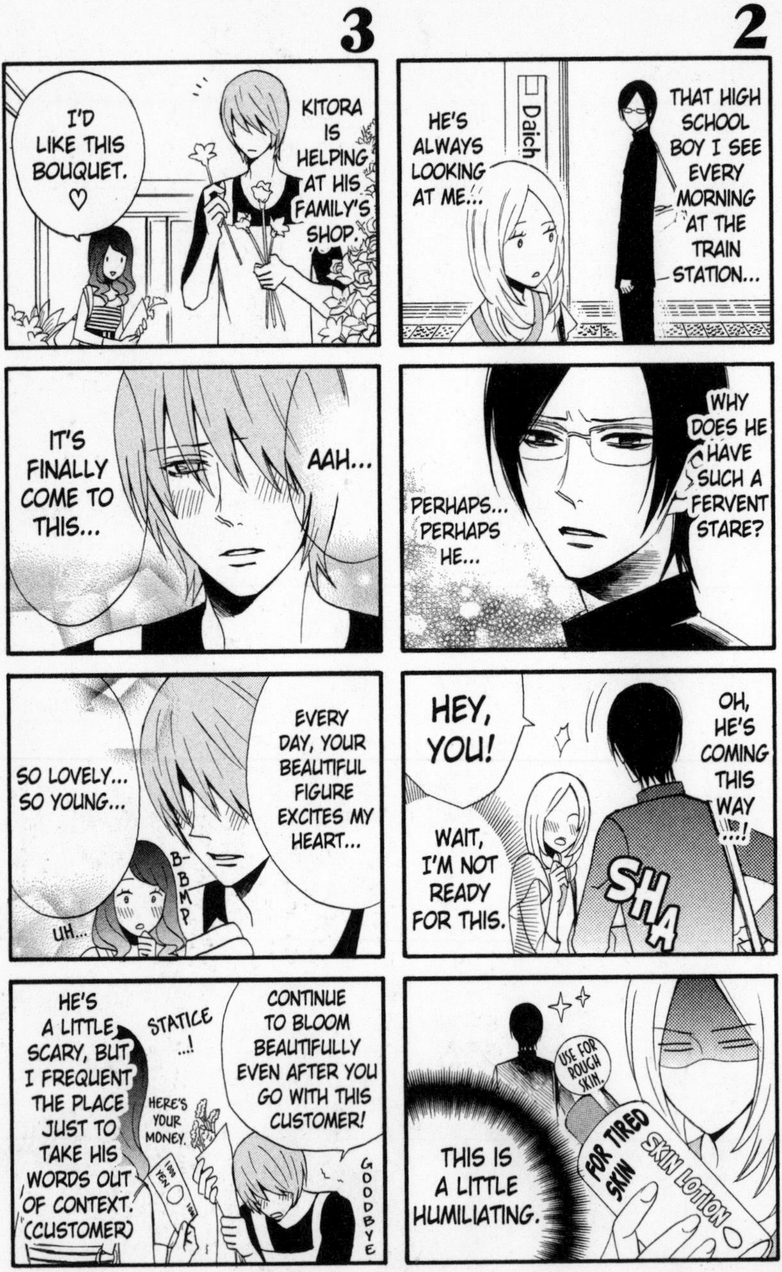
2
THAT HIGH SCHOOL BOY I SEE EVERY MORNING AT THE TRAIN STATION...
Daich
HE'S ALWAYS LOOKING AT ME...
WHY DOES HE HAVE SUCH A FERVENT STARE?
PERHAPS... PERHAPS HE...
OH, HE'S COMING THIS WAY...!
HEY, YOU!
WAIT, I'M NOT READY FOR THIS.
SHA
USE FOR ROUGH SKIN.
SKIN LOTION
FOR TIRED SKIN
THIS IS A LITTLE HUMILIATING.
3
KITORA IS HELPING AT HIS FAMILY'S SHOP.
I'D LIKE THIS BOUQUET. ♡
AAH...
IT'S FINALLY COME TO THIS...
EVERY DAY, YOUR BEAUTIFUL FIGURE EXCITES MY HEART...
B-BMP
SO LOVELY... SO YOUNG...
UH...
GOODBYE
CONTINUE TO BLOOM BEAUTIFULLY EVEN AFTER YOU GO WITH THIS CUSTOMER!
STATICE ...!
HERE'S YOUR MONEY.
1000 YEN
HE'S A LITTLE SCARY, BUT I FREQUENT THE PLACE JUST TO TAKE HIS WORDS OUT OF CONTEXT. (CUSTOMER)

4

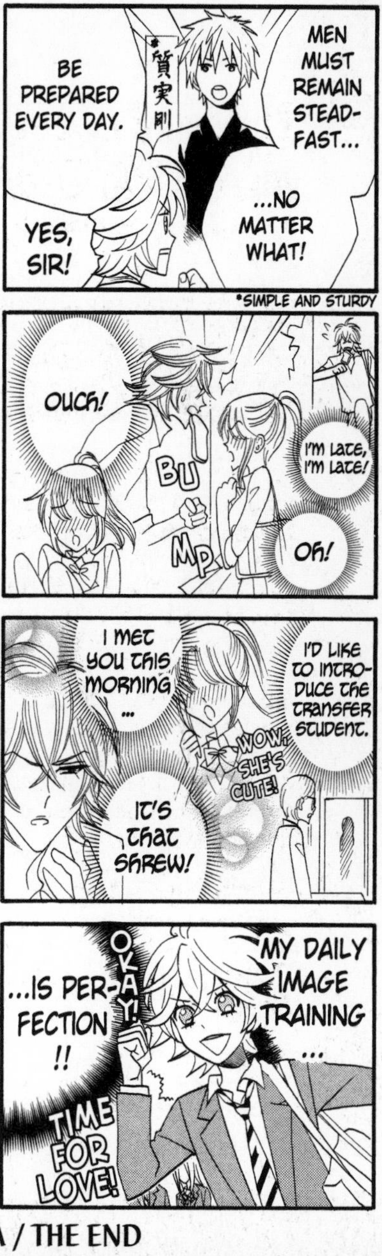
MEN MUST REMAIN STEADFAST...
*質実剛
BE PREPARED EVERY DAY.
...NO MATTER WHAT!
YES, SIR!
*SIMPLE AND STURDY
I'M LATE, I'M LATE!
OH!
OUCH!
BUMP
I'D LIKE TO INTRODUCE THE TRANSFER STUDENT.
I MET YOU THIS MORNING...
WOW, SHE'S CUTE!
IT'S THAT SHREW!
MY DAILY IMAGE TRAINING...
OKAY!
...IS PERFECTION!!
TIME FOR LOVE!

5

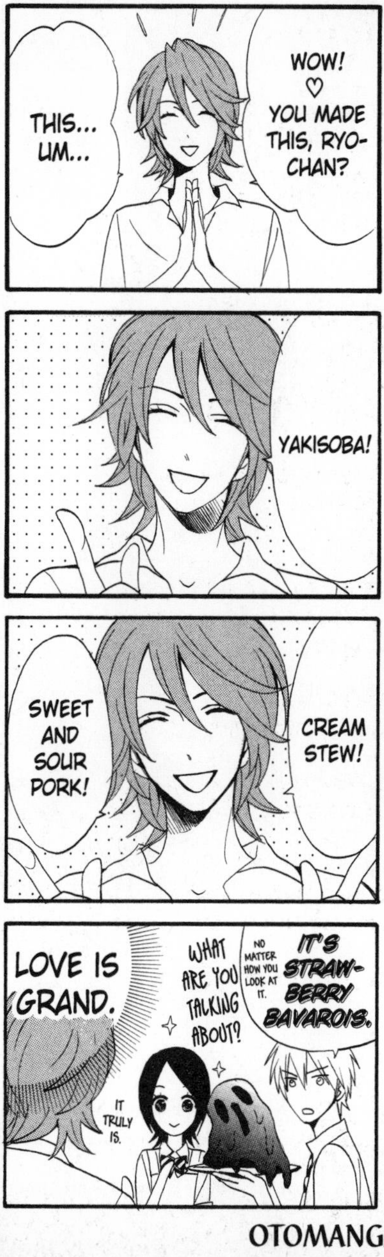
WOW! ♡ YOU MADE THIS, RYO-CHAN?
THIS... UM...
YAKISOBA!
CREAM STEW!
SWEET AND SOUR PORK!
IT'S STRAWBERRY BAVAROIS.
NO MATTER HOW YOU LOOK AT IT.
WHAT ARE YOU TALKING ABOUT?
LOVE IS GRAND.
IT TRULY IS.

OTOMANGA / THE END

Confused by some of the terms, but too MANLY to ask for help?

Here are some **cultural notes** to assist you!

HONORIFICS

Chan – an informal honorific used to address children and females. *Chan* can also be used toward animals, lovers, intimate friends and people whom one has known since childhood.

Kun – an informal honorific used primarily toward males; it can be used by people of more senior status addressing those junior to them or by anyone addressing male children.

San – the most common honorific title. It is used to address people outside one's immediate family and close circle of friends.

Senpai – used to address one's senior colleagues or mentor figures; it is used when students refer to or address more senior students in their school.

Sensei – honorific title used to address teachers as well as professionals such as doctors, lawyers and artists.

Sama – honorific used to address persons much higher in rank than oneself.

NOTES

Page 2 | **Hana to Mame**
The name *Hana to Mame* (Flowers and Beans) is a play on the real shojo manga magazine *Hana to Yume* (Flowers and Dreams) published by Hakusensha, Inc.

Page 3 | **Tsun-sama**
Juta makes this word up by combining *tsundere* and *ore-sama*. *Tsundere* describes a character who is *tsuntsun* (cold or irritable) and later becomes *deredere* (affectionate or sentimental). *Ore-sama* describes a pompous and arrogant person, as it combines *ore* (me) with the honorific *sama*.

Page 18, panel 5 | **Bento**
A lunch box that may contain rice, meat, pickles and an assortment of side dishes. Sometimes the food is arranged in such a way as to resemble objects like animals, flowers, leaves, and so forth.

Page 76, panel 4 | **Mira Jonouchi**
A shojo manga artist who inspired Juta to become a shojo manga artist himself. For more information, see *Otomen* volume 5.

Aya Kanno was born in Tokyo, Japan.
She is the creator of *Soul Rescue* and *Blank Slate*
(originally published as *Akusaga* in Japan's
BetsuHana magazine). Her latest work, *Otomen*,
is currently being serialized in *BetsuHana*.

OTOMEN
Vol. 9
Shojo Beat Edition

Story and Art by | **AYA KANNO**

Translation & Adaptation | **JN Productions**
Touch-up Art & Lettering | **Mark McMurray**
Design | **Fawn Lau**
Editor | **Amy Yu**

Otomen by Aya Kanno © Aya Kanno 2009
All rights reserved. First published in Japan in 2009 by HAKUSENSHA, Inc., Tokyo.
English language translation rights arranged with HAKUSENSHA, Inc., Tokyo.

The rights of the author(s) of the work(s) in this publication to be so identified
have been asserted in accordance with the Copyright, Designs and Patents Act 1988.
A CIP catalogue record for this book is available from the British Library.

Printed in the U.S.A.

Published by VIZ Media, LLC
P.O. Box 77010
San Francisco, CA 94107

10 9 8 7 6 5 4 3 2 1
First printing, February 2011

PARENTAL ADVISORY
OTOMEN is rated T for Teen and is recommended
for ages 13 and up. This volume contains
suggestive themes.
ratings.viz.com

www.viz.com

www.shojobeat.com

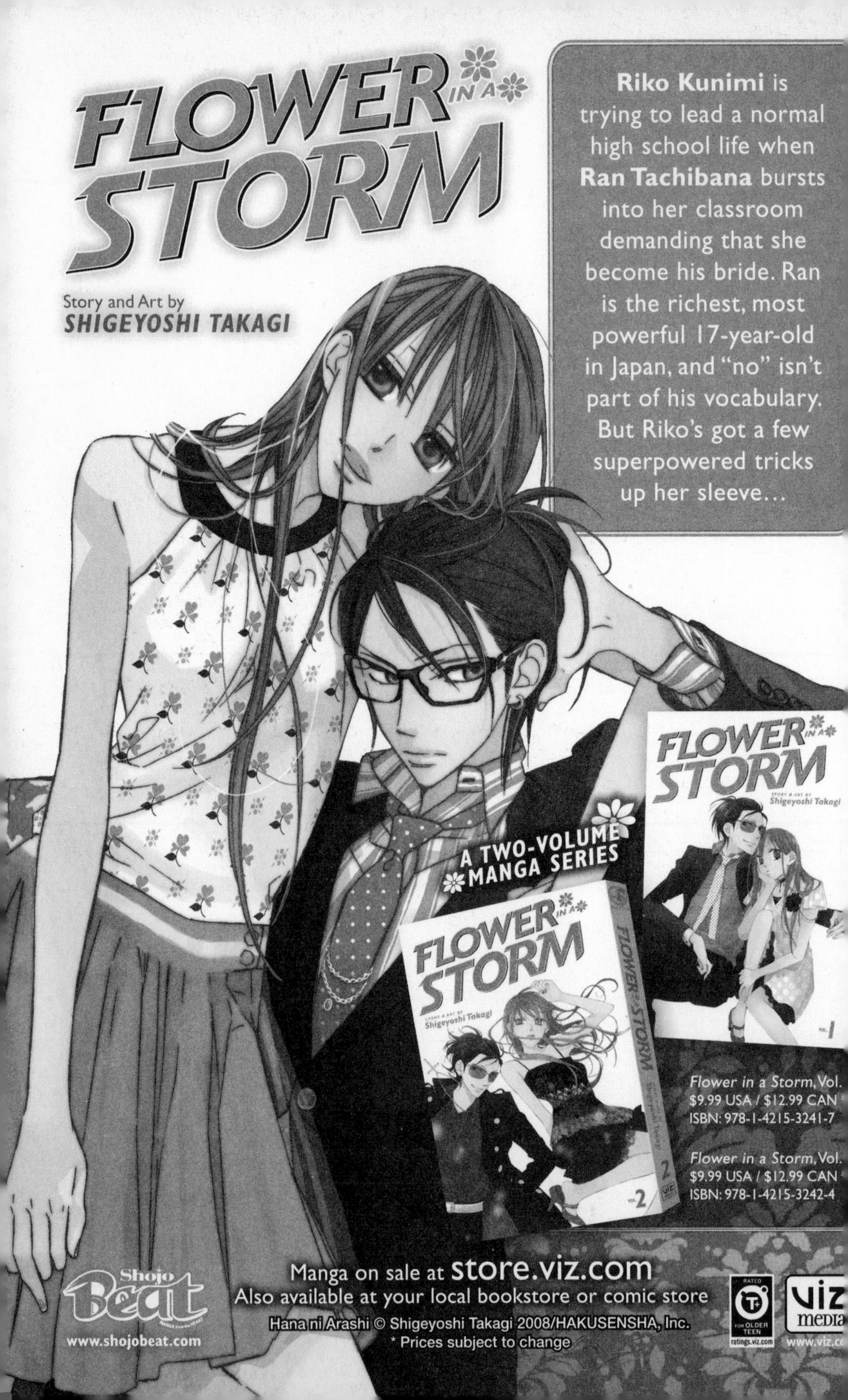
FLOWER IN A STORM
Story and Art by
SHIGEYOSHI TAKAGI
Riko Kunimi is trying to lead a normal high school life when Ran Tachibana bursts into her classroom demanding that she become his bride. Ran is the richest, most powerful 17-year-old in Japan, and "no" isn't part of his vocabulary. But Riko's got a few superpowered tricks up her sleeve...
A TWO-VOLUME MANGA SERIES
FLOWER IN A STORM
STORY & ART BY Shigeyoshi Takagi
VOL. 1
FLOWER IN A STORM
STORY & ART BY Shigeyoshi Takagi
VOL. 2
Flower in a Storm, Vol.
$9.99 USA / $12.99 CAN
ISBN: 978-1-4215-3241-7
Flower in a Storm, Vol.
$9.99 USA / $12.99 CAN
ISBN: 978-1-4215-3242-4
Manga on sale at store.viz.com
Also available at your local bookstore or comic store
Hana ni Arashi © Shigeyoshi Takagi 2008/HAKUSENSHA, Inc.
* Prices subject to change
Shojo Beat
www.shojobeat.com
RATED T+ FOR OLDER TEEN
ratings.viz.com
VIZ media
www.viz.c

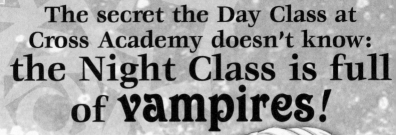

The secret the Day Class at Cross Academy doesn't know: the Night Class is full of vampires!

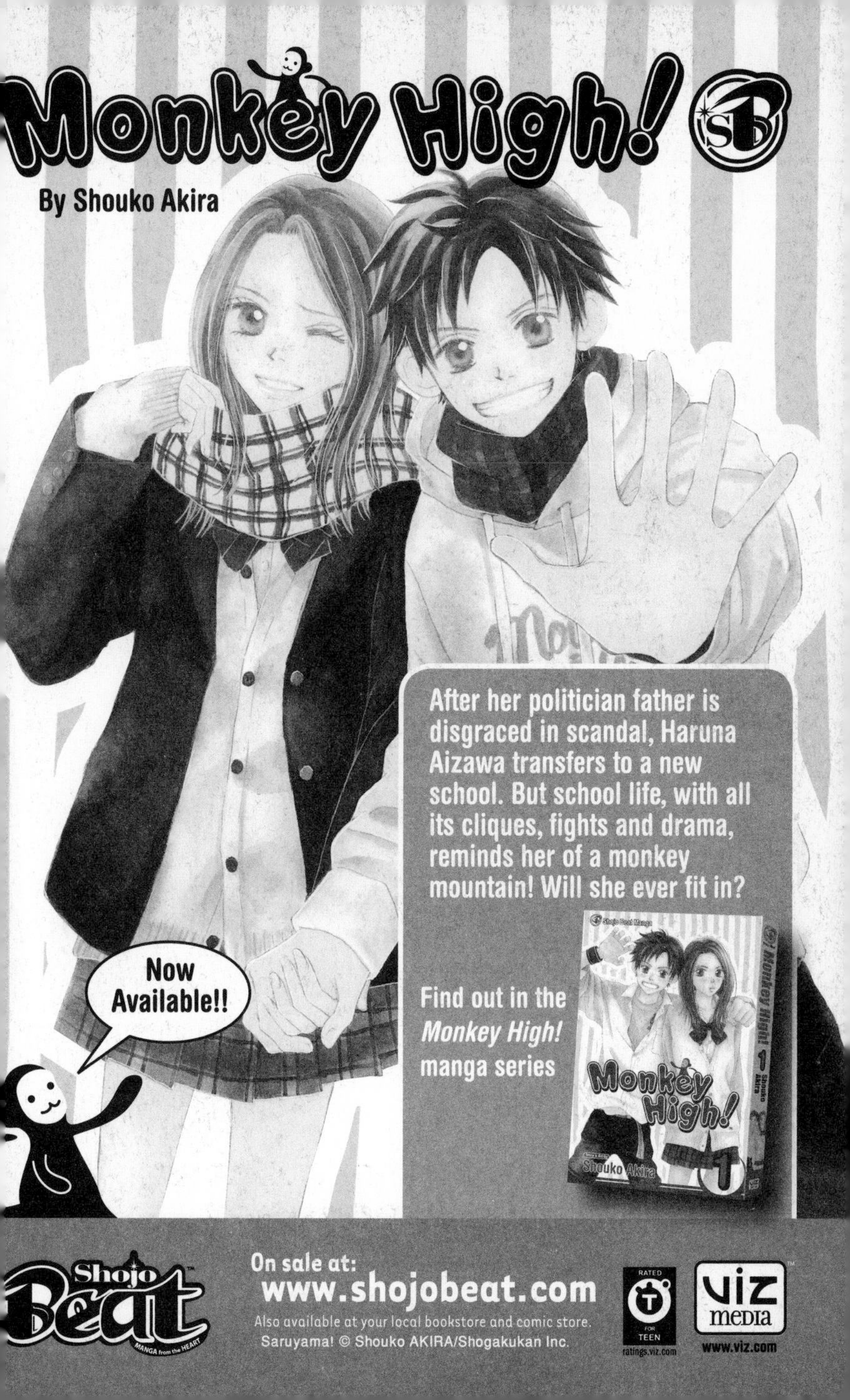
Monkey High!
By Shouko Akira
After her politician father is disgraced in scandal, Haruna Aizawa transfers to a new school. But school life, with all its cliques, fights and drama, reminds her of a monkey mountain! Will she ever fit in?
Now Available!!
Find out in the *Monkey High!* manga series
Monkey High! 1 Shouko Akira
Shojo Beat MANGA from the HEART
On sale at:
www.shojobeat.com
Also available at your local bookstore and comic store.
Saruyama! © Shouko AKIRA/Shogakukan Inc.
RATED T FOR TEEN
ratings.viz.com
VIZ media
www.viz.com

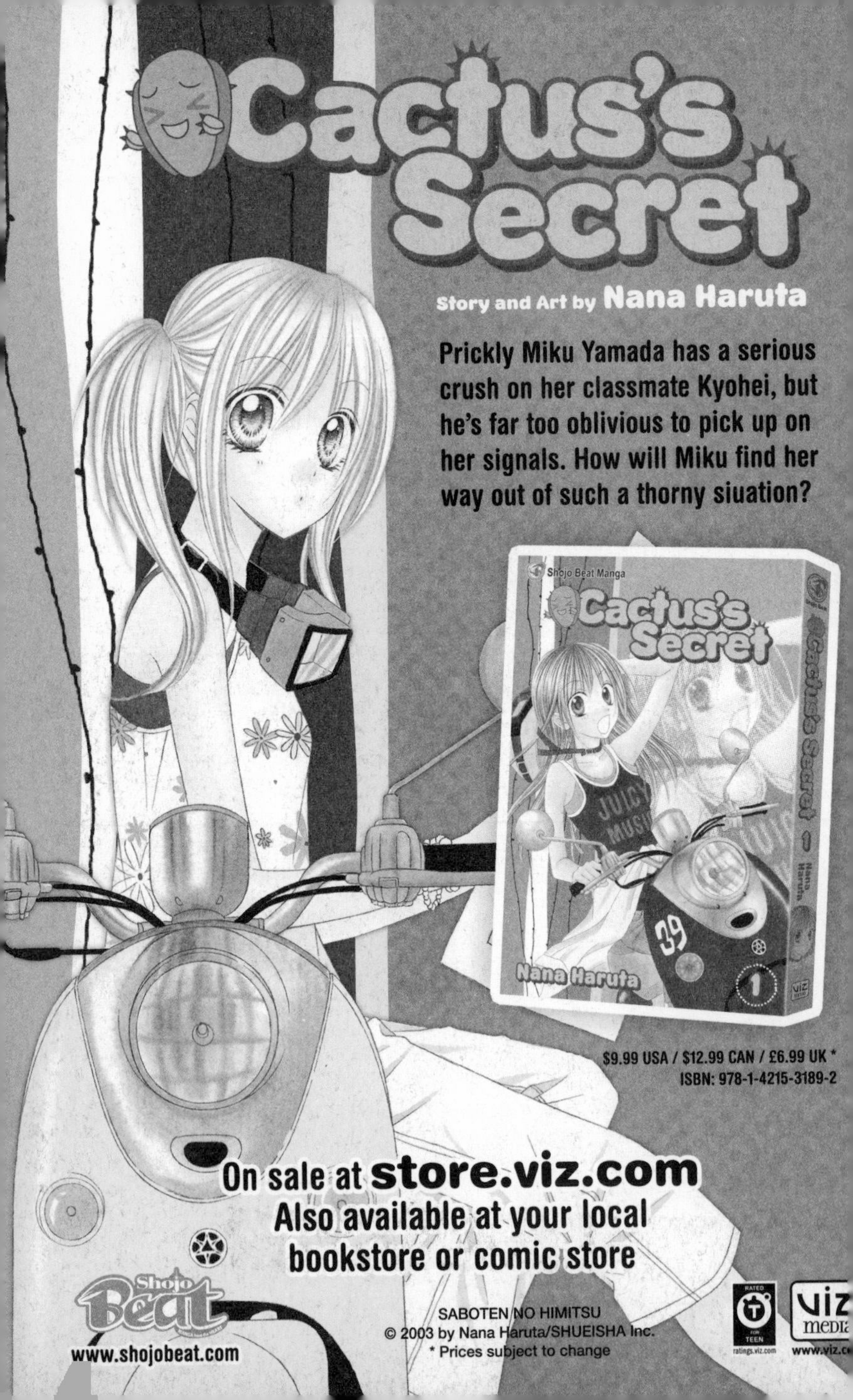
Cactus's Secret
Story and Art by Nana Haruta
Prickly Miku Yamada has a serious crush on her classmate Kyohei, but he's far too oblivious to pick up on her signals. How will Miku find her way out of such a thorny siuation?
Shojo Beat Manga
Cactus's Secret
Nana Haruta
1
$9.99 USA / $12.99 CAN / £6.99 UK *
ISBN: 978-1-4215-3189-2
On sale at store.viz.com
Also available at your local bookstore or comic store
Shojo Beat
www.shojobeat.com
SABOTEN NO HIMITSU
© 2003 by Nana Haruta/SHUEISHA Inc.
* Prices subject to change
RATED T FOR TEEN
ratings.viz.com
viz media
www.viz.c

Can love trump a cursed life?

Sawako's a shy, lonely, pure-hearted student who just happens to look like the scary girl in a famous horror movie! But when she manages to befriend the most popular boy in school, will her frightful reputation scare off her best chance for love?

kimi ni todoke
From Me to You

By Karuho Shiina

kimi ni todoke
From Me to You
Karuho Shiina
kimi ni todoke

Find out in the *Kimi ni Todoke* manga—
BUY YOURS TODAY!

Winner of the 2008 Kodansha Manga Award (shojo category)

On sale at **www.shojobeat.com**

store or comic store.

Shojo Beat MANGA from the HEART

RATED T FOR TEEN ratings.viz.com

VIZ media www.viz.com